Translation / Transformation

Translation is at the heart of psychoanalysis: from unconscious to conscious, experience to verbal expression, internal to enacted, dream thought to dream image, language to interpretation, unrepresented to represented and transference of past to present.

The book's first part discusses the question of translation, literal and metaphoric. Both linguistic and cultural translations are closely tied to specific and significant personalities who were involved in the early history of psychoanalysis and thus in the development of *the IJP*. There was a close relationship between *the IJP* and the visual arts via the Bloomsbury Group. The link between the visual arts and *the IJP* is indeed to be found in its logo, which is taken from a painting by Ingres. The second part of the book approaches transformations between psychoanalysis and the arts from conscious, unconscious and non-represented elements into non-verbal modes, specifically visual, poetic and musical; it also looks at the developments and transformations in psychoanalytic ideas about artistic expression as expressed within the pages of *the IJP*.

This book will be of great interest to psychoanalysts and psychotherapists, and to those interested in the history of psychoanalysis and *the IJP*.

Dana Birksted-Breen, a training and supervising psychoanalyst of the British Psychoanalytical Society in private practice, was General Editor of the New Library of Psychoanalysis (2000–2010), initiating the New Library Teaching Series, and is the Editor-in-Chief of *the IJP* since 2010.

THE NEW LIBRARY OF PSYCHOANALYSIS
General Editor: Alessandra Lemma

The New Library of Psychoanalysis was launched in 1987 in association with the Institute of Psychoanalysis, London. It took over from the International Psychoanalytical Library which published many of the early translations of the works of Freud and the writings of most of the leading British and Continental psychoanalysts.

The purpose of the New Library of Psychoanalysis is to facilitate a greater and more widespread appreciation of psychoanalysis and to provide a forum for increasing mutual understanding between psychoanalysts and those working in other disciplines such as the social sciences, medicine, philosophy, history, linguistics, literature and the arts. It aims to represent different trends both in British psychoanalysis and in psychoanalysis generally. The New Library of Psychoanalysis is well placed to make available to the English-speaking world psychoanalytic writings from other European countries and to increase the interchange of ideas between British and American psychoanalysts. Through the *Teaching Series*, the New Library of Psychoanalysis now also publishes books that provide comprehensive, yet accessible, overviews of selected subject areas aimed at those studying psychoanalysis and related fields such as the social sciences, philosophy, literature and the arts.

The Institute, together with the British Psychoanalytical Society, runs a low-fee psychoanalytic clinic, organizes lectures and scientific events concerned with psychoanalysis and publishes *the International Journal of Psychoanalysis*. It runs a training course in psychoanalysis which leads to membership of the International Psychoanalytical Association – the body which preserves internationally agreed standards of training, of professional entry, and of professional ethics and practice for psychoanalysis as initiated and developed by Sigmund Freud. Distinguished members of the Institute have included Michael Balint, Wilfred Bion, Ronald Fairbairn, Anna Freud, Ernest Jones, Melanie Klein, John Rickman and Donald Winnicott.

Previous general editors have included David Tuckett, who played a very active role in the establishment of the New Library. He was followed as general editor by Elizabeth Bott Spillius, who was in turn

"More than about literal translation, this collection of essays is about the movement of ideas from one culture to another, from one generation to another. Thus temporality infuses this collection, whose original in-depth research findings, by creative authors with deep knowledge in their respective fields (psychoanalysis, art history, archaeology, musical composition), retrace and rediscover the creative journey of psychoanalysis from Vienna to London with its tragic historical background. And so too it considers how cultures take into consideration essential issues in psychoanalysis from other cultures and transform them: translation is transformation. The theme of the Oedipus enigma and excellent reflections on art intermingle in this beautifully illustrated book, in which Dana Birksted-Breen blends these themes in her usual expected talent to conceive and design a collection as this remarkable one and in her revealing introduction. This centenary and anniversary collection of essays marks an historical and seminal milestone in the developing history and the continued evolution of psychoanalysis. A book not to be missed...".

Haydée Faimberg, MD, Training and
Supervising Analyst, SPP, APA, International
Distinguished Fellow of BPAS

"'Language has been invented, translation can be achieved, musical and mathematical notations exist, men compose and paint. And now psycho-analysis attempts to elucidate the barriers and links that hinder or promote the relationships that require a capacity for communication' (Bion, *Cogitations*). The title of the book to celebrate the 100th anniversary of *the IJP* – and I would add the word transmutation – faithfully reflects the task that Freud assigned to psychoanalysis. The task of *the IJP* is well represented in the words of the linguist Hagège, 'it is not only languages that are translated, but also habits and intellectual processes'".

Prof. Dr. Jorge Canestri, Training and
Supervising psychoanalyst AIPsi, APA, Associate
Editor of *the IJP*

"This multi-voice book highlights the foundations upon which the reputation of *the International Journal of Psychoanalysis* is built. Since the time of Freud, this *Journal* has become a reference for English-speaking psychoanalysts, its primary destination, and then for each psychoanalyst all over the world. In addition to the richness of its professional, historical and cultural roots highlighted here, its value derives not only from the independence that an anonymous peer review process provides, but also from a non-partisan approach that respects everyone's positions, in the tradition of the British Psychoanalytic Society responsible for its management".

Jean-Michel Quinodoz, Swiss Psychoanalytical Society, Editor for Europe 1994–2003

Translation / Transformation

100 Years of *the International Journal of Psychoanalysis*

Edited by Dana Birksted-Breen

Routledge
Taylor & Francis Group

LONDON AND NEW YORK

First published 2021
by Routledge
2 Park Square, Milton Park, Abingdon, Oxon OX14 4RN

and by Routledge
52 Vanderbilt Avenue, New York, NY 10017

Routledge is an imprint of the Taylor & Francis Group, an informa business

British Library Cataloguing-in-Publication Data
A catalogue record for this book is available from the British Library

Library of Congress Cataloging-in-Publication Data
Names: Breen, Dana, editor.
Title: Translation/transformation: 100 years of the International
journal of psychoanalysis / edited by Dana Birksted-Breen.
Other titles: International journal of psycho-analysis.
Description: Abingdon, Oxon; New York, NY: Routledge, 2021. |
Series: New library of psychoanalysis | Includes bibliographical
references and index. | Identifiers: LCCN 2020034919 (print) |
LCCN 2020034920 (ebook) | ISBN 9780367563325 (paperback) |
ISBN 9780367560935 (hardback) | ISBN 9781003096399 (ebook)
Subjects: LCSH: International journal of psycho-analysis. |
Psychoanalysis. | Psychoanalysis and art. | Psychoanlysis and literature.
Classification: LCC BF173.T623 2021 (print) | LCC BF173 (ebook) |
DDC 150.19/505—dc23
LC record available at https://lccn.loc.gov/2020034919
LC ebook record available at https://lccn.loc.gov/2020034920

ISBN: 978-0-367-56093-5 (hbk)
ISBN: 978-0-367-56332-5 (pbk)
ISBN: 978-1-003-09639-9 (ebk)

Typeset in Bembo
by codeMantra

Contents

Figures

Acknowledgements

The International Journal of Psychoanalysis grants permission for the publication of the articles below in the book **TRANSLATION/ TRANSFORMATION: 100 Years of the International Journal of Psychoanalysis, edited by Dana Birksted-Breen, published by the New Library of Psychoanalysis, Routledge.**

Chapter 4. Dee McQuillan, previously published:
McQuillan, D. (2019). Publish and be fair? "I am myself strongly in favour of doing it": James Strachey as the candid wartime editor of *The International Journal of Psycho-Analysis*, 1939–1945. *Int. J. Psycho-Anal.*, 100(3):540–566.

Chapter 5. Rachel Blass, previously published:
Blass, R. B. Joan Riviere: The professional and personal struggles of a formidable foundress of *the International Journal of Psychoanalysis*.

Chapter 7. Rachel B. Blass, previously published:
Blass, R. B. *The International Journal of Psychoanalysis* as the voice of psychoanalysis: united and different.

Chapter 9. Carina Weiss:
These are modifications of papers previously published:
Weiss, C. The Enigma of the Hour: Display Case Compendium. *Int. J. Psycho-Anal.*, 100(6):1481–1613 (2019).

Chapter 10. Margot Waddell, previously published:
Waddell, M. (2019). "All the light we cannot see": Psychoanalytic and poetic reflections on the nature of hope. *Int. J. Psycho-Anal.*, 100(6):1405–1421.

Chapter 11, Francis Grier:

This has been previously published in a modified form:

Francis Grier (2019) Musicality in the consulting room, *The International Journal of Psychoanalysis*, 100:5, 827–851, DOI: 10.1080/00207578.2019.1664905

INTRODUCTION
Dana Birksted-Breen

Each day except Sunday I spend an hour on the Prof's sofa (I've now spent 34 altogether) – and the "analysis" seems to provide a complete undercurrent for life. As for what it's all about, I'm vaguer than ever; but at all events it's sometimes extremely exciting and sometimes extremely unpleasant – so I daresay there's something in it. The Prof himself is most affable and as an artistic performer dazzling. He has a good deal rather like Verrall in the way his mind works.[1] Almost every hour is made into an organic aesthetic whole. Sometimes the dramatic effect is absolutely shattering. During the early part of the hour all is vague – a dark hint here, a mystery there -; then it gradually seems to get thicker; you feel dreadful things going on inside you, and can't make out what they can possibly be; then he begins to give you a slight lead; you suddenly get a clear glimpse of one thing; then you see another; at last a whole series of lights break in on you; he asks you one more question; you give a last reply – and as the whole truth dawns upon you the Professor rises, crosses the room to the electric bell, and shows you out at the door.

That's on favourable occasions. But there are others when you lie for the whole hour with a ton weight on your stomach simply unable to get out a single word. I think that makes one more inclined to believe it all than anything. When you positively feel the 'resistance' as something physical sitting on you, it fairly shakes you all the rest of the day.

(Strachey, November 6, 1920; Forrester &
Cameron, 2017, p. 529)

The year is 1920. James Strachey is describing to his brother Lytton his analysis with Freud. He had travelled to Vienna that year to begin psychoanalysis with Freud. Soon his wife Alix also began psychoanalysis with Freud. Freud asked the couple to translate some of his works into English. This initiated their life's work as psychoanalysts and translators; James became Freud's official translator and Editor of the *Standard Edition,* and, with Alix's assistance, began publishing the *New German-English Psycho-Analytic Vocabulary* in 1943. In 1920, *the International Journal of Psychoanalysis* was established by Ernest Jones as the first Editor, under the direction of Freud, and Strachey became the second Editor after Freud's death in 1939. Joan Riviere also met Freud in 1920, starting psychoanalysis with him in 1922 in Vienna. Freud also asked her to translate some of his papers, and she became the translation editor of the *International Journal.* Joan Riviere and Alix and James Strachey were all part of the Glossary Committee set up by Ernest Jones to create a glossary of psychoanalytic terms in English. These form the foundation of psychoanalytic writings in the English language.

Translation and temporality are the Ariadne's thread that, as Editor-in-Chief of the *International Journal,* I chose as a frame for its centenary year: temporality and translation at the heart of psychoanalysis, and translation and temporality at the heart of the development of the *International Journal* over 100 years.

Freud wrote: "How are we to arrive at a knowledge of the unconscious? It is of course only as something conscious that we know it, after it has undergone transformation or translation into something conscious" (1915, p.166). Further work is needed to transform it into language and still further into the written word, with the potential pain and pleasure of this work. Hilda Doolittle, poet and famous analysand of Freud, captures the experience of psychoanalysis, its transformation into the written word, and its strange temporality, paradoxically at once temporal and atemporal:

> …it was not that he conjured up the past and invoked the future.
> It was a present that was in the past or a past that was in the future.
> (Doolittle, 1956, p.16)

Translation/ Transformation was planned as one of the celebrations of the centenary of *the International Journal of Psychoanalysis*; its history is intermingled with and inseparable from the history and development of psychoanalysis. To honour the *International Journal* in its specificity, and to accompany the International Journal Centenary Conferences on the theme of the unconscious, I organized an exhibition, presenting archival material set in conversation with art works. In preparation, I worked with an international group of psychoanalysts and researchers from different countries to research a number of archives, focussing in particular on the theme of translation-transformation. The exhibition, *The Enigma of the Hour, One Hundred Years of Psychoanalytic Thought*, took place at the Freud Museum to coincide with the London Centenary Conference.[2,3]

This book has developed as an extension of the research that was initiated for the exhibition, which focussed specifically on the early history of the *Journal*, the centrality of translation, and the relationship to the visual arts via the "Bloomsbury editors" who were part of the European *Intelligentsia* of the early 20th century, into which *the International Journal of Psychoanalysis* was born. The art installations of the Centenary Celebrations therefore resonated with the early history of those who created *the International Journal of Psychoanalysis*. Some papers elaborate on the short pieces of text that discussed each item exhibited in the Display Case of the exhibition (original letter, object, or small artwork) and presented next to it in the Compendium; other papers were developed during the research but never found their way into the exhibition or the Compendium, and still others are recent contributions on subjects close to the overall theme of translation/transformation.

Translation is at the heart of psychoanalysis; psychoanalysis is a work of translation, the translation from unconscious to conscious, from experience to verbal expression, the transference from past to present, from internal to enacted, from dream thought to dream image, to language and to interpretation. Solms points out:

> Freud was, as he wrote, therefore obliged to invent a "figurative language" peculiar to depth psychology: "We could not otherwise describe the processes in question at all, and indeed we could not become aware of them" (Freud 1920a Freud, S. 1920a. "Beyond the Pleasure Principle" *RSE* 18. *RSE*, 18, 57). Herein lies the tension between discovery and invention in psychoanalysis. Freud was in this sense his own first translator.
>
> (Solms, 2018)

New terms had to be found and decisions about whether to stay close to the way of writing of the original language (German) or of the language being translated (into English). Steiner, in his chapter, describes Freud's own acute awareness of issues of translation between cultures and languages, and he also describes emotional factors involved in choices made by Strachey but also Jones before him, regarding terms to be used in translating Freud:

> Thinking of both terms 'cathexis' and 'anaclitic type', James Strachey, but also Jones if one considers his original input too, managed in some way to 'occupy' to 'besetz', 'cathect' the reader, but also Freud, with their translation, and to reverse their dependency on Freud as a parental figure, making him in a sort of way depend on them, hiding their unconscious phantasies of control, possession, but also of being possessed, in the acoustic skin of those so very cacophonic and mysterious words.
>
> (Steiner, Translation/Transformation, 2020)

The development of psychoanalysis in the English-speaking world is linked to the options which were taken by Strachey for the Standard Edition, and which have been debated ever since. A century later, the question of the translation of Freud is still open to interesting debates and new findings.[4] Notably, it has been suggested that Strachey's translation of certain concepts has obscured the complexity of Freud's conception of psychic temporality, in particular the notion of *Nachträglichkeit*.[5] As an English-language journal, the development of psychoanalysis held within the pages of the *IJPA* is intimately tied to these issues.[6] Strachey, in his obituary of Joan Riviere, writes about her work as "Translation Editor", translating and editing, and the importance of her work as "the foundation on which all our English knowledge of psycho-analysis was first built" (Blass, Chapter 5).

In 1920, the first issue of *the International Journal of Psychoanalysis* – a journal whose history is intertwined with the history of Freud, his research into the unconscious, his unstoppable drive for knowledge – was published: "Our work should go forward on the basis not of our doubts, but of our discoveries", he had written a couple of years earlier (1917, p. 273).[7]

At that time, Freud was still in Vienna, and Europe was only just beginning to recover from the devastation of World War I. An English-language journal seemed the way forward for the diffusion of Freud's ideas in the English-speaking world, and this was made possible, thanks to the dedication and financial capacity of the first editor Ernest Jones. The *Journal* began as a work of translation from German to English, but very soon papers were submitted directly in English, as it became the *Journal* of the international community.

When Freud finally realized his wish to see the diffusion of his ideas via the publication of an English-language journal in 1920 alongside the German journals, he was already at a turning point in his theoretical thinking with the publication that same year of "Beyond the Pleasure Principle" (1920), soon followed by *The Ego and the Id* (1923), taking psychoanalysis in new directions, particularly in the Anglophone world, and often trumping the earlier models.

Freud had been in discussion with Ernest Jones about starting an English-language journal for some years; the first mention of it was apparently in 1913 (see Bruns, Chapter 2), but it was not until after World War I that the idea came to fruition. In the same letter in which he mentions his grief for the recent death of his young wife, Jones tells Freud that the time has now come for an English-language journal:

> At last we are allowed to communicate freely again… I think the time is ripe for an English journal, or edition of the *Zeitschrift* (not identical, of course) owned by the Vereinigung. There is so much to talk over.
>
> You see I can look forward in life, although I have been through hell itself these last three months. It has been an indescribably terrible experience, signifying more even than a tremendous loss—owing to my inner psychical situation and the poignant circumstances of my wife's death. But I am surely winning through, and have learnt very much by it. Yesterday I read your paper on grief and melancholy, 1 which made a great impression on me.
>
> (December 7, 1918, 326)

Freud writes to Jones in December of that year:

> Needless to say we are all impatient to get your contributions to the *Zeitschrift* and see you taking an active part in the new career, opening for 'her ".
>
> (Freud to Jones, 22 December 2018)

Coming not long after the devastation of the World War I, the new *Journal* becomes a sign of survival and of life over death, of creativity and action in the wake of mourning.

In her address given on the occasion of presenting the portrait of Ernest Jones, painted by Rodrigo Moynihan, the Slade artist Sylvia Payne ends by saying:

> One of his most spectacular actions was to fly to Vienna at the time of Hitler's invasion of Austria to help Professor Freud, his family and colleagues. He was instrumental in bringing about their escape to England, and was untiring in the work he did for colleagues and friends who had to escape from the Nazis. It was due to him mainly that Professor Freud was able to spend the end of his life in peace and safety.
>
> (July 3, 1946)

If this was his most spectacular action, it was also down to Jones that the *International Journal* came into being, enhancing the future development of Freud's work. There were many difficulties in getting the *Journal* established – financial, practical, and rivalry – as Bruns and Steiner discuss in their chapters (Chapters 2 and 3, this volume). Different agendas, personal rivalries, and financial issues were at stake. Freud writes to Jones in January 1919:

> As for the journal, I hope you know, that both periodicals, *Zeitschrift* and *Imago*, have become official with the "European" groups. I hope also you have heard by Sachs, that we are setting on foot a ψα Verlag. Now Rank developed the idea at the same time as you, that you should bring out an English edition of the *Zeitschrift* (or both), all the papers getting translated into the two languages.

Meanwhile, Abraham wanted to resuscitate the *Jahrbuch,* which had been the first of a number of psychoanalytic journals started at the turn of the century, this one under the direction of Jung, and which had folded up due to rivalries, disputes, and economic problems. But Freud warns:

> … a third publication would be restricted to the purely Ψα public, which does not have much buying power (…). I am afraid that

the material produced by us in the course of a year might not be sufficient to keep it going. We do not exactly have an abundance of material even for the *Zeitschrift* (...) what England (and America) produce is henceforward to be diverted to the *English Journal of* Ψα.

(1919, p. 401)

At the meeting held at the newly formed British PsychoAnalytical Society on February 20, 1919, "it was resolved that the subscription [to the Society] should be two guineas per annum, which should include the Journal and the Subscription to the International Psycho-Analytic Association" (1920, p. 116).

The International Journal of Psychoanalysis was finally published by the International Psychoanalytical Press (International Psychoanalytischer Verlag) in Vienna, with Jones as Editor and Otto Rank taking charge of things in Vienna. After many delays, the first issue was finally published. Jones writes: "Dear Otto, the Journal arrived today and I was very proud to see it. The get-up is altogether excellent and you are greatly to be congratulated (...)". However, he then adds: "There are only two slight faults in the whole number, that the printing on the front cover is not in the middle and that Fleugel's initials have got altered" (July 30, 1920). One senses Jones's increasing frustration in the next few months:

> Dear Otto, I am afraid that I cannot agree to the journal being issued without my having seen its contents, especially when there are as many and such serious errors as in the pages you sent, so I wired to you yesterday to stop the issue at all cost until I could send you the corrected proofs which I now enclose.
>
> (November 30, 1920)

A few days later, Jones writes:

> Dear Otto, you did the right thing to let the decision about Journal No2 rest with Prof. For my part I would suffer <u>any</u> cost and <u>any</u> delay rather than see the Journal appear with such impossible errors. I cannot describe to you how incredibly foreign such mistakes are as to write New-York instead of New York, and i instead of I; the latter is like writing sachs (his name occurs to me because

he always makes this mistake in English). Such things affect me deeply both for the sake of the Journal and because of my responsibility as editor; the world would not guess that Stern corrected the Journal in place of me, so that I would simply look ridiculous.

(December 3, 1920)

In the first Editorial, Jones sets out the aims of the *Journal*:

The main consideration, though not the only one, that has made this increasingly imperative is the unexpectedly great progress in recent years of the interest taken in our Science by readers not familiar with the German language, and the desirability of making accessible to them the latest researches in the subject. It has long been evident that a periodical published mainly in German could not indefinitely subserve the function of an official international organ, and, since interest in Psycho-Analysis has extended from German-speaking countries to English-speaking countries far more than to any other, it was only a question of time when such a Journal as the present one would have to be founded: with the cessation of the war, the resumption of scientific activities, and the re-establishment of contact between different countries, that time may be judged to have now arrived.

(1920, p. 3, Editorial)

On the occasion of the fiftieth anniversary of *The International Journal*, Anna Freud notes that "behind the scenes, the reasons for establishing an English *Journal* were essentially practical and humble ones". She writes,

The *International Journal* came into being at a period when the publishing house established by Freud in Vienna (*Internationaler Psychoanalytischer Verlag*) had suffered severe financial reverses due to the first world war and its aftermath. There was urgent need for rescue operations.

Anna Freud suggests that it was consequent to the Nazi advances and the subsequent World War II that "the balance between the German and English language became and remained reversed so far as psychoanalysis is concerned" (A. Freud, p. 473, 1969).

When the Verlag was no longer able to subsidize the cost of publishing, printing moved to London, still under the International Psycho-analytical Press. In March 1922, Freud writes to Jones:

> The Verlag has at last found an abode and I trust it will do good work. I am not so well satisfied by the Press. The sphinx in our coat of arms could be supplemented by a snail to give account of the rate of acceleration in its progress. Maybe its mechanism is too complex, I do not see where the fault lies. As we depend for our subsistence on the sale of the English products we throw on the market—the Verlag cannot pay—it is rather a serious affair. Yesterday I got the first two volumes of the *Journal* in exquisite, nay gorgeous, leather-binding. The contents do not correspond to the cover. My wish is that these offsprings of the Anglo-Viennese alliance shall thrive as do the other two you raise in your house.
> (Freud 1922, p. 464, Letter from Sigmund Freud to Ernest Jones, March 2, 1922)

In 1924, after a short period in Lawn House in Hampstead Square, the publishing moved to Baillière, Tindall and Co., who were already the publisher of Jones's *Papers on Psycho-Analysis*. Baillière, Tindall and Co. remained the publisher of the *Journal* until 1989 when the publishing moved to Routledge; then, after a period of self-publishing, it moved to Wiley-Blackwell, and in 2018 back to Routledge, part of the Taylor and Francis group.

Jones persevered throughout, in spite of all the difficulties. Silvia Payne notes:

> Unperturbed by a letter from a London publisher (1924), saying that the latest news from America suggested that 'psycho-analysis was in decline already, the subject having suddenly gone 'flop'', Dr. Jones set the course by which the *International Journal* and the *Library* became highly respected means of communication and worthy archives of psycho-analytic development.
> (Payne 1958, p. 308)

Glover writes about Jones:

> Only those who have had the opportunity of watching Jones at work, as for a number of active years I had the privilege of doing,

can appreciate fully the strain of constantly exercising judgement, balancing opposing interests and producing what is in effect a new book every quarter ... Jones enjoyed the immeasurable advantage of being able to do everything better than everybody else ... The skill with which he maintained the international status of the *Journal* and secured its financial stability ... had to be witnessed to be believed.

(Glover, 1969, *IJPA*, 50, p. 499)

Seventy-five years later, David Tuckett, in the footsteps of Jones (1920), James Strachey (1940), Adrian Stephen (1946), the triumvirate of Willi Hoffer, John Rickman and Clifford Scott (1947), then Hoffer (1949), John D. Sutherland (1960), Joseph Sandler (1969), and Thomas Hayley (1978), writes:

It is to Jones that the *Journal* owes two of its most important and scientific traditions: its non-partisan approach to controversy and its encouragement of the view that judgements concerning the truth and utility of ideas should be based as far as possible on evidential data.

(Tuckett, 1994, p. 1)

Writing in 1945, Adrian Stephen, brother of Virginia Woolf and Vanessa Bell, and third editor following Strachey (both of them were members of the Bloomsbury group), said: "True clinical observations are necessary for the formation of true theory, and true theory is of almost equal importance for the making of clinical observations" (Stephen, 1945, p. 55).

Clearly, however, Jones was not an easy character, though as Riccardo Steiner has noted, his "enormous, obsessive, and often authoritarian labor of control over and motivation of every part of the newborn British Psychoanalytical Society from 1919 onward" (p. xxxi–xxxii) is also what made it possible for him to establish the *Journal*. And Winnicott wrote that:

...those who came in contact with Ernest Jones were often stung by something in his way of making contact. It is not easy to know exactly what it was that people experienced, but whatever it was it had to be accepted. His mother told him he had a sharp tongue. His own Celtic quickness was not always to be matched by a similar quickness in the other person, and this could easily lead to a moment of awkwardness in which there was a sense of something having gone wrong, when in fact all was well. Jones had a keen grip on every subject that he interested himself in, and it would seem that he expected a similar preparedness on the part of those to whom he was talking; when the others were, in fact, not at grips with their subject in a way comparable to his own they were apt to feel a sense of intellectual inferiority, often only too well founded in fact.

(1958, p. 303)

Jones remained the editor until Freud's death in 1939, by which time the *Journal* was very well established. Broadly speaking, the aims and editorial policy of *the Journal* set out by Jones in his first editorial have continued to apply through the century:

...the contents of the Journal will be on the following lines. They will be confined to the subject of Psycho-Analysis and kindred studies having a bearing on Psycho-Analysis. They will thus not attempt to cover the whole field of psychopathology (...), the contents will go beyond the clinical sphere and will embrace as well pure Psycho-Analysis and the other branches of applied Psycho-Analysis, e.g. its relation and application to literature, education, mythology, philology, sociology, anthropology, and so on.

(Jones, 1920, p. 5)

For its fiftieth anniversary, Joseph Sandler stresses the special place and role of the *International Journal* which had been started as the official journal of the IPA:

The *Journal* was started with the intention of representing international psychoanalysis, and it has maintained its identity and function over the past 50 years. This is perhaps all the more remarkable in view of the fact that the administration of the *Journal* has fallen to the lot of the British Society. That this Society has been able to maintain the *Journal* through many difficult periods, and at the same time to preserve the *Journal's* independent identity, reflects the tradition of tolerance which has kept the British Society together even though it has contained so many divergent trends. The *Journal* has never become a partisan vehicle for any one trend in psychoanalysis, even during the years when one point of view appeared to be quite dominant in the British Society.

Although a number of psychoanalytic journals have been started in recent years, the need for an international journal is no less acute than in the past. Indeed, it seems to be all the more necessary nowadays to have an organ which is at one and the same time the guardian of a long tradition and a liberal forum for the different viewpoints within psychoanalysis.

(1969, p. 417)

For its seventy-fifth anniversary, David Tuckett reaffirms the special international role of the *International Journal*:

Freud founded the *Journal* to provide a coherent on-going setting in which all those who were taking part in the growing body of psychoanalytic thought and research could enter into dialogue with one another. From the start it was clear that this dialogue should be international and, although the administration of the *Journal* quite soon became the responsibility of the British Society, an increasingly wide group of colleagues has come to make up the editorial group. They have seen fit to aim the *Journal* at being both the guardian of the psychoanalytic tradition and a liberal forum for the different points of view within psychoanalysis. As such, the *Journal* has successfully represented international psychoanalysis and in doing so has established a unique identity among the publications in our field. The *Journal* has enjoyed the goodwill and co-operation of many colleagues, who advise, write and read it.

(1994, p. 1)

These words are eminently applicable today. In an editorial a few years ago, I wrote:

Being 'international' in my view means publishing the best papers from all traditions. Psychoanalysis has developed in different places along different traditions. Strong traditions are to be valued and fostered. Enabling the creative and focused pursuit of specific ways of thinking and of particular topics of interest is important for our discipline. Difference is to be respected and can also nurture cross-fertilization. Looking at divergences and convergences is important and *The International Journal* is also the place of publication for those who seriously wish to engage with other points of view.

(Birksted-Breen, 2012, p. 3)

I have also emphasized that a core concern of *The International Journal* is:

…the creative space *between* tradition and change, where development stems from psychoanalytic foundations in a dialectical movement of returning to the past and looking forward … [we need] to stay attentive to the questions - what is the psychoanalytical? Where are its parameters? When does it become so changed that it is no longer psychoanalysis? These are not simple questions and need constant discussion if our profession is to retain its solid foundation, providing a frame for creativity. Innovation emerges from previously established parameters and resides in specific, sometimes subtle, shifts in thought.

(Birksted-Breen, 2013, p. 425)

It is also the case that psychoanalysis has been and will always be by its nature countercultural, not least now in its aim to preserve values such as time for reflection in a fast-moving and conflicted world.

★

This book is divided into two parts. Part I discusses the question of translation, both literal and metaphoric – how translation is tied to the significant personalities involved, and its essential role in the development of the *International Journal*. This section starts with the chapter by Weiss and Weiss, who write that "Freud's basic model of the analytic work as an act of decipherment and translation remained relatively unchanged"; they show how Freud used the parallels between archaeology and psychoanalysis to depict his own theory and clinical work, and how archeology is a metaphor for transformations of psychic content and the work of psychoanalysis. In this light, Weiss and Weiss discuss Freud's view of temporality and, in particular, the concept of *Zweizeitigkeit* (literally "two-timedness") in Strachey's translation, an important concept in relation to trauma, repression, and the onset of symptoms.

In the next two chapters, Bruns and Steiner give an insight into the difficulties which were involved in setting up the *International*

Journal, revolving around the significant figures of Freud and his disciples, their personalities, and their affective interrelationships. The question of translation from German to English became an urgent one, and one that had already been a preoccupation of Jones over the previous decade, as Steiner discusses[8]; this issue is addressed by Bruns (Chapter 2), by Steiner (Chapter 3), and by Blass (Chapter 5) from different perspectives. Bruns describes the move from German to English language, Steiner discusses Freud's own immersion in translation and looks at some of the emotional and unconscious factors involved in the translations of Freudian concepts, and Blass focusses on the under-acknowledged important role of as translation editor (Chapter 5).[9]

Women have played a huge role as psychoanalysts, theorists and authors since Freud. But none have played the role of the overall Editor of the *Journal* until today, nor have they been well known for their editorial contribution to the *Journal*. While Blass focusses on Riviere's editorial input, Thompson describes the contribution of Marjorie Brierley, in particular her prolific and interesting book reviews that are both sympathetic and critical (Chapter 6).[10]

The intricacies of the interrelationships of phratry are woven into the history of the *Journal* and the history of the translation of Freud. Riviere, Alix Strachey, and James Strachey were all analysands of Freud. Riviere was an analysand first of Jones and subsequently of Freud. Strachey, Freud's official translator, made use of those translations when he worked on the standard edition (see Blass, Chapter 5). In October 1924, James Strachey writes to his wife Alix about his translation work with Ernest Jones and Joan Riviere:

> I had a very tiresome hour with Jones & Mrs Riviere from 2 to 3 today. The little beast (if I may venture so to describe him) is really most irritating. However, I hope I preserved my suavity. – One thing I foresee fairly clearly. Our names will be ousted from the title-page all right. Mark my words.
>
> (Oct 9, 1924)

James Strachey became the second Editor of *the International Journal of Psychoanalysis* after Freud's death in 1939.

In going through the obituaries of all the editors of the *Journal*, what struck me was how often two things are mentioned: intellectual integrity and a non-partisan approach to psychoanalysis. Winnicott, for instance, writes about Strachey: "the main thing about Strachey is *unassailable intellectual honesty*" (Winnicott, 1969, p. 139). Strachey did not take sides in the controversial discussions between Kleinians and Freudians. He writes to Glover:

> The trouble seems to me to be extremism *on both* sides. My own view is that Mrs K made some highly important contributions to psychoanalysis, but that it is absurd to make out a) that they cover the whole subject b) that their validity is automatic. On the other hand, I think it is equally ludicrous for Miss F to maintain that psychoanalysis is a game reserve belonging to the F family and that Mrs K's ideas are fatally subversive.
> (Strachey letter to Glover, 23 April 1940, General Training Papers 1939–1942: file S-D-02-02)

And of Adrian Stephen, it was said that he:

> ...was supported by his genuine passion for the truth and by a certain satisfaction in debunking nonsense, dishonesty and pretentiousness. He wrote, as he spoke, with difficulty, but he never passed anything slovenly in his own work.
> (Anonymous 1948)

In McQuillan's chapter (Chapter 4), she shows how Strachey was committed to a non-partisan position and to publishing a plurality of views, in particular around issues connected to the controversial discussions which took place during his editorship, and which she links with his lifelong bias towards free speech and heterodoxy. Open-mindedness to different points of view while maintaining a scholarly approach, and a search for truth based on clinical evidence, have been the hall mark of the *International Journal*. Blass, in Chapter 7, shows Ernest Jones's fairness when it came to what she identifies as the first controversy, that between Anna Freud and Melanie Klein. She examines how the journal has evolved over the years as a unifying voice of the analytic community worldwide. This unifying voice includes providing a context for the profound differences that exist within this broad community; Blass posits that an overview of the major discussions of differences of ideas regarding important theoretical and clinical issues that have taken place within *the International Journal of Psychoanalysis* in the course of 100 years

15

demonstrates how the journal has provided such a context. Through researching the history of ideas and controversies, Blass proposes that the aims of the IPA and of the *IJPA* are both convergent in that both wish to open up to free debate, but they are also divergent. The divergence emerges from the way that the *IJPA* has embraced another aim in tension with free debate – that of maintaining "the critical standards that Freud intended for it" with the preservation of the basic tenants of psychoanalysis which he posited: of the unconscious, transference, conflict, resistance.

Part II of the book looks at translation and transformation into representation. From the early days of psychoanalysis, Freud privileged visual representation and transformation into visual images. He writes in *The Interpretation of Dreams*:

> If we now bear in mind how great a part is played in the dream-thoughts by infantile experiences or by phantasies based upon them, how frequently portions of them re-emerge in the dream-content and how often the dream-wishes themselves are derived from them, we cannot dismiss the probability that in dreams too the transformation of thoughts into visual images may be in part the result of the attraction which memories couched in visual form and eager for revival bring to bear upon thoughts cut off from consciousness and struggling to find expression.
>
> (1900, p. 546)

Dreams provided Freud a way to understand the unconscious phenomena because dreams give:

> … a more detailed, intelligible and convincing form of evidence than that produced by conscious mental activity, one that has a more direct bearing on the psychical work of creation, particularly at the three levels on which dreams operate: that of the borderline between the unconscious and the pre-conscious, where drives are given their figurative form in representations and their expression in affects; that of the transformation of mental images into words and vice versa; and, lastly, that of the secondary revision of pre-conscious thoughts through the perceptual-conscious system.
>
> (Anzieu, 1986, p. 6)

And as Anzieu also puts it:

>...like a modern novelist (...) he used material in his dreams to make immediate the psychical realities which he had discovered, and whose existence and nature he wished to make known, in particular the Oedipal organisation of the instincts. While awake, Freud discovered the meaning of dreams; and while dreaming he visualised his discoveries as they came into being and anticipated new ones.
>
> (Anzieu, 1986, p. 6)

In this second part of the book, we approach the question of transformation in two ways: first, in terms of the transformation of conscious, unconscious, and non-represented elements into non-verbal modes of presentation, in particular visual, poetic, and musical; second, in terms of the development within the *International Journal* over a 100 years of the discourse between psychoanalysis and artistic expressions.

Freud used the striking visual image of the Greek myth of Oedipus and the Sphinx from a painting by Ingres as the logo for all the publications he initiated when he established a *Verlag* (press) in Vienna in order to publish his theories without restrictions and censorship; to this day, it remains the logo of *the International Journal of Psychoanalysis*. In Chapter 8, Adele Tutter proposes that Ingres's herocizing representation of Oedipus may have influenced Freud's theorizing about the myth. Tutter contrasts this representation with Francis Bacon's 20th- century representation of a traumatized Oedipus, comparing the two canvases as a springboard for a broad overview of articles on art and psychoanalysis over the 100 years of *the International Journal of Psychoanalysis*. In the next chapter (Chapter 9), Carina Weiss places the interest in the Oedipus theme within the culture of 19th and early 20th centuries in Vienna; she looks at the depiction of Oedipus and the Sphinx on the medal which was gifted to Freud by his closest friends and disciples on the occasion of his fiftieth birthday, and which is closer to Freud's ex libris created by the Art Nouveau painter and graphic artist Berthold Löffler (1874–1960) than to Ingres. In this version, the sphinx is crouching with a human head, which "augments (...) her uncanny epiphany and evokes in a way her erotic danger". Weiss discusses the orthographic mistakes on the inscription on the medal and Freud's reaction.[11]

The next two chapters discuss a different sensibility to psychoanalysis: rather than visual representation, they seek to describe what lies beyond words. Margot Waddell chooses poetry as that which expresses rhythms reaching areas of experience outside simple prose. She describes a move over the century to more complex psychoanalytic insights into the nature of creativity and the centrality of meaning in psychic and artistic life, with the poetic becoming a vital dimension of understanding the unconscious itself. Francis Grier discusses the negligible role that music and musicality have played in psychoanalytic theory and clinical practice, and how this is beginning to change with the deepening and broadening out of psychoanalytic theory to include in a central position the intuitive and non-verbal dimension of musicality. He draws together different aspects of the psychoanalytic situation to bring attention to the ubiquity of music:

> Music is ubiquitous in the psychoanalytic encounter, literally, not just metaphorically. It lies behind the words of both patient and analyst, filling those words – or the silences, or other non-verbal noises and utterances to which we rarely give attention – with meaning, or, in the case of a lack of music, depleting the encounter of emotional resonance.
>
> (Grier, 2019)

The book ends with a chapter by Lucy LaFarge on the Wolf-Man's dream – iconic in the history of psychoanalysis in its reference to Freud's important paper "From the History of an Infantile Neurosis", which brings forth the question of infantile sexuality, the primal scene, and questions of temporality and historical truth. The iconic aspect of the Wolf Man dream is further increased by its plastic representation in the form of the painting that Freud's patient, Sergei Pankieff, presented to Freud. LaFarge discusses the various resignifications of the dream through the pages of the *International Journal*, proposing its duality of conservatism and development.

This chapter on the Wolf-Man's dream, which concludes the book, brings together the themes of the book on translation and transformation in the development of *the International Journal of Psychoanalysis* over the century, with a special focus on writings relating to representation and that which lies beyond words.

Notes

1 *Verrrall was a Classicist and Lecturer at Cambridge, also the uncle of Joan Riviere.*

2 A centenary special issue which includes all the conference papers and the Compendium which accompanied the archival display case of the exhibition is published in *the International Journal of Psychoanalysis* 2019, issue 6.

3 A short film of the exhibition can be found on Vimeo: The Enigma of the Hour – *the International Journal of Psychoanalysis* Centenary Exhibition, conveying the themes of temporality, transformations, and resonances.

4 Nowadays, the *Journal* translates more than half its published papers from other languages, and the *Annuals of Psychoanalysis* translates papers into many languages (Italian, Spanish, Portuguese, French, German, Rumanian, Turkish, Greek, Chinese).

5 See Birksted-Breen D. for a discussion of this (2003), and Weiss H and Weiss C in this volume.

6 *IJPA* was the acronym for *the International Journal of Psychoanalysis* until 2001 when it was changed to *IJP*. For this reason, in this book, when referring to the history of psychoanalysis the acronym *IJPA* is used by the authors. Up to 1998, the word Psycho-Analysis was hyphenated in the title of the *Journal*: *The International Journal of Psycho-Analysis*. From 1999, the hyphen was dropped, and it became *International Journal of Psychoanalysis*.

7 There is currently no extensive and in-depth history of *the International Journal of Psychoanalysis*.

8 For a presentation of the various glossary projects, see IJP 2019.

9 See IJP 2019, pp for a discussion of her role in helping colleagues with their papers.

10 In the exhibition *The Enigma of the Hour,* a special focus was given on four women who played an important and not sufficiently recognized role in their contribution to the early days of the *Journal*. For a presentation of the role of Alix Strachey and Anna Freud, see *IJP* 2019 issue 6 The Enigma of the Hour: Display Case Compendium pp. 1481–1613.

11 Adele Tutter (2019, p. 400) suggests that there could have been an unconscious meaning behind or attributed to the misspelt inscription accompanying the Oedipus and the Sphinx. KΛEIN (Greek, *famous*) is *misspelled* KLEIN (German, *small*). She suggests that

> Freud (...) might easily have interpreted the mistake to mean that his colleagues (or, more precisely, the one that made the misspelling) *unconsciously* felt that "Siegmund" had solved a small, insignificant

riddle, rather than a famous one. Thus, even if Freud disregarded the archaic spelling of his name, the potentially meaningful "shrinking" of his achievement may have contributed to his dramatic response to the medal—and, perhaps, to his later refusal to translate its inscription for Jones.

(Tutter, 2019)

References

Anzieu, D. (1986). Freud's Self-Analysis. *Int. Psycho-Anal. Lib.*, 118:1–596.

Birksted-Breen, D. (2003). Time and the *Après-coup*. *Int. J. Psycho-Anal.*, 84(6):1501–1515.

Birksted-Breen, D. (2012). "Editorial." *Int. J. Psycho-Anal.* 93(1):3–4. doi: 10.1111/j.1745-8315.2011.00550.x

Blass, R. (2019). The Enigma of the Hour: Display Case Compendium. *Int. J. Psycho-Anal.*, 100(6):1481–1613.

Doolittle, H. (1956). *Tribute to Freud; With Unpublished Letters by Freud to the Author.* New York: New Directions Books.

Freud, S. (1915). [SEN159a1] The Unconscious. *The Standard Edition of the Complete Psychological Works of Sigmund Freud, Volume XIV (1914–1916): On the History of the Psycho-Analytic Movement, Papers on Metapsychology and Other Works*, 159–215.

Freud, S. (1920). Beyond the Pleasure Principle. *RSE*, 18:57.

Freud, S. (1922). Letter from Sigmund Freud to Ernest Jones, March 2, 1922. *The Complete Correspondence of Sigmund Freud and Ernest Jones 1908–1939*, 463–464.

Freud, A. (1969). Remarks on the Fiftieth Birthday of the International Journal of Psycho-Analysis. *Int. J. Psycho-Anal.*, 50:473–474.

Forrester, J., and Cameron, L. (2017). Bloomsbury Analysts. In *Freud in Cambridge* (pp. 505–612). Cambridge: Cambridge University Press.

Grier, F. (2020). The Inner World of Beethoven's Ninth Symphony: Masculine and Feminine? *Int. J. Psycho-Anal.*, 101(1):84–109.

Jones, E. (1920). "Editorial." *Int. J. Psycho-Anal.*, 1:3–5.

Meisel, P., and Kendrick, W. (eds.) (1986). *Bloomsbury/Freud: The Letters of James and Alix Strachey, (1924–1925).* London: Chatto & Windus.

Stephen, A. (1945). "(1) Ruminations of a Scientific Secretary1." *Int. J. Psycho-Anal.*, 26:52–55.

Tuckett, D. (1994). The 75th Volume. *Int. J. Psycho-Anal.*, 75:1–2.

Winnicott, D. W. (1958). "Ernest Jones." *Int. J. Psycho-Anal.*, 39:298–304.

Winnicott, D. W. (1969). James Strachey – 1887–1967. *Int. J. Psycho-Anal.*, 50:129–132.

---Part One---

A PROMENADE THROUGH HISTORY AND THE CENTRAL PLACE OF TRANSLATION

TRANSLATION AS A METAPHOR, THE ROLE OF ARCHAEOLOGY IN FREUD'S DECIPHERING OF THE HUMAN MIND

Heinz Weiss and Carina Weiss

Freud, the "archaeologist"

In a letter to his early biographer, Stefan Zweig, Freud admits that he has

> sacrificed a great deal for my collection of Greek, Roman and Egyptian antiquities, have actually read more archaeology than psychology, and that before the war and once after its end I felt compelled to spend every year at least several days or weeks in Rome.
>
> (Freud 1931, p. 402)[1]

Very probably, Freud started collecting art objects in a systematic way after his father's death in October 1986 (Forrester 1994, pp. 227, 230–234).[2] He began with copies of Renaissance works, but switched soon over to original antiquities from the Egyptian, Greek, and Roman periods, later also to Asiatic art objects. Many items he bought himself, and many he got as presents from friends, disciples, followers, and also from patients.[3]

In fact, towards the very end of his life, his collection of antiquities had amounted to more than 3,000 pieces, some of which have subsequently been published in various archaeological journals and volumes (Engelmann 1976; Weiss & Weiss 1984, 1985; Gamwell &

Wells 1989; Corcoran 1991; D'Agata 1994; Forrester 1994; Reeves & Uemo 1996; Marinelli 1998; Śliwa 1999; C. Weiss 2011).[4]

When the authors of this article had the opportunity to visit Freud's house, 20 Maresfield Gardens, London, immediately after the death of his daughter Anna in spring 1983, it conveyed the impression of an antique tomb, with its treasures still unchanged even after a long period of time (Figures 1.1–1.3). This was the first time that parts of his collection were subject to scientific research and subsequent publication (Weiss & Weiss 1985).

If we trace back Freud's interest in archaeology to his personal life, we may detect its origins to his childhood (cf. Cassirer Bernfeld 1951), when the ruins of an old castle nearby his hometown Freiberg (Moravia) evoked his spirit of discovery and perhaps initiated his identification with famous discoverers like Heinrich Schliemann who had excavated the ruins of Troy in the 1870s; Sir Arthur Evans, excavator of the temples of Karnak; or Thomas Young and Jean-François Champollion, who had succeeded to decipher the enigmatic hieroglyphs on the Rosetta Stone from Egypt by comparing

© carina und heinz weiss

Figure 1.1 20 Maresfield Gardens, the house, May 1983, copyright Carina and Heinz Weiss.

© carina und heinz weiss

Figure 1.2 20 Maresfield Gardens, Freud's study, May 1983, copyright Carina and Heinz Weiss.

them to the demotic and ancient Greek versions of the text on the Hellenistic stele displayed since 1802 in the British Museum.[5]

Repeatedly Freud mentions his fascination of archaeology and in particular his longing to visit the antique sites in Italy (Pompeii, Rome) in his letters to Wilhelm Fließ.[6] There is some evidence that Freud's interest in W. Jensen's (1903) novel *Gradiva* (Freud 1907) was motivated by an hidden identification with the protagonist, young archaeologist Norbert Hanold, who had travelled to Pompeii to meet the reappearance of a girl he had loved in his childhood, as it was for Freud his early girlfriend Gisela Fluß. The descriptions he gives in his autobiographical fragment on *"Screen Memories"* (Freud 1899; Bernfeld 1946) reveal some striking parallels to the imagery of Jensen's novel (Weiss & Weiss 1989; C. Weiss 2018).

Another important link to archaeology was Freud's relationship with his friend from school days, Emanuel Loewy, one of the few persons outside his family with who he was on first-name terms. Since 1891, Loewy held a professorship of classical archaeology at the University of Rome. He used to visit Freud once a year and is likely to have further stimulated and sustained his interest in archaeology.

© carina und heinz weiss

Figure 1.3 20 Maresfield Gardens, a glass cabinet with Egyptian, Etruscan, and other antiquities in the study, May 1983, copyright Carina and Heinz Weiss.

From 1896 onwards, Freud began to acquire antiquities and copies which are mentioned in his letters to Fließ.[7]

Amongst Freud's many art dealers were Ludwig Pollak in Rome and Robert Lustig in Vienna. In a letter to the authors, Lustig remembers Freud as an expert and keen collector of Egyptian, Greek, Etruscan, and Roman antiquities. He visited him regularly to introduce new items and sometimes even exchanged objects with him, like the side piece of a Roman sarcophagus which was placed on the top of one of his bookshelves (Figures 1.4 and 1.5).

These objects, together with his journeys to Italy and Greece, deepened his interest in ancient culture and accompanied his scientific work from its very beginning up to his last paper on Moses and monotheism (Freud 1939). The antiquities were objects of devotion, charms to keep away the roughness of everyday life, sometimes used to explain his theory (Doolittle 1956). Acquiring and giving away, the collection stayed in perpetual movement during Freud's lifetime. Antiques were gifted to his closest disciples like the gemstones which adorned the rings of the members of the "Secret Committee" or were given to family members and friends. Sometimes they were

© carina und heinz weiss

Figure 1.4 20 Maresfield Gardens, fragment of a Roman sarcophagus on top of a bookshelf, May 1983, copyright Carina and Heinz Weiss.

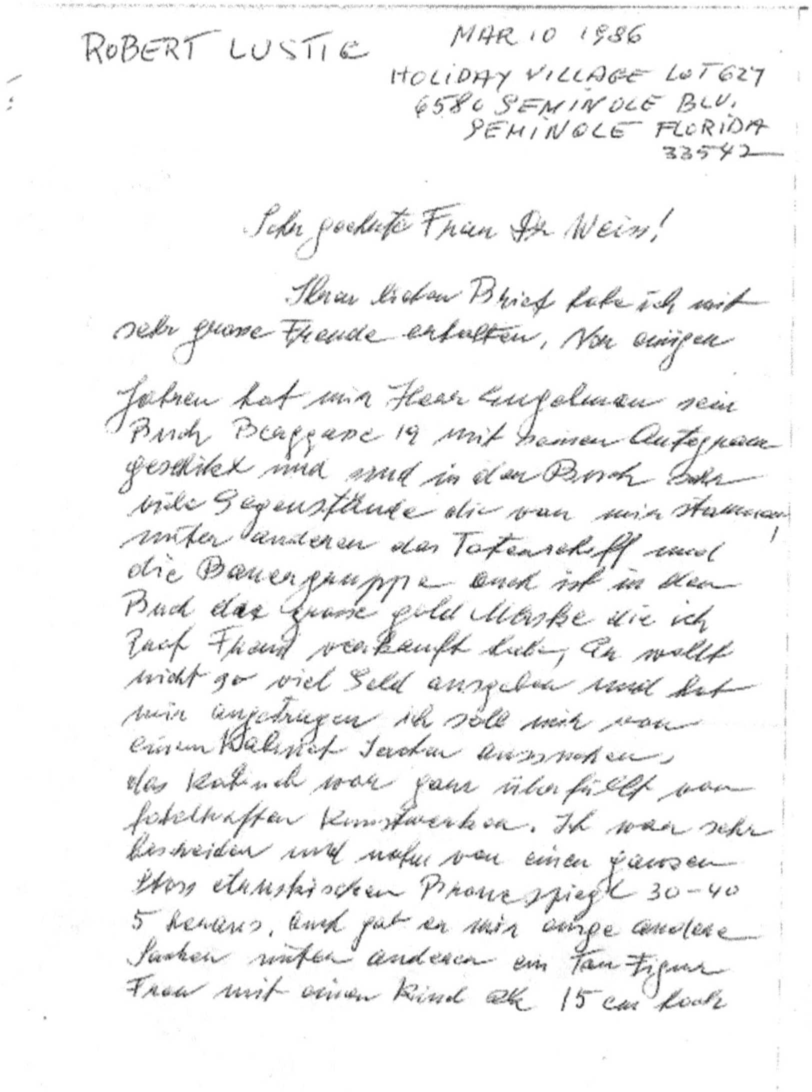

Figure 1.5 Front page of a letter March 10, 1986, by Robert Lustig to Dr. Carina Weiss, copyright Carina and Heinz Weiss.

exchanged with art dealers to acquire better or more desired items (Berthelsen 1987, pp. 47–48; Forrester 1994, pp. 229–230; C. Weiss 2011, 2016).

(Re)construction, decipherment, and translation

Freud's comparison of the work of the archaeologist to that of the psychoanalyst seems all present in his work. He also published a number of papers on antique history and mythology (Freud 1910b, 1911b, 1916–1917a, 1932, 1939, 1940). The aim is always to uncover the foundations underneath the surface, to decipher a meaning, and to examine its various transformations. Already in his *Studies on Hysteria* (Freud 1895), he draws the parallel between the symptoms of a hysteric patient and a "pictographic script which has become intelligible after the discovery of a few bilingual inscriptions" (p. 129).

One year later, in 1896, he extends this comparison when he writes:

> Imagine that an explorer arrives in a little-known region where his interest is aroused by an expanse of walls, fragments of columns, and tablets with half-effaced and unreadable inscriptions. He may content himself with inspecting what lies exposed to his view, with questioning the inhabitants (…) who live in the vicinity, about what tradition tells them of the history and meaning of these archaeological remains, and with noting down what they tell him - and he may then proceed on his journey. But he may act differently. He may have brought picks, shovels and spades with him, and he may set the inhabitants to work with these implements. Together with them he may start upon the ruins, clear away the rubbish, and, beginning from the visible remains, uncover what is buried. If his work is crowned with success, the discoveries are self-explanatory: the ruined walls are part of the ramparts of a palace or a treasure-house; the fragment of columns can be filled out into a temple: the numerous inscriptions, which, by good chance, may be bilingual, reveal an alphabet and a language, and, when they have been deciphered and translated, yield undreamed-of information about the events of the remote past, to commemorate with the monuments were built. *Saxa loquuntur!*
> (Freud 1896, p. 191)

By quoting the motto of stone gravers, palaeontologists, and geologists *saxa loquuntur* – the rocks begin to speak[8] – Freud refers to a model of decipherment, where the meaning of a text can be discovered by means of reconstruction and translation. Every trace, every transcription contains the testimony of its origin, even if parts of it were lost and had to be supplemented by meaningful construction.

Freud discovered the "bilinguals" he was looking for in the language of dreams, and later on in the manifestations of the transference. Both could be seen as transcripts by which the enigmatic language of symptoms became gradually understandable as a meaningful narrative.

Although Freud altered and extended his metapsychological assumptions in subsequent decades, his basic model of the analytic work as an act of decipherment and translation remained relatively unchanged. Thus, in accordance with his argument from 1896, he wrote some 40 years later in "*Constructions in Analysis*":

> His [the analyst's] work of construction, or, if it is preferred, of re-construction, resembles to a great extent an archaeologist's excavation of some dwelling-place that has been destroyed and buried or of some ancient edifice. The two processes are in fact identical, except that the analyst works under better conditions and has more material at his command to assist him, since what he is dealing with is not something destroyed but something that is still alive – and perhaps for another reason as well. But just like the archaeologist builds up the walls of a building from the foundations that have remained standing, determines the number and positions of columns from depressions in the floor and reconstructs the mural decorations and paintings from the remains found in the debris, so does the analyst proceed when he draws his inferences from the fragments of memories, from the associations and from the behaviour of the subject of the analysis. Both of them have an undisputed right to reconstruct by means of supplementing and combining the surviving remains. Both of them, moreover, are subject of many of the same difficulties and sources of error. One of the most ticklish problems that confronts the archaeologist is notoriously the relative age of his finds; and if an object makes its appearance in one particular level, it often remains to be decided whether it belongs to this particular level or whether it was carried down to that level owing to some subsequent disturbance. It is easy to imagine the corresponding doubts that arise in the case of analytic constructions.
>
> (Freud 1937, p. 259)

As we will see, the latter problem is not just a methodological one, but closely connected to Freud's conceptions of "bi-temporality" (*"Zweizeitigkeit"*) and "afterwardness" (*"Nachträglichkeit"*). But when he published his paper on *"Constructions"*, this was in itself a time of critical personal change, the year before he was forced to emigrate and to move to London. It was Marie Bonaparte who helped him to escape the Nazi terror and who also succeeded to arrange for the greatest part of his collection to follow him to his London exile. Single pieces of his collection were personal gifts from her.

When Freud speaks in the aforementioned quotation of the "mural decorations and paintings" as the aim of the archaeologist's reconstructions, he seems to allude to his fascination for antique Pompeii. From 1900 onwards, he had acquired several pieces of Pompeian wall paintings which decorated his Viennese consulting room (see Engelmann 1976; letter to Fließ from May 8, 1901). His first visit to the antique city in 1902 was an overwhelming impression, and in the same year when he had published his study on *Gradiva* (Freud 1907), he had discovered the original of the Gradiva relief in the Vatican museums and acquired a plaster copy of it. Thus, with the wall paintings on his side and the Gradiva relief placed above the couch whilst analysing his patients, he must have felt like working in a Pompeian house (Figure 1.6).

However, Pompeii was not only a striking example of the archaeologist's work of reconstruction through careful excavation, rearrangement, and combination. It also served as a metaphor for the unconscious being preserved underneath the forces of repression. Just like antique Pompeii remained preserved, *because* it was covered underneath the ashes of mount Vesuvio (Figure 1.7), the repressed memories and wishes remain powerfully alive as long as they are denied access to the conscious – a parallel that Freud himself had mentioned towards one of his patients, known under his eponymous name, the "Rat Man".[9]

Perhaps one might say that what Freud later on described as the "timelessness" and "immortality" of the unconscious (Freud 1915b, p. 187; 1920, p. 28; 1933, p. 73) was pre-figured by the destiny of antique Pompeii (H. Weiss 2011). As an expert who was familiar with contemporaneous archaeology, he must have heard of the innovative methods of Professor Giuseppe Fiorelli (1823–1896), chair of archaeology at Naples University and director of the excavations in Pompeii from 1860 to 1875. Fiorelli had not only established the

Figure 1.6 20 Maresfield Gardens, study, Pompeian wall paintings, May 1983, copyright Carina and Heinz Weiss.

meticulous method of studying archaeological sites layer by layer but also invented the method of pouring plaster into the cavities of the lava ashes to regain the corpses of the victims (C. Weiss 2018). This came about as a sensational finding at this time which stimulated the novelist's interest in "revenants" (Gautier 1852; Hawthorne 1860) and shows striking resemblances to what Freud called the "return of the repressed" (Freud 1915a). Now everyday life, the social relations, clothes, and facial expressions of the inhabitants of Pompeii came to the forth and could be examined in detail. In a similar way, Freud emphasized the vividness of the repressed memories which are contained in a negative form in the imprints of the neurotic symptoms.

Nevertheless, in psychoanalysis, the language of these memories has to be translated, since there is no direct access to the unconscious. Like in archaeology, the testimonies of the past have always to be put into a meaningful context. What the analyst gets to see, layer by layer, therefore, are not the historical events as such, but

POMPEI · VEDUTA GENERALE DEL FORO CIVILE

Figure 1.7 Pompeii, view over the forum towards Mt. Vesuvio (historical photograph, Ricordo di Pompei, 32 vedute, N. 227, undated, Edizioni A. Scrocchi, Milano).

transformations of their narratives, sometimes represented as pictographs, which have to be translated through the methods of comparison, supplementing, and interpretation.

Translation and transference

One example for this is Freud's examination of the meaning of dreams. Very much like Egyptian hieroglyphs, the meaning of the dream pictures is not expressed in their apparent iconography, but has to be unravelled by decoding the underlying language. The dream-thoughts and the dream-content, Freud writes, "are presented to us like two versions of the same subject-matter in two different languages" (1900, p. 277). Or, to put it more precisely:

(…) the dream-content seems like a transcript of the dream-thoughts into another mode of expression, whose characters and syntactic laws it is our business to discover by comparing the original and the translation. (…) The dream-content (…) is expressed as it were in a pictographic script, the characters of which have to be transposed individually into the language of the dream-thoughts.

He argues that one might be led into error if "we attempted to read these characters according to their pictorial value instead of according to their symbolic relation" (p. 277). Instead, the pictography of the dream is comparable to a rebus where each separate element has to be replaced by a syllable or a word:

> The words which are put together in this way are no longer nonsensical but may form a poetical phrase of the greatest beauty and significance. A dream is a picture-puzzle of this sort and our predecessors in the field of dream-interpretation have made the mistake of treating the rebus as a pictorial composition: and as such it has seemed to them nonsensical and worthless.
>
> (p. 278)

Freud was already familiar with antique script-systems when he visited Charcot in Paris (1885/1886) where he saw the Obelisk at the Place de la Concorde. He admired Charcot's collection of antique art[10] and was fascinated by the Egyptian and Assyrian collections in the Louvre:

> There were Assyrian kings - tall as trees and holding lions for lapdogs in their arms, winged human animals with beautifully dressed hair, cuneiform inscriptions as clear as if they had been done yesterday, and then Egyptian bas-reliefs decorated in fiery colours, veritable colossi of kings, real sphinxes, a dreamlike world.[11]

A childhood dream showing his sleeping mother being carried away by persons with bird-like heads reminded him of Gods from an Egyptian tomb relief (Freud 1900, p. 589). The figure originated from an illustration in the Phillippson Bible which was in the possession of the family. Rosenfeld (1956), Flem (1982; 1992), and Niederland (1988) have speculated about the significance of the many archaeological illustrations in this book for Freud's later scientific interests and biography. When Abraham announced his study on Amenhotep IV and the cult of Aton (Abraham 1912), he expressed his gratitude for the "first lessons in Egyptology" he had obtained from Freud in 1907.[12] In Freud's personal collection, there

34

were many objects of Egyptian origin, some of which were exposed on book shelves (Figure 1.8) and in a glass cabinet (Figure 1.3).

However, Freud's use of the terms "transcript", "transposition", and "translation" is interesting also for another reason. Because it was here, in the area of dreams, that he used already the term "transference" to designate the way in which an unconscious wish is transposed into another context, be it a neurotic symptom, the day residues of the manifest dream-content, or the patient's relation to the analyst.[13] Thus, "transference" does not simply mean reproduction, but also transcription, translation, or reassignment. In fact, the German word *Übertragung* (transference) means "handing over" as well as "transmission" and "translation". "Transferring" a text, especially in Freud's time, would mean to translate its meaning into another language. Consequently, Freud emphasized in his postscript to the "Dora" case (1905, p. 116) that the "transferences" are not merely "facsimiles" or "reprints" of the patient's original impulses and phantasies, but some of them have to be considered as modifications and "revised editions".

© carina und heinz weiss

Figure 1.8 20 Maresfield Gardens, study, Egyptian figurines in a bookshelf, May 1983, copyright Carina and Heinz Weiss.

Later on in Freud's writings "transference" was closely connected to the phenomenon of the "repetition compulsion". "We soon perceive", Freud explains in his seminal paper "Remembering, Repeating and Working Through" (1914, p. 151), "that the transference is itself only a piece of repetition". But he adds, the repetition is, in turn, "a transference of the forgotten past (...) to all (...) aspects of the current situation". Thus, transference and repetition supplement each other. Transference is a form of repetition, but, vice versa, repetition is brought about through "transference" as a form of transcription and transformation.

The same thought can be found in Freud's letters to Fließ where he repeatedly states that the psychic content is deposited in different "scripts" which overlay and superimpose each other. Already in 1896, he supposes "that our psychical mechanism has come into being by a process of stratification", where the memory traces are "subjected from time to time to a re-arrangement in accordance with fresh circumstances – to a *re-transcription*" (p. 233).[14] These successive registrations, he adds, "represent the psychical achievements of successive epochs of life" (p. 235). Hence, his later comparison is with the city of Rome where the different phases of the town's history are to be found in the stratification of various overlapping layers (Freud 1930, pp. 69–71). Transcription, translation, and transformation can therefore be seen as an oscillating process promoting psychic development. They seem to include some sort of symbolic activity, albeit in a primitive form, like primary process functioning. As we shall see, these considerations had an influence on Freud's notions of time and remembering.

Bi-temporality ("Zweizeitigkeit"), afterwardness ("Nachträglichkeit"), and the time of the unconscious

In her seminal paper "Time and the après-coup", Dana Birksted-Breen (2003) has elaborated Freud's complex ideas on time and temporality. She shows that the model of genetic continuity and the more dialectical concept of afterwardness (*Nachträglichkeit* or *après-coup*) do rather supplement than contradict each other. Afterwardness results from bi-temporality ("*Zweizeitigkeit*"), a concept that is difficult to grasp since Strachey used different translations for the German word.

We find the term *Zweizeitigkeit*, for instance, in Freud's *An Autobiographical Study* (1925b) where he speaks of the bi-temporality (in Strachey's translation: "diphasic onset") of the development of human sexuality.[15] Already in his *Three Essays* from 1905, there is a paragraph on the "bi-temporality of object choice" (Freud 1905, p. 99). He uses the term in his analysis of the Schreber case (Freud 1911a, p. 55), in "Totem and Taboo" (1912–1913, p. 112) and discusses the bi-temporal symptom formation in anxiety hysteria in his paper on repression (Freud 1915a, p. 258).[16]

It is clear bi-temporality means that "inscriptions" are made at two different times which seems to imply that they are stored in different layers of the human mind. Therefore, Freud's notion of bi-temporality is closely connected to his concepts of trauma, regression, and the return of the repressed. Insofar, afterwardness can be seen as resulting from the bi-temporality of mental life, that is, the continuous to and fro between past, present, and future. In other words: alongside genetic continuity, there is a permanent process of "re-transcription" which assigns retrospectively and prospectively meaning to our past and to our future. Or, as Freud puts it in his early paper on *Screen memories*:

> It may be indeed questioned whether we have any memories at all *from* our childhood: memories *relating to* our childhood may be all that we possess. Our childhood memories show us our early years not as they were but as they appeared at the later periods when the memories were aroused.
>
> (Freud 1899, p. 321)

In the same paper, he differentiates between positive and negative, and retrogressive and anticipatory,[17] screen memories (S.E., p. 319, G.W., p. 550). And even when he does not mention the term there, he gives a plain exposure of the concept of *Nachträglichkeit*.

If we move a step forward and interpret the concept of "bi-temporality" in a more contemporaneous way, we may see it as hinting at *two different forms of temporality* which coexist and supplement each other: one which draws a *linear concept of time* where each new experience follows the previous one, and the other a *dialectical model* which depicts a loop from the present to the future reassigning the meaning of our past from an anticipated later point of view. It was this model of temporality that attracted the attention of analysts like Jacques Lacan (1964, 1966) in France and Wolfgang Loch (1988, 1993) in Germany.

At least one could read Freud's "Note on the Mystic Writing Pad" (1925a) in such a way. In this paper, he returns to his early formulations from his *Project* (1895) and his letters to Fließ[18] (Freud 1950). Concerning the relationship between the perceptual apparatus, memory, and time, he recalls the antique idea of memory-formation by writing with a stylus on a wax tablet where the impressions are preserved as traces and inscriptions (Figure 1.9).

However, so as to make room for new perceptions to be stored on a limited space, the memory traces must at least temporarily disappear.[19] Only then new perceptions can emerge and re-transcriptions can take place. What results is a complex oscillation between preservation and extinction, continuity and disruption, synchrony and diachrony, and past and presence. At the end of his paper, Freud goes as far as to speculate that the unconscious, via the system *Pcpt.-Cs.*, stretches out from time to time: "feelers (…) to the external world and hastily withdraws them as soon as they have sampled the excitations coming from it" (Freud 1925a, p. 230). He assumes that this discontinuous method of working "lies at the bottom of the origin of the concept of time" (p. 230).

Figure 1.9 Wood tablet covered with wax used as a writing pad in the Roman Empire. 1st century A.D. Museo de Santa Cruz, Toledo, Spain. https://fr.wikipedia.org/wiki/Fichier:Tablette-de-cire.jpg Auteur: Codex. Wikimedia Commons, File tablette de cire.

Timeless phantasies or phantasies of timelessness?

At this point, one might ask how this assumption fits in with Freud's ideas on the "timelessness" and "immortality" of the unconscious? Is the unconscious really timeless or must there be at least a preconception of time as one of the "basic facts of life" (Money-Kyrle 1971)? Freud's paper on *"Transience"* (Freud 1916) seems to point in this direction, since it is the acknowledgement of finitude and loss that allows the individual to face reality and to appreciate what we can get from it. Here, as well as in *Mourning and Melancholia* (Freud 1916–1917b), Freud comes perhaps closest to the Kleinian notion of time which is closely linked to the experiences of the depressive position. Whenever transience is acknowledged, full reversibility is never possible (H. Weiss 2018). This is in contrast with the more primitive, paranoid-schizoid, and borderline modes of experiencing time which give rise to catastrophic fears, persecutory guilt, and endless repetitive cycles beyond symbolization and repair (Birksted-Breen 2003; Weiss 2003, 2009; Bell 2006).

For that reason, some authors have questioned Freud's ideas about the timelessness of the unconscious. They see it as a misreading of Kant's transcendental philosophy (Hanly 2009) or perhaps as an expression of nineteenth-century romantic idealism (H. Weiss 2018). Andre Green has introduced the concept of "heterochronicity" (Green 2002, 2007, 2009), that is, the idea that different modes of experiencing time may coexist and operate simultaneously in the human mind. These may include even very primitive "proto-temporal" experiences[20] at the origin of what we call the perception of time.

Of course, like the psychic apparatus, psychoanalytic theory is never static and is itself subject to transformations and "re-transcriptions" in the course of its development. In view of narcissistic and borderline pathologies, we tend to see "timelessness" today not just as a quality of the system *"Ucs."*, but rather as a defence against the experience of time. Several mechanisms like "slicing", "significant forgetting" (Riesenberg-Malcolm 1990, 2004), "unpicking the tapestry" (Birksted-Breen 2003), "freezing" (Giovacchini 1967), or "romantic erotization" (Weiss 2008) have been identified to understand the retreat into timeless states of mind (Weiss 2009, 2017; Steiner 2018). In those withdrawals, there is a longing for timelessness, and perhaps in view of those pathologies, it might be more appropriate to speak of *phantasies of timelessness* rather than of *timeless phantasies*.

These themes are issues of future debate. Of course, phantasies of timelessness are a universal motive in mythological and utopic thinking, as it was for Freud his immersion in antique history and his collection of antique art objects. "These things put me in a good mood and speak of distant times and countries", he writes to Fliess in August 1899, when he was planning "to tramp on foot to my beloved Salzburg" on the next rainy day, "where I actually unearthed a few Egyptian antiquities last time".[21]

Many of his journeys had taken him to antique sites in Italy and Greece, like the voyage to Athens with his brother Alexander in 1904 (see Freud 1936), where he saw Schliemann's former assistant and follower in Troy, Professor Wilhelm Dörpfeld, on the boat, but was too shy to approach him,[22] or the journey he undertook with Ferenczi to Sicily in 1910. After visiting the antique temples of Segesta, Selinunt, and Agrigento, they reached Syracuse, where Freud collected a bundle of papyrus leaves from the ancient fountain of Arethusa.[23] Perhaps it was the same bundle of dried papyrus leaves which, for many years, decorated the Gradiva relief over his couch (Figure 1.10).

Figure 1.10 Vienna, Berggasse 13 consulting room, plastercast Gradiva relief with papyrus, 1938, reproduced from Engelmann, 1976.

As Susanne Cassirer Bernfeld (1951, p. 110) recalls, Freud's house-maid Paula used "to warn newcomers to the couch to keep away from them, since at the slightest touch they would dissolve in a rain of dust".

Notes

1 Freud's statement is confirmed by the vast amount of archaeological literature in private library (Davies 1998).

2 Already as a young student, Freud showed some interest in collect-ing; see the auction list of nonsense objects found in Lichtenberg (1742–1799) which he copied for his friend Eduard Silberstein. Freud (1874). Letter from Sigmund Freud to Eduard Silberstein, 2 December 1874. The Letters of Sigmund Freud to Eduard Silberstein 1871–1881, pp. 72–76.

3 See correspondence between Sigmund Freud and Sándor Ferenczi: Let-ters from 8 February–17 May 1910 (Brabant, Falzeder, Giampieri-Deutsch 1993). Gifts from patients: See the recollections of the "Wolf-Man" in Gardiner (1971, p. 150).

4 There is no complete catalogue of Freud's collection up to the present.

5 Champollion 1922 – Rosetta Stone, Brit. Mus. Inv. Nr. EA24. For the huge bibliography, see http://www.britishmuseum.org/research/collection_on-line/collection_object_details.aspx?objectId=117631&partId=1&search-Text=rosetta+stone&page=1; Rieber (2012) pp. 45–47. Freud mentions Champollion in his Leonardo paper (Freud 1910a, p. 156).

6 See, for example, the letters from 6 December 1896, 5 November 1897 and 23 October 1898 (Freud 1887-1904).

7 See letters from 6 December 1896 and 17 July 1897. The origins of Freud's collection and the significance of the antique objects for his private life are depicted in Weiss & Weiss (1984, 1989) and Gamwell (1989).

8 Refering to Lukas VII.

9 "(…) and I illustrated my remarks by pointing to the antiques standing about in my room. They were, in fact, I said, only objects found in a tomb, and their burial had been their preservation: the destruction of Pompeii was only beginning now that it had been dug up" (Freud 1909d, p. 176; Forrester 1994, p. 224).

10 See letter to Martha Bernays from 20 January 1886 (Freud 1873–1939, p. 194).

11 Letter to Martha Bernays from 19 October 1885 (Freud 1873–1939, pp. 173–174).

12 Letter to Abraham from 11 January 1912 (Falzeder 2002, p. 146).

13 See Freud (1900, pp. 183, 200, 531, 597).

14 Letter to Fließ from 6 December 1896 (Freud 1887–1904).
15 In Strachey's translation "diphasic onset" (Freud 1925b, p. 36). Concerning Freud's use of the term *"zweizeitig"* (bi-temporal) in the context of the development of human sexuality, see also Freud 1923, G.W., pp. 221–222; 1926b, G.W., p. 239; 1926f, G.W., p. 304; 1939, G.W., p. 180.
16 In Strachey's translation, second phase (S.E. vol.14, p. 156). Concerning Freud's use of the term *'zweizeitig'* (bi-temporal) in the context of symptom-formation, see also Freud (1916–1917a, G.W., p. 311; 1926a, G.W., p. 142).
17 Again Strachey's translation "pushed-forward" does not exactly catch the meaning of the German "vorgreifend" which is "anticipatory".
18 See letter 52 from 6th December 1896.
19 Freud's special interest in one of his ushebti Inv. 3269 is referred by several scholars to the palimpsest that occurs in its inscription, cf. Corcoran (1991, p. 24).
20 We would like to thank Leonard Weiss, Munich, for this comment.
21 Letter to Fliess from 6 April 1899 (Freud 1897–1904, p. 366).
22 See Jones (1955, p. 25).
23 Letter to Sándor Ferenczi from 2 October 1910 (Freud 1973, 1939, p. 282).

References

Abraham, K. (1912), Amenhotep IV. 'Echnaton'. Psychoanalytische Beiträge zum Verständnis seiner persönlichkeit und des monotheistischen Aton-Kultes. *Imago* 1(4), 334–360.

Bell, D. (2006), Existence in time. Development or catastrophe. *Psychoanal. Q.* 75(3), 783–805.

Bernfeld, S. (1946), An unknown autobiographical fragment by Freud. *Am. Imago* 4A(1), 3–19.

Birksted-Breen, D. (2003), Time and the après-coup. *Int. J. Psycho-Anal.* 84, 1501–1515.

Brabant, E., Falzeder, E., and Giampieri-Deutsch, P. (1993), *The Correspondence of Sigmund Freud and Sándor Ferenczi Volume 1, 1908–1914.* Cambridge, MA and London: Harvard University Press, 1–571.

Cassirer Bernfeld, S. (1951), Freud and archaeology. *Am. Imago* 8(2), 107–128.

Champollion, M. (1822), *Lettre à M. Dacier relative à l'alphabet des hiéroglyphes phonétiques.* Paris: Firmin Didot.

Corcoran, L.H. (1991), Exploring the archaeological metaphor. *Annu. Psychoanal.* 19, 19–32.

D'Agata, A.-L. (1994), Sigmund Freud and Agean archaeology: Mycenean and Cypriot material from his collection of antiquities. *Stdie Micenei ed Egeo-Anatolici* 34, 7–36.

Davies, E. (1998), Eine Welt wie im Traum. Freuds Antikensammlung. In: Marinelli, L. (ed.), *Meine ... alten und dreckigen Götter. Aus Sigmund Freuds Sammlung.* Wien: Sigmund Freud – Museum, 94–102.

Doolittle, H. (1956), *Tribute to Freud.* New York: Pantheon.

Engelmann, E. (1976), *Berggasse 19. Sigmund Freud's Home and Offices, Vienna 1938.* New York: Basic Books.

Falzeder, E. (Ed.) (2002), *The Complete Correspondence between Sigmund Freud and Karl Abraham.* London and New York: Karnac.

Flem, L. (1982), L'archéologie chez Freud. Destin d'une paasion et d'une métaphore. *Revue de Psychanalyse* 26, 71–93.

Flem, L. (1992), *L'homme Freud.* Paris: Editions du Seuil.

Forrester, J. (1994), 'Mille e tre': Freud and collecting. In: Elsner, J., and Cardinal, R. (eds.), *The Cultures of Collecting.* London: Reaktion Books, 224–251.

Freud, S. (1873–1939), *Letters* (Ed. Freud, E.L.). London: Hogarth, 1961.

Freud, S. (1895), Studies on hysteria. *S.E.* II.

Freud, S. (1896), The aetiology of hysteria. *S.E.* III, 191–221.

Freud, S. (1897–1904), *The Complete Letters of Sigmund Freud to Wilhelm Fliess* (Ed. Masson, J.M.). Cambridge, MA and London: Harvard University Press, 1985.

Freud, S. (1899), Screen memories. *S.E.* III, 299–322.

Freud, S. (1900), The interpretation of dreams. *S.E.* IV/V.

Freud, S. (1905 [1901]), Fragment of an analysis of a case of hysteria. *S.E.* VII, 1–122.

Freud, S. (1907), Delusions and dreams in Jensen's Gradiva. *S.E.* IX, 7–93.

Freud, S. (1909), Notes upon a case of obsessional neurosis. *S.E.* X, 151–318.

Freud, S. (1910a), Leonardo da Vinci and a memory of his childhood. *S.E.* XI, 57–138.

Freud, S. (1910b), The antithetical meaning of primal words. *S.E.* XI, 155–161.

Freud, S. (1911a [1910]), Psycho-analytical notes on an autobiographical account of a case of paranoia (dementia paranoids). *S.E.* XII, 1–82.

Freud, S. (1911b), Great is Diana of the Ephesians. *S.E.* XII, 342–344.

Freud, S. (1912–1913), Totem and taboo. *S.E.* XIII, 1–161.

Freud, S. (1914), Remembering, repeating and working through. *S.E.* XII, 145–156.

Freud, S. (1915a), Repression. *S.E.* XIV, 146–158.

Freud, S. (1915b), The unconsious. *S.E.* XIV, 166–204.

Freud, S. (1916 [1915]), On transience. *S.E.* XIV, 303–307.

Freud, S. (1916–1917a), A mythological parallel to a visual obsession. *S.E.* XIV, 337–338.

Freud, S. (1916–1917b [1915]), Mourning and melancholia. *S.E.* XIV, 237–258.

Freud, S. (1920), Beyond the pleasure principle. *S.E.* XVIII, 7–64.

Freud, S. (1923 [1922]), 'Psychoanalyse' und 'Libidotheorie'. *G.W.* 13, 211–233.

Freud, S. (1925a), A note upon the 'mystic writing pad'. *S.E.* XIX, 225–232.

Freud, S. (1925b), Autobiographical study. *S.E.* XX, 7–70.

Freud, S. (1926a), Hemmung, symptom und angst. *G.W.* 11, 21–115.

Freud, S. (1926b), Die Frage der Laienanalyse. Unterredungen mit einem Unparteiischen. *G.W.* 14, 207–286.

Freud, S. (1930), Culture and its discontents. *S.E.* 21, 64–145.

Freud, S. (1932), The acquisition and control of fire. *S.E.* XXII, 187–193.

Freud, S. (1933), New introductory lectures on psycho-analysis. *S.E.* 22, 5–182.

Freud, S. (1936), A disturbance of memory on the acropolis. *S.E.* XXII, 239–248.

Freud, S. (1937), Constructions in analysis. *S.E.* XIII, 257–269.

Freud, S. (1939 [1934–1938]), Moses and monotheism. Three essays. *S.E.* XXIII, 7–137; *G.W.* 16, 103–246.

Freud, S. (1940 [1922]), Medusa's head. *S.E.* XVIII, 273–274.

Freud, S. (1950), Pre-psychoanalytic publications and unpublished drafts. *S.E.* I.

Freud, S. (1926). Psycho-analysis. *G.W.* 14, 299–307.

Gamwell, L. (1989), The origins of Freud's antiquities collection. In: Gamwell, L., and Wells, R. (Eds.), *Sigmund Freud and Art. His Personal Collection of Antiquities.* New York: State University; London: Freud Museum, 21–32.

Gamwell, L., and Wells, R. (Eds.) (1989), *Sigmund Freud and His Art. His Personal Collection of Antiquities.* New York: State University; London: Freud Museum.

Gardiner, M. (Ed.) (1971), *The Wolf-Man.* New York: Basic Books.

Gautier, T. (1852), Arria Marcella, un souvenir de Pompej. *Revue de Paris.*

Giovacchini, P. (1967). The frozen object. *Int. J. Psycho-Anal.* 48, 61–67.

Green, A. (2002), *Time in Psychoanalysis. Some Contradictory Aspects.* London: Free Associations Books.

Green, A. (2007), The construction of heterochrony. In: Perelberg, R.J. (Hg.), *Time and Memory.* London: Karnac, 1–22.

Green, A. (2009), From the ignorance of time to the murder of time. From the murder of time to the misrecognition of temporality in psychoanalysis. In: Glocer Fiorini, L., and Canestri, J. (Hg.), *The Experience of Time. Psychoanalytic Perspectives.* London: Karnac, 1–20.

Hanly, Ch. (2009), A problem with Freud's idea of the timelessness of the unconscious. In: Glocer Fiorini, L., and Canestri, J. (Hg.), *The Experience of Time. Psychoanalytic Perspectives.* London: Karnac, 21–34.

Hawthorne, N. (1860), *The Marble Faun*. Columbus: Ohio State University Press, 1968.

Jensen, W. (1903), Gradiva. Ein pompejianisches Phantasiestück. In: Urban, B., and Cremius, J. (Hrsg.), *Der Wahn und die Täume in W. Jensens 'Gradiva' mit dem Text der Erzählung von Wilhem Jensen*. Frankfurt a.M.: S. Fischer, 1973, 23.

Jones, E. (1955), *Sigmund Freud. Life and Work*, vol. 2. London: Hogarth.

Lacan, J. (1964), *Les Quatres Concepts Fondamentaux de la Psychanalyse. Le Séminaire, Livre XI*. Paris: Editions du Seuil, 1973.

Lacan, J. (1966), *Écrits*. Paris: Èditions du Seuil.

Loch, W. (1988), Rekonstruktion, Konstruktion, Interpretation – Vom Selbst-Ich zum Ich-Selbst. Jahr. *Psychoanal.* 23, 37–81.

Loch, W. (1993), *Deutungs-Kunst. Dekonstruktion und Neuanfang im psychoanalytischen Prozeß*. Tübingen: Edition diskord.

Marinelli, L. (Ed.) (1998), *"meine... alten und dreckigen Götter." Aus Sigmund Freuds Sammlung. Sigmund FreudMuseum*. Frankfurt a.M.: Stroemfeld.

Money-Kyrle, R. (1971), The aim of psychoanalysis. *Int. J. Psycho-Anal.* 52, 103–106.

Niederland, W.G. (1955), Die Phillipsonsche Bibel und Freuds Faszination für die Archäologie. *Psyche Z – Psychoanal.* 42(1988), 465–470.

Reeves, N., and Uemo, Y. (Eds.) (1996), *Freud as Collector. A Loan Exhibition from the Freud Musuem, London*. Tokyo: Gallery Mikazuki.

Rieber, R.W. (2012), *Freud on Interpretation: The Ancient Magical Egyptian and Jewish Traditions*. New York, Dordrecht, Heidelberg and London: Springer.

Riesenberg-Malcolm, R. (1900), As-if: The phenomenon of not learning. *Int. J. Psycho-Anal.* 71, 385–392.

Riesenberg-Malcolm, R. (2004), Bedeutsames Vergessen: Eine klinische Untersuchung. Jahrb. *Psychoanal.* 48, 9–26.

Rosenfeld, E.M. (1956), Dream and vision. Some remarks on Freud's Egyptian birth dream. *Int. J. Psycho-Anal.* 37, 97–105.

Śliwa, J. (1999), *Egyptian Scarabs and Seal Amulets from the Collection of Sigmund Freud*. Kraków: Polskiej Akademii Umiejetnosci.

Steiner, J. (2018), Die Verleugnung der Zeit in der Phantasie des Garten Eden. In: Weiss, H., and Horn, E. (eds.), Zeitlose seelische Zustände. Frankfurt a.M.: Brandes & Apsel, 91–114.

Weiss, C. (2011), Geschnittene Steine gekauft. Antike Gemmen aus dem Besitz von Sigmund Freud. In: Benthien, C., Böhme, H., and Stephan, I. (eds.), *Freud und die Antike*. Göttingen: Wallstein, 69–113.

Weiss, C. (2016), "Geschnittene Steine gekauft" – Carved stones acquired. Antique gems of the collection Sigmund Freud. Unpublished Lecture, New York.

Weiss, C. (2018), Gradiva and the flowers of oblivion. Unpublished Lecture, New York.

Weiss, C., and Weiss, H. (1984), Eine Welt wie im Traum. Sigmund Freud als Sammler antiker Kunstgegenstände. Jahrb. *Psychoanal.* 16, 189–207.

Weiss, C., and Weiss, H. (1985), Ein Blick in die Antikensammlung Sigmund Freuds – sechs ausgewählte Vasen. *Antike Welt* 16, 43–53.

Weiss, C., and Weiss, H. (1989), Dem Beispiel jener Forscher folgend. Zur Bedeutung der Archäologie im Leben Freuds. *Zeitschrift für Geschichte der Psychoanalyse* 2, Heft 3, 45–71.

Weiss, H. (2003), Zeiterfahrung und depressive Position. *Psyche.* 57, 857–873.

Weiss, H. (2008), Romantic perversion: The role of envy in the creation of a timeless universe. In: Roth, P., and Lemma, A. (eds.), *Envy and Gratitude Revisited.* London: International Psychoanalytic Association, 152–167.

Weiss, H. (2009), *Das Labyrinth der Borderline-Kommunikation. Klinische Zugänge zum Erleben von Raum und Zeit.* Stuttgart: Klett-Cotta.

Weiss, H. (2011), Pompeji und das Problem der Zeitlichkeit bei Freud. In: Benthien, C., Böhme, H., and Stephan, I. (eds.), *Freud und die Antike.* Göttingen: Wallstein, 143–158.

Weiss, H. (2017), *Trauma, Schuldgefühl und Wiedergutmachung. Wie Affekte innere Entwicklung ermöglichen.* Stuttgart: Klett-Cotta.

Weiss, H. (2018), Is reversibility an illusion? Reflections on the 'reversibility principle' (H. Rey). In: Weiss, H., and Horn, E. (eds.), *Zeitlose seelische Zustände.* Frankfurt a.M.: Brandes & Apsel, 115–139.

2

FOUNDING *THE INTERNATIONAL JOURNAL OF PSYCHOANALYSIS*

A chapter of psychoanalytical science and association policy

Georg Bruns

Introduction

The beginning of the *IJPA* is usually marked by Jones's letter of 7 December 1918 to Freud, in which he writes the oft-quoted sentence: "I think the time is ripe for an English journal, or edition of the *Zeitschrift*[1] (not identical, of course) owned by the *Vereinigung*[2]" (Freud & Jones 1993, p. 326). Steiner (1994, p. 883) also points out that Jones's letter outlines the plan for an International Psychoanalytical Association (IPA)-sponsored English-language publication for the first time. Jones himself mentions in the editorial of the first issue of *The International Journal of Psycho-analysis* that such plans had been aired years earlier, but postponed: "The question was discussed, indeed, but postponed, at the last International Congress, at Munich in 1913" (Jones 1920, p. 3). However, neither in the minutes of the Munich Congress nor elsewhere in the IPA Korrespondenzblatt (bulletin) for the years 1913 or 1914 is such discussion mentioned.

However, in 1913, there was a reason to consider the issue of an English-language psychoanalytic journal, namely, the publication of such a journal in the USA. The first psychoanalytic journal in English, *The Psychoanalytic Review: A Journal Devoted to Understanding of Human Conduct*, was first published there in 1913. The *Review* had been co-founded by the Washington psychiatrist William Alanson White and the New York neurologist and psychiatrist Smith Ely Jelliffe (Barnett 2013). Both Jelliffe and White were members of the American Psychoanalytic Association; Jelliffe was also the member of New York Psychoanalytic Society. But in founding the *Psychoanalytic Review*, they did not act in cooperation and agreement with the IPA; it was their private venture. They had never met Freud, had no psychoanalytical training, and had no closer contact with the leading groups of psychoanalysis at the time. In addition, they were obviously not aware of the differences between Freud and Jung that had emerged since 1911, after Jung (1911) had published the first part of his work *Psychology of the unconscious*. In 1912, Jung had given lectures in New York, and for the first issue of the *Psychoanalytic Review*, Jelliffe and White relied on them as contributions. Later, after they had learned that the contradictions between Freud and Jung could no longer be overcome at that time, Jelliffe justified the choice of contributions in the *Review* as follows: [The *Review*] "aims to be catholic in its tendency, a faithful mirror of the psychoanalytic movement, and to represent no schisms or schools but a free forum for all" (Barnett 2013, p. 12). Its first issue opened with a congratulatory letter and a paper by Jung, "The Theory of Psychoanalysis", based on Jung's lectures presented the prior year at Fordham University (ibid.). In 1913 and 1914, the controversies between Freud and Jung culminated. Freud therefore refused to publish in a journal whose editors were so intimate with Jung (ibid., p. 17). Furthermore, he believed that the psychoanalytic literature should remain centralized for a while until it had found enough interest and contributors in America to fill a journal (ibid.). Nevertheless, as early as 2 June 1913, he wrote to Brill: "… the English-speaking journal cannot be avoided…" (ibid., p. 14).

Forerunners to *the International Journal of Psychoanalysis (IJP)*

In this letter by Freud to Brill dated 2 June 1913, the idea of an English-language psychoanalytic journal under the auspices of the *Association* seems to have been expressed in writing for the first time. However, we can assume that before mentioning it in writing to Brill, the subject had been raised in the newly constituted "Secret Committee" (see below). For in 1913, Freud, together with some colleagues, also founded the *Internationale Zeitschrift für ärztliche Psychoanalyse,* renamed *Internationale Zeitschrift für Psychoanalyse* in 1920 (in the following text referred to as *IZP*), the first issue of which was published in the spring of 1913. From the beginning, the subheading of this new journal carried the designation: "Official Organ of the International Psychoanalytic Association". It would be surprising if, during the planning of the *IZP,* the Secret Committee did not also discuss creating an English-language psychoanalytic journal. Freud was the publisher of the *IZP,* with Ferenczi, Rank, and Jones acting as co-editors, the latter in particular to also underscore the international nature of the *IZP.*

The *IZP* was neither the first psychoanalytic journal nor the first of the IPA's journals. The first psychoanalytic periodical was the *Jahrbuch für psychoanalytische und psychopathologische Forschungen (Yearbook for psychoanalytic and psychopathological research),* with Eugen Bleuler and Sigmund Freud as the publishers and Carl Gustav Jung as the editor. The *Jahrbuch* was published from 1909 to 1914 by Franz Deuticke, Leipzig/Vienna. The contributions were almost exclusively psychoanalytical in nature, with psychopathological contributions being very rare. One was Bleuler's famous text dating from 1912, "Das autistische Denken" ("Autistic Thinking"). In 1911 and 1912, Jung had published his text "Changes and Symbols of the Libido"[3] in two parts in the *Jahrbuch.* This contributed decisively to the break between Freud and Jung, because the view of the libido expressed in it deviated markedly from Freud's concept of the libido. In the face of this conflict, Jung resigned as editor of the *Yearbook* in 1913, as did Bleuler as co-publisher, with Freud becoming the sole publisher. To make the change clear, for the sixth volume in 1914, the *Jahrbuch* was renamed *Jahrbuch der Psychoanalyse. Neue Folge des Jahrbuchs für psychoanalytische und psychopathologische Forschungen. (Yearbook of Psychoanalysis. New series of the Yearbook for Psychoanalytic and Psychopathological Research.)*

With this volume in 1914, the *Jahrbuch* ceased publication. Due to its history and contributions, it had too many associations with Jung, who had worked on it as editor for five years. In addition, presumably in order to clearly emphasize a change of direction, Freud therefore published two contributions in this volume as frontispieces and closing articles framing the other essays: the volume opened with Freud's text "On Narcissism" (1914a), which as well as offering an organized and developed version of his recent scattered remarks on narcissism provided a scientific analysis of Jung's ideas. In it, he dealt with Jung's critique of the libido theory, refuting it. Jung had challenged Freud's view of narcissistic libido in Schreber's case and, in general, advocated a broader notion of the libido not merely based on sexuality. The closing text of the volume *The History of the Psycho-Analytic Movement* (Freud 1914b) presented the organizational history of psychoanalysis and Freud's role in it. Both texts together can thus be understood as a symbolic effacement of Jung within psychoanalysis, in that Freud refuted Jung and rendered him insignificant in the publication he had previously edited.

The first journal published by the IPA that had been founded in 1910 was issued in 1911: the *Zentralblatt für Psychoanalyse. Medizinische Monatsschrift für Seelenkunde* (Central Review of Psychoanalysis. Medical Monthly of Psychology). Freud was the publisher, and the editors were Adler and Stekel. At the time *Zentralblatt* was founded, the tensions between Freud and Adler were already becoming serious. Adler, who had been a member of the Wednesday Psychological Society (Nunberg & Federn 1962) since its foundation in 1902, had been developing his own theory about the origins of neurosis since about 1906. He assumed an organic insufficiency, which would be compensated by performance changes in the central nervous system. He further developed this theory into a theory of a sense of inferiority and a "male protest" against this feeling. According to this theory, aggressive striving thereby seeks to gain a sense of superiority; it is a striving for a sense of validity. He saw the origin of neurosis in this conflict (Handlbauer 2010). In principal, this was an early narcissistic theory. Freud, on the other hand, advocated repressed and suppressed sexuality as the cause of neurosis within the framework of his libido theory.

Freud's and Adler's different viewpoints came to a head in 1911, culminating in Adler leaving the Wednesday Society and the IPA that same year. In the autumn of 1911, he also resigned as editor of the *Zentralblatt*, justifying this step in a brief explanation: Freud saw their scientific differences as so serious that, in his view, joint publication of a journal was inopportune. Therefore, he, Adler, was voluntarily leaving the editorial staff of the *Zentralblatt* (Adler 1911).

Stekel remained as the sole editor of the *Zentralblatt*. A conflict arose between him and Freud at the end of 1912, when Freud wanted to replace him with another editor, Viktor Tausk. Stekel refused to step down. The contracts with the publishing house granted him a strong position, so Freud could not remove him from his post. Freud then resigned as publisher (Marinelli 2005). On 24 November 1912, the Executive Board of the IPA, still with Jung as the president and Riklin as the secretary, decided to withdraw the recognition of the *Zentralblatt* as the official organ of the IPA and to no longer publish the Korrespondenzblatt (Bulletin; see later) of the IPA in the *Zentralblatt* (Jung & Riklin 1913, p. 111). The withdrawal of the IPA cost the *Zentralblatt* its readers and its authors. It began to flounder due to the lack of contributions. Publications became increasingly rare and contained hardly any original contributions. It ceased publication at the end of 1914.

The "Secret Committee" and the *IZP*

In the second half of 1912, various developments coincided: the emergence of a small group of talented psychoanalysts from various countries who were avowed followers of Freud and who formed the Secret Committee with Freud's support, the loss of the *Zentralblatt*, and the escalation of the Freud–Jung controversy that, in April 1914, culminated in the resignation of Jung from his position as president of the IPA. The Secret Committee was decisively involved in this.

The group of strict supporters of Freud, who, together with him, was to form the Secret Committee at the end of 1912 and beginning of 1913, consisted of Sándor Ferenczi, Hanns Sachs, Otto Rank, Karl Abraham, and Ernest Jones. Years later, in 1920, Eitingon joined this group. The idea of a special group, which consistently supported Freud and his theories, arose when, probably in July 1912, Ferenczi, Rank, and Jones met in Vienna and had a talk about the theoretical and personal differences between Freud and Jung. On 30 July 1912, Jones wrote to Freud telling him about this meeting:

> One of them, I think it was Ferenczi, expressed the wish that a small group of men could be thoroughly analyzed by you, so that they could represent the pure theory unadultered by personal complexes, and thus build an unofficial inner circle in the Verein and serve as centers where others (beginners) could come and learn the work. If that were only possible it would be an ideal solution.
>
> (Freud and Jones 1993, p. 146)

Although Jones was apparently not the author of this "unofficial inner circle" idea, he was the one who transmitted it to Freud, thus making himself the spokesman for the group. Freud replied by return mail from Carlsbad on 1 August 2012:

> What took hold of my imagination immediately is your idea of a secret council composed of the best and most trustworthy among our men to take care for the further development of ΨA and defend the cause against personalities and accidents when I am no more. You say it was Ferenczi who expressed this idea, yet it may be mine own shaped in better times, when I hoped Jung would collect such a circle around himself composed of the official headmen of the local associations. Now I am sorry to say such a union had to be formed independently of Jung and of the elected presidents... First of all: This committee had to be strictly secret in his existence and his actions. It could be composed of you, Ferenczi and Rank, among whom the idea was generated. Sachs... and Abraham could be called next, but only under condition of all of you consenting.
>
> (Ibid., pp. 147–148)

A week later (7 August 1912), Jones wrote to Freud of a "united small body, designed, like the Paladins of Charlemagne, to guard the kingdom and policy of their master" (ibid., p. 149).

In his letter of July 30, Jones not only presents himself to Freud as a faithful follower being a member of the Secret Committee, but also as someone who, independently of this group, is pondering the future of psychoanalysis. After telling Freud about his efforts to gain colleagues for psychoanalysis in London, he expresses concern for the future of psychoanalysis when he talks about its possible future leaders. "I get a little pessimistic at times when I look around at the men who must lead for the next thirty years" (Freud & Jones 1993, p. 146). He makes critical remarks about four leading minds at the time: Jung, Stekel, Rank, and Ferenczi. He implicitly presents himself as the most suitable leader in considering the future and appropriate leadership for psychoanalysis. A few sentences later, however, he also seems to reconfirm that he is still a member of a small group whose two other members he has just put down: "Ferenczi, Rank and I had a little talk on these general matters in Vienna. They were rather disappointed with the whole Zurich attitude at the moment…". As a solution, voiced by Ferenczi, the idea of a small group of men came up in the course of the three-way conversation "…thoroughly analysed by you… and thus build an unofficial inner circle in the Verein…" (ibid., p. 146). Freud's analysis would be like a consecration that would bestow special knowledge and abilities and would allow access to the inner circle of the IPA. Freud apparently sees such a loyalty to himself as a prerequisite for higher tasks in the IPA and also comments accordingly on Jones's leadership issue:

> Whatever the next time may bring, the future foreman of the ΨA movement might come out of this small but select circle of men, in whom I am still ready to confide in spite of my last disappointments with men.
>
> (Ibid., p. 148)

Freud was enthusiastic about the idea of a group of faithful followers. He introduced the terms "committee" and "council" for such a group (August 1, 2012, ibid., pp. 147–148). Besides Jones, he suggested Ferenczi and Rank as well as Sachs and Abraham. On 12 August, he communicated with Ferenczi about "forming a secret committee to oversee the development of psychoanalysis" (Wittenberger 1995, p. 202). Ferenczi, Jones, Sachs, and Rank met in Vienna at the beginning of October 1912 (Schröter 1995, p. 521). Abraham was not present at the meeting, but was being wooed by the others; Ferenczi, Rank, and Jones approached him in the summer and autumn of 1912 to persuade him to join the committee. Freud also made an effort to win him over. After much hesitation, Abraham definitively joined the committee in the summer of 1913 (Schröter 1995, p. 522).

This group became the Secret Committee of the early IPA. The committee worked closely with Freud and found together to accomplish two tasks: the founding of the *Internationale Zeitschrift für Ärztliche Psychoanalyse (IZP)* and the enforcement of Jung's resignation as the central president of the IPA. The Secret Committee brilliantly completed both the tasks. The *IZP,* founded in the first step, could be used to approach the second task, the removal of Jung, through a concerted critical engagement with his theories.

It had become necessary to found the *IZP* after the IPA had lost *Zentralblatt.* The experiences with Adler and Stekel at *Zentralblatt* and with Jung at *Jahrbuch* encouraged Freud in his quest to obtain a journal that was loyal to him and his ideas. He thus filled the important positions of the *IZP* with colleagues whose loyalty he trusted, the group that was to form the Secret Committee. He himself was the publisher, while Ferenczi, Rank, and Jones were the co-editors. In 1919, Abraham and Hitschmann joined; the latter was not a member of the Secret Committee. In 1920, Rank assumed the editing tasks alone, and van Emden and Oberholzer additionally joined the previous editorial staff. Their participation was now called "Mitwirkung" (cooperation).

The *IZP* was published since 1913 by the Hugo Heller publishing house in Vienna. Since 1912, the journal *Imago* had also been published there, with Freud as publisher and Rank and Sachs as co-editors. Freud wanted to emphasize the international nature of the *IZP* and strengthen its international connections. For this reason, he included Jones in the editorial group. He subsequently sought the approval of the members of the IPA at the fourth Congress of the IPA in Munich on 7/8 September 1913: "A proposal by Prof. Freud to include Prof. Jones of London on the editorial staff of the *Internationale Zeitschrift*, in consideration of the Anglo-American field of interest, finds approval" (Abraham 1914b, p. 407).

The first task the Secret Committee had to fulfil was to strive against Jung's modified theory of libido (Jung 1911, 1912). Ferenczi (1913) was the first to publish a careful and critical paper in the *IZP* in response to Jung. In 1914, several other articles were published on Jung's writings, again in the *IZP*. The most important of them were Abraham's (1914a) critical discussion of nine lectures Jung had given in the USA in 1912, and Eitingon's argument against Jung's modified concept of the unconscious (Eitingon 1914). After this series of critical articles, Jung resigned in April 1914 from his post as president of the IPA. The Secret Committee had won its first battle with a coordinated scientific action based on its publishing power in the *IZP*.

From the first volume, the *IZP* also contained the *Korrespondenzblatt der Internationalen Psychoanalytischen Vereinigung* (Giefer 2007) of the IPA. This was created in 1910 with the founding of the IPA to provide members with information about the IPA and its local groups. It informed about the members of the local groups, later of the societies, about scientific meetings, meetings of the members, their decisions, but also about lectures by psychoanalysts in the regional groups as well as in public. Likewise, it reported on when and how psychoanalysis was discussed and written about in public, such as in newspapers.[4] The first six editions (1910/1911) appeared as individual print runs exclusively for the members of the IPA. From the end of 1911 until the beginning of 1913, the *Korrespondenzblatt* was affiliated to the *Zentralblatt*. With the founding of the *IZP* in 1913, it became part of this journal. As the central president of the IPA, Jung was acting editor for the *Korrespondenzblatt* in the first few years until 1913, with Riklin as secretary. In later years, it was mostly edited by the secretary of the IPA. With the downfall of the *IZP* in 1941, the *Korrespondenzblatt* also went under. Accompanying the founding of the *IJPA*, from 1920, the English equivalent of the *Korrespondenzblatt* was published as the *Bulletin of the International Psycho-Analytical Association*. It was published for the last time in the *IJPA* in 2000, after having appeared irregularly, with intervals of several years between issues since 1987.

Imago was a parallel journal to the *IZP* since 1912. Its subtitle *Journal for the Application of Psychoanalysis to the Humanities* highlights its editorial programme, namely, to apply psychoanalysis to the humanities and cultural studies. However, the date of its first appearance, 1912, was no accident: a year earlier, Jung had submitted the first part of his great work "Psychology of the Unconscious: a study of the transformations and symbolisms of the libido, a contribution to the history of the evolution of thought" (Jung 1911/Engl. 1916), in which he had developed a theory on the nature of the libido that, in parts, diverged from that of Freud. In it, he had dealt in detail with cultural history, religions, and cultural symbols. Freud and his followers wanted to oppose it with their version of a psychoanalytic cultural theory. Therefore, the editorial structure of *Imago* was given by Freud: he was the publisher, and he installed two followers as co-editors: Rank and Sachs. They became members of the Secret Committee that was about to be founded. *Imago* was the first psychoanalytic journal in which Freud consistently asserted and established his conception of psychoanalysis, in this case for the field of psychoanalytical cultural theory. The assumption that *Imago* was the template for the *IZP* and for the later *IJPA* seems justified, for the two later journals were formed on the same principle, to fill the roles of publisher, editor, and co-editors with proven followers and to place Freud himself in a central position. In this form, the journals were a key element in the implementation of Freudian scientific policy.

The editorial introduction of the first issue of *Imago*, "Entwicklung und Ansprüche der Psychoanalyse" [Development and Claims of Psychoanalysis] (Rank & Sachs 1912), gives a condensed account of the entire Freudian theory to date. In the final section it says that myths and cults allowed humans a symbolic fulfilment of their wishes and that they had merged with religion in the early history of humankind. "Religion is thus also one of the numerous forms of compromise: it liberates the path to higher civilization and secretly satisfies the repressed instincts" (ibid., p. 16). This is a formulation of Freud's clear and rational theory of religion, the most important expression, and the central supporting element of all cultural developments in early societies: it is a compromise between human instinctual drives and their control, formed in the same way as a neurotic symptom. This theory is the counterpart to Jung's mythical-mystical conception of religion. Significantly, Jung's name is not mentioned in the entire editorial.

Jones's path to psychoanalysis

In 1913, Jones was not just co-editor of the *IZP* but also became a member of the Secret Committee. At 34, he was still a young man and already belonged to the inner circle of the psychoanalytic movement. His path to achieving this was somewhat surprising, as he grew up far from Vienna, in South Wales, and also far removed from the intellectual milieu of early psychoanalysis.

Born on 1 January 1879, the son of an accountant and general secretary of a steel mill in South Wales, he attended Gowerton Village School and a grammar school in Swansea. Then, having gained a scholarship at the age of 14, he went to a very prestigious Welsh college, Llandovery (Maddox 2006, pp. 12–14). He stood out for his intelligence and curiosity. In 1895, at the age of 16, he began a preclinical study of medicine in Cardiff (ibid., p. 18) and moved to London in 1898 to begin three years of clinical training at University College Hospital (UCH) (ibid., p. 22). During this time, he dealt intensively with neurology (ibid., pp. 27–28) and surgery (p. 29). He received high recognition from his teachers for his professional knowledge. However, a lofty attitude and spiteful side to him also emerged:

Jones was a good pupil, but a poor colleague. Nurses disliked being ordered about by him. Junior students resented his know-it-all manner and his readiness to contradict. The sharp tongue was also an insulting one. To judge from his later correspondence, offensive phrases such as 'stupid'... and 'despicable race'... fell as easily from his pen as from his tongue... [Later] he could see that he could have been correctly considered 'opinionated, tactless, conceited, or inconsiderate'.

(Ibid., pp. 28–29)

He was a successful student; in April 1900, he became a licensed doctor at the age of 21 and completed his medical qualification. "In his examination for the Bachelor of Medicine (MB) qualification in 1901 he won first class honours, a university scholarship and two gold medals" (p. 29). After two temporary residential appointments at UCH, he took other posts. With the New Year of 1903, he moved on to become resident medical officer at the North-Eastern Hospital for Children, Bethnal Green. There he ran into difficulties, because he had been absent without permission, and so he had been asked to resign (pp. 31–32). "...this forced resignation in November 1903 unquestionable brought ruin. He was never to hold a serious hospital appointment again" (p. 32).

In January 1904, he applied to the National Hospital. To his surprise, despite his splendid references, the two gold medals, and the first-class honours in the Doctor of Medicine examination, he did not get the job. He had to learn "that he was a marked man – marked as awkward and irascible" (p. 33). Another examination made him a member of the Royal College of Physicians, but it did not help him to get a full-time hospital job (ibid.).

Jones undertook various smaller jobs. In 1905, together with a colleague, Wilfred Trotter, he opened a practice in Harley Street, London. They subscribed to a large number of scientific journals and began to publish themselves. At Trotter's request, he read a review by Clark (1896) of Freud's *Studies in Hysteria* in the magazine *Brain* and was fascinated. In the *Monthly Journal of Psychiatry and Neurology*, he read Freud's case presentation on Dora (Freud 1905), and he read a report by Putnam on the treatment of hysteria using the Freudian method in the first issues of the *Journal of Abnormal Psychology* in April 1906 (Maddox 2006, pp. 38–40). Now Jones wanted to perform psychoanalysis. He started to do so in 1906.

It seems that Jones's medical career in London, despite his talents in those years, had reached a dead end since 1904 due to his lofty and idiosyncratic behaviour. The new psychoanalysis, which had not arrived in medicine and was still unknown in London, could offer him a way out. In order to understand the almost exclusively German texts, he and Trotter learned German from a private tutor (ibid., p. 40). He first published an essay on some experiences from his own psychoanalytical treatments in the *Journal of Abnormal Psychology* in 1907/1908 (ibid., pp. 57–58).

In September 1907, he attended the "Congress of Psychology and Psychotherapy" in Amsterdam, where he met Jung. The latter was very taken by him and wrote to Freud that he had met a promising young Englishman who was also working psychoanalytically and might do much good for psychoanalysis (ibid., p. 51).

Jones and the international departure of Freud

Jones entered Freud's life when he was expanding his sphere of activity beyond Vienna and Austria-Hungary. The year 1907 brought a major widening of Freud's personal and professional contacts that was to prove significant for him in the years to come. Until then, everyone interested in psychoanalysis and Freud's circle, whom Freud also met in person, lived in Vienna or in the surrounding area. However, as Eissler remarks, Freud "by no means found personalities who would be suitable for a deep friendship" among the Viennese colleagues (Eissler 1982, p. 8). With a few physicians living abroad who were interested in his publications and theories, Freud exchanged correspondence, for example, with Jung and Abraham. The only major exception was Wilhelm Fließ in Berlin until 1900, when the rift took place (Masson 1985). However, the letters became increasingly rare and reserved until contact finally dwindled out in 1904. Eissler (1982) notes of the correspondence that began between Freud and Jung in 1906 that Freud felt "connected by the deepest friendship" to Fließ after the break with Breuer until about 1902, but that he was "deeply offended by him… So there was a vacuum in his friendship" (p. 8). This vacuum was filled by the foreign visitors, who came to see Freud in Vienna from 1907 onwards. However, with the exception of Jung, Freud never developed as deep and amicable a relationship with anyone as he had had with Breuer and Fließ. It seems as if the recent disappointment with Jung had prevented Freud from ever entering into a deep male friendship again.[5] The new relationships were much more influenced by Freud's professional goals, and they were more stable.

At first, new contacts were transmitted through Eugen Bleuler, the internationally renowned director of the Zurich psychiatric Burghölzli clinic. The first visitor from Zurich was Max Eitingon (Nunberg & Federn 1962, p. 77[6]) in January 1907. At the time he was working as a volunteer at the Psychiatric University Hospital Zurich, also known as the Burghölzli. He participated in two Wednesday-evening sessions at Freud's home on 23 January (ibid.) and 30 January 1907 (ibid., p. 87). Six weeks after Eitingon's visit, at the beginning of March 1907, two other Swiss doctors came to see Freud in Vienna. They were Carl Gustav Jung and Ludwig Binswanger, who were also working at the Burghölzli. Jung and Binswanger attended the Wednesday-evening meeting on 6 March 1907 (ibid., p. 131). In December 1907, someone else working at the Burghölzli, Karl Abraham, visited Freud. He, too, had been exchanging letters with Freud since the beginning of the year and had moved from Zurich to Berlin shortly before his visit. He was a guest at the Wednesday evening session on 18 December 1907 (ibid., p. 254). Freud's invitation to a presentation on modern theories of hysteria at the "Congress of Psychology and Psychotherapy" in Amsterdam in September 1907, which he did not take up (ibid., p. 157), also testifies to the fact that he was becoming increasingly recognized internationally.

A next important step in internationalization was the first International Psychoanalytic Congress in Salzburg on 27 April 1908 (Rank 1911). There were 38 participants (Nunberg & Federn, p. 366f). More than half of them, that is, 20, were from Austria-Hungary, eight from Germany, seven from Switzerland, two from the United Kingdom, and one from the United States. Only four participants came from non-German-speaking regions, two from London, one from New York, and one from Geneva. Abraham Brill from New York, however, was born in Galicia, which belonged to Austria-Hungary, and grew up speaking German. He emigrated to America at the age of 15. In this respect, the internationality of this congress hardly went beyond the German-speaking countries.

Freud and Jones met for the first time at this congress. Since 1906, Jones had been dealing not only with psychoanalysis but also with the German psychiatry, and did not yet seem clear in his mind which interested him the most. In October 1907, he took part in a one-month course for postgraduates given by Emil Kraepelin in Munich, who was internationally known for his systematology of psychiatric disorders. There he also got to know Otto Gross, a psychiatrist interested in psychoanalysis, who frequented the Munich bohemian scene and propagated free love. Gross became psychotic himself and was treated at the Burghölzli. Jones had an affair with his wife Frieda Gross, which can be traced from the correspondence between them (Robinson 2013). The propagation of free love by Gross and other psychoanalysts worried Freud, as he feared for the public reputation of psychoanalysis. According to Robinson, this affair by Jones led Freud to focus his attention on countertransference (Freud 1910). He may have been reminded of the entanglement between Jung and Sabina Spielrein.

Jones also gave a lecture at the congress in Salzburg: "Rationalisation in every-day life" (Rank 1911, p. 126). He then went to Vienna for a few days. On 6 May 1908, he was a guest, along with Brill, at the Wednesday Society (Nunberg & Federn 1962, p. 368). He had thus gained access to Freud's inner circle of early psychoanalysts.

Jones's admission to the inner circle of early psychoanalysts

Jones was very anxious to maintain his connection with Freud. From Vienna, he travelled back to Munich, where for two months he once more worked alongside Kraepelin at the psychiatric hospital. He first wrote to Freud on 13 May 1908, just a few days after he had left Vienna (Freud & Jones 1993, p. 1), and reported, among other things, that Kraepelin had mentioned Jung's publications with appreciation and that in Toronto, where Jones was to relocate to in the summer of 1908, there were plans to set up a psychiatric clinic modelled on the Munich clinic led by Kraepelin.

He kept up the correspondence with Freud from Toronto, where he arrived in September 1908. He wrote of his contacts with American psychiatrists and psychotherapists, the planned psychotherapeutic congress in Boston in May 1909, in which he himself lectured on "Psycho-analysis in Psychotherapy" (ibid., p. 13), and his efforts to teach American psychiatrists about Freud's writings. Freud praised him for these efforts on 22 February 1909 (ibid., p. 18). On 28 February 1909 (ibid., pp. 19–20), he informed Jones of the invitation to Clark University, Worcester, Massachusetts, and the planned trip there in September. Jones and Brill, Freud's most important liaison in the USA, met Freud at Worcester (Freud 2002, p. 306). Freud himself perceived the recognition he received at Clark University as a breakthrough. He later wrote:

> As I stepped on to the platform at Worcester to deliver my Five Lectures on Psycho-Analysis [1910a] it seemed like the realisation of some incredible day-dream: psycho-analysis was no longer a product of delusion, it had become a valuable part of reality.
>
> (Freud 1925, p. 51)

Jones was alive with agility and drive. During his four years in Canada, from 1908 to 1912, at the end of 1908, he contacted a group of philosophers and neurologists in Boston, including William James and Morton Prince, who was editor of the *Journal of Abnormal Psychology* (Maddox 2006, p. 70). Jones was involved in founding the American Psychopathological Association in May 1910. "Morton Prince was appointed president, Putnam and Jones were officers, and the 'Journal of Abnormal Psychology' became its official organ. Prince made Jones an associate editor..." (Maddox 2006, p. 83). His initial activities as a pathologist and neurologist at the Ontario Asylum for the Insane, Toronto (p. 68), and as a demonstrator in anatomy and physiology at the University of Toronto (p. 69), gave him time for a flood of publications, including in the *Journal of Abnormal Psychology*: "Of the thirty-two contributors listed on the contents page for the April-May 1910 volume, most had one article on the inside pages; the prolific Jones was represented by eleven contributions. Putnam was full of admiration" (p. 83). This gives the impression that very early on, after meeting Freud personally in April 1908, Jones felt like an ambassador of psychoanalysis and represented it by giving psychoanalytic lectures, writing essays, and recommending that his colleagues read Freud's writings.

During the years in Canada, soon after Freud's visit to Clark University, Jones decided to devote himself entirely to psychoanalysis. On 17 October 1909, he wrote to Freud: "... I determined not only to further the cause by all the means in my power, which I had already decided on, but also to follow your recommendations as exactly as possible" (Freud & Jones 1993, p. 29). On the one hand,

Freud regarded Jones critically, pointing out, for example, his hostile behaviour towards Brill that did not serve the cause of psychoanalysis:

> You treated our good friend Brill with unmistakable hostility and disdain, no doubt also out of personal motives, in other words, complex related motives. Now, I think the cause is too great and vast and we would not accomplish anything by means of clever delaying tactics. One could too easily run the risk of becoming deceitful and hide the essentials, which is in direct conflict with the spirit of ΨA.
>
> (Ibid., p. 32)

Or he touched upon his doubts about Jones's faithfulness:

> I remember the first time when I got aware of this my attitude towards you, it was a bad one; when you left Worcester after a time of dark inconsistencies from your side and I had to face the idea that you were going away to become a stranger to us. Then I felt it ought not to be so...
>
> (Ibid., p. 132)

On the other hand, to some extent, he enthusiastically acknowledged Jones's commitment to the cause of psychoanalysis. When Jones wrote to him in July 1911 that he was leaving Canada due to unfulfilled job promises and the unwillingness of his wife to stay there, he praised him greatly for his activities in Canada. On 9 August 1911, he flattered him:

> You have, as it were, conquered America in no more than two years, and I am by no means assured which way things will go, when you are far. But I am glad you are returning to England, as I expect you will do the same for your mother-country...
>
> (Ibid., p. 112)

Jones understood this humorously formulated instruction of Freud's, which also referred to his narcissistic feelings of grandiosity. He accepted it, so that on 10 May 1912, a few days before he left Toronto, he replied in the same tone at the end of his last Canada letter to Freud: "There now remains only Brazil, China and Greenland to be penetrated. Still I do think with all the opposition that we shall suffer like Alexander for want of worlds to conquer" (ibid., p. 142).

The International Journal of Psycho-Analysis: delays

In fact, it is fair to say that from then on, Jones dedicated his life to conquering the world for psychoanalysis. He became Freud's principal intermediary to the English-speaking world. As a member of the Secret Committee and the editorial staff of the *IZP,* he belonged to the IPA's inner circle of power around Freud. He had noticed during the disputes Freud had had with Adler and Jung how emphatically Freud represented and enforced his conception of psychoanalysis. He had seen that Freud was a thinker, scientist, physician, and writer, but also active in organizational matters: he had gathered a circle of followers, and had founded journals, a publishing house, and an international scientific association. He had not done everything himself, but delegated many activities to his students and companions. However, Freud apparently attentively watched the proceedings and intervened when necessary, often by encouraging others to take action. Organizational challenges no doubt appealed to Jones, because he had a strong urge to act and a pronounced organizational talent.

In 1913, two local psychoanalytic groups existed in English-speaking countries: since February 1911, the "New York Psychoanalytic Society" (Gieler 2007, CB V/1911/1 – Korrespondenzblatt No. 5, April 1911); since October 1913, "The London Psycho-Analytical Society" (Abraham 1914b, p. 411). In addition, in the USA, in May 1911, the "American Psychoanalytic Association" was formed as a superordinate structure. Jones, as a participant, reported in detail to Freud on the circumstances of its foundation on 22 May 1911 (Freud & Jones 1993, pp. 102–104). The fact that organizations were being founded showed the increasing and sustained interest in psychoanalysis in these countries. Thus, the establishment of an English-language psychoanalytic journal entered onto the agenda of the IPA, as Freud's letter of 2 June 1913 to Brill demonstrates (Barnett 2013, p. 14).

However, in 1913, Freud and his colleagues were not prepared to establish an English-language journal. After the experience with Adler, Jung, and Stekel, Freud was anxious to keep the publication organs of the IPA under his control, so that they represented psychoanalysis based on his thinking. At that time, he did not think this was guaranteed either in the USA or the United Kingdom. In a letter to White, in 1914, on why he did not support the founding of the *Psychoanalytic Review,* he wrote the following: The *Review* was created more for economic than scientific reasons (Barnett 2013, p. 16).

Psychoanalysis was not yet developed enough in America to have a journal of its own, and at present, it is rather more served by centralized production of psychoanalytic literature, as in the *IZP* (ibid., p. 17). Finally, its closeness to Jung spoke against it: "This judgment of the *Review* is further supported by Jelliffe's intimacy with Jung..." (ibid., p. 17). Jones did not value the professional qualities of his American counterparts very highly, either. Seven years later, on 26 October 1920, he wrote in a circular letter to the other members of the Secret Committee: "I doubt if there are six men in America who could tell the difference between Vienna and Zurich, at least at all clearly" (Wittenberger & Tögel 1999, p. 118).

However, even within the London Psycho-Analytical Society, only a segment of the members shared the views of the IPA. Jones thus sought to cleanse the society. In a clever manoeuvre, he invited only the faithful members to a general assembly on 20 February 1919 to disband the existing society and create a new cleansed one: "Owing to the fact that certain members of that Society had adopted views which were in contradiction to the principles of Psycho-Analysis the objects of that Society were negatived" (Reports of the International Psycho-Analytical Association 1920a, p. 115). The attending members of the London Psycho-Analytical Society requested the dissolution of the Society. This was decided upon. "It was then resolved that a British Psycho-Analytical Society be formed, that application be made for affiliation to the International Psycho-Analytical Association..." (ibid.). Thus, at a single meeting, Jones got rid of the old London Society and its disreputable members, in the same breath founding a cleansed British Society.

Not only did the undeveloped scientific state of psychoanalysis in England and the USA prevent the founding of an English-language journal before World War I, but also the limited resources did not permit a new magazine on top of the *IZP*. With the start of the war in 1914, the organizational development of psychoanalysis came to a standstill. On 7/8 September 1913, the fourth congress of the IPA took place in Munich, the last meeting before the war (Abraham 1914b, p. 406). The fifth IPA congress planned for September 1914 in Schandau near Dresden or in Heidelberg (ibid., p. 407) was cancelled because of the war. It took place four years later on 28/29 September 1918 in Budapest, a few weeks before the end of the war (Ferenczi & von Freund 1919, p. 52). It was just a torso of a congress, with participants almost exclusively from Vienna and

Budapest, with only three coming from Germany and two from the Netherlands. Psychoanalytic publications also suffered from the effects of the war – during the three years, from 1916 to 1918, only one volume of the *IZP* was published, in 1918, instead of the usual annual volumes. *Imago* was also published less frequently: instead of a complete annual volume, a single volume was published for 1915 and 1916 and likewise a single volume for the three years 1917–1919.

The Verlag[7] and the *International Journal of Psycho-Analysis*

The war conditions hindered correspondence and visits, so a new journal was unthinkable during the war years. Immediately after the end of the war, Jones urged Freud to found an English-language journal in the cited letter of 7 December 1918. Apparently, Freud and Rank had already developed the same plan, for, on 24 January 1919, Freud replied:

> Now Rank developed the idea at the same time as you, that you should bring out an English edition of the Zeitschrift (or both), all the papers getting translated into the two languages. That means the extension of the Verlag and the forming of an English affiliation.
>
> (Freud & Jones 1993, p. 331)

Jones's ideas differed from Rank's – the two met in Switzerland – and after the meeting, Jones let Freud know: "We get on splendidly together…" (ibid., p. 337; March 17, 1919).

Before the war, the disputes between Freud/Adler and Freud/Jung and the founding of a journal with the *IZP* that was faithful to Freud took priority. After the war, the spread of psychoanalysis in English gained much greater weight. Germany and Austria-Hungary were the losers of the war. They lost not only large parts of their territories but also cultural influence worldwide. At the end of the 19th century and beginning of the 20th century, German was one of the international languages of science, along with English and French. In most disciplines of natural science, it was the leading scientific language and was often used by scientists from other countries when they first published their research (Reinbothe 2011). German was one of the languages of communication in international scientific organizations. After the war, the Academies of Sciences of the allies imposed a science boycott on Germany and the countries which had been allied with it (ibid., pp. 56–58). Scientists from Germany and Austria and the German language were excluded from international scientific associations, congresses, and publications. The boycott of the German language and the anti-German attitude made an English-language psychoanalytic journal all the more urgent after the war.

The opportunity was favourable, because the Hungarian entrepreneur Anton von Freund, having himself undergone analysis by Freud (Marinelli 2009, p. 39ff), had decided during the war to promote psychoanalysis after the war ended. Along with his brother, he was the heir of a brewery and a food manufacturing company. While other similar companies had collapsed during the war, he had been able to increase production and earn high profits. He intended to use the money to set up a large psychoanalytic centre in Budapest and to provide a large sum for the establishment of a psychoanalytic publishing house.

And, so, in 1919, the *Verlag* was established in Vienna and held out the prospect of becoming independent from any publisher. Otto Rank became its director. Unfortunately, the financial capital of the *Verlag* soon proved to be limited because there were restrictions on transferring money from Budapest to Vienna. Additionally, high inflation devaluated the capital which had been transferred to Vienna (ibid., pp. 46ff). From the beginning, the *Verlag* was underfinanced. Nevertheless, it started in 1919.

The task of the *Verlag* was to publish psychoanalytical books and journals. It had at the beginning three journals, the *Internationale Zeitschrift für aerztliche Psychoanalyse (IZP)* since 1919, *Imago* since 1919, and *the International Journal of Psychoanalysis (IJPA)* since 1920. Prior to this, the publisher Hugo Heller had published *Imago* (from 1912) and the *IZP* (from 1913). *IZP* and *IJPA* had identical names in the two different languages in order to show their close relationship. *Imago* and *IZP* were already official organs of the IPA, and the *IJPA* obtained this status when a resolution was passed at the Business Meeting of the IPA Congress in The Hague in September 1920.

The donation from Anton von Freund was used to establish a foundation. This foundation was administered by Freud himself, supported by an advisory committee which consisted of Abraham,

Ferenczi, v. Freund, Jones, Rank, and Sachs (Wittenberger & Tögel 1999, p. 40f; Marinelli 2009, p. 51). The advisory committee was identical to the Secret Committee except for von Freund, who, as donator, completed the circle. However, von Freund died in 1920 from sarcoma. The *Verlag* was organized as a limited-liability company (Schröter 2015, p. 108), "GmbH" in German, with five shareholders: Eitingon, Ferenczi, Freud, Jones, and Rank (Wittenberger & Tögel 2003, p. 233). Rank was the director of the *Verlag* and governed it. Important decisions required consultation of the other shareholders. This constellation was a perpetual source of conflict between Jones and Rank. Freud clarified these responsibilities after Jones complained about Rank because he felt left out by a decision Rank had made (ibid., p 233f).

In 1919, *The International Psychoanalytic Press* was established as a branch of the *Verlag*. Some months before that, Jones had already opened, together with Eric Hiller, a London bookseller, a "Shop" for psychoanalytic books which was a mixture of a bookshop and a lending library. The British members of the IPA had given money for establishing the shop. Though shop and *Press* stayed separate organizations, their activities merged. Hiller also worked as a secretary and translator for the *Press*. The shop as well as the *Press* incurred financial deficits. These deficits were one reason for conflicts between Jones and Rank. But there were more: The production of the *Journal* was complicated – the *Press* had an office in London, but the *Journal* was printed in Vienna like the *Zeitschrift*; the first print of an issue was controlled in London, a corrected print had to be done again in Vienna. All this took much time, and the *Journal* issues were always delayed (Marinelli 2009, p. 162f).

Other areas of conflict were Jones's agreement with the English publisher Unwin to sell psychoanalytical books – the *Verlag* had to pay a quota of the proceeds to Unwin (ibid., p. 157f), and Rank was upset. It was another source of the *Verlag's* losses. In 1920, Freud and Rank started negotiations with the Austrian banker and publisher Kola, who also possessed another large publishing house and was interested in buying the *Verlag* (ibid., p. 164f); Jones was afraid that the *Press* would lose its independence. At the end of 1920, Jones, Hiller, and Rank agreed upon closing the office of the *Press* in London and to move Hiller to Vienna where he could more easily check proofs and, as a native speaker, work on translations (ibid., p. 163). The *Press* only retained a pro forma postal address in London.

The status of the *Press* was complicated. Though it was a branch of the *Verlag*, its formal legal status in Great Britain was that of a purely British firm because when the *Press* was founded, a peace treaty had not yet been signed. So Jones opposed the sale of the *Verlag* to Kola.

As we were still 'at war' when our Press was founded it had to be legally a purely British firm, and its relation to the Verlag is based on private understanding only. Even now, for an Austrian firm to have a branch in London involves very cumbrous restrictions...
(Wittenberger & Tögel 1999, p. 93)

In the end, the sale failed.

The start of *the International Journal of Psychoanalysis*

The planned English journal was to be the official journal of the IPA for the English-speaking countries. Freud and the Secret Committee planned this *Journal* according to the same principles on which they had planned *Imago* and the *IZP* a few years before, namely, filling the key positions with Freud's loyal supporters. The economic control of the *Journal* was guaranteed by its affiliation with the *Verlag*. Content control had to be carried out by the publisher and his employees.

Since 1913, Sigmund Freud was editor-in-chief of the *IZP*, with Rank, Ferenczi, and Jones on the editorial staff. The status quo was maintained until 1918. In 1919, Abraham and Hitschmann joined the editorial staff. Structural changes took place in 1920: Freud remained the head as director, Rank became the managing editor, and was supported by a group of subeditors (Abraham, van Emden, Ferenczi, Hitschmann, Jones, and Oberholzer). Its internationality was thereby emphasized: van Emden practised in The Hague, Oberholzer in Zurich, Abraham in Berlin, Ferenczi in Budapest, and Jones in London. The members of the Secret Committee continued to form a clear majority in the structures of the *IZP* and held the key positions.

The *IJPA* was structured in a similar fashion. From the beginning in 1920, Freud was director of the *IJPA,* and Jones was still provisional editor; other members of staff had not yet been appointed. At the IPA conference in The Hague in September 1920, Jones was confirmed as the publisher. In addition, "an editorial committee, to be appointed later, consisting of three American and two British members" was to be appointed (Reports of the International Psycho-Analytical Association 1920b, p. 210). In 1921, the members of the editorial committee were appointed, although not without conflict, especially with respect to the American members (Jones, circular letter October 26, 1920, in: Wittenberger & Tögel 1999, p. 118). The Americans were Brill, Frink, and Oberndorf, the British Bryan and Flügel. They were presented on the cover page with the phrase, "with the assistance of". In 1922, this group was extended to include Abraham, Bose, van Emden, Ferenczi, Oberholzer, and Rank. With the exception of Bose and Bryan, they were all also members of the editorial staff of the *IZP*. Once more, the leading positions held by Freud and Jones were staffed by members of the Secret Committee, which was also represented in the extended editorial committee with Abraham, Ferenczi, and Rank.

The rush with which the *IJPA*, still unfinished in its editorial structure and in the composition of its staff, appeared in its first issue in July 1920 was due to competition with the American psychoanalyst Samuel Tannenbaum. He had approached Jones in 1918 to ask his support for an English-language psychoanalytic journal that he wanted to publish. Jones had dissuaded him by pointing out that there was already another psychoanalytic journal in the USA, the *Psychoanalytic Review*, which left no room for another private journal (Marinelli 2009, p. 160; Freud & Jones 1993, p. 343). He had also promised Tannenbaum to take him on as co-editor of the planned *International Journal*. However, he did not keep this promise when the *IJPA* was actually planned in detail. He had heard from Brill that Tannenbaum did not have a good reputation in New York (ibid.). When Tannenbaum realized that he had been ousted, he immediately resumed his plans for his own journal. Now Jones and Rank feared that Tannenbaum could use his journal to forestall the *IJPA* and usurp the planned name. They thus did all they could to be quicker than Tannenbaum. Nevertheless, Tannenbaum's journal appeared a few months before the *IJPA*, but with the name *Psyche and Eros*. Rank, the director of the *Verlag*, and Jones still compared the first issue of the *IJPA* with Tannenbaum's journal. Rank wrote to Jones on 4 August 1920 that the *IJPA*, despite some shortcomings, was "at any rate more beautiful and better than Tannenbaum's journal" (quoted from Marinelli 2009, p. 161). When *Psyche and Eros* had to cease publication in 1922, Rank and Ferenczi, on seeing the last issue, wrote a circular letter to the other members of the Secret Committee: "However, I believe that we can chalk the failure of Psyche & Eros up to our own success..." (Wittenberger & Tögel 2003, p. 186).

One-and-a-half years after Freud and the Secret Committee had decided to publish the *IJPA*, the first volume was issued. It opened with a letter from Ferenczi, which he had already written in October 1919 in his position as president of the IPA. In it, he emphasizes that among the many current tasks of the IPA, "none [were] to be more urgent or important than the reconsideration of the position of our literary organs" (Ferenczi 1920, p. 1). The *Internationale Zeitschrift für Psychoanalyse* could no longer fulfil its role as an international body. It was necessary to publish

> ... a distinct journal in the English language, in close contact with the *Zeitschrift*, and if possible under a similar editorship. The new Journal would rank equally with the *Zeitschrift* and *Imago* as an official organ of the 'International Psycho-Analytical Association', with special reference to the English speaking public...
>
> (Ibid.)

He had therefore asked Ernest Jones, along with Otto Rank, the director of the *Verlag*, to take on this task (ibid., p. 2). Jones (1920) emphasizes in his editorial that with the spread of psychoanalysis, especially in English-speaking countries, the need for an English-language journal had arisen and that "... with the cessation of the war, the resumption of scientific activities, and the reestablishment of contact between different countries, that time may be judged to have now arrived" (p. 3).

Excursus: the "Translation Monopoly"

Jones had been busy with translation issues since returning from Canada to England. Firstly, Freud's texts were increasingly translated into English; secondly, there were no uniform views on the translation of Freudian terms; and, finally, psychoanalysis, with its emphasis on sexuality, was viewed critically in British medical publications as well as in other periodicals and newspapers (Steiner 1991). In 1918, the collected writings of Jones appeared in a second edition, to which he attached a glossary for 80 psychoanalytic terms (ibid., p. 368). This glossary was a springboard for further related activities by Jones (ibid., p. 369). He formed a "Glossary Committee" with members of the British Society. This was to develop obligatory translations of psychoanalytic terms into English, and its work "culminated in the very idea of a *standard* edition" (Solms 2018, p. 14). The intention was to gain control over the terminology of English-language psychoanalytic literature (Freud & Jones 1993, p. 538; Steiner 1994; Marinelli 2009, p. 176). Jones's goal was also, with the help of the *Press,* "to distinguish between trustworthy psa books and the otherwise published…" (Freud & Jones 1993, p. 538). Marinelli (2009, pp. 141–176) calls this goal of creating a binding and generally used translation of Freud's German terminology in the English-speaking world in connection with translation of Freud's works for the *IJPA* and for the books of the *Press* a "translation monopoly" (ibid., p. 141). The Glossary Committee included Alix and James Strachey, Joan Riviere, Barbara Low, John Rickman, John Carl Wing, Douglas Bryan, and Jones himself (Steiner 1991, p. 378).

James Strachey relied on the work done there when the Standard Edition was published. The translation represented in the Standard Edition is essentially subject to three main criticisms: (1) it contains translation errors (e.g. Mahony 1992); (2) it has a basic tendency to erase the humanistic cultural background and the literary quality of the Freudian texts, so that a humanistic Freud becomes a medical one (e.g. Bettelheim 1983); and (3) the language of the Standard Edition is rendered scientific and is Latinized, so that Freud's everyday language and his colloquial terms for psychoanalytic concepts would become sterile and technical in translation (e.g. Ornston 1982). Strachey's translation for the Standard Edition proves, however, that Jones had achieved his goal "to achieve an hegemonic control of the translation of Freud and his efforts to lay the foundations of the way Freud had to be translated into English" (Steiner 1991, p. 390). In addition, the Standard Edition had probably become the first reading of Freudian texts practically all over the world, as English became the lingua franca and German was spoken by only a few psychoanalysts beyond the German-speaking world. Only France likely differed, since Jean Laplanche (1991) created an elaborate translation project of Freud's writings in the 1980s. Marinelli (2009, p. 147f) recognizes that the Standard Edition provides a good translation of Freud given the cultural background in England, but criticizes the fact that it gives the impression of finality and is not open to a changing understanding of a foreign language. However, with its canonized translation of Freud, it brought about a common usage for psychoanalytic terms in the English-speaking world. Solms also acknowledged in his presentation of the Revised Standard Edition of Freud's work that Strachey had followed the rules of English scientific literature and, if available, had relied on well-rehearsed translations, such as translating "das Ich" as "the ego", as it is in philosophical writings (Solms 2018, p. 18). Likewise, he used the familiar terms developed by the Glossary Committee, which have been in common usage in English since then. There was little point in replacing Strachey's translations with new translations that would probably be unsatisfactory in other respects (ibid., p. 15).

The German-French linguistic philosopher and writer Georges-Arthur Goldschmidt (1988) compares the German and French languages. According to him, the German language is very physical:

> It is as if the German language is the original surge of the sea, maintaining its sway, ebb and flow... The whole German language is based on the alternation of raising and lowering of the ribcage, on ascent and descent, back and forth in space... In German, everything originates from the body, returns to it, goes through it.

The German word *"Leib"* (corps, body), for example, is etymologically derived from "Leben" *(la vie, life)*. *"Leib"* has a different meaning from *"Körper"* (body), which etymologically originated from the Latin "corpus". In French, there is only one word for both *Leib* and *Körper: le corps* (ibid., p. 17[8]). Goldschmidt juxtaposes the semantic spheres of the two terms: one could say that *"Leib"* stands for vital physical processes and sensations, *"Körper"* rather for a form or a container – the best-known phrase, however, is the dead "Corpus Christi".

According to Goldschmidt, the German language is spatially oriented and based around root words such as *stand, lie, sit*, verbs that express a movement in space. Through a large number of prefixes such as *an (at, on), ab (off), auf (upon)*, and *unter (under)*, a lot of words can be formed, each with several meanings. These root words have no equivalent in French (ibid., p. 18).

The scientific language and the language of philosophy would also be close to the physical and to everyday life.

The first chapter of Hegel's 'Phenomenology of Mind' consists only of words that even a five-year-old child can understand... The deeper the German 'philosophy' is, the simpler and more concrete its language, at any rate very close to the *bodily feeling* [nahe dem *leiblichen Empfinden*] ...

(Ibid.)

Scientific terms were replaced in everyday use by words used in everyday life that immediately evoke images. The word for "pancreas", for example, is *Bauchspeicheldrüse* (*belly* plus *saliva* plus *gland* – salivary gland of the belly) (ibid., p. 23).

Solms also refers to the other scientific usage of the German language: "... in German scientific writing it is conventional to use everyday descriptive words for the equivalent technical terms" (Solms 2018, p. 14).

But a slightly different accent is perhaps more appropriate: in German-language usage, at least four different fields of application can be distinguished: everyday language, which is simply structured, very variable, and versatile; literary language, which is complex, elaborate, possibly sophisticatedly constructed, and comprises a large vocabulary; technical language for engineers, tax consultants, computer scientists, and so forth; and scientific language, which is used in academic disciplines and which is elaborate, very differentiated, and based on precisely defined conceptual meanings.

The literary language usually avoids foreign words, most of which come from Latin or Greek. Therefore, literary language sounds simple at first, almost like everyday language, but it is not. Its melody, however, is close to everyday language and it sounds familiar, although it may contain neologisms. This creates associative connections. Sometimes academic authors have a literary language. So did Freud. He had a precise and subtle literary language in which he could invent new words and present new facts. However, it was anything but everyday language.

It may perhaps be said that the use of German language in the sciences – and this is certainly particularly true for the language of psychoanalysis – is, by association, frequently deeply rooted in everyday experience and engages in the sensual experience through onomatopoeic consonance and terms close to experience (e.g. *"Bauchspeicheldrüse"*). These affective associations are difficult to maintain in translations. For the English language, similar limitations of translatability from German may exist in some respects as for the French language.

Transfer of the IJPA from the *Verlag* to the British Psycho-Analytical Society

It soon turned out that the production of the *IJPA* caused high costs which were not covered by the sale. The rationalization efforts such as Hiller's move to Vienna and the relocation of all technical and most editorial work steps to Vienna also did not lead to a reduction in losses. So the problems of the *Verlag* persisted. It only survived, after the death of von Freund, because of another benefactor, Max Eitingon (Schröter 2015, p. 109f), who repeatedly compensated for its financial losses. Eitingon came from a wealthy family of a Jewish fur merchant. His father moved his business and his family from Moscow to Leipzig in 1893, and later the family moved to New York (Schröter 2004). Based on his financial support and expertise, Eitingon adopted a supervisory role at the *Verlag* from 1921 (Jones 1957, p. 32). But it was clear that at some point the *Verlag* would have to pay for itself and that Freud would not be able to continue his constant search for a financier. Drastic changes seemed inevitable.

On 26 November 1922, Freud sent a circular letter to the members of the Secret Committee and informed them that the *Verlag* and he himself had decided not to continue subsidizing the *Press* and the *Journal* because of their ongoing deficit which the *Verlag*, struggling with its own financial problems, could not compensate any more (Wittenberger & Tögel 2003, p. 231ff). Concerning the future of the *Press*, he outlined three possible scenarios (ibid., p. 234f): (a) production and distribution of the *IJPA* and books are done together with the other books and journals of the *Verlag* in Berlin where a printing house would start working for the *Verlag* in 1923, because after the devaluation of the mark, it was much cheaper there than in Vienna, (b) the *Press* returns with its production and sale to London and maintains intimate relationships to the *Verlag*. The problem: the production in London was much more expensive than in Berlin or Vienna, (c) production, economic responsibility, and distribution are given from the *Verlag* to an English publishing house, while editorial competences remain in the hands of the *Verlag*.

In the following months, the members of the Secret Committee discussed the *Press* in their circular letters. Three topics dominated this discussion: the conflicts between Jones and Rank, the relation-ship *Verlag/Press,* and the losses of the *Verlag* produced by the *Press.*

Not only was there a complicated legal relationship between the *Verlag* and the *Press* (see earlier in the chapter), but also a clash of dif-ferent interests. Although as director of the *Verlag* Rank wanted to publish psychoanalytic books and the *Journal* in English, it was more important to him that the *Verlag* should not make a protracted loss. Jones's priority, on the other hand, was to publish psychoanalytic lit-erature in English in a controlled manner, best of all in a publishing house owned by psychoanalysts.

In the face of constant losses by the *Press,* first and foremost Freud sought to save the *Verlag* and was prepared to sacrifice the *Press.* In a letter to Eitingon (11 January 1923), he wrote about a donation he had received for the *Verlag* that he wished to conceal from the mem-bers of the Secret Committee, because: "If I announce the donation, he (Jones) will certainly demand that we continue to nourish the poorly managed Press..." (Freud & Eitingon 2004, p. 318).

In the letter from 26 November 1922, Freud also stated that the decision on the future of the *Press* must be made in England: "... Rather, the English will have the free choice between several pos-sibilities and we in Vienna... will certainly not make the decision, even if Jones expressly leaves it in our hands" (Wittenberger & Tögel 2003, p. 234). Jones was ambivalent about leaving the decision to the English. On the one hand, he repeatedly fought for a high degree of independence for the *Press* and complained vehemently in the Secret Committee (circular letters of December 4 and December 8, 1922), because he felt Rank had ignored him in the decisions concerning the *Verlag* and the *Press* (ibid., p. 244f and 249ff), but on the other hand, he wanted to keep the *Verlag* and the Viennese on board the *Press:* "... I cannot agree with Professor's point of view that the fu-ture of the Press must be decided in London" (ibid., p. 250). The financial aspect of the deficit adjustment probably may not be ex-pected to have played a minor role.

As Rank wrote in the newsletter of 20 December 1922 to the members of the Secret Committee, at the end of 1922, Storfer, a Viennese psychoanalyst who was to become involved in publishing in 1923, and Hiller, Jones's man in Vienna, had prepared an account of the financial transactions between the *Verlag* and the *Press* since the founding of the *Press* up until the end of 1922. According to this, the *Press* owed the *Verlag* £700 sterling. This calculation also took into account the grants which the English psychoanalysts had once donated to the *Verlag* (ibid., p. 262). Fed up with the constant wrangling, Freud wrote to Jones on 7 January 1923: "I think the English are bad to collaborate with and the only chance is they should do the work for themselves" (Freud & Jones 1993, p. 508). The *Press* survived for the time being, and Freud continued to support it. However, he did not want it at the expense of the *Verlag*. He granted Jones the rights to and profit from the sale of his books in America (November 4, 1923):

> I never thought that the American sales of the translations of my books (which ones?) could be so vital for the Press... I am prepared to let the Press have the American rights to my books for a period of two years, that is, until 31 December 1925, provided that during this period it retains its independence.
>
> (Ibid., p. 530f)

Freud's decision to no longer compensate the losses of the *Press* caused by the *IJPA* through the *Verlag* was irrevocable. At the beginning of 1923, the production and the press of the *IZP* and *Imago* was contracted out to a printing company in Berlin. The editors of both journals remained in Vienna. From 1923 onwards, the *IJPA* was technically and editorially produced in London. It was a difficult transitional period, since at first a publisher could not be found as a cooperation partner. On the 1923 title page of the fourth volume, *The International Psycho-Analytical Press* was still given as the publisher, while Lawn House, Hampstead Square, London, was listed as the printer. In 1924, Baillière, Tindall, and Cox, London, became the publisher and remained so for several decades, with the added line: "Published for the Institute of Psychoanalysis". The *Series of the Psychoanalytic Library*, previously also published in the *Press,* was henceforth issued by the Hogarth Press.

With the *Verlag's* withdrawal from the *Press*, the latter and the *IJPA* published by the *Press* were transferred from the *Verlag* to the British Psycho-Analytical Society. The British Society led by Jones kept the *IJPA* alive. The institutional connection between the *IZP* and the *IJPA* on the joint publication by the *Verlag* was thereby dissolved. However, a close scientific and personal connection remained. In 1925, the editor (*IZP*) or director (*IJPA*) of both magazines was Sigmund Freud. Jones was on the editor's staff and copy editors of both magazines (as publisher of the *IJPA*), as were Abraham, Bose, Brill, Van Emden, Ferenczi, Oberholzer, and Wulff.

The programme of contents of the *IJPA*

In his editorial for the first edition of the *International Journal*, Jones (1920) outlines the tasks that were to be fulfilled. In technical terms, it was intended to make Freud's work available in English, to be a forum for English-language psychoanalytical literature, to be an "Official Organ of the International Psycho-Analytical Association", and to be an information bulletin on the association's affairs for IPA members, as well as to produce quasi-official views on topics, "systematically comprehensively codifying all that is published on the given subject" (ibid., p. 3). As to content, Jones indicated a cooperation between the *Journal*, the *Zeitschrift,* and *Imago* in his editorial to the first issue: "An arrangement has been made whereby a mutual exchange of articles, abstracts and other material may be effected between the *Journal* on the one hand and the *Zeitschrift* and *Imago* on the other whenever this is found suitable" (Jones 1920, p. 5).

The four regular major categories of content contributions included the Original Papers, which were in-depth theoretical and clinical contributions, Shorter Communications, being short and mostly clinical contributions, the Book Reviews, and the Bulletin of the International Psycho-Analytical Association. In some volumes, there were discussion forums, such as in Volume 8, 1927, a discussion on lay analysis with 38 contributions, in which practically all the well-known analysts of the time had participated. A volume very occasionally contained congressional reports, as did Volume 8, 1927, with a collection of several reports of a "Symposium on Child Analysis".

The Original Papers documented most clearly the scientific activities of the authors; they represented the scientific core of the *IJPA*. The origin of these contributions therefore sheds light on the state of development of psychoanalysis in the regions where it was already practised at that time. The first volume, in 1920, offered a rich programme. It gathered original articles and reviews of recent literature from different languages such as English, French, Dutch, Spanish, and Italian. It also included articles on special themes by Hitschmann, Abraham, Ophuijsen, Ferenczi, and Hug-Hellmuth, 26 reviews of books by English-speaking authors, and additionally reports of the

IPA and of the Sixth IPA Congress in The Hague in 1920. This first volume demonstrates significant effort to present the internationality of psychoanalysis and especially what English-speaking psychoanalysts and authors could contribute to psychoanalysis.

The idea to publish papers in parallel in the *IJPA* and in the *IZP* was partially realized. During the first years, the exchange of papers was one-sided insofar as many more papers which had first been published in the *IZP* or in *Imago* were, after translation, reprinted in the *IJPA*. This was conducive to making previously published psychoanalytic literature available to English readers. The *IJPA* usually published current papers from *IZP* in the same or in the following year. Vice versa, papers of English-speaking authors were less commonly published in the *IZP* after they had been printed in the *IJPA*. First it happened in 1927 (Table 2.1, Column 6 "later in Ger").

In the first two years of the *IJPA*, special efforts were made to prove that the English-speaking world was also able to provide

Table 2.1 Primary and secondary publication language of original papers, 1920–1935

Year	Orig Engl	Transl Ger	Total Or Ps	simult IJ+IZ	Prior in Ger	Later in Ger
1920	9	7	16	4	3	
1921	7	4	11	3	1	
1922	4	9	13	2	7	
1923	1	7	8		7	
1924	4	13	17	1	12	
1925	11	11	22	7	4	
1926	7	19	26	20	4	
1927	7	6	13		6	1
1928	5	12	17	2	10	1
1929	18	15	33	19	5	3
1930	17	11	28	10	2	1
1931	13	8	21	4	4	
1932	4	9	13	5	4	1
1933	10	6	16	4	2	
1934	9	10	19	4	6	1
1935	16	8	24	7	5	3

Orig Engl: Originally English Papers.
Transl Ger: Papers translated from German.
Total Or Ps: Totality of Original Papers.
Simult IJ+IZ: Papers simultaneously published in *IJP* and *IZP*, that is, in the same year.
Prior in Ger: Papers published in German one or more years before being published in *IJP*.
Later in Ger: Papers published in German one or more years after being published in *IJP*.

qualified psychoanalytical texts (Table 2.1). The years 1922 with four English original papers and 1923 with only one brought a menacing collapse of its own scientific productivity (Table 2.1, Column 1 "Orig Engl"). In 1923, there was a severe economic crisis after the *Verlag* had stopped subsidizing the *Press*. The uncertainty over the continued existence of the *IJPA* apparently also stifled scientific creativity. However, Jones and the British Society managed to overcome this crisis. The number of original papers written in English increased again. In 1929, there was with 33 (Table 2.1, Column 3, "Total Or Ps") an unusually high number of original papers, 18 of them primarily in English (Table 2.1, Column 1 "Orig Engl"; Figure 2.1). For the first time after the first two years, they exceeded the number of those translated from German. This continued to be the case in the following years until 1932, when of 13 original papers, only four had been written in English and nine were translations. In the following years, the primarily English written original papers predominated again (Table 2.1, Columns 1–3; Figure 2.1).

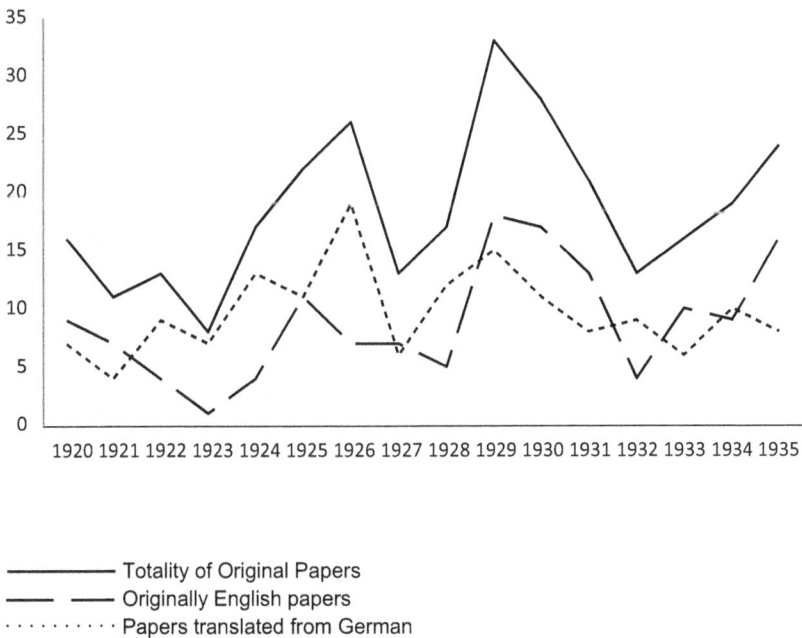

Figure 2.1 Original papers of *the IJP* 1920–1935; originally English papers compared to papers translated from German.

German-language journals from which selected articles were republished in the *IJPA* in the 1920s and 1930s were the *IZP, Imago,* the *Zeitschrift für Psychoanalytische Pädagogik* (Journal for psychoanalytic pedagogy), and the *Almanach der Psychoanalyse* (Almanac of psychoanalysis). They all were periodicals of the *Verlag.*

Since the beginning of the 1930s, psychoanalysts who had emigrated from German-speaking countries to Great Britain and America were increasingly among the *IJPA's* authors. They also changed their language of publication. In 1935, the emigrated authors of papers that were originally written in English included, for example, Alexander, Bergler, Eidelberg, Alfred Gross, Schilder, and Wittels.

Since 1927, original papers from the *IJPA* had also been reprinted in the German-language periodicals *IZP* or *Imago* (Table 2.1, Column 6). These changes show that English-speaking psychoanalysts had become more independent and creative in their scientific productivity and were increasingly leaving the phase of learning from German-language psychoanalysis behind.

A few years later, the question of whether a psychoanalyst wanted to publish a work in the *IJPA IZP, Imago,* or in another journal was settled. The 1937 volume was the last of the *IZP* and *Imago* for the time being, for on 13 March 1938, Austria was annexed to the German Reich. On 15 March, the National Socialists began to liquidate the *Verlag* in Vienna. Thus, the basis for the publication of the two journals *IZP* and *Imago* and others was lost. Although a collated journal, the "Internationale Zeitschrift für Psychoanalyse und Imago", continued to be published for a further three years from 1939 to 1941, after the emigration of most psychoanalysts from Germany and Austria and following Freud's death in September 1939, and in view of the disfiguring influence of the Nazis on the remnants of psychoanalysis remaining in Germany and Austria, psychoanalysis no longer had the power to sustain and continue an international German-language psychoanalytic journal. Anyone who now wanted to publish as a psychoanalyst in a journal along Freudian lines and wanted to reach an international readership could do so in the *IJPA*.

Concluding remarks

The founding of the *IJPA* was in the interest of Freud, who, at least following his trip to the United States at Clark University in Worcester, Massachusetts, had subsequently sought to spread his new science of psychoanalysis throughout the world in 1909: "... it seemed like the realisation of some incredible day-dream..." (Freud 1925, p. 52). Together with the members of the Secret Committee and other colleagues, he developed ideas on the scientific and organizational structure of psychoanalysis. Independent publication possibilities played an important role in this. He took his first steps in this direction with the founding of the German-language journals *Imago* and *Internationale Zeitschrift für Ärztliche Psychoanalyse* already before World War I. However, the more important step towards internationalization was the founding of *the International Journal of Psychoanalysis*. After the World War I, Freud was able to found an international psychoanalytical publishing house, the *Verlag*, along with his closest associates and with the help of an extremely generous donation granted to him by the Hungarian entrepreneur Anton von Freund. It published psychoanalytic books and the three IPA journals *Imago (since 1919)*, *IZP (since 1919)*, and *IJPA (since 1920)*, and later also other journals.

After the first issue of the *IJPA* in 1920, this new journal took ten years to become independent in terms of content, as could be seen by the growing number of original papers written in English. Furthermore, there was a lively exchange with the *IZP* and *Imago* and the mutual acquisition of works originally published in the other journal. The political developments with the expulsion of psychoanalysis and psychoanalysts from Central Europe by the National Socialists led to the downfall of *Imago* and the *IZP*. The *IJPA* was the only surviving journal of the three and, following on from Freud's thinking and developments, continues the tradition of psychoanalysis, which has since widened into a broad spectrum. Hand in hand with the general political developments and consequent organizational ones, the focus of international psychoanalysis shifted from the central European centres of Vienna and Berlin to other centres such as London and New York. The development of the *IJPA* was, and remains, interwoven in these processes. In this respect, it reflects not only the history of science and associations of psychoanalysis but also a piece of contemporary history.

Notes

1 "Zeitschrift" – abbreviation of *Internationale Zeitschrift für Psychoanalyse*.
2 "Vereinigung" or "Verein" – abbreviation of *Internationale Psychoanalytische Vereinigung (IPV)*, used by its members.

3 Jung, C.G.: Wandlungen und Symbole der Libido: Beiträge zur Entwicklungsgeschichte des Denkens (Changes and Symbols of Libido. Contributions to the developmental History of Thinking). Part one 1911, part two 1912. Both were published together in English in 1916: Psychology of the Unconscious: a study of the transformations and symbolisms of the libido, a contribution to the history of the evolution of thought. See references.

4 Two examples illustrate how the *Korrespondenzblatt* reported on the public perception of psychoanalysis. (a) "'Rascher's Jahrbuch für Schweizer Art und Kunst' [Rascher's Yearbook for Swiss Character and Arts], edited by Konrad Falke, Zurich, 1912, contains an article by C. G. Jung: Neue Bahnen der Psychologie [New ways of psychology]. On this occasion a longer press feud in the 'Neue Zürcher Zeitung' (January 14–15, 25, 27–28 and February 1), introduced by a co-editor of the newspaper, was unleashed. He expressed himself in several articles on the dangers of psychoanalysis, against which he called on public opinion to help. The content of the articles does not offer anything new or remarkable, but is a repetition of the usual lay errors and misunderstandings. In this polemic, against which the Psychoanalytical Association could only react with a public protest, Forel also mingled in an unpleasant way. The new thing he brings forward is that he distinguishes psychoanalysis with and without o. To the psychanalysis without o he counts as the true representatives of science some of his followers... The editorial staff of the Zurich literary magazine 'Wissen und Leben' [Knowledge and Life] offered to include a final word in the above-mentioned press feud. The article was published on February 15. The matter has caused quite a stir in other Swiss cities, too" (Korrespondenzblatt 1912, p. 480). (b) "Psychoanalysis was the main topic of discussion in the psychiatric section of the recently concluded International Medical Congress in London. The speakers were Prof. Dr. Pierre Janet of Paris, the greatest French authority in the field of psychopathology, and Dr. C. G. Jung of Zurich. Janet's presentation was quite negative towards the psychoanalytic method. In the discussion that followed the presentations, Prof. Jones (Toronto) and Dr. Eder (London) used examples to show that Janet's presentation was largely based on inadequate reviews of the original German works in English and French journals. A long series of misunderstandings and depositions in Janet's lecture were due to this quite insufficient information and to prejudiced judgement. The debate was heavily attended and did not result in any lasting objections against the psychoanalytic method on the part of the opponents. The closing words of the president of the psychiatric section Sir George Savage, the elderly senior of English psychiatry, acknowledged the scientific nature of the

psychoanalytic method and especially underlined the lack of scientific reasons for the opposition. This complete victory of the new method deserves to be especially emphasized because its scientific nature was denied not only by doctors, but also by less competent laymen in the daily press. In the discussion, Dr. Jung particularly emphasized the fact that the psychoanalytic method and the sexual theory of nervous diseases, which Freud had set up, are two different things that should not be confused" (Korrespondenzblatt 1913, p. 636).

5 Obviously there was a strong ambivalence between Freud and Jung at an early stage already. Freud passed out twice in the presence of Jung, for the first time on 20 August 1909 in Bremen at the beginning of their joint trip to Clark University in the USA, second time on 24 November 1912 in Munich, when he sought advice from some colleagues for his dealings with Stekel. Freud and Jung felt that their relationship was like a father–son relationship. Before Freud's first fainting in 1909, Jung had talked extensively about bog corpses, which Freud had felt like a latent death wish towards him. After the fainting in 1912, Jung had felt that when Freud woke up he had looked at him, Jung, "as if I were his father..." (Jung 1961, p. 161). That is, in his fantasies Jung took over the father's place at that moment – the elimination of the "father" Freud. For more details, see: Bruns (2004).

6 All page references to Nunberg & Federn refer to the German edition of the minutes.

7 "Verlag" – abbreviation for *Internationaler Psychoanalytischer Verlag (International Psychoanalytical Publishing house)* as used within the IPA; the parent company of the Press.

8 All page references to Goldschmidt refer to the German edition of Goldschmidt 1988.

References

Abraham, K. (1914a): Besprechung zu: C. G. Jung, Versuch einer Darstellung der psychoanalytischen Theorie. Neun Vorlesungen, gehalten in New-York im September 1912 (Comments on: C.G. Jung, Attempt to Present the Psychoanalytic Theory. Nine Lectures, Given in New York in September 1912). Jahrb. f. psychoanalyt. Forsch., Bd. V. Buchausgabe: Wien, F. Deuticke 1913. *Internat. Zschr. Psychoanal.*, 2(1):72–82.

Abraham, K. (1914b): Korrespondenzblatt der Internationalen Psychoanalytischen Vereinigung. *Internat. Zschr. Psychoanal.*, 2(4):405–417.

Adler, A. (1911): Erklärung (Statement). *Zbl. Psychoanal.*, 1(10–11):433.

Barnett, A.J. (2013): The Psychoanalytic Review: 100 Years of History. *Psychoanal. Rev.*, 100:1–56.

Bettelheim, B. (1983): *Freud and Man's Soul.* A.A. Knopf, New York.

Bleuler, E. (1912): Das autistische Denken (Autistic thinking). *Jb. Psychoanal. Psychopathol. Forsch.*, 4(1912):1–39.

Bruns, G. (2004): Zwei Ohnmachten Freuds in der Begegnung mit Jung. Eine Reminiszenz an seine Herzneurose und den Ambivalenzkonflikt in Männerfreundschaften (Two faintings of Freud in the encounter with Jung. A reminiscence of his heart neurosis and the ambivalence conflict in male friendships). *Jb. Psychoanal.*, 48(2004):105–133.

Clark, J.M. (1896): Reviews and abstracts: Studien über Hysterie. *Brain*, 20(1896):401–414.

Eissler, K.R. (1982): *Psychologische Aspekte des Briefwechsels zwischen Jung und Freud (Psychological Aspects of the Letters between Freud and Jung).* Fromman-Holzboog, Stuttgart (Jahrbuch der Psychoanalyse, Beiheft 7).

Eitingon, M. (1914). Über das Ubw. bei Jung und seine Wendung ins Ethische (The Ucs according to Jung and its Turn into the Ethical). *Internat. Zschr. Psychoanal.*, 2(1):99–104.

Ferenczi, S. (1913): Besprechung zu: C. G. Jung, Wandlungen und Symbole der Libido. Beiträge zur Entwicklungsgeschichte des Denkens (Comments on: C.G. Jung, Changes and Symbols of Libido. Contributions to the Developmental History of Thinking). (Jahrbuch für psychoanalytische und psychopathologische Forschungen, III. u. IV. Band, 1911 und 1912. Auch separat bei F. Deuticke, Wien 1912, Preis K. 12.-, 422 S. samt Index.). *Internat. Zschr. Psychoanal.*, 1(4):391–403.

Ferenczi, S. (1920): Open Letter. *Int. J. Psychoanal.*, 1(1920):1–2.

Ferenczi, S., & Freund, A. (1919). Korrespondenzblatt der Internationalen Psychoanalytischen Vereinigung. *Internat. Zschr. Psychoanal.*, 5(1):52–57.

Freud, S. (1905): Fragment of an Analysis of a Case of Hysteria (1905 [1901]). *SE* 7:1–122.

Freud, S. (1910): The Future Prospects of Psycho-Analytic Therapy. *SE* 9:139–152.

Freud, S. (1914a): On Narcissism. *SE* 14:67–102.

Freud, S. (1914b): On the History of the Psycho-Analytic Movement. *SE* 14:1–66.

Freud, S. (1925): An Autobiographical Study. *SE* 20:1–74.

Freud, S. (2002): *Unser Herz zeigt nach dem Süden. Reisebriefe 1895–1923 (Our Heart Points to the South. Letters from Journeys 1895–1923).* Edited by Tögel, C., and Molnar, M., Aufbau-Verlag, Berlin.

Freud, S., & Eitingon, M. (2004): *Sigmund Freud – Max Eitingon. Briefwechsel 1906–1939, Bd. 1 (Sigmund Freud – Max Eitingon. Exchange of Letters 1906–1939, Vol. 1).* Edited by Schröter, M., Edition diskord, Tübingen.

Freud, S., & Jones, E. (1993): *The Complete Correspondence of Sigmund Freud and Ernest Jones 1908–1939.* Edited by Paskauskas, R.A., The Belknap Press of Harvard University Press, Cambridge, MA and London.

Giefer, M. (Ed., 2007): Das Korrespondenzblatt der Internationalen Psychoan-alytischen Vereinigung 1910–1941. Ursprünglich publiziert als CD-ROM im Selbstverlag (2007) (The Bulletin of the International Psychoanalytical Association 1910–1941. Originally Self-Edited as CD, 2007) https://www.luzifer-amor.de/index.php?id=179 (accessed 9 August 2019).

Goldschmidt, G.-A. (1988): Quand Freud voit la mer – Freud et la langue allemande. Buchet/ Chastel, Paris. (In German: Als Freud das Meer sah. Freud und die deutsche Sprache [*When Freud Saw the Sea. Freud and German Language*]. Translated by Grosse, B., 1999, Fischer, Frankfurt a.M., 2005).

Handlbauer, B. (2010): *Die Freud-Adler-Kontroverse (The Freud-Adler Controversy)*. Psychosozial-Verlag, 2. Ed., Gießen.

Jones, E. (1920): Editorial. *Int. J. Psychoanal.*, 1(1920):3–5

Jones, E. (1957). *Sigmund Freud Life and Work, Volume Three: The Last Phase 1919–1939*. The Hogarth Press, London.

Jung, C.G. (1911): Wandlungen und Symbole der Libido: Beiträge zur En-twicklungsgeschichte des Denkens. Erster Teil (Changes and Symbols of Libido. Contributions to the Developmental History of Thinking. Part One). *Jb. Psychoanal. Psychopathol. Forsch.*, 3(1):120–227. (*Psychology of the Unconscious: A Study of the Transformations and Symbolisms of the Libido, a Contribution to the History of the Evolution of Thought. Part 1 and 2.* Translated by Hinkle, B.M., 1916, Kegan Paul Trench Trubner, London).

Jung, C.G. (1912): Wandlungen und Symbole der Libido: Beiträge zur En-twicklungsgeschichte des Denkens. Zweiter Teil (Changes and Symbols of Libido. Contributions to the developmental History of Thinking. Part two). *Jb. Psychoanal. Psychopathol. Forsch.*, 4(1):162–464.

Jung, C.G. (1961): *Erinnerungen, Träume, Gedanken von C.G. Jung (Memories, Dreams, Thoughts of C.G. Jung)*. Edited by A Jaffé. Walter-Verlag, Olten-Freiburg/Br., 1971.

Jung, C.G., & Riklin, F. (1913): Korrespondenzblatt der Internationalen Psychoanalytischen Vereinigung I/1913. *Internat. Zschr. Psychoanal.*, 1(1913):111–116.

Korrespondenzblatt der Internationalen Psychoanalytischen Vereinigung. (1912): Bericht der Ortsgruppen 1911/12. *Zbl. Psychoanal.*, 2(8):475–480.

Korrespondenzblatt der Internationalen Psychoanalytischen Vereinigung. (1913): Ortsgruppe Zürich. *Internat. Zschr. Psychoanal*, 1(6):621–636.

Laplanche, J. (1991). Specificity of terminological problems in the transla-tion of Freud. *Int. R. Psycho-Anal.*, 18:401–406.

Maddox, B. (2006): *Freud's Wizard. The Enigma of Ernest Jones*. John Murray, London.

Mahony, P. (1992): A Psychoanalytic Translation of Freud. In: Ornston, D.G. (Ed.), *Translating Freud*. Yale University Press, New Haven, CT, pp. 24–47.

Marinelli, L. (2005): Zentralblatt für Psychoanalyse. International Dictionary of Psycho-analysis. 2005. *Encyclopedia.com*. 17 Juli 2019: https://www.encyclopedia.com/psy-chology/dictionaries-thesauruses-pictures-and-press-releases/zentralblatt-fur-psychoanalyse.

Marinelli, L. (2009): *Psyches Kanon. Zur Publikationsgeschichte rund um den Internationalen Psychoanalytischen Verlag (Psyche's Canon. The History of Publications around the Internationaler Psychoanalytischer Verlag)*. Wien: Turia + Kant.

Masson, J.M. (Ed., 1985): *The Complete Letters of Sigmund Freud to Wilhelm Fließ 1887–1904*. The Belknap Press of Harvard University Press, Cambridge, MA.

Nunberg, H., & Federn, E. (Eds., 1962): *Protokolle der Wiener Psychoanalytischen Vereinigung (Minutes of the Vienna Psychoanalytic Society. Vol 1. International Universities Press, New York)*. Bd. 1. Fischer, Frankfurt a.M., 1976.

Ornston, D.G. (1982): Strachey's Influence: A Preliminary Report. *Int. J. Psychoanal.*, 63(1982):409–426.

Rank, O. (1911). Bericht über die 1. private Psychoanalytische Vereinigung in Salzburg am 27. April 1908. (Report on the 1. Private Psychoanalytical Congress in Salzburg, 27 April 1908). *Zbl. Psychoanal.*, 1(3):125–129.

Rank, O., & Sachs, H. (1912): Entwicklung und Ansprüche der Psychoanalyse (Development and Aspirations of Psychoanalysis). *Imago*, 1(1912):1–16.

Reinbothe, R. (2011): Geschichte des Deutschen als Wissenschaftssprache im 20. Jahrhundert (History of German Language as Language of Science in the 20th century). In: Eins, W., Glück, H., & Pretscher, S. (Eds.), *Wissen schaffen – Wissen kommunizieren. Wissenschaftssprachen in Geschichte und Gegenwart (Creating Knowledge – Communicating Knowledge. Languages of Science in Historical and Present Times)*. Harassowitz Verlag, Wiesbaden, 2011, pp. 49–66.

Reports of the International Psycho-Analytical Association. (1920a): Bul. Int. Psychoanal. Assn., *Int. J. Psychoanal.*, 1(1920):114–124.

Reports of the International Psycho-Analytical Association. (1920b): Sixth Congress of the International Psycho-Analytical Association. Bul. Int. Psychoanal. Assn., *Int. J. Psychoanal.*, 1(1920):208–221.

Robinson, K. (2013). A Portrait of the Psychoanalyst as a Bohemian: Ernest Jones and the 'Lady from Styria'. *Psychoanal. Hist.*, 15(2):165–189.

Schröter, M. (1995): Freuds Komitee 1912–1914. Ein Beitrag zum Verständnis psychoanalytischer Gruppenbildung (Freud's Committee 1912–1914. A Contribution to Understanding the Formation of Psychoanalytical Groups). *Psyche – Z Psychoanal.*, 49(1995):513–563.

Schröter, M. (2004): Einleitung: Der Steuermann. Max Eitingon und seine Rolle in der Geschichte der Psychoanalyse. (Introduction: The Helmsman. Max Eitingon and His Role in Psychoanalytic History). In: Schröter, M. (Ed.), *Sigmund Freud – Max Eitingon. Briefwechsel 1906–1939, Bd. 1 (Exchange of Letters 1906–1939, Vol. 1).* Edition diskord, Tübingen.

Schröter, M. (2015): Max Eitingon's Rise and Decline: The Berlin Years. *Psychoanal. Q.,* 84(1):103–123.

Solms, M. (2018): Extracts from the Revised Standard Edition of Freud's Complete Psychological Works. *Int. J. Psychoanal.,* 99(2018):11–57.

Steiner, R. (1991). To Explain Our Point of View to English Readers in English Words. *Int. Rev. Psycho-Anal.,* 18:351–392.

Steiner, R. (1994). 'The Tower of Babel' or 'After Babel in Contemporary Psychoanalysis'?—Some Historical and Theoretical Notes on the Linguistic and Cultural Strategies Implied by the Foundation of the International Journal of Psycho-Analysis, and on Its Relevance Today. *Int. J. Psycho-Anal.,* 75:883–901.

Wittenberger, G. (1995): *Das "Geheime Komitee" Sigmund Freuds. Institutionalisierungsprozesse in der Psychoanalytischen Bewegung zwischen 1912 und 1927 (Sigmund Freud's "Secret Committee." Processes of Institutionalization of the Psychoanalytic Movement 1912–1927).* Edition Diskord, Tübingen.

Wittenberger, G., & Tögel, C. (Eds., 1999): *Die Rundbriefe des "Geheimen Komitees" (The Circular Letters of the "Secret Committee").* Bd. 1 (Vol. 1): 1913–1920. Edition discord, Tübingen.

Wittenberger, G., & Tögel, C. (Eds., 2003): *Die Rundbriefe des "Geheimen Komitees" (The Circular Letters of the "Secret Committee").* Bd. 3 (Vol. 3): 1922. Edition discord, Tübingen.

3

"THE DEEP OPEN SEA"[1] "L'ALTO MARE APERTO"

Some notes on psychoanalysis and translation, focusing on the early vicissitudes of the first British attempts to translate Freud

Riccardo Steiner

To start my paper, I have chosen what the Italian writer Primo Levi wrote in a paper called "Del tradurre ed essere tradotto" ("To translate and on being translated"), because Levi, with his usual clarity and empathy, draws attention to the contradictory emotional reactions that even the most skilled translator must face when encountering the "other" or "the unfamiliar" during the process of translation:

> For many people at a more or less conscious level, anyone who speaks another language is a foreigner by definition, an outsider, a stranger and different from me and someone different is a potential enemy or at least a barbarian.
>
> (Levi, 1985)

What I find so interesting and unusual considering the vast literature on translation is what at one moment Levi describes as the emotional experience of being translated: "It is not a weekday or a weekend job", Levi claims, "it is a sort of passiveness similar to that of the patient on the surgeon's table or the psychoanalyst's couch, rich nevertheless in violent and contradictory emotions" (Colarossi, 2015).

What I quoted from Levi's paper therefore seems to me an extremely apt, and as I will try to show, even surprising starting point for what I want to develop in this paper. First of all, I try to understand what Freud meant by translation and the relationship he established between translation and his work. Then I will look at the first attempts to translate him by the English pioneers of the British Psychoanalytical Society in the early 1920s and even before, and how complex and unique was their attempt to face "the unfamiliar", which led to the monumental *Standard Edition (S.E.),* translated by James Strachey with the help of his wife in the 1950s.

The complexity and the uniqueness of the translation of Freud also help us study the problems related to the links between translation and psychoanalysis. Besides the role played by specific cultural, institutional, financial, and socio-political factors, those first translators were all directly or indirectly analyzed, or at least emotionally deeply influenced in their private and professional life, by the living Freud. They were also influenced by the "other", the "unfamiliar", that Freud was still discovering – the unconscious – and by their own unconscious, their own "unfamiliar" in their interaction with him.

The process of systematically translating Freud into English started with Jones, who was the mastermind of the first plans to translate Freud, but also the mastermind of the *S.E.,* and who, with his *Glossaries* of the language of Freud, created what I have called a sort of English Tower of Babel of the English language of psychoanalysis "which lasted more than 50 years and is partially still lasting today" (Steiner, 1994). The case of Abraham Brill and his pioneering work of translating Freud into Anglo-American deserves another paper, but from time to time, I will mention his contributions too.[2]

But why choose to discuss the creation of the *S.E.,* some could ask. After all, it is only the English translation of Freud. Well, besides the strange context in which the translation was conceived compared with the other translations of Freud's work, I think one cannot deny that the historical vicissitudes of the diaspora of the European and mainly Jewish analysts during the years of Nazi persecution, which involved at times painful processes of adaptation (Steiner, 1999, 2000, 2003 [2016]), meant that English supplanted German as the official language of the IPA. Due to the approval of Anna Freud, who collaborated with Strachey from a young age in Vienna, the *S.E.* became, and is still today, at least partially, the global version of Freud for the IPA and elsewhere.

And due to its "iconic" quality, and the personalities and intellectual stature of its translators, the *S.E.* influenced and still influences directly or indirectly the other attempts to translate Freud – as if it were a sort of "septuagint"[3] of Freud's *Gesammelte Werke* (collected works). Although, of course, today, in what I have called the era of liquid psychoanalysis (Steiner, 2012), our relation to Freud is enormously different and distant compared with those pioneers.

I will now summarize some ideas about Freud and his views on translation.[4] I will first of all try to illustrate what Freud meant by translation as such, starting with his pre-analytical years and the environment in which he grew up and studied – his vital need to translate in order to try to become acquainted with and integrated within the dominant language and culture of the Austro-Hungarian Empire.

As a Jew and so belonging to a minority group, and coming to Vienna with his family as a small child from a remote province of the Austro-Hungarian Empire, Freud was brought up learning to speak Yiddish, Czech, and, of course, Austro-German and Hebrew.

Of enormous importance for him was his experience of translating Ancient Latin and Greek and English at the Sperlgymnasium in Vienna. One should not forget that, besides his interest in so many other languages and cultures like Spanish or Italian, Freud translated some Essays of J. Stuart Mill while he was still a student at the University of Vienna, becoming a sort of professional translator from his beloved English (Jones, 1953; Molnar, 1999). And a few years later, he translated some work of Charcot and Bernheim from French into German (Freud 1892, 1893). But one should also consider his correspondence and some other translations that he carried out when he was already a practicing psychoanalyst. "Grosso modo", one could say that Freud's views on translation as such were not so different from those of a learned European at that time, and could be condensed in the famous motto "traduttore traditore", which Freud used in his book on jokes (1905 [1968], *S.E.* 8, p. 38). He had a rather conservative, prudent view of how to translate, wanting to respect the text of the original as much as possible, as he had learned at school.

At the same time, if we look at *The Interpretation of Dreams* (1900 [1968], *S.E.* 4) and at the famous Chapter 6 on "The Dream Work" (p. 277), as well as the *Introductory Lectures on Psychoanalysis* (1916–1917) ([1968], *S.E.* 15, XI, p. 170), where Freud deals with dreams, to mention just a few texts, one can see his real interest in translation; we see this in his account of the "dream work" and the manifest and latent content of the dream, and the need to retranslate the manifest content into the "unfamiliar" – the unconscious dream thoughts of the latent content. His engagement with translation is also visible in his notion of the non-verbal or verbal language of the symptoms of his patients, which he related to the dream work when he claimed that the dream could be understood if one was able to "translate" the manifest distorted content of the dreams, or even of the symptoms, into the original latent, unconscious content of thoughts, wishes, and phantasies. If one considers all these forms of translation in his work, then Freud can be seen as one of the revolutionary pioneers of what R. Jakobson (1959 [1971], p. 264) called, in a landmark paper on translation, the inter-semiotic type of translation or "transmutation": a translation that allows figurative language to be translated into verbal language, and vice versa (Mahony, 1980, 1987, 2003; Steiner, 1980, 1981, 1988; Eco, 2003).[5]

Therefore, Freud's insistence that the activity of the analyst can be compared to that of a translator in reality means comparing the activity of the analyst to that of an inter-semiotic translator, if not a semiotician. Aside from the dream, just think of the importance that non-verbal and verbal communication has for Freud, along with Breuer, in trying to make sense of all the descriptive vignettes of the symptoms of their patients in *Studies on Hysteria* (1895). But also remember the marvellous examples of non-verbal communication that Freud later describes in the Dora case (Freud, 1905 [1968], *S.E.* 8, p. 78).

I think that Freud's notion of "Übersetzung" ("translation") in the case of the dream (Freud, 1900, 1968, *S.E.* 4, p. 277), but also in the symptoms both of patients and the so-called normal people, and the problems related to the application of psychoanalysis to sociocultural artistic phenomena, raises the question of whether in psychoanalysis there can be a translation without a component of personal interpretation.

Looking at some of Freud's statements, I would also like to put forward the view that in our activity as psychoanalyst translators, we are, in reality, more the interpreters of an oral text than what Freud meant by translators of a sort of written text.[6] Or we are both at the same time. This coexistence of the oral interpreter and the translator can perhaps better explain the difficulties we have in translating,

91

in interpreting as psychoanalysts, the mobility of the unconscious and the ever-changing interactions and communications between analyst and patient, as well as the impossibility of working on a proper fixed, written text. This is all due to the "unfamiliarity" of the unconscious, the "demonic", as Freud calls it in *The Interpretation of Dreams* (1900 [1968], *S.E.* 5, p. 614) and in the Dora case (1905 [1968], *S.E.* 7, p. 81). Not to mention the uncertainties of our results when we try to interpret-translate cultural or sociopolitical phenomena using psychoanalysis.

Indeed, in stressing the possibility of translating dreams, free associations and symptoms, and of even understanding the transference as a translation,[7] in *The Interpretation of Dreams* and in many papers up to the end of his life, he constantly stressed the impossibility of a total, perfect translation/interpretation of the dreams and of the symptoms of his patients, and in the end of the transference too.[8] Just remember his famous statement in *The Interpretation of Dreams* about the impossibility of a total translation/interpretation, what he calls "the dream's navel ... the spot where the dream reaches down to the unknown" (1900 [1968], *S.E.* 5, p. 525).

Although I am drastically summarizing and simplifying Freud's views, these are Freud's ideas about translation and the relationship between translation and psychoanalysis that Brill, Jones, and later on the Stracheys, and even J. Riviere, found themselves confronted with when they contacted Freud in Vienna or, later on, when they went to Vienna to be treated by Freud and to learn how to better translate him; these engagements with Freud were not simply meetings between professionals who had to discuss how to translate a written text or to discuss ideas. They were unique, "unfamiliar" situations, where very often Freud as an interpreter and translator analyzed these analysts through written correspondence, at times during their meetings in Vienna, like in the case of Jones (Paskaukas, 1993) and Brill, or on his couch, like in the case of J. Riviere and the Stracheys. At the same time, however, he would discuss their translations of the written text of his work, and he took all sorts of liberties with them, which went far beyond what he had written on the necessity of being as objective as possible, even in translating dreams where the confused manifest content had to be taken with extreme seriousness. At one moment, as if he knew about Saint Jerome, the father of the Western translators, Freud even compared the translation of the manifest content of the dream to the care one has to take when confronted with the attempt to translate *"ein heiligen text"* (the sacred text; *Die Traumdeutung*, 1900 [1968], *G.W.* II/III, p. 518).[9]

The liberties that Freud took with his translators went much further than what he wrote in his paper on technique and how to deal with patients in analysis during those years (1911/12/13 [1968] *S.E.* 12). I would like now to illustrate this unique situation between Freud and his translators, which gave rise to all sorts of amusing, extraordinary, and also disturbing problems.

A few paragraphs above, I mentioned in passing Brill and his breakdown. But in what follows, I would like to focus on what Otto Rank at one moment in an unpublished letter to Jones on 2 February 1921, polemically termed Jones's attempt to establish *"Die Weltmachstellung des Britischen Reichs"* –"The fostering of the world power of the British Reign", or Empire, as one might say (Steiner, 1988). Rank was referring to Jones's obsessive plan to become the only reliable English-speaking translator and editor of Freud's work. Indeed, Jones had been the first to contact Freud, along with A. Brill, to discuss the issue of translating his work in 1908 when they first met in Vienna after the International Meeting in Salzburg. And Freud nominated Brill as his translator in America (Brill, 1938; Jones, 1959; Steiner, 1984, 1987, 1988; Maddox, 2007; Kuhn, 2014, 2017). Jones started to develop his own plans concerning the translation of Freud's work into English when he went to Canada in 1908. There is no doubt that he felt very ambivalent and excluded by Freud's choice of Brill as his translator (Jones to Freud, 18 December 1909; Brill, 1938; Paskaukas, 1993, pp. 34–35).

Therefore, contrary to what has very often been claimed by those who have studied the translation of Freud in the *S.E.*, like Bettelheim (1983), Meisel & Kendrick (1986), J. Ornston (1982, 1985, 1988), and others, Jones played a pivotal and fundamental role in organizing the first translations of Freud. Jones started this work in the first decade of 1900, much earlier than the Stracheys and Joan Riviere, who went to Vienna in the early 1920s to learn how to translate Freud, consulting Freud even during their analyses with him (Steiner, 1987, 1988).

If one looks at the evidence coming from the documents I studied, one can easily come to the conclusion that Jones was responsible for the beginning of the standardization of the technical language of Freud, using terminology coming from Ancient Greek and Latin, or rooted in those languages. Terms like "ego", "super ego", "instinct", "interpretations of dreams", "mind", "repression", "transference", "unconscious", and so on, which have been criticized by Lacan (1966), Bettelheim (1993), and many others, who attributed the terms only to Strachey, were gradually created by Jones, who also used the work of other American translators of Freud like A. Brill, H. Chase, and others. In Britain, Havelock Ellis's reviews and paper on Freud, of which Jones knew about (1945), were also particularly influential to the technical vocabulary of Freud.[10] And along with Brill (1912), Jones started to create the first rudimentary English *Glossaries of Psychoanalysis* from 1912 onwards (Steiner, 1989; Linstrum, 2014).[11] I will now try to briefly explain the very complex cultural, institutional, and even sociopolitical reasons behind Jones's wish to translate the technical language of Freud, and then to edit his work in the way he did, which resulted in gaining hegemonic control of Freud's psychoanalysis in English-speaking countries.

Since the first decade of the 20th century, Jones was absolutely convinced that psychoanalysis could only survive and be accepted as a natural science. One has only to read the numerous letters he wrote to Freud from Canada in 1908 to 1910 (Steiner, 1987, 1988, 1999; Paskaukas, 1993). Due to the difficulties and oppositions to psychoanalysis in Canada and the USA, and from the British medical establishment at the time, Jones felt that the language of psychoanalysis needed to imitate that of the natural sciences; like physics, chemistry, biology, physiology, neurology, experimental psychology, and modern psychiatry, psychoanalysis had to be as "monosemic" as possible, rooted in ancient Greek and Latin terms, the *lingua franca* of the technical vocabulary of the European but also the American natural sciences of that time. It was a condition *sine qua non* for the survival of psychoanalysis that any misinterpretation and superficial use of it must be avoided, both in Britain and in the United States. Jones never changed those views throughout his whole professional life (Steiner, 1987 [1995]).

There is no doubt that Jones could have found some of those terms rooted in ancient Greek and Latin in the original German work of Freud. Indeed, Freud had studied as a neurologist, a physiologist, and then as a doctor and psychiatrist, reading the same texts Jones read and studied, particularly those of the French psychiatrists and neurologists like Bernheim, Charcot, Binet, Janet, and so forth.

However, the standardization planned and gradually implemented by Jones from 1908 to 1909, his attempt to "familiarise the unfamiliar" in psychoanalysis, led to a rather rigid codification, to a sort of linguistic corset, or rigid linguistic scaffolding, and too often to a partial, reductive, scientific interpretation of psychoanalysis. Jones would impose his own views about what should be considered psychoanalysis, avoiding what he saw as the too dangerous and speculative aspects of Freud's thinking. Think about Jones's letter to Freud about the death drive (Jones to Freud, 1 January 1930, p. 667; Freud to Jones, 26 January 1930: Pakaukas, 1983, p. 668), along with Jones's great difficulties in dealing with Freud's views on telepathy (Jones to Freud, 25 February 1926: Jones, 1958; Paskaukas, 1993, p. 592). All this would have long-standing implications and would even influence the creation of the *S.E.* and James Strachey's translation style (Strachey, 1968, "General Introduction", *S.E.* 1 pp. XII–XXII) more than 30 years after the publication of Jones's first *Glossaries*.[12]

Coming back to England from North America in 1913 (Jones, 1959; Maddox, 2007; Kuhn, 2015, 1917) after having founded The London Psychoanalytic Society in 1913 and the British Psychoanalytical Society in 1919, Jones worked very hard to develop psychoanalysis, which had started to become more popular during World War I (Rapp, 1990; Graves & Hodge, 1994; Hinshelwood, 1995; Richard, 2000; Forrester, 2003, 2008; Johnson, 2006; Shepards, 2007; Kuhn, 2014, 2017). At the same time, he tried to gradually create a group of translators (J. Riviere, the Stracheys, and others) of Freud and other psychoanalysts, keeping them completely under his control.[13]

Even Freud and Anna Freud were once members of Jones's Glossary Committee, which he organized in 1920 when he founded *the International Journal of Psychoanalysis* and the *International Library of Psychoanalysis*, and when he became a long-standing President of the IPA (Jones to Freud, 26 January 1922: Pakaukas, 1993, p. 456). In 1924, Jones published the first official *English Glossary of Psychoanalytic Terms* (Steiner, 1989, 1991), where all the terms that he had already created in America with the help of Brill, Chase, and others, and the more recent ones like cathexis, anaclitic type, parapraxis, were put forward as the words that should be used to translate Freud and psychoanalysis[14]; he suggested that they should be used in *the International Journal of Psychoanalysis* and to translate the books for the International Library.

With time, these words became the "familiar language" of psychoanalysis, as I have already mentioned, although this expression needs to be taken with a pinch of salt ("The English Tower of Babel of Psychoanalysis", Steiner, 1994; Amati-Mehler, Canestri, & Argentieri, 1993), and not only in the English-speaking countries.

At the same time, with regard to editing and publishing *the International Journal of Psychoanalysis* and *International Press*, Jones tried to get rid of all his possible rivals in translating or editing Freud into English: Brill in America, Otto Rank in Vienna, other translators, and even Freud's relatives like his nephew E. Bernays.[15]

Jones's total, obsessive, dedication to his plan, what Freud in a letter to Jones called his Chinese rigidity (27 July 1921; Paskaukas, 1993, p. 434) – his intelligence, but also his ruthlessness in implementing it, and the prodigious energy he spent in trying to control all that was translated, edited, and published of Freud's work in English – at one moment compelled a furious Rank to write to Jones on 2 February 1921 that he had in mind fostering the world power of the British reign, or one could also say the empire of psychoanalysis.

One should also consider the sociopolitical situation of those years. The Austro-German Empire had been defeated at the end of World War I, but the British Empire, in spite of all these changes, was still alive and thriving and imposing its rules. At times, Jones seemed to incarnate the superior self-assurance of a British imperial official brought up before World War I (Meisel & Kendrick, 1986; Hobsbaw, 1987). Jones had in mind his own plan to gradually differentiate psychoanalysis as it was understood in London, from the one that was understood in Vienna. Just think of the support that Jones gave a few years later, together with the Stracheys, to Melanie Klein and her wish to come to work in London (Steiner, 1985). Jones had some rough but precise ideas about translation and how to translate. He had a genuine interest in those issues.

Curiously enough, even Jones, like Freud and Brill, came from a minority group. He was Welsh, and from his childhood, he had to accept and submit to the language of the old invader of Welsh – Imperial English. Like Freud, but on a more minor scale, Jones learned how to translate in his public school (Jones, 1959), and he was well acquainted with ancient Latin, some rudiments of ancient Greek, and he knew French and Italian very well (Jones, 1959; Steiner, 1991). Already when he was in America, Jones claimed that the translations of Freud's works should be as literal as possible, as was necessary for any respectable scientific text (1913). This is something that Freud would not have disagreed with. But the standardization of the technical language adopted by Jones was not really a literal translation. He did not act as an invisible translator, to paraphrase the famous expression of a leading contemporary theoretician of translation (Venuti, 1995). It was a very performative kind of translation.

At this point, I would like to put forward the hypothesis that there could have been some personal reasons that motivated Jones, which might perhaps better explain his obsessiveness, the fury he expressed towards his sibling rivals in this project of translating Freud, and his own reactions to Freud. Please do not misunderstand me: by pointing to these personal reasons, I do not want to claim that all the work Jones did should be "reduced" to or explained by his personal problems, conflicts with Freud, and his sibling rivals. The same has to be remembered when I will deal with Joan Riviere and with the Stracheys.

But the first attempts to translate Freud have to be understood in all their complexity. This complexity includes all the personal fights, and conscious or less-conscious interactions, and the projections between the translators and between the translators and Freud, whose enormous power over them and difficulties in handling their transferences and his own countertransference one cannot deny. Remember that those were also the years in which he wrote and published *Totem and Taboo* (1913) [1968], *S.E.* 13).

All this can perhaps help to explain the long-standing quasi-iconic and untouchable status that the Stracheys, the heir of those first attempts at translation, achieved with the publication of *The Standard Edition of Freud*. Although the expression *Standard Edition* was first used by Jones in the 1920s (Jones to Freud, 29 February 1920; Paskaukas, 1993, p. 371; Steiner, 1988).

In a letter to his wife Alix, dated 27 March 1924, James Strachey refers to the "erogenous Jones" (Meisel & Kendrick, 1986, p. 244). If one studies the correspondence between Freud and Jones (1908–1939; Paskaukas, 1993), there is plenty of evidence of the enormously charged and very often ambivalent relationship between Jones and Freud during the first 15 years of their professional and personal relationship, when Jones was gradually organizing his hegemonic plan and creating the first *Glossaries* of Freud's language. Freud was extremely interested in having his work translated and published in the English-speaking countries, and he had great admiration for Jones's intelligence and his organizational and political skills, but he was also very suspicious of some aspects of his personality.

Several times, Freud had to deal with the tragicomic troubles of the "erogenous Jones", his sexual adventures and misadventures with female patients in London and in Canada (Jones, 1959; Maddox, 2007; Kuhn, 2014), and the serious problems that those erotic adventures created more than once for the cause of psychoanalysis (see for instance, Freud to Jones, 14 February 1914, in Paskaukas, 1993, pp. 124–125). Jones never literally lay on Freud's couch, but he seemed to do it by letter. Had I the chance, I could quote several letters where Freud boldly analyzed Jones's problems and Jones analyzed himself too, asking Freud for help and forgiveness for his behaviour. Freud used his extremely powerful analytical tools as "translator interpreter" of Jones's troubles and symptomatic disturbances in various ways. At one moment in 1912, having taken into analysis Jones's then-mistress, Loe Kann, and after some long personal discussions with Jones in Vienna (Jones, 1959), Freud became worried about Jones and sent him to Ferenczi to have some analysis. Freud and Ferenczi discussed Jones's problems in their correspondence, and Freud discussed them with Loe Kann, which upset Jones.

Freud could be blatantly harsh and judgemental when dealing with Jones's behaviour, but also very seductive and kind. Jones experienced him as an enormously idealized parental figure (Jones to Freud, 30 January 1912, in Paskaukas, p. 130), but Jones nevertheless felt that he could never be completely loved or accepted as he would like to (Jones, 1959; Maddox, 2007). He felt excluded and at times persecuted by Freud because of the "erogenous" aspects of his life, having at one point to reassure Freud that he was now "a reformed character" (Jones to Freud, 31 October 1916; Paskaukas, 1993, p. 320). More than once, Freud pointed out the duplicity of Jones's character (see, for instance, Freud to Jones, 31 October 1909, in Paskaukas, 1993, pp. 32–33, or Freud to Jones, 7 January 1923, in Paskaukas, 1993, p. 507). At the same time, Jones wanted enormously to please Freud, to show him how much he wanted to work for the cause of psychoanalysis. Carrying out the translation of Freud's work and the creation of the *Standard Edition* of Freud's work, was his life goal (Steiner, 1987; Jones to Freud, 10 April 1922, p. 473), to become, one might say, his preferred son. The mixture of personal, cultural, and political institutional issues related to the translation of Freud's work therefore became quite incredible at times.

Furthermore, according to Jones (1959), it did not help that he was not a Jew, compared with the affectionate relationships Freud had with Brill, Abraham, Rank, Ferenczi, and others. Nor did his failed attempts to court the young Anna when she came to England in 1914 particularly help, arousing Freud's worries and anxieties (Freud to Jones, 22 July 1914, Paskaukas, 1993, p. 214). Some of his letters to Freud on his translation and editing plans, and his resentful words in his biography of Freud (1958, p. 58), where he claimed that Freud never understood the complexity and importance of the problems of translating his work, do seem to show that his plan to have total control of the translations and impose his *Glossary* could be understood as an attempt to be the only one to possess Freud, at least in English; that he wanted to own him as his own Freud, at least in translation, getting rid of all his rival siblings or trying to keep them under his autocratic control.

It is outside the scope of this paper to address Jones's competitive dealings with Jung and Ferenczi, along with other potential rivals. One might be tempted to say that for Jones, Freud's text represented some sort of concrete equivalent to a mother, whom Jones had to absolutely possess, as well as a father, to whom he had to submit, and not only identify with, but also triumph over by imposing his own translation and interpretation of Freud's work (Jones to Freud, 18 December 1909; 19 June 1910; Paskaukas, 1993, pp. 34 & 61).

Jones openly admitted his envy and jealousy (Jones to Freud, 7 February 1909; Freud to Jones, 31 October 1909; Jones to Freud, 18 December 1909; Paskaukas, 1993, pp. 15, 32–34). Some of Jones's siblings, like Joan Riviere and the Stracheys, were analyzed by Freud, a matter that was not easy for Jones to overcome, although he had recommended them to Freud. This never-satisfied wish can be seen in one of Jones's letters to Freud (30 July 1912, 1993, p. 146), which seems to anticipate the later famous Secret Committee of the ring (Grosskurt, 1991). Quoting Ferenczi, Jones clearly expressed his wish to be part of a small group of people analyzed by Freud, so that "they could represent the pure theory unadulterated by personal complexes" (sic). Jones said it would remain "an ideal solution" for him (see also Freud to Jones, 1 August 1912; Paskaukas, 1993, pp. 147–148).

Jones's rivalry is also apparent in the relationship between Jones, Joan Riviere, and Freud. Joan Riviere was an ex-patient of Jones, a formidable British woman, intellectual and passionate (Hughes, 1991; Bower, 2018). She did not have a university education but had learned German and was a naturally gifted translator, speaking and writing in impeccably elegant English. Probably in the end she was the best translator of some of Freud's work, as Gay (1990) and others (Bachman, 2008) have acknowledged.[16]

Riviere decided to go to Vienna to be psychoanalyzed by Freud, from February until October 1922 (Freud to Jones, 25 June 1922; Paskaukas, 1993, p. 491), after having had the most confusing, erotized, and disappointing analysis with Jones, as one can see from her passionate letters to Jones in the Archives of the British Psycho-analytic Society (see also Jones to Freud, 22 January 1922; Paskaukas, 1993, pp. 453–454).

Jones admired her intelligence, and in 1916, he appointed her as a translator under his control of some of Freud's and other psycho-analysts' work, supporting her wish to contact Freud. When she went to Vienna, Riviere discussed with Freud her ongoing translation of his *Introductory Lectures on Psychoanalysis* (1916–1917 [1922]), which Jones was strictly supervising (Jones, 1922, p. 6).

Here, the personal translation that Riviere had to submit to in her analysis with Freud, the discussion with him of the actual translation of his work, the role that Riviere should have had in those translations and editorial work, which she felt Jones was not acknowledging, created a colossal confusion. Added to this was the role played by Freud, who genuinely admired her intellectual gifts, but was rather seductive with her, taking technical liberties in and out of analysis (Freud to Jones, 23 March 1922, 6 April 1922, 11 May 1922, Paskaukas, 1993, pp. 464, 468–469 and 475–476). He also wished to support Riviere against Jones's need to control her. What happened between the three of them did not really have much to do with sharing ideas about how to translate in the most objective way!

The letters exchanged between Freud and Jones in February, March, and September 1922, about Riviere's character and problems, Jones's way of dealing with her neurotic character, and the issue of translation, are some of the most amusing and extraordinary of the whole correspondence of Freud and Jones (Paskaukas, 1993), and perhaps of his whole correspondence with friends and colleagues.

Had I the chance to reveal in detail the sort of saga that went on in those months between Freud, Jones, and Riviere, one would be amazed. There was infantile fury, there was Jones's jealousy, which Freud pointed out to him, and there was brutal confrontation with Jones regarding the mistakes he made in Riviere's analysis (Freud to

Jones 23 March 1922, 6 April 1922, 11 May 1922, 4 June 1922, and esp. 25 June 1922; Paskaukas, 1993, pp. 464, 468, 475, 483–484, 491).

Jones's fear of losing control over the English translation of Freud's work due to Freud's support of Riviere, who had become a terrible rival sibling to him, probably unconsciously reminding him of the rivalry with his actual sister (Jones to Freud, 12 February 1910; Paskaukas, 1993, pp. 44–45), became enormous and totally irrational (Jones to Freud, 26 May 1922, Paskaukas, pp. 481–482). As I have previously mentioned, at one moment, Brill had a breakdown around the same time, when Freud, persuaded by Putnam, Jones, and others, complained about his translations.

If one reads some of the letters that Jones wrote to Freud about Riviere, he did not seem very mentally and emotionally balanced in that period. Such were the unconscious emotions, phantasies, and conflicts mobilized by the way in which Freud's translations were taking place. At one moment, Jones even accused Riviere of making mistakes because she was not a doctor and did not know the technical language, and because of her psychical complexes, which she had projected into the translation (Jones to Freud, 10 June 1910; Paskaukas, 1993, p. 489).

But were Jones's attempts to translate Freud without any unconscious complexes or motivations? He even had to reassure Freud that he did not sleep with Joan Riviere when she was his patient (Jones to Freud, 1 April 1922; Paskaukas, p. 467). And then, of course, there were Riviere's own difficult personal problems, which both Freud and Jones discussed in their correspondence, alongside issues about the translation and editing of Freud's work.[17] But Freud also discussed Jones's letters with Riviere, causing further anger and tension in Jones (Jones to Freud, 22 May 1922; Paskaukas, 1993, p. 478).

Riviere was never granted the post of Translator Editor or *redacteur en chief* of *the International Journal of Psychoanalysis* which she really wanted, and which Freud also wanted her to have (Freud to Jones, 6 April 1922, p. 468, Freud to Jones, 17 May 1922; Paskaukas, 1993, p. 477). Incidentally, Freud explicitly told Jones that he wanted Riviere to translate several of his papers, taking them "away from the other people" (Freud to Jones, 12 May 1922, Paskaukas, 1993, p. 475), obviously increasing Jones's anxiety and envy.

Jones's envious patriarchalism, and the need to keep Riviere in a sort of inferior position, nevertheless prevailed. Jones only gave Riviere the title of "Revising Translator", not of Translator Editor of the *International Journal* (Jones to Freud, 10 June 1922; Pakaukas, 1993, p. 488). And later, she was overtaken as Freud's translator by the Stracheys who admired her (Strachey, 1962), but who were also, at times, rather ambivalent towards her work (Meisel & Kendrick, 1986). Riviere's translations, however, and the way the Stracheys used and absorbed them in their work, should deserve a proper study. But I think one should also consider her wish to give up translating Freud. She always admired him and wrote a moving obituary in 1939 when he died, but later on she became a follower of Melanie Klein. Freud, who was always fond of her, nevertheless accused her of becoming a sort of Jungian "heretical" for the importance she gave, following Klein, to the phantasy life of the child in relation to the early superego (Freud to Jones, 1927; Paskaukas,1993, pp. 36 & 635).

In her book on Joan Riviere (1991, p. 58), Hughes reported that Herbert Rosenfeld, who had become Riviere's supervisor for some of her psychotic patients, after having been supervised by her as a student in the 1940s, said that Riviere claimed that Freud seemed more interested in her as a translator than as a patient. No doubt there must have been some deep difficulties in Riviere, which would have remained after Freud's analysis, and could at least partially explain Riviere's decision to become a Kleinian – which in those years was quite a courageous choice – as well as her gradual disinterest in the translation of Freud.

Another chapter of this saga occurred when James Strachey went to Vienna in 1920 to be analyzed by Freud, with the support of Jones, and at the same time he agreed to collaborate with Jones to work on the Glossary that Jones was gradually putting together. He had just married Alix, who incidentally at that time had a better knowledge of German than James had. It had been Jones who recommended James Strachey to Freud (Meisel & Kendrick, 1986, Jones to Freud, 7 May 1920, Paskaukas, 1993, p. 378). When the Stracheys arrived in Vienna, James very soon started to be analyzed by Freud, and Freud also started to analyze his wife Alix, due to the symptoms of severe agoraphobia that she had suddenly developed in Vienna (J. Strachey to Lytton Strachey, 6 November 1920).

Fascinated by their culture and personalities, Freud gave James and Alix a paper to translate what he had just written, "A child is being beaten", just a few weeks after they had both first laid down on his couch in October 1920. After that, Freud chose them as his best translators. Then he gave James *Massen Psychologie* (*Group Psychology*), and then he asked both of them to translate the Case Histories.

Freud's appreciation of their work as translators lasted until the end of his life. The confusion between their personal analyses, the translations they had to submit to in the process of analysis in order to face their "unfamiliar", along with discussions about how to translate Freud's work and its "unfamiliarity", the sibling rivalries between them, and also between them and Joan Riviere who was in analysis with Freud at the time, and last but not least, the role played by Jones from London, raise all sorts of questions.

As with Freud, Jones, and Riviere, I would like to spend a few words on the cultural and social backgrounds of James and Alix Strachey before they went to Vienna. James Strachey came from an extremely elitist, cultivated, but also very aloof English family, reflected in his upbringing and in his aloof but extremely elegant late-Victorian spoken and written English (Holroyd, 1968 [1994]; Caine, 1998, 2005; Linstrum, 2014; McQuillan, 2017).

Like Freud and partly even Jones, James learned ancient Greek and Latin as an adolescent at Saint Paul's Public School in London, before going to Cambridge. But as a child, he had already learned French from his very cultivated mother. Despite their differences in social class and upbringing, there were some similarities in what James Strachey, Freud, and Jones learned at school and the experience Strachey had as a translator of ancient Latin and Greek. Both James and Alix were experiencing uncertainties in their private life and professions when they went to Vienna. Like his brother, the famous writer Lytton Strachey, and others of the secluded group of Cambridge's "Apostles", as an adolescent and young man James practised what at the time they called "high sodomy" (Holroyd, 1968; Deacon, 1985; Hale, 1998; Lubenow, 1998; Ley, 2005; Taddeo, 2012). And those were not easy years for this sexual choice because homosexuality was legally forbidden. Both James and Alix, who also came from a rather sophisticated family and had more than one female lover, were members of the Bloomsbury avant-garde group (Holroyd, 1994; Caine, 2005; MacQuillan, 2017). What Freud and even Jones had to fight for in order to become part of a middle class, was taken for granted by James and Alix.

All this, and much more of course, could explain Strachey's way of translating Freud later on as an English man of science of the 19th century ("General Preface", 1968, *S.E.* 1, pp. III–XXII). In spite of the difference in Jones's social class, upbringing, and culture, James ended up sharing *grosso modo* Jones's "view of Freud as a man of science", since their first attempts to translate Freud (Steiner, 1988). With regard to how to translate Freud (see James to Alix, 1925, p. 162; Meisel & Kendrick, 1986, pp. 201–202), Strachey had in mind the late-Victorian men of science he met in his family since he was a young boy, including his father.

Jones, of course, made it clear to Freud and to the Stracheys that the last word on Strachey's translations of Freud's work – which Jones had to accept, though not without some anxieties – would be his own (Jones to Freud, 6 May 1921; Pakaukas, 1993, p. 421). Openly, he did not have the same problems of rivalry that he had with Joan Riviere, although the fact that the Stracheys belonged to such elevated and socially different families and cultural environment should not be forgotten in Jones's ambivalent feelings towards them (Jones to Freud, 22 May 1922; Paskaukas, 1993, pp. 478–479). And as in the case of Riviere, Jones had to face the fact that the Stracheys were analyzed by Freud and therefore had personal access to him, from which he was excluded.

The letters of the Stracheys, including some of Freud's statements concerning their analyses, nevertheless show the personal, although not always positive, side of what the Stracheys went through in Vienna.[18] As well as being analyzed simultaneously by Freud, they took Anna Freud to the opera (Steiner, 1995), at a time when Anna was still in analysis with her father, and when she was the patient in "A child is being beaten" (1919) without the Stracheys knowing this (Young Bruhel, 1988)[19]; they also had to discuss their translations on Sunday afternoons at Freud's house, so James wrote to his mother, Lady Strachey, on 9 March 1921 (Holroyd, 1968, p. 442).[20] Freud took all sorts of liberties with them. Of course, those were different times, and one is reminded of the *Rabbe meg* (the Rabbi could do it), as M. Schur, quoting a Yiddish motto, told Jones many years later (1955), referring to the technical liberties Freud took with other patients.

With the Stracheys seeing Freud every Sundays, after six hours of weekly analysis with him (remember what I quoted from Primo Levi's paper on the weekend job of translating, or of being on the couch of a psychoanalyst!), it must have been a rather surreal, "unfamiliar", experience of reciprocal gratification and possession, both for Freud and for the Stracheys.[21]

One might say, with the benefit of hindsight, that the presence of transferences and counter-transferences, anxieties related to primitive possession and to being possessed, as well as anxieties about intrusions and being intruded upon, must have been rather complicated and difficult to sort out (along with their own personal problems). Freud had decided to take into analysis Alix and James Strachey, claiming that he wanted to "sondieren the possibility of this kind of analysis" (James Strachey to Lytton Strachey, 6 November 1920). But who was "sondieren" (sounding out) whom?

In a letter to Lytton on 6 November 1920, which has been quoted by Meisel and Kendrick (1986, p. 30) and others, James describes his treatment, idealizing Freud, and comparing him to the great British scholar of ancient Greek, J. Verrall, an uncle of Joan Riviere, whom he met in Cambridge as a student and greatly admired. Feeling the enormous privilege of having been given the clinical *Case Histories* to translate, in a letter to Lytton dated the 16 February 1921, James gives another portrait of Freud, feeling full of gratitude and admiration for his extreme friendliness and for being so complimentary towards Alix and himself: "by character and nature he is exceedingly respectable and conservative – without a trace of crankiness or even advanced views. In Vienna of course he is entirely unknown". James goes on to tell his brother that he went to a bookshop and asked for one of his books, but he was told that they had "never heard his name".

Enormously fascinated by Freud and perhaps seduced by his kindness, James Strachey accepted all that Freud asked him and his wife to do (Jones at one moment called him "an effeminate", and later on insisted on his upper-class laziness; Jones to Freud, 22 May 1922, Paskaukas, 1993, p. 479). But when he wrote to his brother and friends, was it only his dry, British upper-class sense of humour that led James to use metaphors like "the professor's dissecting table" or "the scalpel of the professor" to describe his experience in analysis with Freud? (James to Lytton Strachey, 15 October 1920; to E. M. Keynes, 6 June 1921, in Dostaler & Marsi, 2000, p. 240).

Let us not forget the difficulties Freud faced in analyzing James Strachey, as he wrote to Jones (Freud to Jones, 9 December 1921; Paskaukas, 1993, pp. 446–449). Both the Stracheys analyses were stopped abruptly by Freud after Alix's "serious illness": a terrible pneumonia. In the summer of 1922, Freud sent them back to Jones. According to Freud, they were ready to work as analysts. He had already highly recommended the Stracheys to Jones a year before as "extremely nice, cultured although rather queer people" (Freud to Jones, 14 July 1921, Paskaukas, p. 431).[22]

But in what Strachey wrote to Jones at that time (Strachey to Jones, 18 May 1922) or to his brother Lytton (22 June 1922), there was clear discomfort in having to stop the analysis at that point. Although Freud seemed very satisfied with the way Alix had responded to his treatment, she had further treatment later in Berlin by Karl Abraham, who she considered was a much better analyst than Freud (Alix to Strachey, 9 February 1925; Meisel & Kendrik, 1986, p. 198). And at one point, James wanted to go to Berlin too to be analyzed by Abraham (Alix to James, 29 April 1925) but instead he had further treatment in London with James Glover (James to Alix, 28 April 1925). Later on, Alix went into analysis with Edward Glover and then with Sylvia Payne (Meisel & Kendrick, 1986, p. 308). And both Stracheys, particularly Alix, were instrumental in discovering Klein's work in Berlin and helping her to come to London.

Were the events I have briefly summarized concerned only with how to objectively translate Freud? Without exaggerating the validity of my views at this point, I will briefly try to show that some traces of this incredible tour de force, the multiple analytic "translations" and proper translations that went on between all these people, must have left some traces in the translation of Freud's work too.

Curiously enough, the Archives give us the chance to study how in 1921 James Strachey came to conceive of two of the most iconic terms in the *Standard Edition*.[23] In a "virtuoso" letter to Jones (27 November 1921) on the various ways in which Freud uses *Besetzung* in German, James makes proposals on how to translate it, showing his extraordinary knowledge of ancient Greek. Strachey proposed "*cathexis* from the Ancient Greek", "catechein to occupy", as a translation of the various complex ways that Freud used *Besetzung* in German, which can mean "being occupied", "being invested", or "to occupy, to invest". And with the help of Jones, Strachey created "anaclitic type" as a translation of "*Anlehnungstyp*", which in German means "leaning upon", dependence on a parental figure'.[24]

Strachey's use of the Ancient Greek *cathexis* and *anaclitic* comes from authors such as Aristotle, Plato, Tucidides, Teofrastus, and even Homer, as I have found out from consulting the famous Liddel–Scott's (1898) *A Greek English Lexicon,* which was extremely well known at the time. The very reliable Rocci (2011) also refers to Aeschylus for the ancient Greek "*catekeini*".

In a playful way, I would like to put forward the idea that if one studies very carefully the letters between James and Jones, the way in which James, with Jones's support, translated the two terms cathexis and anaclitic type, seems in some ways to encapsulate the complexity of the relationship that James and Jones had with Freud. Through their translation, James and Jones compelled the other English translators (like Alix Strachey, Rickman, Riviere, and, in the end, even Brill, 1931), the English reader, and Freud himself to depend on the distancing, esoteric language they used (Gay, 1988), creating a very performative version of Freud's original text. Thinking of both terms "*cathexis*" and "anaclitic type", James Strachey, but also Jones, managed in some way to "occupy", to "*besetzen*", and "cathect" the reader — as well as Freud — with their translation, thereby reversing their dependency on Freud as a parental figure, making him sort of depend on them; in this way, they hid their unconscious phantasies of possession and of being possessed in the acoustic skin of these cacophonic and mysterious words.[25]

And one should not forget that in one way or another, James and Jones cathected and were cathected by Freud's editing and translation and biography (in the case of Jones) until the end of their lives. Incidentally, "*cathexis*" (Steiner, 1984) but also "anaclitic type" certainly did not help the English-speaking reader to understand that there could be a link between the original "*besetzen*" and "to occupy" or "to invest", particularly when referring to an object, and what later on Klein described as some of the characteristics of projective identification.[26]

In this final part of my paper I would like to make some comments on what today, due to all sorts of changes inside and outside psychoanalysis, and our different relationship with Freud and his work, has become the revised *Standard Edition*. This version has been enriched with the neurological and other unpublished writings of Freud, edited with a gigantic effort by Mark Solms (2020: in process), also using the ground-breaking philological and editorial work in German of Grubrich Simitis, who deepened the monumental editorial work carried out by Strachey for the *S.E.* Of course, all this reflects our different views and new discoveries about many aspects of the life and work of Freud, and the different cultural but also sociopolitical time in which we are living and thinking and practising psychoanalysis in comparison with the first translators of Freud's work in English. Inevitably, all this will arouse new criticism and proposals.

The life of great written masterpieces in every field of the humanities and sciences is intrinsically bound to the possibility of being translated anew.

I nevertheless would like to stress again that the incredible, "unfamiliar" saga of personal internal and external issues that constitutes the prehistory which led to the *S.E.*, the phantoms of the personal experience that those translators had with Freud and between themselves, which lie behind the translation but also inside the very language that was chosen to translate Freud, and which contributes to the iconic status of the *S.E.* All this is, of course, unique, and is also due to the intellectual and cultural status of the translators and to the hegemonic role of the British Psychoanalytical Society in supporting the translation of the *S.E.* with the help of Anna Freud and the financial support of American analysts after World War II (Steiner, 1988). But the saga that I just mentioned can be taken as an example and reminder.

There will never be a perfect and final translation of Freud (Steiner, 1988).[27] And there will never be the possibility of entirely excluding from the translation of Freud all sorts of institutional, financial, sociopolitical and cultural issues, pressures, and interests, along with the unconscious personal factors and "complexes" of the translators (as Jones referred to Riviere). The inevitable unconscious aspects of the translator will affect further translations of Freud, or of any other psychoanalytical author, and even our attempts to understand and translate each other in our field today.

It could be a very interesting matter to discuss whether the unconscious personal factors can influence translation in general, and whether translators and theoreticians of translations today should take into account the subjectivity of the translator, or what we call in our technical language, resistances (Venuti: 2013). Even today, we have to deal with our unconscious conflicts between Eros, which tries to link, and Thanatos, which tries to fragment or confuse, in our unconscious narcissistic projections or projective identifications, in trying to understand and translate the other. What I have just suggested could mark the very important contribution that psychoanalysis could make to addressing the inevitable limits of any attempt to translate and interpret. One could say, paraphrasing Freud: translation terminable or interminable. I can only really hint at these issues in this paper.

What I have just said, nevertheless, tunes in with what contemporary theorists of translation are claiming from their own point of view: we can try to reach, to understand, and to translate the "alterity of the other", the unfamiliarity, only by approximation (Jakobson, 1967 [1972]; Steiner, 1975; Eco, 1990, 2003; Venuti 1995, 2000, 2013; Ricoeur, 2004). Nevertheless, despite all limitations and approximations, we have to go on trying to translate, as Freud actually claimed in "Some elementary lessons on psychoanalysis" – his last, unfinished work written in London in October 1938.

And thinking about the year and months in which he wrote his last statements, his thoughts sound even more poignant and moving, as if he was a real heir and reincarnation of the defence of reason that we can find in the great thinkers of the European Enlightenment.

Indeed, after having stressed the importance not only of the unconscious but also of being conscious, as "the only light which illuminates our path and leads us through the darkness of mental life", Freud claims, "In consequence of the special character of our discoveries, our scientific work in psychology will consist in translating unconscious processes in to conscious ones and thus filling in the gaps in conscious perceptions" (1940, 1938 [1968], *S.E.* 23, p. 286).

His words reminded me of the redeeming power that Primo Levi attributed to the possibility and activity of translating during "the darkness of the mental life" in the Shoah'; one can find all this in a chapter of Primo Levi's book *Se questo e' un uomo /If This Is a Man* (1958, 1987). I started my paper quoting from Primo Levi's paper "To translate and on being translated" (1985, 2015), and I want to finish with what one can read in Levi's *If this is a Man* in the chapter *"Il canto di Ulisse"*, which is one of the most famous episodes of *The Inferno* in Dante's *Divine Comedy*.

At Auschwitz in 1944, to cope with the brutality of the work he was compelled to do, Levi tried to remember something for his young Polish friend called Pikolo; he wanted to remember how to translate from ancient Italian into French Dante's famous words, where Ulysses invites his old friends to go beyond the forbidden boundaries, to face *"l'alto mare aperto"* (the deep open sea) after reminding them of their courage. This effort to remember and find the right words to translate helped Levi to survive, to keep his mind alive, to make of the *"l'alto mare aperto"*, the "deep open sea", a metaphor for the freedom to go on thinking, and hoping, and translating, in order to discover and to know others, or to know about what makes us all human beings, as Dante himself said through Ulysses' speech, quoted by Levi:

> *Fatti non foste a viver come bruti,*
>> *ma per seguir virtute e conoscenza* (2005, p. 102)
>> For brutish ignorance your mettle was not made;
>> You were made men to follow after knowledge and excellence (1982, p. 119)
>> These words applied even in the Inferno, the hell inside the barbed wires of a concentration camp. They might apply today, inside the refugee camps.

At the end of this paper, I would like to express the following wish: that we, as psychoanalysts, can use in the broadest possible way the specific knowledge and experience we have acquired in our daily work of the sort of abysses of total isolation, pain, and despair, as well as destruction and self-destruction, that the narcissistic incapacity, or the wish not "to translate", understand, and tolerate our unconscious and that of the other, can lead to.

Thinking of what is happening today, at the new barbed wires, the new walls already existing or planned to be built in the next future between people and countries, I wish that we as psychoanalysts could use our experience and knowledge to help in whatever way we can, to keep open the contacts, the exchanges, the need to know and accept the different cultures and identities and languages of others, and the necessity of translating them, to be open to what Dante and Levi meant by *l'alto mare aperto*.

We cannot exist as proper human beings without constantly "translating", without being open to understanding and tolerating and accepting the otherness of the others. Although we can never completely translate the alterity of the other, and as Ricoeur says (2004, p. 7), we have to accept and take inspiration from Freud's "mourning process" – mourning the absolute perfect translation of the other. This acceptance is also "le Bonheur de la traduction", the pleasure, and I would add, the justification of the need to translate. We cannot exist in a total personal, cultural, sociopolitical, "monosemic" isolation. History and our clinical experience tell us that such isolation is the grotesque anteroom that could lead once again to tragic totalitarianism.

Acknowledgements

I would like to thank Dr Birksted-Breen PhD, Dr C Humble PhD, D MacMillan PhD, M Molnar, the librarian and the archivist of the BPSA, Mr S Morris and Mr Ewan O'Neill, for the generous help they have given to me to write and edit this paper.

This paper is dedicated to my friends and colleagues J. Amati Mehler, J. Canestri, and S. Argentieri. This is a revised version of a much longer paper, which I am currently developing. I read a version of this paper in The Hague at the European Congress of Psychoanalysis in April 2016.

Notes

1 "The Deep Open Sea". Primo Levi (1975), pp. 188–189; Levi (1958), p. 101. This chapter is written for my friends and colleagues, J. Amati Mehler, J. Canestri, and S. Argentieri. I would like to thank Dee MacQuillan for the generous help she has given to me to write this paper. This is a short version of a much longer paper which I am currently developing. I read this version in The Hague.

2 Incidentally, if there is another significant example of the complex, emotional, unconscious relationship between Freud and his translators, and the unique interaction which took place between them, this is the case of Brill, who worked productively with Freud for many years, but then had a breakdown after Freud openly complained about his translations in the early 20s (Brill, 1938; Jones, 1956 [1958]; Hale, 1971a, vol. 1; 1971b; Steiner, 1987; Morr, 1995); Rundbriefe, signed by Freud and O Rank Wien 20 and 21 October 1920, p. 102 and 26 October 1920, p. 156; Henberg Toegel eds., 1999, vol. 1; see Freud's letter to Jones, 11 December 1919, Paskakas, 1993, p. 360, where Freud calls him "a crazy Jew" (meschugge).

3 The "Septuagint" is a translation of the Old Testament from Hebrew into Koine spoken Greek by 70 wise Jewish scholars around 3rd century BCE. This "iconic" translation influenced, for better and worse, further translations of the Old Testament in other languages. Koine Greek, also known as Alexandrian dialect, common Attic, Hellenistic or Biblical Greek, was the common supra-regional form of Greek spoken and written during the Hellenistic period, the Roman Empire, and the early Byzantine Empire, or late antiquity.

4 These ideas in this chapter will be developed in a future project.

5 P. Mahony has noticed this in his very important paper. At the time, I did not know about the existence of his paper. I came to some similar conclusions, but Mahony's paper provides fuller articulations.

6 In the long version of my paper I try to show how Freud seems to bring back the old notion of interpreter as interpreter of an oral text, and of the translator of a written text, which, for more than 2,000 years, were considered as the same activity in our Western culture and given the same name. Only starting with the Italian and European Renaissance did the activity of the translator as a translator of a written text start to be clearly differentiated from that of the interpreter of an oral text (Berman, 1988; Folena, 1991; Lepschy, 2010).

7 Freud uses "*Übersetzung*" and "*Übertragung*" as synonymous to define the transference (1900 [1968], *G.W.* II/III, pp. 4 & 28, (1900 [1968], *S.E.* 4, pp. 277–278). Besides what one can find in Freud's previous work, it was in treating Dora that he discussed the importance of the *Übertragung*, translated as a transference by Brill and Jones in the first decade of the 20th century (1905 [1968], *S.E.* 7, p. 116; Steiner, 1987, 1989, 1991).

8 But see also Freud's*Vorlesungen zur Einführung in die Psychoanalyse* (1916–1917 [1968], *G.W.* 10, p. 175; *Introductory Lectures to Psychoanalysis* (1916–1917 [1968], *S.E.* 15, p. 173.

9 Saint Jerome, who lived during the 3rd century AD, and who translated the *Bible* from Hebrew into Latin, is considered the father of the theory of translation in Western Christian culture. In a very important letter to Psammacus on translation called "*De optimo genere intepretandi*" (395 AD [1879], Steiner, 1975, Folena, 1991; 2 Lepschy, 2010), he claimed that in translating he rendered the ancient texts in a liberal way, not "*verbo e verbo*" (word for word), except for the Holy Scripts "*ubi etiam verborum ordo est mysterium*" (where even the order of the words is mystery). He tried to translate them as literally as possible. Echoes of Saint Jerome and what he said about the Holy Scripts can be found at the end of one of the most important and complex papers on translation of the 20th century (W. Benjamin, "*Die Aufgabe des Übersetzers*" / "The Task of the Translator", 1923 [2000], p. 23.

10 The translator of Freud's five famous lectures on psychoanalysis given at Clark University in the USA in 1909.

11 Linstrum's 2014 study contains very important observations on Strachey as a translator, and archival research. Unfortunately, concerning Jones and the first attempts to translate Freud, he makes me say exactly the contrary of what I wrote in my papers on this issue (Steiner, 1987, 1988, 1991).

12 After all, A. Strachey's *A New German-English Psychoanalytical Vocabulary* (1943), used by the Stracheys for the *S.E.,* is nothing else than

an expansion of the original Glossary created by Jones, following his decisions.

13 Whether Jones's views were completely correct is a rather complex question. There is no doubt, even without having to totally share Forrester's (2003, 2008) and Kuhn's (2014, 2015) very stimulating recent research on Jones and the diffusion of psychoanalysis in Great Britain in the early 20th century, that Jones (1959) exaggerated his role as the unique first defender and propagandist of Freud's work in Great Britain and even in America.

14 The term parapraxis was created by Jones around 1917–1918 and not by Strachey, as Bettelheim and many others believe.

15 Jones used Stedman's *A Practical Medical Dictionary* (1913) to standardize some of Freud's language, using ancient Greek or Latin terms. "Parapraxis" is quoted by Stedman. To bring to fruition his projects, Jones had to face Freud's clumsiness in selling the copyrights and right to translate some of his work to the Americans and his relative E. Bernays. It was to become an endemic problem, which later delayed the publication of the *S.E.* (Jones, 1958, 1959; Steiner, 1987, 1995).

16 J. Strachey, as I discuss further in a future paper, appreciated Riviere's translations too. But in the end, he standardized them, absorbing them in his *S.E.* All these issues do pose the problem of the role played by gender even in the translation of Freud's work. Just think of the autocratic way that Jones ran the whole enterprise in those years. He was supporting other translators too, like Ms Baines, C Hubback, a descendant of J Auden, who was particularly dear to him. He was helped by B Low, C Flugel, J Rickman, H Stoddart, and even his last wife Katherine Jokl, but they were all under his control.

17 As I discuss further in a future paper, J. Strachey appreciated Riviere's translations too. But in the end, he standardized them, absorbing them in his *S.E.* All these issues do pose the problem of the role played by gender in the translation of Freud's work. Just think of the autocratic way that Jones ran the whole enterprise in those years.

18 For instance, Freud complained about James's way of speaking in English, which he, like others (Holroyd, 1968), found "very strange, a torture to my attention" (Freud to Jones, 12 October 1920, Paskaukas (ed.), 1993, p. 393). He complained, "if not admonished", James's laziness in translating (Freud to Jones, 7 February 1921, op. cit, p. 409). At times he preferred Alix as a patient; James was slow. "James Strachey has not yet overcome his scepticism but his wife is progressing nicely" (Freud to Jones, 9 December 1921, op. cit, p. 446).

19 When Alix got seriously ill, Anna helped James and brought a pint of fresh milk to Alix every day. (L. Strachey to Carrington, 15 February 1922, in Levy, ed., 2005, p. 506). And besides regularly lending them

the *New Republic* (James to Lytton Strachey, 29 March 1921), S. Freud discussed *Queen Victoria,* Lytton Strachey's book, with his brother James (James to Lytton, 20 April 1921). Freud expressed his preference for *Eminent Victorians* over Lytton's biography of Queen Victoria (Lytton to James Strachey, 14 February 1922, in Levy, op. cit, pp. 505–506).

20 In his letter to Lytton of 6 November 1921, James told him that he went to analysis "every day except Sunday."

21 I am referring to what Levi says, that translating is not a weekend job, or what he says when he compares the process of translation as the surgeon's table or the couch of the psychoanalyst.

22 Freud to Jones, 23 March 1922 (Paskaukas, 1993, p. 464). See also Jones to Freud, 1 April 1922, p. 466.

23 Add as a footnote – (J. Strachey to E. Jones, 27 November 1921, in Ornston, 1985; and J. Strachey to E. Jones, 18 May 1922, with the collaboration and the final "imprimatur" of Jones: E. Jones to J. Strachey, 24 May 1922).

24 See Jones's Glossary (1924). It might be of some interest that in her 1922 translation of Freud's *Introductory Lectures on Psychoanalysis,* Riviere translates *"Anlehnungstyp"* as "anaclitic type" with a long explanatory note, but does not use *"cathexis",* etc., to translate *"Besetzung".*

25 Besides the discussion with Strachey, I am referring to *"parapraxis",* etc.

26 According to Strachey, Freud did not like *"cathexis"* (Strachey in Freud, 1894, [1968], *S.E.* 3, p. 63) and even discussed with him *"anaclitic"* (Strachey to Jones, 18 May 1922). *Cathexis* was nevertheless later accepted as a neologism in the Oxford Dictionary. And Freud used *cathexis* to write one of his articles for the *Encyclopedia Britannica* later on (1926 [1968], *S.E.* 20, p. 266).

27 As I have tried to show, Jones nevertheless thought that only he and Strachey and some of his colleagues could properly translate Freud (Steiner, 1987).

References

Amati-Mehler, J. Canestri, J., & Argentieri, S. (1993): *The Babel of the Unconscious.* New York: New York Psychoanalytical Press.

Benjamin, W. (1923, 1973): *The Task of the Translator in Illuminations.* London: Fontana Collins, pp. 69–82.

Berman. (1988): De 'la translation' a 'la traduction'. *TTR: Traduction, Terminologie, Redaction,* Vol. 1, No. 8, pp. 87–125.

Bettelheim, B. (1983): *Freud's Man Soul.* New York: Knopf.

———. (1983). *Freud and Man's Soul.* New York: Knopf.

Brill, A. (1912): *Psychoanalysis His Theories and Practical Applications.* New York: Sanders.

————. (1931): *Revised Translation of Freud's The Interpretation of Dreams*. New York and London: Unwin & Allen.

————. (1938): *The Basic Writing of S Freud*. New York: The Modern Library.

Caine, B. (1998): The Stracheys and psychoanalysis. *The History Workshop Journal* Vol. 45, pp. 142–169.

————. (2005): *Bombay to Bloomsbury: The History of the Strachey Family*. Oxford: Oxford University Press.

Colarossi, M. (2015): Translating and being translated by P. Levi, in *Parallel Texts: World Reflections on Line*, pp. 3–8.

Dante, A. (1982): *The Inferno*, translated by A Mandelbaum. New York: Random House.

————. (2005): *La Divina Commedia*. Milano: Mondadori.

Deacon, R. (1985): *The Cambridge Apostles*. New York: Farrer, Strauss & Giroux.

Dostaler, G., & Maris, B. (2000): Dr Freud and Mr Keynes on money and capitalism, in J. Smithin (ed.), *What is Money?*. London: Routledge, pp. 235–254.

Eco, U. (1990): *I limiti dell 'Interpretazione*. Milan: Bompiani.

————. (2003): *Dire quasi la stessa cosa*. Milan: Bompiani.

Folena, G. (1991): *Volgarizzare e Tradurre*. Torino: Einaudi.

Forrester, J. (2003): Freud in Cambridge. *Critical Quarterly* Vol. 46, No. 2, pp. 1–27.

————. (2008): Psychology and psychoanalysis: Cambridge and London, Myers, Jones and McCurdy. *Psychoanalysis and History* Vol. 10, No. 1, pp. 37–93.

Freud, S. (1894)[1968]: *The NeuroPsychoses of Defence*. S.E. 3. London: Hogarth Press.

————. (1900)[1968]: Die Traumdeutung. *G.W.* II/III.

————. (1900)[1968]: *The Interpretation of Dreams*. S.E. 4/5. London: Hogarth Press.

————. (1905)[1968]: *A Case of Hysteria*. S.E. 7. London: Hogarth Press.

————. (1905)[1968]: *Jokes and Their Relationship to the Unconscious*. S.E. 8. London: Hogarth Press.

————. (1913)[1968]: *Totem and Taboo*. S.E. 13. London: Hogarth Press.

————. (1916–1917)[1968]: *Vorlesungen zur Einführung in die Psychoanalyse*. *G.W.* X.

————. (1916–1917)[1968]: *Introductory Lectures on Psychoanalysis*. S.E. 15/16. London: Hogarth Press.

————. (1919)[1968]: *A Child Is Being Beaten*. S.E. 17. London: Hogarth Press.

————. (1920)[1968]: *Beyond the Pleasure Principle*. S.E. 18. London: Hogarth Press.

————. (1926)[1968]: Two Articles for the *Encyclopaedia Britannica. S.E.* 20. London: Hogarth Press.

————. (1940, 1938)[1968]: *Some Elementary Lessons in Psychoanalysis. S.E.* 23. London: Hogarth Press.

Freud, S., & Jones, E. (1908–1939)[1993]: *The Complete Correspondence between Sigmund Freud and Ernest Jones.* R. A. Paskaukas (ed.). Cambridge, MA: Harvard University Press.

Gay, P. (1988): *Freud: A Life for Our Time.* New York: WW Norton.

————. (1990): *Reading Freud.* New Haven, CT and London: Yale University Press.

Graves, R., & Hodge, A. (1994): *The Long Week End. A Social History of Great Britain.* London: Faber & Faber.

Hale, K. (1998): *Friends and Apostles. The Correspondence between R. Brooks and J. Strachey (1905–1914).* New Haven, CT and London: Yale University Press.

Hale, N. (1971a): *Freud and the Americans.* New York: Oxford University Press.

————. (1971b): *James Jackson Putnam and Psychoanalysis.* Cambridge, MA: Harvard University Press.

Hobsbaw, E. (1987): *The Age of Empire.* London: Weidenfeld and Nicholson.

Holroyd, M. (1968): *Lytton Strachey: A Critical Biography – The Years of Achievement,* vol. 2. London: Heinemann.

————. (1994): *Lytton Strachey.* London and New York: Norton Books.

Hinshelwood. (1995): Psychoanalysis in Britain: points of cultural access (1883–1918). *The International Journal of Psychoanalysis* Vol. 76, No. 1, pp. 135–151.

Hughes, A. (ed.) (1991): *The Inner World of J. Riviere.* London: Karnac.

Jakobson, R. (1959)[1971]: On linguistic aspects of translation, in *Selected Writings,* vol. 2. The Hague: Mouton, pp. 260–266.

————. (1967)[1972]: Language and culture. *Sciences of Language* (Tokyo) Vol. 12, No. 3, pp. 3–18.

Jerome, Saint (390 A.C). (1879): *De Optimo Genere interpretandi Epistula L.V Pannachium in Ouvres de Saint Jerome.* Paris: Delagave.

Johnson, G. (2006): *Psychodynamic Psychology and British Modernist Fiction.* London: Palgrave Mc Millan.

Jones, E. (1913): 'Introduction to C Payne' in Hitschmann, E. (1913). Freud's Theories of the Neuroses. *Journal of Nervous and Mental Disease,* pp. 2–5.

————. (1922a): *Preface to Joan Riviere's Translation of S. Freud's Introductory Lecture on Psychoanalysis (1916–17).* London: Allen & Unwin.

————. (1922b): Unpublished Letter to James Strachey, 22 May 1922. Archives of the British Society. E Jones's Papers.

————. (1924): *Introduction to The Glossary of Psychoanalytic Terms*. London: Balliere and Tindall.

————. (1956, 1958). *The Life and Work of Sigmund Freud*, vol. 2 and 3. London: Hogarth Press.

————. (1959): *Free Associations*. London: The Hogarth Press.

Kuhn, P. (1917): *Psychoanalysis in Britain 1893–1913*. New York and London: Lexinton Books.

————. (2014): Observing Ernest Jones discerning the work of Sigmund Freud (1905–08). *Psychoanalysis and History* Vol. 16, No. 2, pp. 5–54.

————. (2015): The Dark Regions of the mind. A reading of the indecent assault in E. Jones' dismissal from the West End Hospital for nervous diseases. *Psychoanalysis and History* Vol. 17, No. 1, pp. 3–65.

Kuhn, P. (2017) *Psychoanalysis in Britain 1893–1913 Histories and Historiography*. New York: Lexinton Books.

Lacan, J. (1966): *Ecrits*. Paris: Du Seuil.

Levi, P. (1958): *Se questo me' un uomo*. Torino: Einaudi.

————. (1985): *Del Tradurre e dell'essere tradotto in Dall'atrui mestiere*. Torino: Einaudi.

Levy, P. (ed.) (2005): *The Letters of Lytton Strachey*. New York: Farrar.

Liddell, H. G., & Scott, R. (1898): *A Greek English Lexicon*. Oxford: Clarendon Press.

Mahony, P. (1980). Toward the Understanding of Translation in Psychoanlysis. *Journal of the American Psychoanalytic Association*, Vol. 28, pp. 461–475.

————. (1987): *Towards an Understanding of Translation in Psychoanalysis in Psychoanalysis and Discourse*. London: Tavistock.

Meisel, P., & Kendrick, W. (1986): *The Bloomsbury Freud*. London: Chatto and Windus.

Morr, E. (1995): A. A. Brill first American translator of Freud in Alexander F and others, in *Psychoanalytic Pioneers*. New York: Transaction Books, pp. 210–223.

Paskaukas, A. (ed.) (1993): *The Complete Correspondence of Sigmund Freud and Ernest Jones (1980–1939)*. Cambridge, MA: Harvard University Press.

Rank, O. (1921): Unpublished Letter to E Jones, 2 February 1921. Archives of the British Psychoanalytic Society. E Jones's Papers.

Ricoeur, P. (2004): *Sur la Traduction*. Paris: Bayard.

Riviere, J. (1922): *Translation of S Freud Introductory Lectures on Psychoanalysis (1916–17)*. London: Allen & Unwin.

Rocci, E. (2011): *Vocabolario Greco Antico Italiano*. Rome: Roma Societa Dante Alighieri, p. 10.

Schur, M. (1955): Unpublished letter to E Jones, 30 September 1955. London: Archives of the British Psychoanalytic Society, E Jones' Papers.

Shepards, B. (2007): *A War of Nerves Soldier and Psychiatry*. Cambridge, MA: Harvard University Press.

Stedman, T. L. (1913): *A Practical Medical Dictionary*. W Wood: New York.

Steiner, G. (1975): *After Babel*. Oxford: Oxford University Press.

Steiner, R. (1980/1988): Paths to Xanadu. *International Review of Psycho-Analysis* Vol. 15, No. 4, pp. 415–454.

———. (1981): Es Ludens in F Fornari ed. *La Comunicazione Spiritosa*. Florence: Sansoni.

———. (1984): Unpublished Paper. James Strachey and the History of the English Translation of Freud, given on 28 May. London: The British Psychoanalytic Society.

———. (1987): M A Worldwide International Trademark of genuineness. *International Review of Psycho-Analysis* Vol. 14, pp. 13–102.

———. (1988): Die Weltmachstellung des Britischen Reichs, in E. Timms, & N. Segal (eds.), *Freud in Exile*, pp. 181–195. Yale University Press: New Haven.

———. (1989). It is a New Kind of Diaspora.... *International Review of Psycho-Analysis* Vol. 16, pp. 35–72.

———. (1991): To explain our point of view to English Readers in English Words. *International Review of Psycho-Analysis* Vol. 18, pp. 351–392.

———. (1994): The Tower of Babel or after the Tower of Babel in contemporary psychoanalysis. *The International Journal of Psychoanalysis* Vol. 75, No. 5 and 6, pp. 883–890.

———. (1995): Et in Archiviom ego. *The International Journal of Psychoanalysis* Vol. 76, pp. 739–759.

———. (1999): Endliches und Unendliches Exil. *Forum der Psychoanalyse* Vol. 15, pp. 360–373.

———. (2000): *It is a Kind of New Diaspora*. London: Karnac Books.

———. (2003, 2016) Einige Bemerkungen über die theoretischen and klinischen Entwicklungen in der Psychoanalyse nach die Auflösung der WPV, in W. Burian, et al., *Trauma der Psychoanalyse?* (pp. 119–144). Gießen: Psychosozial-Verlag.

———. (2012) *IPA Bulletin*. pp. 35–37.

Strachey, A. (1943): *A New German-English Psychoanalytical Vocabulary*. London: Balleire and Tyndall.

Strachey, J. (1920): Unpublished letter to Lytton Strachey, 15 October 1920, The British Library Archives: Strachey's Papers.

———. (1921a): Letter to E Jones 27 November 1921 in Orston (1985).

———. (1921b): Letter to his mother Lady A Strachey, 7 March 1921, in M Holroyd.

———. (1921c): Letter to M Keynes in Dostalar Maris (2000).

———. (1921d): Unpublished letter to Lytton Strachey, 16 February 1921, The British Library Archives: Strachey's Papers.

————. (1921e): Unpublished letter to Lytton Strachey 29 March 1921, The British Library Archives: Strachey's Papers.

————. (1921f): Unpublished letter to Lytton Strachey 20 April 1921, The British Library Archives: Strachey's Papers.

————. (1921g): Unpublished letter to Lytton Strachey 6 November 1921, The British Library Archives: Strachey's Papers.

————. (1922a): Unpublished Letter to E Jones 18 May 1922 Archives of the British Society, E Jones' Papers.

————. (1922b): Unpublished Letter to L Strachey 22 June 1922, The British Library Archives: Strachey's Papers.

Taddeo, J. A. (2002): *Lytton Strachey and the Research for Modern Sexual Identity*. New York: The Harrington Press.

Timms, E., & Segal, N. (eds.) (1988): *Freud in Exile*. New Haven, CT: Yale University Press.

Venuti, L. (1995): *The Translator's Invisibility*. London: Routledge.

————. (2000): *The Translator Reader*. London and New York: Routledge.

————. (2013): *Translation Changes Everything*. London and New York: Routledge.

Wittenberger, G., & Toegel, C. (eds.) (1999): *Die Rundbriefe des "Geheimen Komitees"*, vol. 1. Tuebingen: Diskord.

PUBLISH AND BE FAIR? "I AM MYSELF STRONGLY IN FAVOUR OF DOING IT"

James Strachey as the candid wartime editor
of *The International Journal of Psycho-Analysis,*
1939–1945

Dee McQuillan

Introduction

This is an examination of the history of James Strachey's work as the editor of *The International Journal of Psycho-Analysis* during a time dominated by the internal strife within British psychoanalysis and the great international conflict of World War II. The references to the war made here are necessarily brief, specific ones, but in everything that follows, its enormity needs to be borne in mind.

Strachey was only the second editor of the *Journal:* Ernest Jones had been firmly in control of since its beginnings in 1919. From the primary sources, it has been possible to give an account of how Strachey came to be in charge of the *Journal*, why he was suited to the role, and also to provide an example of what he was like as an editor dealing with colleague-contributors. Perhaps the most surprising discovery was the evidence that James Strachey had wanted to make both the papers and the ensuing discussions of the Controversies public through the *Journal*. It is argued here that this wish was due both to his long-held belief in free speech and candour, and because he was so strongly set against splitting the British

Psycho-Analytical Society. As he had expressed it to James Glover in a letter in April 1943, "I feel that any suggestion of a 'split' in the society ought to be condemned and resisted to the utmost" (King and Steiner 1991, 32–33). In fact, the proceedings of the Controversies were not printed in the *Journal,* and some thoughts as to why this was will be offered here, but Strachey did succeed in publishing papers directly related to the debate by fostering investigation into the subject of internal objects. He also gave space to new writers and a plurality of theories, including the nascent object relations theories of D.W. Winnicott and John Bowlby.

The main sources drawn upon are the contents of the *Journals* themselves used alongside what letters and documents survive in the Archives of the British Psychoanalytical Society (ABPS) and the Wellcome Library Archive.[1] Another major, parallel source is *The Freud-Klein Controversies 1941–45* edited with commentaries by Pearl King and Riccardo Steiner (King and Steiner 1991). Details from Strachey's earlier life come from the very many 20th-century Strachey papers archived at the British Library. Jones's tenure at the *Journal* is a related topic, but beyond this article's remit and the space available. The *Journal,* with its associated publication *The International Review of Psycho-Analysis,* has published two studies of its own history by Riccardo Steiner, the first of which is dedicated to its foundation, linguistic strategies, and cultural significance. The second paper addresses the International Psycho-Analytic Association's political decisions during the 1930s, with reference to how these were reflected in the papers and information Jones chose to print in the *Journal,* and how that changed and the *Journal* re-engaged with political topics once Britain entered the war in 1939 (Steiner 1994, 2011, introduction, 558 f.). There is also much material on the *Journal* in *The Complete Correspondence of Sigmund Freud and Ernest Jones* (Paskauskas 1993), in the correspondence of contemporary analysts and International Psycho-Analytical Society Bulletins.[2]

The following abbreviations are used: the British Psycho-Analytical Society is referred to here as the Society and *The International Journal of Psycho-Analysis* as the *Journal*; ABPS is Archives of the British Psychoanalytical Society; BL is British Library; PEP is Psychoanalytical Electronic Publishing (www.pep-web.org); SE is The Standard Edition of the Complete Psychological Works of Sigmund Freud; and WLA is Wellcome Library Archive.[3]

How Strachey became editor

In 1939, James Strachey began to take over the role of editor of *Journal*. A couple of strange occurrences marked the beginning of his editorship. The first was that Dr Sylvia Payne wanted to know how and when the decision to give him the position was made. And the second involved a shared effort with Melanie Klein to publish a paper on Don Juan for the final *Journal* of 1939, which was to be dedicated to Ernest Jones but their plan [went awry].

In November 1939, Payne, who was business secretary of the Society and was also on its Publishing and Training Committees and hence increasingly a force to be reckoned with, wrote to Ernest Jones about James Strachey's appointment. She questioned Jones's decision to make Strachey editor and reminded him that his unilateral decisions were a cause of dissatisfaction.[4] Strachey was in effect editing the *Journal* already, as will be shown later in the chapter. Furthermore, Payne was highly likely to have known this because, with Strachey and Dr Edward Bibring, she was credited in the publication as being on the editorial committee arranging the Ernest Jones's sixtieth birthday tribute edition. My estimate is that Payne's chief motive in writing to Jones was to put the irregularity on the official record, because she at least was already sensitive to the pressure to reform the way offices were distributed within the Society. The ABPS records Jones's announcement in June 1939 of his staged withdrawal from executive work, including his membership of the Training Committee and charge of the *Journal*. The same meeting recorded that the board as a whole had decided to postpone a decision regarding the future editor.[5] And yet Jones went ahead and awarded a plum job to James Strachey, whom Dr Adrian Stephen at least regarded as a great favourite—"that lickspittle Strachey" (MacGibbon 1997, 158–159).

Monopolies and seeming favouritism were recorded by King and Steiner as one important, non-theoretical factor in the development of the Controversies. Addressing the period of 1941–1943, Riccardo Steiner has written,

> Feelings were running strong for and against the need for a revision of the constitution in favour of limiting tenure of offices and the possibility of holding multiple offices in the Society.
>
> (King and Steiner 1991, 33)

From 1941, strong feelings and calls for reform would be voiced repeatedly by Barbara Low, and Doctors Melitta Schmideberg, Karin Stephen and Adrian Stephen. Possibly, Jones's reply to Payne's questions about the change of editorship was not particularly contrite,

> November 10th 1939
>
> Dear Doctor Payne,
>
> Some time ago I asked Mr Strachey to discuss the matter of editorship with you. It is of course a matter for the board, not for myself, and I think it would be worth while to have a board meeting after the ordinary meeting in December; there are also other matters to discuss [...]
>
> Things seemed to be pointing so definitely towards Strachey that when I left London I handed all the *Journal* apparatus, correspondence, etc. to him. If you prefer to have a board meeting at a different time from the ordinary meeting please do so; it is only a matter of attendance.
>
> Yours sincerely
>
> E.J.[6]

Behind Jones's off-hand manner were well-founded anxieties about an invasion of Britain by Germany. His wife Katherine was Jewish, and he had seen Nazism in Austria in 1938 (Steiner 2011). Also, suddenly he had fewer patients (Brome 1985, 200); likely reasons for this include the conscription of men into the armed forces which began immediatcly war was declared, after which followed the direction of women under 30 into working for the war effort.[7] From September 1939, the government began evacuating children out of the major British cities and many adults relocated as well. Jones had decided to be based at his house at Elsted, West Sussex, and it has been said that his preferred solution to the crises without and within was that the Society would put itself into a state of near-suspension for the duration of the war (Maddox 2006, 245; Schmideberg quoted in King and Steiner 1991, 64). Arguably, the seemingly precipitate and high-handed awarding of the editorship by Jones could be classified as bad group psychology but it was rather canny individual psychology. In 1939, Jones knew James Strachey a great deal better than Payne did, and had made up his mind that Strachey tended to evade excessive workloads. Perhaps he acted quickly as he anticipated a polite refusal.

On the subject of work and Jones's relations with the Stracheys, there is some comedy in the letters in *Bloomsbury/Freud* (Meisel and Kendrick 1986) and the Freud-Jones letters (Paskauskas 1993) as Jones tried to put Alix and James Strachey to work as he and Freud had planned, and they amused themselves keeping him waiting for their translations, criticizing his delusions about being a good proof-reader, and referring to him as "the Erogenous Jones" (Paskauskas 1993, 486 on Freud's catching translators for Jones; Meisel and Kendrick 1986, 189 and 244). During the 1920s, Jones had complained several times to Freud, for example, writing in 1928 that as Strachey's analyst, Freud should know all about Strachey's "intolerance of work" (Paskauskas 1993, 638). That quality is relative: Jones had driven himself exceptionally hard and demanded a great deal from others, whereas Strachey had other things he liked to do.[8] And Jones rather undermines his own criticism by stating the fact that Strachey had eight patients a day in 1928 (Paskauskas, as mentioned earlier).

The Society had other members with experience of publishing, particularly Dr John Rickman who ran the Institute's book publishing, edited for *The British Journal of Medical Psychology,* and wrote for *The Lancet;* it also had talented writers in Joan Riviere, Ella Freeman Sharpe, and Edward Glover, so in the interests of fairness, there probably should have been discussions about the editorship.[9] But James Strachey was particularly well-qualified in the practicalities of putting a magazine together. From 1909 to 1915, he had worked on the political weekly magazine *The Spectator.* Strachey had been a socialist since his student days and became what he termed an "ultra-pacifist" in the lead-up to World War I; *The Spectator's* political colours were then pretty much as they are now, and he only got the job because his mother had asked the proprietor and editor, who was also a Strachey, to employ him. According to the letters he wrote to his brother Lytton, the post gave him money for concerts, restaurants, and travel, which he enjoyed, but at times it threatened to bring a return of a depressive tendency that had afflicted him as an undergraduate.[10] He would complain, "I've spent eight hours and a half today bolstering up the ruling classes in a dingy room".[11] As World War I began, he refused to give his cousin, the editor, any commitment to volunteer to fight. He left *The Spectator* once it was clear that the government would implement conscription, and he made his conscientious objection in March 1916.

However, his time at *The Spectator* had been productive in as far as it enabled him to learn the trade of editorial production from start to finish. Strachey had worked alongside an assistant editor called C.L. Graves, who was highly respected for his skills and dedication (Sanders 1953, 219).[12] Strachey's standard of written English was already high – witness the letters to Rupert Brooke (Hale 1998, ff.) – but in that office he would have been instructed in checking and marking-up copy, passing page proofs, and working with the printers. He wrote letters to writers on the editor's behalf. He would also have been trained to impose an official house style, for example, approved spellings, nouns meriting capital letters, numbers to be either expressed as words or numerals, preference for single or double quotation marks, and the approved abbreviation for et cetera. In other words, as a young man working beside Graves at *The Spectator,* he would have learned a form of standardization.

To return to the late 1930s, there were other circumstances, such as Strachey being given the title of translation editor in 1938 and offering his curious paper on the problem of Akhenaten to the *Journal* in 1939 that point to the likelihood that he had been serving as a de facto assistant or deputy prior to the Jones's sixtieth birthday tribute. The Institute's board accepted Jones's decision in December 1939 and gave Strachey a three-year term and an advisory committee that comprised Dr Marjorie Brierley with Rickman and Payne.[13]

Klein's Don Juan is not Strachey's

The "apparatus" that Jones passed over to Strachey probably included the many commissioning letters, manuscripts, and proofs of articles that producing the *Journal* would have generated and of which, sadly, so little has survived. (It is likely that there was just too much editorial paperwork to keep.) This makes the correspondence between Strachey and Klein in 1939–1940 doubly precious: naturally it is valuable for the typescript of Klein's Don Juan, and additionally it gives some sense of what the work of the *Journal* was, and of what Strachey was like as an editor.

In the 1930s, the *Journal* was published in four parts a year. The last part of 1939 was scheduled to be a tribute to Ernest Jones on his sixtieth birthday. As mentioned earlier, Payne and Bibring were on the committee for this issue, but Strachey was the most involved: it is his name and address that were printed in the *Journal* for contributions to be sent to, and we have evidence that he was editing the papers. Strachey referred in correspondence to that issue as "The Jones Heft" (meaning an issue or number of a publication); when it appeared, it carried a good portrait photograph of Jones and an uncredited dedication on page 222, describing the issue as "offered by his friends and colleagues from around the world in gratitude for his unceasing efforts on behalf of the psycho-analytical movement", even though British analysts may have wondered if the word "unceasing" was justified given Jones's decisions and actions since war was declared. In composition, the Heft was the last genuinely international *Journal* for several years. Thirty-one analysts from seven countries wrote papers, some of which were closer than others in reflecting upon Jones's particular contributions to psychoanalysis.

Documents, in the form of handwritten letters from Strachey and typed letters and papers from Klein at the WLA, tell us that Klein too planned to make a contribution to The Jones Heft, on the subject of Don Juan.[14] On 29 October 1939, Strachey chased Melanie Klein for her contribution, giving her 7 November as "the positively last possible day" for sending the text. He said there were few British papers, and it really was her patriotic duty to send him something (the last part I take to be intended as humorous encouragement). On 9 November, he wrote her a three-and-a-half-page letter to "just remind you of a few of the events connected with it". These were that Bibring had first requested a contribution from her on 15 March, after which she and Strachey had agreed a deadline of 1 September, but in view of the crisis, a delay seemed reasonable.[15] Finally, on 28 October, he had told her that 7 November was the last possible day and held up the printing, but the paper arrived on 9 November. He continued, "it was essential to send the paper off immediately. On looking at the manuscript, however, I saw that it was far from being in a condition for the printers". Furthermore, "your covering letter made quite clear that you were contemplating all kinds of further alterations, abbreviations, and discursions". He said it would be dishonest of him not to add that, "it gives me an impression of being hastily put together", and that, "as it stands it would not do justice to your work". Here, we see that although the received opinion regarding Strachey's character was that he was a gentle, self-contained man who gave an impression of being shy or vague, he was perfectly able to be strict as an editor (Bell 1997, 221; Winnicott 1969, 130; Roazen 1995, 238).

The two agreed that the Don Juan paper would be revised, and Klein continued to try to work on it.[16] Meanwhile, she sent an emotional, reparative apology to Jones for having missed his Heft, writing that,

> the magnitude of the happenings we are now going through and the problem of what the future will bring to mankind, quite apart from my own personal life, had for weeks such a strong hold on me that my whole impulse to write vanished.[17]

She then tried to negotiate with Strachey on the precise form of words which would explain her paper's non-appearance in the Jones's tribute edition; however, the *Journal* merely noted that papers by Klein and Rickman could not be included but would appear subsequently.[18]

Klein's paper

The idea for Klein's paper seems to have come from a few paragraphs on Don Juanism that she had written in *Love, Hate and Reparation* (Klein and Riviere 1937, 84–87). For the Jones's tribute, she took the idea much further, using "the Don Juan type" to examine anxieties and underlying depression based on her hypothesis that depressive feelings can begin early, possibly at one-year-old. Klein does not precisely define the clinical type but writes of a "characteristic attitude to women" that makes Don Juan-esque men unhappy or ill if they try to be faithful to one partner.[19] Her main source was André Obey's play.[20] James Strachey, aficionado of Mozart and Haydn and the author of the Glyndebourne Opera's plot synopses, was of the opinion that this play sounded atypical: he wrote, "What one naturally thinks of is the figure in Molière or in Da Pointe (Mozart)".[21]

That criticism may be questionable: whilst it is true that the Obey play was hardly familiar in Britain then, and is unknown now as the full script of the version she saw seems to be lost, the difficulty could have been solved by putting Obey's Don Juan in the title of the paper and providing a synopsis. And the salient points of the paper came from Klein's attention being caught by two unusual attributes particular to that play: first, some words given to the Don describe a devouring beast within that feeds on women; second, Obey portrayed him as haunted by death, and dying by suicide, that is, by his own means rather than divine or infernal intervention.

Necessarily, in analyzing Don Juanism, Klein had to consider adult sexuality, but she explained it through infancy and childhood by connecting early depressive feelings to a great capacity for genital enjoyment caused by the genital being imbued with oral qualities and impulses. She wrote,

> My contention is" [...] "that the depressive features which this particular Don Juan manifests are latent in all Don Juans, whatever the superficial picture they present may be. In those who do not show depression on the surface, I nevertheless believe that their attitude towards women is one of the ways in which they master and keep at bay anxieties which are ultimately of a depressive nature.[22]

In its preoccupation with depression, the paper is closely related to her 1935 "A Contribution to the Psychogenesis of Manic-Depressive States". Granted, Don Juan was not completed, but it is indicative of what Juliet Mitchell has observed, "For Klein, the depressive position comes to incorporate and replace the psychic centrality that Freud accorded to the later Oedipus complex" (Mitchell 1986, 116).

Strachey had written to Klein that the case history material she supplied did not seem to have any relation to the Don Juan character.[23] This seems to be an unfair comment in the example of Child A, but is more justified in the three-page history of a man who will only sleep with the same woman three times: the latter seems less to the point. He had sent his marked-up copy of what Klein had written in November back to her to work on, but he seemed rather to jump at the chance when instead she wrote to him in February 1940 suggesting what he called the "Mourning" paper. This was the paper she had read at the Paris Congress, and may also have been presented to the Society on 21 February 1940 at Marjorie Brierley's invitation.[24] It was published in the *Journal* as "Mourning and Its Relation to Manic-Depressive States" (Klein 1940) and is a major milestone in Klein's theoretical development on depression, orality, and a depressive position.

Forcing depression on everyone?

Two letters at the Wellcome from Joan Riviere to Klein show that the latter had consulted her on her Mourning paper.[25] In her second letter, Riviere referred to the growing disagreement within the British Society. She wrote,

> The other point is more difficult. It concerns the question of "mourning" as a good thing! Naturally, "normal" people take that for granted, both instinctively, & understand it scientifically, that a person should be able to feel grief. But we know this was very much disputed before by Melitta and Glover, and there are a lot of people who, consciously or not, have a tendency to agree with their attitude. Moreover, they also tend to feel, as M. obviously does, that your views represent a wish to force depression on everybody.

Riviere's advice to Klein was to "give less of a handle" to those who are inclined to feel persecuted about depression, guilt, and sorrow: "I wondered if you could in any way deal with these resistances already in the paper & to some extent forestall such a reaction". But Riviere's letter to Klein was too close to the deadline, and Strachey again refused to delay and also refused to take on added printing costs. He calculated that one footnote alone of the several requested by Klein would come to £10.[26] Of course, the significance of Riviere's suggested amendments is far greater than demonstrating the trials of an editor: here again in correspondence we find early signs of the Society's internal conflicts. Melitta Schmideberg (Klein's daughter) and Edward Glover are identified as opponents of Klein and Riviere's use of the conditions of mourning and depression; they are depicted too as feeling persecuted, and in the same letter Riviere writes that in 1936, Ella Freeman Sharpe "had attacked my paper" [on the Negative Therapeutic Reaction] "saying in so many words such analysts want to force their patients into depression".[27]

"Untranslated Freud"

Strachey's time as editor of the *Journal* is marked by his return to translation work. His and his wife Alix Strachey's contributions to the *Sigmund Freud Collected Papers* (including volume III, the Case Histories, which were all their own work) were published in 1924–1925; next, he translated *An Autobiographical Study* for publication in 1927; after that he did not accepted any long text by Freud despite requests from the latter.[28] What changed after 1939 was that, in common with most analysts who had been based in Britain before 1938, James Strachey's patient numbers had gone down because of the war. And Freud's death was a great change. Strachey, who had been analyzed by him from 1920 to 1922 and always recalled him warmly, was probably glad to make the first translation of *An Outline of Psycho-Analysis* and to run it in the special Freud edition, which was the *Journal*'s first instalment in 1940.[29]

Several other important factors were at work in his return to translating. An active, positive factor was Ernest Jones's immediate proposal upon Freud's death that a grand Memorial Edition of Freud in English should be created. Strachey obliged by drafting a letter to influential people and potential donors, and Jones negotiated with publishers; however, in 1940, the former evidently was not initially keen to take on the work, because he noted on a letter of Jones's, "Not inclined to be involved—anyway not unless paid. *Journal* takes up too much time".[30] (The Memorial project was repeatedly delayed and ended in disappointment.)

What he did do as Editor was, in 1940, to introduce the heading "Untranslated Freud". The Editorial Note on page 469 read,

> Since all of his major works have already been translated, it is not to be expected that anything of outstanding importance will be included here. Nevertheless, much will be found which is of very great interest and nothing, perhaps, that does not exhibit in some degree the originality of its author's mind.

The title marks a new stage of Freud in English and in Strachey's translating life. The *Journal* at this time did not credit translators, but the prefaces in the later *Standard Edition of the Complete Psychological Works of Sigmund Freud* identify all of the 1939–1946 translations run by the *Journal* as James Strachey's work.[31] At the same time that James was engaged with his Untranslated Freud, Alix Strachey was working on recording the expansion of psychoanalytic terms and recommending particular words for her book *New German-English Psycho-Analytic Vocabulary* (A. Strachey 1943). The book reflects the fact that the number of psychoanalysts and their publications in the *Journal* or elsewhere had grown. She established a style for German compound words, and the value of her research was generously acknowledged in *The Language of Psychoanalysis* (Laplanche and Pontalis 1973, xv). My estimation is that papers by other authors for the *Journal* that needed translating from German from 1939 to 1945 would have been translated by either Alix or James Strachey.[32] As the war went on, the amount of non-Freud translating done by the *Journal* diminished substantially, and, on a point of detail, these translations were almost never credited and the translators were likely to have worked unpaid.

John Forrester once made an extempore remark about Strachey having resumed translating Freud, "Partly to fill up the *Journal* because he had very little copy during the war"; these words may not have been entirely serious, and certainly they are contradicted by the paper shortages that will be described later.[33] Publishing Freud in English had always been the top priority of the *Journal*, so it was logical that Strachey should be compiling a Freud bibliography in order to find shorter or older texts that were not yet translated into English.[34] In 1945, the *Journal* ran Strachey's "List of English Translations of Freud's Works" (Strachey 1945). His acknowledgements for help with the List show he had reached out to American analysts in a way that Jones might have been uncomfortable with; of course, American analysts now included many talented, well-informed European émigrés, but in the first place, Strachey had never been biased against American analysts or their publications, unlike Jones whose attitude was often competitive. As Editor Strachey also began to run many more ab-stracts from the US periodical *The Psychoanalytic Quarterly* than had previously been the case, for example, giving good coverage to a Symposium on Neurotic Disturbances of Sleep held in Los Angeles (International *Journal* of Psycho-Analysis 1942, 23:49–68) and to pa-pers given at the Chicago Psycho-Analytical Society (International *Journal* of Psycho-Analysis 1944, 25: 1–8 and 13–19).

On the subject of translation, the enduringly important topic both of the specific words and the tone adopted by the *Journal* and Interna-tional Psycho-Analytic Library (the latter also founded by Jones and based in London under his control) is one that has been considered in depth by Riccardo Steiner in several papers. In "A Worldwide Inter-national Trade Mark of Genuineness?" he gave careful proof of how far back Jones's wish to determine the English into which Freud and the other pioneers were translated went: Jones had been working away at this objective since 1909, the date when Strachey left the Univer-sity of Cambridge. Steiner demonstrates that when the Stracheys trans-lated, they followed a template which Jones, A.A. Brill, and Harry W. Chase, translator of Five Lectures on Psycho-Analysis, had set-up in consultation with Freud (Steiner 1987, 70–72). Although Joan Riviere and the Stracheys were part of the 1920s Glossary Committee, Jones continued to oversee the official language of psychoanalysis in English closely at least until 1939.[35]

In "'The Tower of Babel', or 'After Babel in Contemporary Psychoanalysis?'" Steiner considered the *Journal* specifically, giving a detailed account of its foundation, of Jones's hopes and ambitions, and its course through to the 1980s. From the primary sources, he argues that Jones was hegemonic in both his organizational and cultural objectives and the *Journal* had a clear hegemonic purpose. "Jones and the British Society regarded the *Journal* as a kind of cultural weapon, particularly where the linguistic side of the enterprise was concerned" (Steiner 1994, 884). Unlike Strachey's period in charge, during Jones's editorship, there would have been many papers to translate into English, and with these there was a determined effort to use consistent terms; Steiner wrote,

> It is difficult to tell whether Jones fully realized the extraordinary implications of his plan Yet, this plan was also, indeed mainly, based on a complex control of the language in which psychoanalysis was written, spoken and transmitted in the English speaking world. It formed the basis of a monopoly sanctioned in many ways by Freud himself, if only, at times in a rather luke-warm fashion.
>
> (Steiner 1994, 889)

Part two: belt-tightening and the ideal of an open forum 1941–1945

Belt-tightening

The resources available to the *Journal* reduced rapidly after France and Britain declared war in September 1939.[36] In terms of potential writers, many British psychoanalysts directed their time and energy into war work in various forms. Beyond the areas under Allied control, potential European contributors' lives were in turmoil, to put it mildly, and anyone who had the will and stamina to write from occupied Europe would have faced censorship and unreliable postal services. The non-UK-based contributors for Strachey's years in charge were almost entirely Americans, headed by Clarence Oberndorf, the official American editor for the *Journal*.[37]

Part of the *Journal*'s usual formula was, first, to have substantial sections of book reviews, and second, to make abstracts from articles of psychoanalytic interest run in international periodicals, but increasingly foreign journals and imported books were not reaching Britain. Non-fiction publishing in Britain was generally reduced, not only by the rationing (outlined later), but also by a reduction in the number of people wanting or being able to afford reference books.[38] To fill the gap, the *Journal* relied upon its two excellent US contributors, analysts Lucile Dooley and Clara Thompson, for reviews and abstracts.

By 1943, the *Journal* was restricted to 192 pages of thin paper a year. This caused a drastic reduction of its scope, given that it had been 523 pages in 1938, 515 in 1939, and 504 in 1940. As seen in his letter quoted later, Strachey proposed to the Society's Board and Publishing Committee that the *Journal* should switch to producing only two editions a year, an arrangement that was accepted and had to continue after the war. In addition, labour shortages, as Strachey had tried to explain to Melanie Klein during the long negotiations over her Don Juan amendments, meant that printing work was being done more slowly. Physical restrictions upon importing wood or paper, or using power to produce pulp for paper, or on the use of electric lights (the urban black-outs) which reduced print works' hours, were all elements that shaped the history of the World War II *Journal*.

Strachey to Payne

Another letter takes us further into the Controversies and describes the exigencies that war conditions were forcing upon the *Journal*. It was written by James Strachey to Sylvia Payne in February 1943, and it implies that by now they knew each other better, and had been discussing the bad feelings and behaviour within their Society. In full, the letter is two pages long. The reference is to Susan Isaacs's discussion paper on phantasy, the first paper of the Discussions of Scientific Differences given in two parts on 13 January and 17 February 1943.[39]

[...] "I shan't be able to come to the adjourned discussion on Susan Isaacs next week. (I thought, by the way, the last one went off very well. The fact that so many non-partisan English members criticized the paper took the wind out of Anna's sails. I was also delighted at Melitta's disgracing herself so completely.) If the question of printing the proceedings in the *Journal* comes up again, the following facts should be borne in mind:-

Each of the four quarterly issues of the Journal is now limited to 48 pages (by Govt. restriction of paper). This includes space ear-marked for the Bulletin of the I.P.A. as well as space for abstracts & reviews.

If printed in full, Susan Isaacs' paper would fill about 22 pages and last time's discussion about 15: together, 37 pages. If next week's discussion is equally long, the grand total would be 52 pages, or four more than the whole of one issue of the Journal.

At least two similar discussions seem to be in view.

I mention these facts so as to show that the question of printing the discussion in the Journal is not so simple as it might seem. I am myself strongly in favour of doing it in some form or other, especially as there is a very great shortage of other material for the Journal. But the problem of editing and summarizing the discussions would, in the circumstances, be a delicate one.

But perhaps the whole question is one for the consideration of the Board. Which leads me to

(4) If and when the Board meets, my private agenda is slightly changed: (a) Desirability of concentrating on two double numbers yearly.

(b) Disposal of stocks of back numbers. [The question of the American price of the Journal can stand over.]

Yours sincerely, James Strachey[...]"[40]

The letter is evidence that acrimony within the Society about the acceptability of Kleinian metapsychology was reaching a peak. It had been decided to hold a series of Discussions of Scientific Differences, ostensibly to improve understanding, although of one side only: the Kleinian one. The group working closely with Melanie Klein was to explain their concepts, theories, and technique. Edward Glover was determined to connect theoretical divergences to the question of what should be taught to trainees at the Institute, while other analysts were equally determined to see their Society reformed to give members more say and to restrict the tenure of the key offices.[41] The realpolitik centred on Glover, who had been thought of as Jones's natural successor until he turned into a persistent critic of Klein in concert with Melitta Schmideberg who was his analysand.

The International Journal of Psycho-Analysis
as an open forum: a hypothesis

With what he had to say – privately – about Isaacs, Anna Freud, and Schmideberg, it might seem as if Strachey were back at the top of his satirical-sarcastic form, as expressed in his 1924–1925 letters to his wife (Meisel and Kendrick 1986 ff.). But note too that he was strongly in favour of publishing Isaacs's presentation: how serious the dismissive-sounding remark about lack of material was should be gauged against Strachey's repeated and often genuinely funny uses of bathos and understatement in private letters. Contradictoriness was evident in Strachey's attitudes to the Controversies: he mocked, refused to take sides, attended only one or two of the Discussions of Scientific Differences, yet was at the same time convinced that it was important that a split in the Society be condemned and resisted to the utmost (King and Steiner 1991, 32–33).[42]

The letter to Payne shows he was prepared, in his powerful position as editor, to let the Controversialists publish. Here, and almost invariably throughout his life, James Strachey's bias was towards free speech and heterodoxy. Because he left so many letters, it is possible to state that he had canvassed for women's suffrage in 1909, was active against censorship in the theatre in 1912, had joined the Union for Democratic Control during World War I (the organization aimed for more accountability in foreign policy), and at the same time volunteered to work at the National Council Against Conscription, with the aim of lobbying for himself and others to be allowed to refuse conscription into the military.[43] So he had a track record of supporting free speech and campaigning for rights to self-determination, as well as one for making satirical remarks.

Strachey was also on the Training Committee by 1943, and one attempted peace offering he made there was to suggest that training was run as an open forum (King and Steiner 1991, 602–609). Anna Freud referred to that open forum idea in her crucial statement in September 1943. She wrote that,

> In a former meeting of the Training Committee Mr Strachey has put forward the suggestion that the analytic Institute might form an open forum where current analytic theories and techniques are taught without giving preference to any one among them.

She doubted such a forum's effectiveness (King and Steiner 1991, 632–634). On the basis of the contents of the *Journals* of which he was editor, it seems a reasonable hypothesis that Strachey was pursuing the same idea by offering an open forum for exchange and debate in the *Journal*. The range of authors and theoretical approaches he managed to get into the *Journal* during his tenure, and the aforementioned letter to Sylvia Payne in February 1943 in which he said he would like to print not only the papers but also the discussions that followed them, give support to this line of argument.

An open forum approach was in keeping with Strachey's ideals for the Society expressed in a memorandum to the Training Committee written in February 1943. He had called for "each of us to be a little sceptical about his own conclusions and a little ready to consider other people's and to put up with a little uncertainty upon a few questions". He referred his fellow training analysts to "Freud's view of our science as something incomplete and susceptible to modification", and recommended tolerance, patience, and dialogue (King and Steiner 1991, 603–609). And yet, at times in private letters, Strachey himself seemed to be in danger of pursuing tolerance in a pretty dogmatic tone (King and Steiner 1991, 32–33, 680–681).

But the *Journal* did not publish Isaacs's presentations during Strachey's editorship.[44] Nor did it run any of the Discussions, despite these being taken down by shorthand writers. Inevitably, there must have been several factors at work, including the authors' positions: for instance, Susan Isaacs may not have been ready to put her contribution to the Discussions into print. And, as Strachey had told Payne, paper rationing would have made complete publishing very difficult. But we also know from Strachey's letter to Payne, quoted earlier, that the question of printing the proceedings in the *Journal* had been raised, by someone or some people, and that Strachey was strongly in favour of doing this in some form, despite the page reduction.[45] So what had happened? My assessment of the balance of probabilities is that the Society's Council would not permit publication of the transcripts, edited or not. From 1942, Ernest Jones had resumed involvement on the Society's committees, and despite the *Journal*'s reduced wartime circulation, he would have been prone to veto anything that he might conceive of as lessening its worldwide status.[46] Glover was so dead-set against Klein's group that it may be justified to surmise that he would have resented giving them such space in the *Journal*, while Payne, in an earlier letter to Jones, had expressed reluctance to publicize the British Society's difficulties using – and this is a traditional English expression – the term, washing the dirty linen in public.[47]

The closest the *Journal* came to running a main discussion paper was with Klein's "The Oedipus Complex in the Light of Early Anxieties" (1945), which is related, but by no means identical, to her presentation to the Discussions of Scientific Differences made on 7 and 21 March 1945 under the heading "The Emotional Life and Ego-Development of the Infant with Special Reference to the Depressive Position". Isaacs's Phantasy paper – again evolved from the original presentation – appeared in 1948, by which time the trio of Willi Hoffer, John Rickman, and Clifford Scott were in charge of the *Journal*.[48] What Strachey appears to have done instead, in pursuit of an editorial policy along the lines of an open forum, was to promulgate work with a bearing upon the Controversies.

He also favoured papers that either were topical in the larger sense, that is, psychological analysis of war and aggression, or were specific clinical studies of current problems like panic and dislocation of families. Paying attention to current events would have been a priority he had learned at *The Spectator* decades before, and he also shared the Bloomsbury Circle's attraction to news and what is new.[49] The declaration of war had made paying attention to international conflict an easier editorial decision for Strachey than it had been for Ernest Jones: Steiner's 2011 paper considers Jones's difficult position as president of the International Psycho-Analytic Association and editor of the *Journal* during the rise of Nazism, when he had the humanitarian obligation and desire to protect Jewish analysts but also a political dilemma about supporting psychoanalytic societies that were under Nazi or Axis control. As a result, there had been little engagement with European politics in the *Journal* in the 1930s, whereas, as Steiner observes, editions from 1939 had a strong sociopolitical interest, including lively contributions from Jones on quislingism and the concept of normal mind (Steiner 2011, 521–525; Steiner 2019).[50]

In terms of Kleinian papers related to the subjects of the Controversies, the *Journal* ran Susan Isaacs's 1940 "Temper Tantrums in Early Childhood in Their Relation to Internal Objects", her 1943 "An Acute Psychotic Anxiety Occurring in a Boy of Four Years", and the 1945 "Notes on Metapsychology as Process Theory"; the latter is especially interesting with regard to the attempts at finding common ground during the Discussions of Scientific Differences, as it was written in response to Marjorie Brierley's paper of the previous year (Brierley 1944). Although Paula Heimann's Discussion of Scientific Differences presentation, "Some Aspects of the Role of Introjection and Projection in Early Development", was also not reproduced, the *Journal* had carried its precursor, "A Contribution to the Problem of Sublimation and Its Relation to Processes of Internalization" (Heimann 1942).

Schmideberg and Glover's work continued to appear in the *Journal* right until the latter resigned from the British Society at the end of 1943. Supporting the supposition that Strachey wanted to run the *Journal* like an open forum, he also published papers by Anna Freud's associates Kate Friedlander and Barbara Lantos, and asked Dorothy Burlingham to review books. Certainly, he would have welcomed papers from Anna Freud and the implication of her friendly letter to him on 19 July 1940 is that he had been asking her to write.[51] Anna Freud wrote, "I myself have been lazy lately as far as writing is concerned; but when I improve I shall let you know. Thank you for asking".[52] The excuse of laziness seems likely to have been a polite deflection: these war years in London following the loss of her homeland and father were difficult ones for Anna Freud; see Young-Bruehl 1988.

From 1929 to 1951, Anna Freud did not appear in the *Journal*, except in her role as an official of, and compiler of bulletins for, the International Psycho-Analytical Association.[53]

Papers on technique or as an aid to training

To say something of Strachey's activities and interests aside from translation, as a training analyst since 1928 he had specialized in giving practical seminars on technique, which he liked to call the "instrument of psychoanalysis", and that became his other main research subject alongside Freud's writings. His interest was demonstrated not only in his 1934 and 1937 papers but also in his 1943 Memorandum to the Training Committee (King and Steiner 1991, 602–609) and in a series of handwritten notes for lectures at the ABPS.[54] The Memorandum asked the Training Committee to address,

[...] what are the essentials of this valid technique. That must be our first and principal task. It is one which, in spite of the greater attention it has received in the last ten years, is still far too much neglected. Its actual details continue to be wrapped in an unholy mystery. ... what do we really know about one another's actual way of behaving as analysts? Maybe we should be shocked if we did. Maybe it would turn out that our basic methods are more in agreement than we fear.

(King and Steiner 1991, 608)

As a result of Strachey's putting this question, Brierley, Anna Freud, Klein, Payne and Ella Freeman Sharpe wrote valuable accounts of their methods. (King and Steiner 1991, 618–660).

Both papers on technique and what might be classified as teaching or training papers feature in the *Journal* during the war years, and the latter were perhaps especially valuable to colleagues because it was difficult to attend training. Edward Bibring's "The Development and Problems of the Theory of the Instincts" surely is the outstanding example of a guide for students (1941). Other studies that might have served as teaching papers from these years include Paul Schilder on anxiety neuroses (1941), Edward Glovers on dissociation (1943), Ludwig Eidelberg considering slips of the tongue (1944), and Otto Fenichel on contemporary concepts of trauma (1945). Arguably, Edoard Weiss on analysis of psychic defence (1942), Richard Sterba on the activity of the analyst (1944), and the papers on Sándor Ferenczi (as mentioned later) follow Strachey's line of enquiry into analytic technique.

On the subject of Ferenczi

Strachey had attended the 1924 Salzburg Congress at which an official symposium on the relationship of psychoanalytic theory and practice was held in response to Ferenczi and Rank's challenges in their book *The Development of Psychoanalysis* (1925), and he was also at the Wiesbaden Congress where Ferenczi read his famous "Confusion of Tongues" paper. From Strachey's 1934 paper and from his manuscript notes on technique at the ABPS, in which he planned to lecture on Ferenczi as a "post-Freudian" theorist to trainees at the Society, it is clear that he believed Ferenczi's work deserved thought and attention.[55] Under his editorship, in 1942, the *Journal* included a fascinating, long paper called "The Therapeutic Technique of Sándor Ferenczi" by Izette De Forest, an American psychoanalyst who had been Ferenczi's patient in 1925.[56] It was the *Journal*'s first descriptive account from an analyst working closely in Ferenczi's methods, and the most significant paper on Ferenczi in the *Journal* since Michael Balint wrote on the final goal of treatment (Balint 1936).[57]

Ferenczi's methods, as described, were so different that Strachey added a cautionary preface on page 120,

> The technical procedure described in this paper differs, as its author makes quite plain, from that recommended by Freud and generally adopted by his pupils. The paper raises in a clear- cut form a number of problems in connection with the therapeutic process—problems concerned, in particular, with the handling of the transference and counter-transference—which are of primary importance: it therefore offers an admirable basis for equally clear-cut criticism.

Strachey wrote that he hoped to publish in a subsequent issue, views on whether the procedure can be approved or rejected; possibly, he also hoped to further his own point that more needed to be known about ways of behaving as analysts.

De Forest outlined Ferenczi's three technical principles as, first, "a constantly maintained and thoroughly studied emotional relationship between analyst and patient"; second, concentration of the analytic drama upon the figure of the analyst; and third, "a continual heightening of the patient's emotional tension until the original trauma or traumatic sequence shall have been and explored. These principles represent Ferenczi's outstanding contributions to psycho-analytic therapy" (De Forest 1942, 121–122). One of the original elements of De Forest's paper is her description of the use of what she called drama,

> We are asked: "Is not the dramatic element a dangerous threat to the success of the technique?" "May it not get out of hand, or seem to the patient like a playful game or artificial trick?" Attention should here be called to the fact that the patient should not sense the drama of the analysis to the extent that the analyst does, if at all. He should only be conscious of his capacity for feeling more and more strongly as the analysis proceeds. The analyst, on the other hand, with a firm grip on the reality of the situation, is merely responding to the patient's increasing emotional strength.
> (De Forest 1942, 138)

Clara Thompson, also an American based in New York, was analyzed by Ferenczi in the summers of 1928 and 1929.[58] She wrote a
response saying that, in her judgement, Ferenczi had a tendency to
carry his ideas to extremes, and the "idea of admitting one's fallibil-
ity to the patient" could be understood as inviting mutual analysis.
"To admit to a patient that one is wrong is one thing. To enter
into extensive free association as to one's unconscious motives in
making the error is quite another" (Thompson 1943, 65). On the
other hand, "Two of his ideas I have found of great value: i.e. that
the analytic situation is a human situation involving the interaction
of two personalities, and that no therapeutic results are possible unless the patient feels and is accepted by the analyst". Here, wrote
Thompson, "The difficulty lies in the definition of the word 'love.'
I think Ferenczi was not entirely clear on this matter" (Thompson
1943, 64–65). She issued a strong caution against any practice making the analytic situation dramatic.

New writers

The one sense in which the difficulties of communications in wartime were of some benefit to the *Journal* was that new contributors
got the chance to write. My understanding of Strachey's character
and behaviour is that he would have wanted to include new people
anyway.[59] And it might have been the case that the pre-war tendency to give priority to the papers of psychoanalytic grandees in
the *Journal* had never been to his liking, because in the middle of a
draft briefing paper on the subject of training during Controversies, he came up with this rather odd sentence, "Thus we shall all
agree that failure to have read an article by Federn published in the
Zeitschrift in 1926, though regrettable, is not a ground for exclusion".
War made it absolutely necessary for him to seek out different writers. Here, again, we come up against the disadvantage of not knowing how the *Journal* had previously acquired its writers because so
few documents have survived.[60] A sensible guess is that some papers
were sent speculatively, but others were sought out. In the letters to
Michael Balint at the ABPS, there is one from Strachey taking the
initiative and offering to translate and publish the "Identification"
chapter of Alice Balint's book on child psychology.[61]

During Strachey's editorship, John Bowlby, Ignacio Matte-Blanco,
and Marion Milner were all published in the *Journal* for the first

141

time; Ronald Fairbairn had his first substantial, non–clinical *Journal* paper; and Roger Money-Kyrle, who had contributed very many abstracts and book reviews since 1927, also achieved his first *Journal* paper in his own right. This last was "Some Aspects of Political Ethics from the Psycho-Analytical Point of View" (1944), which engaged directly with the morality of World War II, including being keenly critical of pacifists. Hardly surprisingly, Matte-Blanco, Milner and Fairbairn all examined aspects of internal objects. In his way, Bowlby did so too, but negatively, writing in "The Influence of Early Environment in the Development of Neurosis and Neurotic Character",

> It is my belief that both good and bad mothers exist in fact as well as in phantasy, and that a child's emotional development is very dependent upon his mother's unconscious feelings about him. It seems probable that most mothers are reasonably good but that the mothers of neurotic children are frequently bad, in the sense that they have very strong feelings of hatred and condemnation towards their children or else make inordinate demands from them for affection.
>
> (Bowlby 1940, 178)

The *Journal* also gave Bowlby 45 pages (in two instalments) on his "Forty-Four Juvenile Thieves: Their Characters and Home-Life", where he reported on the methods of assessment and clearly communicated his absorption with children's family circumstances, remarking upon "the degree of association between the Affectionless Character and a history of mother–child separation" (Bowlby 1944, Part II, 109).

Matte-Blanco at this time was interested both in "id-impulses" during treatment, on which subject he was quite close to Strachey's 1934 and 1937 work on technique (but cited Bibring 1937 instead),[62] and in the analysis of internal objects. Thence his paper "On Introjection and the Processes of Psychic Metabolism" uses both drives theories and the new Kleinian work. What he wrote was in part drawing upon Paula Heimann's presentation. He said:

> I do not know how far she would agree with me, however, in what I am about to say. The process of assimilation which she has so aptly described is carried, in my opinion, to an extent which

involves the actual disappearance of what has been called the internal object.

(Matte–Blanco 1941, 26–27)

Fairbairn, as is fairly well-known, wanted to rewrite Abraham's revision of libido theory,

> Nevertheless, my own findings leave me in equally little doubt that the paranoid, obsessional and hysterical states—to which may be added the phobic state—essentially represent, not the products of fixations at specific libidinal phases, but simply a variety of techniques employed to defend the ego against the effects of conflicts of an oral origin.

Further, he questioned whether the "anal phases" are not in a sense an artefact (Fairbairn 1941, 252 and 264). Fairbairn's 1944 "Endopsychic Structure Considered in Terms of Object-Relationships" is quite dazzling in its innovative metapsychology, with a dramatis personae of egos and internal objects named by him, such as internal saboteur and rejecting object. Probably, this is one of the intellectual high points of the *Journal* during those years; its confidence is summed up in Fairbairn's words: "unless it is assumed that internal objects are structures, the concept of the existence of such objects becomes utterly meaningless" (Fairbairn 1944, 76).

Marion Milner contributed first a case history of a suicidal female child, which she had read to the Society in June 1944, and then an investigation based on the same case in which she set herself the task of analyzing how an academic psychology book would approach the material (Milner 1944, 1945). She used *General Psychology* by Sebastian (W.J.H.) Sprott, Professor of Psychology at the University of Nottingham, translator of *The Future of An Illusion*, and an old friend of James Strachey.[63] Milner made a reasonable case for some comparisons between what she and her child patient expressed as internal objects and Sprott's conceptual language, for example, in his having written that "the organism may take an external objective into itself" (Milner 1945, 148).

Although D.W. Winnicott qualified as an analyst in 1934, until Strachey took over, it seems that he too, like Money-Kyrle, had been given reviews to write but had not yet had a paper of his own published in the *Journal*. Possibly Winnicott was too busy, first with

143

hospital and then with war work, and perhaps Ernest Jones had not encouraged him. A passage in King and Steiner (1991, xxiv) might also indicate that Winnicott was subject to a reluctance or difficulty in writing: "from a letter to Susan Isaacs (dated 13 June 1942) Klein had problems with him because he did not give her his contributions early enough for her or the group to vet them, and he had made a number of 'blunders'". Although it would be interesting to be able to say either that Strachey used their analytic bond to pressurize Winnicott into writing, or that something about having his old analyst as editor enabled Winnicott finally to contribute several thousand words for the *Journal*, I have not found any indications in the archive sources.[64] In 1941, Winnicott's lively and illustrative "Observation of Infants in a Set Situation", which is the spatula play paper, was published.[65] In 1945, "Primitive Emotional Development" appeared in the *Journal*. Here Winnicott presented his thesis of "three processes which seem to me to start very early: (1) integration, (2) personalization, and (3), following these, the appreciation of time and space and other properties of reality—in short, realization" (Winnicott 1945, 139). In the language he used and the lines of thought pursued, the paper was another radical development in object relations theory.

The examination of internal objects

From a theoretical perspective, the most distinctive characteristic of the *Journal* from 1939 was this increasing concentration on internal objects and other theories of object relations. Indeed, the whole subject runs throughout the 1940s issues like the analogy of the red thread of the English Navy woven into its ropes, which Freud had liked and borrowed from Goethe (Freud 1905, 22–23 fn2). The increasing use of the term and concept of internal objects by Melanie Klein and the analysts associated with her was one of the planes on which the Society seemed at risk of splitting, and the papers he published show that Strachey sought to address the crisis through the *Journal*. With Marjorie Brierley and Alix Strachey, he began a project of identifying meanings and encouraging dialogue. Arguably, the first paper in the process was Brierley's "A Prefatory Note on 'Internalized Objects' and Depression" in the 1939 Jones Heft.[66] Brierley was distinguished by her quiet manner and high intellect, and like Payne and Strachey, was intent on avoiding a schism. The Controversies armistice initiative of May 1942, which called for ordinary courtesy and a self-denying ordinance against vendettas, was her idea (Hayman 1994, 384; King and Steiner 1991, 163–165). After Strachey, she was the analyst most involved with the *Journal's* work from 1940 to 1945.[67]

Brierley wrote that "internalized objects" may seem to contravene the idea of the tendency of the ego towards synthesis because the so-called normal person was generally regarded as having succeeded in making a relative whole of himself. At this point, her thinking was that internalized objects only announce themselves in severe neuroses and borderline cases, especially with marked depression. She offered an interesting hypothesis, which was that dominance of either introjection or projection in an individual creates a natural bias: those of an introjecting tendency may be too uncritical of the existence of internal objects, whereas "people who make habitual use of projection mechanisms seem likely to have far more difficulty in appreciating that 'internalized objects' are in any sense real" (Brierley 1939, 242).

Next, Alix Strachey wrote a short and careful paper, drawing some distinctions between uses of the term "internal". In "A Note on the Use of the Word 'Internal'" (1941), she discerned three broad categories with some overlap. First, mental states and things belonging to the mind; second, objects, situations, and events created by imagination as they appear in dreams, delusions, and phantasies; and third, objects, situations, and events that are specifically believed to be inside a person, acknowledging the latter "is a special case of Class 2— of imaginary things" (Strachey 1941, 37). She wrote that we often confuse the sense in which we use the word internal; "when we say 'internal', we do not always know if we mean 'mental', 'imaginary' or 'inside'". Alix Strachey thought that to call an object internal when arguing clinically created the danger of seemingly having proved the patient experienced it as specifically inside of him when actually it might be that "we have discovered nothing to show that this is so", and it could rather be the case that the analyst has made internal (in the sense of meaning imaginary), equivalent to internal meaning supposed by the patient to be inside.

Our misuse of the word "internal" is a symptom rather than a cause of the difficulty we have in distinguishing between what is inside, what is mental and what is imaginary; and … this difficulty is inherent in the nature and status of phantasies about the things inside one's own body and other people's bodies.

(Strachey 1941, 42–43)

Brierley's second publication on the subject, "'Internal Objects' and Theory" (1942), is distinctive in that she identifies a failure to distinguish between percepts (objects of perception) and concepts when turning from clinical events to theory; she had consulted fairly closely with James Strachey on this distinction, as he is quoted on page 108.[68] She wrote that, although it is recognized that theoretical formulations have little place in interpretations to patients, "On the whole we are less vividly alive to the corresponding conclusion that perceptual terms have little place in theory". Evidently the paper was intended to move the debates within the Society onwards, as she requested that as many members as possible report their clinical findings, and that a ban was observed about "the public interpreta-tion of any Member's suspected bias as an illegitimate method of ar-gument". Brierley's written tone is forthright. Citing Alix Strachey's article, she wrote: "We must ask Melanie Klein to which of these types of object she is referring at any given instance" (Brierley 1942, 107). And she continued,

It is manifestly unfair, as Joan Riviere once said in discussion, to label as an animist any one engaged in investigating the phenom-ena of animism. But Melanie Klein's methods of description do sometimes give rise to uneasy doubts as to whether her views are not, in fact, animistic. She is so keenly alive to the child's actual beliefs that she sometimes gives the impression of explaining her theory in terms of these beliefs.

(Brierley 1942, 109)

As Brierley and the Stracheys had probably intended, her 1942 pa-per was responded to or reacted against when the Discussions of Scientific Differences began in January 1943. Susan Isaacs addressed Brierley's 1942 and 1937 papers when she commenced presenting to the Discussions. This developed into a discourse, with the two pursuing differences over whether the percept or concept distinction made by Brierley was justified, then went further, with Brierley in-troducing the idea that,

146

[...] the general theory of psycho-analysis, in its most abstract definition, is a psychology of mental processes and their organization. For such a psychology, mind ceases to be a thing, or entity, and becomes a nexus of activities, a sequence of adaptive responses.

(Brierley 1944, 97)

Isaacs responded directly via the *Journal*, writing that,

In her present emphasis on mental phenomena as processes, and her view that metapsychology is a theory of mental process, Dr. Brierley is thus bringing closer together Freud's later metapsychology (those major elements in it which do the fullest justice to his own clinical discoveries), and the views of outstanding general psychologists.

(Isaacs 1945, 59)

The Brierley-Isaacs exchanges continued after Strachey's tenure despite Isaacs's failing health, notably with her "The Nature and Function of Phantasy" (1948). And yet it would be wrong to give the impression that there was just the remarkable two-woman exchange. Many of the British papers about object relations in the *Journal* during the period are involved in citing, reciprocating, refuting, synthesizing, or furthering the contributions of others.[69] For example, Matte-Blanco (1941) is majorly based upon Heimann's earlier presentation on sublimation (duly acknowledged); Heimann then published a version of her presentation in the *Journal* in 1942 in which she both acknowledged and took issue with what he had written (Heimann 1942, 16); and then, if we follow onto King and Steiner, we find Heimann's further theorizing on internal objects and introjection presented at the Discussions of Scientific Differences in June 1943 as "Some Aspects of the Role of Introjection and Projection in Early Development", with the responses of Brierley, Friedlander, Payne, Hedwig Hoffer, Isaacs, Glover, and Sharpe (King and Steiner 1991, 502–561). A nodal diagram of all the cross-referencing would be a wonderful thing, and one requiring a great deal of space.

Through the *Journal*, by publishing topics related to the Discussions of Scientific Differences, Marjorie Brierley and James Strachey together had supported debate and opened up discussion within the Society of new research and theories. It may not be an exaggeration to describe this as a shared thinking space. For a short while, it was available to everyone in the British Society, but after the Anna Freudians withdrew in January 1944, it was shared by the remaining British Freudians and non-Kleinians, the Middle Way-ers and the associates of Melanie Klein.[70] This was still a remarkable achievement, but as we know, it was one that Edward Glover rejected entirely, and about which Anna Freud had almost insuperable reservations.

Victory in Europe was celebrated in May 1945. Eight months later, in the board meeting minutes book, it was noted that Mr Strachey had indicated that he would not be able to continue as editor of the *Journal*. Adrian Stephen was appointed as the next editor.[71] Strachey gave no particular reason, but the original agreement was only three years' service, the holding of offices in the British Society and Institute had been reformed, and projects for a complete works of Freud had restarted.

Conclusions

Because the *Journal* was cut off internationally due to World War II, and because the Society was absorbed in questions as to how the infant or child self is formed, its wartime editions have a particular continuity: the same concerns and questions reoccur, and there are noticeable and highly interesting themes, some of which have been picked out here. The pressure from great external threats caused by World War II and of perceived internal dangers within psychoanalysis brought about conditions in which some resemblance might be found between British psychoanalysis and an experiment with organisms in a bell jar in which several different strains of object relations analysis grew rapidly under pressure. New theories and practices evolved under stress and then spiralled out to make a universe of British object relations, the growth of which has slowed but still continues. These new forms were, as Michal Shapira's study *The War Inside* demonstrated, put to work particularly in treating and caring for children and thus contributed to shaping post-war Britain (Shapira 2013). And, by dint of being the editor of the *Journal*, James Strachey got to publish some of the most important research first.

The research presented here demonstrates that Strachey was a capable editor in terms of instigating and editing papers, of encouraging new writers, of being strict with senior ones when necessary, and of attending to costs and schedules. It was important to him that the *Journal* reflected current events, including strife on several fronts.

A more timid editor might have hesitated to engage with the Controversies and stuck to papers on safer subjects; on the other hand, any kind of partisan editor could have exacerbated matters. As for what he thought of the work of an editor, Strachey once jotted down some word associations, including "Midwife" written above the word "Editor".[72] The conclusion made here is that as editor, he had functioned somewhat like a midwife who assisted in the labour of various brainchildren of the Society during the Controversies period. As his jottings implied, Strachey does not deserve to take the credit for the originality of those who wrote for the *Journal* in his era, such as Klein, Isaacs, Fairbairn, Winnicott, and Bowlby, but arguably he does deserve credit for letting them put their findings in print at a time when every proffered opportunity within the Society was scrutinized for bias or self-interest. As has been discussed, a hypothesis is made here that Strachey aimed to operate the *Journal* as he had recommended that psychoanalytic training should be run: as an open forum. It has been demonstrated that Strachey was minded to publish a great deal of the presentations and debate of the Discussions of Scientific Differences in the *Journal*. That would have been a radical action: to imagine what the impact might have been, it would have meant that all members of the British Society would have been kept equally informed, along with anyone else outside of the war zones to the extent that the *Journal* could reach them.

In the course of studying the individual I *Journal*s alongside The Freud–Klein Controversies (King and Steiner 1991) in order to write this article, another meaning of Strachey's time as editor has grown in significance. It is incorrect to use the title Independent Group in 1940–1945, but there were clear Middle Way-ers in the Society who were in favour of dialogue and worked to prevent a schism. Prominent among these were Sylvia Payne, Marjorie Brierley, James Strachey, and Ella Freeman Sharpe, who, between them, held the balance of power in the Training Committee from 1942 to 1944. Sylvia Payne was increasingly acting as chief executive to the Society; Marjorie Brierley exerted herself in organizing and contributing to the Discussions of Scientific Differences; and Strachey, as Riccardo Steiner has written, orchestrated the Training Committee's reports (King and Steiner 1991, 262). Sharpe was very much her own woman but would act to preserve the unity of the Society, and, following King and Steiner 1991 (665–667), she finally and politely became exasperated with the politicking. In terms of the number of candidates qualified, she was the most effective training analyst (King and Steiner 1991, 193–195). With James Strachey also as editor, the communications power of the *Journal* was available to Middle Way-ers objectives. Of course, these objectives could and still can be questioned and criticized: we see a definite concentration of power in four pairs of hands, though arguably that was an improvement on Jones's patriarchal–aristocratic government. Any verdict on the matter is, inevitably, subjective. Mine is to read Brierley, Payne, and Strachey, along perhaps with Sharpe who was less in communication but generally in agreement, as making a benign alliance to keep the Society from falling apart, and to argue that James Strachey made an important contribution by seeking to ventilate some of the heat and noise generated by conflict over concepts of internal objects through the *Journal*.[73]

Riccardo Steiner's 1994 paper shows how hard Ernest Jones had worked to establish the *Journal* as the authoritative voice of scientific and medically acceptable psychoanalysis. As editor number two and the pre-eminent British male lay analyst of his era, Strachey was less medically and hierarchically orientated and more interested in fostering debates. World War II severely limited the international content available to him and cut down the size and frequency of the *Journal*, and it is important to remember this qualification, but because of his belief in free speech, the ideal of an open forum, and his aim to avoid a schism, James Strachey's editions of the *Journal* were decidedly contemporary and open-minded. They have a dynamic quality because he, with Brierley and probably also with Alix Strachey for support and editorial back-up, engaged with change by facing internal and external strife realistically, taking a pluralistic approach to theory, and striving to provide an accurate reflection of a remarkable period of conflict and creativity.

Notes

1 The word "survived" is deliberate: documents from the editorial work of the *Journal* in its early decades are scarce in the ABPS, though the publishers' accounts and letters (S–C–03–01 and 02) are better represented.

2 Interesting items about the *Journal*'s history appear sporadically within the *International Journal of Psycho-Analysis*: for example, in Glover's mildly satirical recollections "In Praise of Ourselves" (1969), or in a letter reminding readers of Ferenczi's role in instigating the *Journal* written by Falzeder and Dupont (2000).

3 The word psycho-analysis was always hyphenated at the time, though by the end of the *Standard Edition* work, Strachey wished it were not (see *SE* vol. I, p. xviii, fn 2).

4 ABPS S-C-0-2-A-07.

5 ABPS S-A-03-A, Society minutes book 15 June 1939.

6 6ABPS S-C-0-2-A-07.

7 Compulsory registration for women aged 20–30 was introduced in the Second National Services Act in December 1941.

8 His interests included classical music, opera, theatre, and ballet: as Winnicott wrote in the official obituary, "Strachey had grown up" [...] "in this third area, the area of cultural experience" (Winnicott 1969, 130). And he also enjoyed crossword puzzles and reading detective novels (Meisel and Kendrick 1986, 219–220; BL AddMS 60688 to Noel Olivier, August 1935).

9 However, after 1939, when Anna Freud was in London and closely involved in her father's copyrights, Riviere, as a Kleinian, was a less likely choice as either editor or for further translation work.

10 BL AddMS 60706–60712 correspondence of James and Lytton Strachey.

11 BL AddMS 60708 to L Strachey 19 April 1910.

12 BL AddMS 60710 to L Strachey 11 August 1915.

13 13ABPS S-A-04, Institute board minutes 6 December 1939.

14 WLA Klein PP-KLE-C.91.

15 The crisis being the invasion of Poland and declaration of war by France and Britain.

16 Alix and James Strachey had experienced the problems of getting Klein's abundance of theories, ideas, and examples into English in 1924, when Alix worked with her on six lectures given to the British Society that summer. Alix Strachey wrote about Klein's impulse to rewrite and expand, "as soon as she begins rewriting it fresh efflorescences will blossom out from every nook and cranny" (Meisel and Kendrick 1986, 267).

17 WLA Klein PP-KLE-C.91 to Jones 29 November 1939.

18 WLA Klein PP-KLE-C.91 to Strachey 20 November 1939.

19 WLA Klein PP-KLE-C.91 Typescript p. 1A. Grosskurth made a connection to traits of the men in Klein's own life, "quite clearly she had Emmanuel, Arthur and Koetzel in mind" (Grosskurth 1986, 236).

20 The radical French theatre La Compagnie des Quinze performed the play at the Globe Theatre. Klein's copy of the pro-gramme is in WLA Klein PP-KLE-C.91. Obey wrote three versions of Don Juan; apparently, only the final one, The Man of Ashes, has survived, whereas Klein is likely to have seen an early Don Juan by the same playwright performed in 1934. See Ackroyd (1935) and Knowles (1968).

21 WLA Klein PP-KLE-C.91 letter from Strachey 15 November 1939.

22 WLA Klein PP-KLE-C.91 Typescript p. 16.

23 23WLA Klein PP-KLE-C.91 letter from Strachey 15 November 1939.

24 24WLA Klein PP-KLE-C.91 letters from Strachey 15 February 1940 and Brierley 17 January 1940.

25 WLA Klein PP-KLE-C.91 from Riviere 2 April 1940 and 8 April 1940.

26 26WLA Klein PP-KLE-C.91 from Strachey 13 April 1940. As a guide, a minimum of £500 now (https://www.measuringworth. com/ calculators/ppoweruk/).

27 27WLA Klein PP-KLE-C.91 from Riviere 8 April 1940.

28 See Paskauskas 1993, 637–638 regarding Freud and Jones's failed attempts to get Strachey to translate *The Future of an Illusion*. He did translate the relatively short but important "Constructions in Analysis" for the *Journal* in 1938. It is clear that between 1927 and the outbreak of war, Alix Strachey was doing more work as a translator than her husband was, translating Abraham (with Douglas Bryan), Klein, and Sigmund Freud.

29 Freud's *An Outline* is the paper most sought after from the *Journals* of 1939–1945 via the PEP search.

30 30ABPS P17-F-A-01 from Jones 9 March 1940 with Strachey's dated addition 8 April 1940.

31 The Stracheys were precise in recording either single or shared credits, and therefore, it seems Alix Strachey had not translated any Freud during this particular period.

32 Alix Strachey also reviewed German and English books in the 1940–1942 *Journals* (unless the abbreviation of "A.S." used indicated Adrian Stephen, which seems less likely) and probably assisted with editing and proof-reading.

33 Talk by John Forrester on Bloomsbury and Psychoanalysis at the Freud Museum, 8 November 2013 (https://thefreudmuseum.podbean. com/e/freud-in-bloomsbury/).

34 The Gesammelte Werke project was being worked on in London from 1940, and for a while, there was a bibliography research group that included Bribring.

35 Perhaps the most interesting example is the long letter in the ABPS, reference P04-C-E-14, written by Strachey to Jones in 1922 about a translation for besetzung, explaining his rationale for cathexis and seeking the latter's approval for its introduction.

36 An expression of preparation for a period of famine or other forms of scarcity.

37 The *Journal*'s subscription revenues must have fallen due to poor communications and exchange rates.

38 Hardback reference books were expensive then, compared with now. For example, publishers often asked for the return of review copies, and a copy of Moses and Monotheism in 1939 might now cost the equivalent of £108.10, using the multiple of average income calculation (https://www.measuringworth.com/calculators/ppoweruk/).

39 How the Discussions were entitled varies. I have tried to stick to Discussions of Scientific Differences for the presentations made by Isaacs, Heimann, and Klein and the responses to these, and to use the word Controversies in a broader sense to include all topics in contention, for example, also organizational reform and leadership problems.

40 ABPS P17-F-D-01 from Strachey 12 February 1943.

41 The complete text of King and Steiner 1991 is available on PEP (www.pep-web.org). Informative shorter accounts include Hayman 1994, King 1994, and Robinson 2011.

42 His resistance to schism and clear resentment of the Controversialists is shown in a letter in which he likened himself to Mercutio in Romeo and Juliet, and inveighed against "(bloody foreigners)" (King and Steiner 1991, 32–33).

43 Letter to Rupert Brooke 5 January 1909 (Hale 1998, 54); A. Stephen diary 4 July 1909 (MacGibbon 1997, 65); subscription receipt for the Union of Democratic Control and letter from Harold Wright of the National Council Against Conscription to Strachey 25 March 1916, both in the Strachey Trust Private Papers.

44 The transcript of Isaacs' presentations published in King and Steiner 1991 differs substantially from Isaacs' "The Nature and Function of Phantasy" (1948).

45 ABPS P43/C/A/18 Strachey's impulse to publish candidly was continuing as in the letter to Michael Balint of October 1943 referred to later in the chapter, Strachey also stated that he was thinking of running his own Training Committee presentation quoted earlier here (in "slightly castrated form") in the *Journal*. That document is described as Discussion Memorandum in King and Steiner 1991, 602–616.

46 Again, see Steiner 1994 and 2011 for the history of the *Journal* under Jones's direction.

47 ABPS S-C-02-A-07 to Jones 9 August 1941. In the letter, Payne was protesting at problems around a book on analytic technique in which Glover included criticisms of Klein's work, to which Klein had objected. The book contributed to anxiety within the Society.

48 Chosen to represent the Anna Freudian, non-aligned (or British Freudian or Middle Group – Rickman was no longer counted as part of Klein's group), and the Kleinians within the Society, which underlines the point made here that the editorship carried political power.

49 For example, BL AddMS 60710 11 August 1915, a description written to Lytton of how C.L. Graves and he had delayed printing, worked late, and so got news of the fall of Warsaw into *The Spectator*.

50 My thanks to Riccardo Steiner for letting me read the English version of his new paper which is a further examination of the work of British analysts on war and social conflict in the war and inter-war years: "Zu den ersten Versuchen Britischer Psychoanalytiker, die gesellschafts-politischen Probleme ihrer Zeit zu analysieren", Jahrbuch der Psycho-analyse, 2019 vol. 78.

51 Before the Controversies, James and Alix Strachey had been on good terms with both Anna Freud, who had helped generously when Alix was gravely ill in Vienna in 1922, and with Klein, whom Alix had met in Berlin in 1924 and whose 1925 lectures in London he had proposed and assisted.

52 ABPS P17-F-B-03.

53 Multiple factors may have influenced her absence from the *Journal*, e.g. work at the Hampstead Nurseries, what stage she was at with research and theorizing, and – perhaps – a preference for publishing books rather than papers. However, as the subject here is the *Journal*, the criticisms of Anna Freud's 1927 *Introduction to the Technique of Child Analysis* that Jones had published in it should not be ignored.

54 53ABPS P17-C-C-01 and 02. Rosnick (2017) also includes the text of Strachey's Opening Remarks at a Practical Seminary.

55 ABPS P17-C-C-01 Notes numbered page 3, written on the reverse of a page proof of "The Psychology of Sexual Abstinence", there-fore dated 1943 or later. Adler, Jung and Rank are also on his list of post-Freudian theorists, which gives another indication of Strachey's pluralism. Klein too was on the list as, according to Strachey at least, her theories were post-Freudian.

56 For a short biography, see https://www.psychoanalytikerinnen.de-usa_bi-ografien.html#Forest. Also Brennan, BW. "Ferenczi's Forgotten Messen-ger, the Life & Work of Izette de Forest", American Imago 66, 427–455.

57 Alice Balint's 1943 paper, "Identification" also says something of Ferenczi's methods.

58 For a short biography, see https://www.psychoanalytikerinnen.de/.

59 He would have noticed that lay analysts particularly had few alterna-tive periodicals in which they could publish theoretical papers.

60 Another gap is the lack of information on how the *Journal's* content was approved post-Jones: did Strachey need to give a list of the pro-posed contents to the Publishing Committee?

61 ABPS P43/C/A/18 to Michael Balint, 19 October 1943. Balint, A. 1943 "Identification" *International Journal of Psycho-Analysis*: 97–107. The original was *A Gyermekszoba Pszichologiája, published in Budapest*

in 1931. The book was later published in English as *The Early Years of Life: A Psychoanalytic Study* (1954).

62 Matte-Blanco had Strachey as one of his control analysts.

63 Without more evidence, it is impossible to say if Milner's choice of Sprott was a coincidence.

64 Winnicott was in analysis with Strachey for ten years.

65 Adam Phillips noted that the observational part of that paper was presented in what he finds a "freer" form in 1936 as "Appetite and Emotional Disorder" to the British Psychological Society. His observation that the 1941 text is more organized suggests a possibility that Strachey had edited the paper (Phillips 1988, 72–74).

66 There is textual evidence that the paper was adapted for the Jones Heft. Jones's work is only referred to in footnotes 1and 2, whereas the closing paragraph (p. 245) refers to "our comparative study" of two works by Abraham and Klein, to which Brierley's text may originally have been an introduction.

67 Brierley contributed many abstracts and book reviews and remained an assistant editor of the *Journal* until 1978.

68 Throughout this paper, she changed from "internalized objects" to referring to internal objects.

69 Possibly, there were a few incidences of furthering confusion as well.

70 The term Middle Way-ers is used to indicate those few individuals who took actions intended to support dialogue and compromise. Strictly speaking, the Independent stream of the British Psychoanalytical Society dates to a later period (Robinson in Lowenberg and Thompson 2011, 217).

71 70ABPS S-A-04-01 Institute board minutes of 7 January 1946 and 27 May 1946.

72 ABPS P17-C-C-01 Strachey notes B beginning with "voyeur".

73 The ventilation metaphor is Strachey's. In ABPS P-17-C-C-02 Opening Remarks Typescript p. 25 fn, he had written that the safeguard both against inefficient therapy and false theorizing from what takes place during therapy "is thorough and constant ventilation of the transference itself".

References

Aykroyd, P. 1935. *The Dramatic Art of La Compagnie des Quinze*. London: E. Partridge Limited.

Balint, A. 1943. "Identification." *International Journal of Psycho-Analysis* 24: 97–107.

Balint, M. 1936. "The Final Goal of Psycho-Analytic Treatment." *International Journal of Psycho-Analysis* 17: 206–216.

Bell, A. O., ed. 1997. *Diaries of Virginia Woolf*, vol. 1. London: Hogarth Press.

Bibring, E. 1941. "The Development and Problems of the Theory of the Instincts." *International Journal of Psycho-Analysis* 22: 102–130.

Bowlby, J. 1940. "The Influence of Early Environment in the Development of Neurosis and Neurotic Character." *International Journal of Psycho-Analysis* 21: 154–178.

Bowlby, J. 1944. "Forty-Four Juvenile Thieves: Their Characters and Home-Life 1940." *International Journal of Psycho-Analysis* 25(19–53): 107–128.

Brierley, M. 1939. "A Prefatory Note on 'Internalized Objects' and Depression." *International Journal of Psycho-Analysis* 20: 241–245.

Brierley, M. 1942. "'Internal Objects' and Theory." *International Journal of Psycho-Analysis* 23: 107–112.

Brierley, M. 1943. "Theory, Practice and Public Relations." *International Journal of Psycho-Analysis* 24: 119–125.

Brierley, M. 1944. "Notes on Metapsychology as Process Theory." *International Journal of Psycho-Analysis* 25: 97–106.

Brome, V. 1985. *Ernest Jones – Freud's Alter Ego*. London: Caliban Books.

De Forest, I. 1942. "The Therapeutic Technique of Sándor Ferenczi." *International Journal of Psycho-Analysis* 23: 120–139.

Eidelberg, L. 1944. "A Contribution to the Study of Slips of the Tongue." *International Journal of Psycho-Analysis* 25: 462–470.

Fairbairn, W. D. 1944. "Endopsychic Structure Considered in Terms of Object-Relationships." *International Journal of Psycho-Analysis* 25: 70–92.

Fairbairn, W. R. 1941. "A Revised Psychopathology of the Psychoses and Psychoneuroses." *International Journal of Psycho-Analysis* 22: 250–279.

Falzeder, E., and J. Dupont. 2000. "Sándor Ferenczi." *International Journal of Psycho-Analysis* 81: 805–805.

Fenichel, O. 1945. "The Concept of Trauma in Contemporary Psycho-Analytical Theory." *International Journal of Psycho-Analysis* 26: 33–44.

Ferenczi, S., and O. Rank. 1925. *The Development of Psycho-Analysis*. Trans. C. Newton. New York: Nervous & Mental Disease Publishing.

Freud, S. 1905. *Jokes and Their Relation to the Unconscious. The Standard Edition of the Complete Psychological Works of Sigmund Freud*, Vol. VIII. London: Institute of Psychoanalysis/Hogarth Press, 1960.

Glover, E. 1943. "The Concept of Dissociation." *International Journal of Psycho-Analysis* 24: 7–13.

Glover, E. 1969. "In Praise of Ourselves." *International Journal of Psycho-Analysis* 50: 499–502.

Grosskurth, P. 1986. *Melanie Klein: Her World and Her Work*. New York: Knopf.

Hale, K., ed. 1998. *Friends and Apostles*. New Haven, CT: Yale University Press.

Hayman, A. 1994. "Some Remarks about the 'Controversial Discussions'." *International Journal of Psycho-Analysis* 75: 334–358.

Heimann, P. 1942. "A Contribution to the Problem of Sublimation and Its Relation to Processes of Internalization." *International Journal of Psycho-Analysis* 23: 8–17.

Isaacs, S. 1940. "Temper Tantrums in Early Childhood in Their Relation to Internal Objects." *International Journal of Psycho-Analysis* 21: 280–293.

Isaacs, S. 1943. "An Acute Psychotic Anxiety Occurring in a Boy of Four Years." *International Journal of Psycho-Analysis* 24: 13–32.

Isaacs, S. 1945. "Notes on Metapsychology as Process Theory: Some Comments." *International Journal of Psycho-Analysis* 26: 58–62.

Isaacs, S. 1948. "The Nature and Function of Phantasy." *International Journal of Psycho-Analysis* 29: 73–97.

Jones, E. 1941. "The Psychology of Quislingism." *International Journal of Psycho-Analysis* 22: 1–6.

Jones, E. 1942. "The Concept of a Normal Mind." *International Journal of Psycho-Analysis* 23: 1–8.

King, P. 1994. "The Evolution of the Controversial Issues." *International Journal of Psycho-Analysis* 75: 335–342.

King, P., and R. Steiner, eds. 1991. *The Freud-Klein Controversies 1941–1945*. London: New Library of Psychoanalysis.

Klein, M. 1940. "Mourning and Its Relation to Manic-Depressive States." *International Journal of Psycho-Analysis* 21: 125–153.

Klein, M. 1945. "The Oedipus Complex in the Light of Early Anxieties." *International Journal of Psycho-Analysis* 26: 11–33.

Klein, M., and J. Riviere. 1937. *Love, Hate and Reparation*. London: Hogarth Press/Institute of Psycho-Analysis.

Knowles, D. 1968. *French Drama of the Inter-war Years, 1918–1939*. London: Harrap.

Laplanche, J., and J. B. Pontalis. 1973. *The Language of Psychoanalysis*. Trans. D. Nicholson-Smith. London: Karnak Books.

MacGibbon, J. 1997. *There's the Lighthouse*. London: James James.

Maddox, B. 2006. *Freud's Wizard – The Enigma of Ernest Jones*. London: John Murray.

Matte-Blanco, I. 1941. "On Introjection and the Processes of Psychic Metabolism." *International Journal of Psycho-Analysis* 21: 17–36.

Meisel, P., and W. Kendrick, eds. 1986. *Bloomsbury/Freud*. London: Chatto & Windus.

Milner, M. 1944. "A Suicidal Symptom in a Child of Three." *International Journal of Psycho-Analysis* 25: 53–61.

Milner, M. 1945. "Some Aspects of Phantasy in Relation to General Psychology." *International Journal of Psycho-Analysis* 26: 143–152.

Mitchell, J. 1986. *The Selected Melanie Klein*. London: Penguin.

Money-Kyrle, R. E. 1944. "Some Aspects of Political Ethics from the Psycho-Analytical Point of View." *International Journal of Psycho-Analysis* 25: 166–170.

Paskauskas, R. A., ed. 1993. *The Complete Correspondence of Sigmund Freud & Ernest Jones 1908–1939*. Cambridge, MA: Harvard University Press.

Phillips, A. 1988. *Winnicott*. London: Fontana Paperbacks.

Roazen, P. 1995. *How Freud Worked*. Lanham, MD: Jason Aronson.

Robinson, K. 2011. "A Brief History of the British Psychoanalytical Society." In *100 years of IPA: the Centenary History of the International Psychoanalytical Association, 1910–2010*, edited by P. Lowenberg, and N. L. Thompson. London: International Psychoanalytical Association/ Karnac Books, Ch 18, 196–223.

Rosnick, P. 2017. "Opening Remarks at a Practical Seminary by James Strachey." *The International Journal of Psychoanalysis* 98: 729–754.

Sanders, C. R. 1953. *The Strachey Family 1588–1932*. Durham, NC: Duke University.

Schilder, P. 1941. "Types of Anxiety Neuroses." *International Journal of Psycho-Analysis* 21: 209–228.

Shapira, M. 2013. *The War Inside*. Cambridge: Cambridge University Press.

Steiner, R. 1987. "A World Wide International Trade Mark of Genuineness?—Some Observations on the History of the English Translation of the Work of Sigmund Freud, Focusing Mainly on His Technical Terms." *The International Review of Psycho-Analysis* 14: 33–102.

Steiner, R. 1994. "'The Tower of Babel' or 'After Babel in Contemporary Psychoanalysis'? – Some Historical and Theoretical Notes on the Linguistic and Cultural Strategies Implied by the Foundation of the Int. J. Psycho-Anal., and on its Relevance Today." *International Journal of Psycho-Analysis* 75: 883–901.

Steiner, R. 2011. "In All Questions, My Interest Is Not in the Individual People but in the Analytic Movement as a Whole." *The International Journal of Psycho-Analysis* 92: 505–591.

Steiner, R. 2019. "Zu den ersten Versuchen Britischer Psychoanalytiker, die gesellschaftspolitischen Probleme ihrer Zeit zu analysieren", *Jahrbuch der Psychoanalyse:* 78: 211–256.

Sterba, R. 1944. "The Formative Activity of the Analyst." *International Journal of Psycho-Analysis* 25: 146–150.

Strachey, A. 1941. "A Note on the Use of the Word 'Internal'." *International Journal of Psycho-Analysis* 22: 37–43.

Strachey, A. 1943. *A New Psycho-Analytic Vocabulary*. London: Bailliere, Tindal & Cox/Institute of Psycho-Analysis.

Strachey, J. 1945. "List of English Translations of Freud's Works." *International Journal of Psycho-Analysis* 26: 67–76.

Thompson, C. 1943. "The Therapeutic Technique of Sándor Ferenczi': A Comment." *International Journal of Psycho-Analysis* 24: 64–66.

Weiss, E. 1942. "Psychic Defence and the Technique of its Analysis." *International Journal of Psycho-Analysis* 23: 69–80.

Winnicott, D. W. 1941. "The Observation of Infants in a Set Situation." *International Journal of Psycho-Analysis* 22: 229–249.

Winnicott, D. W. 1945. "Primitive Emotional Development." *International Journal of Psycho-Analysis* 26: 137–143.

Winnicott, D. W. 1969. "James Strachey 1887–1967." *International Journal of Psycho-Analysis* 50: 130–132.

Young-Bruehl, E. 1988. *Anna Freud: A Biography.* New York: Summit Books.

JOAN RIVIERE

The professional and personal struggles
of a formidable foundress of *the International
Journal of Psychoanalysis*

Rachel B. Blass

She chose to spend her time and energy (...) in helping others to
write.

(Heiman, 1963)

Joan Riviere (1883–1962) is best known as a leading Kleinian analyst, an early colleague of Melanie Klein, who made some significant contributions to the analytic literature, especially in her 1936
"A contribution to the analysis of the negative therapeutic reaction"
and, to a lesser extent, in her papers on female sexuality (e.g., 1929)
(Figures 5.1 and 5.2).

While she did not present a paper at the famous Controversial Discussions held at the British Society in the 1940s, her role as clarifier
and advocate of the Kleinian school is also commonly recognized,
in part due to papers she contributed to earlier controversies in 1927
and 1936 (Blass Chapter 7, this volume) as well as her 1952 edited
book *Developments in Psychoanalysis*, in which she includes and intro-
duces the papers of the Controversial Discussions. She also notably
represented and elucidated Kleinian psychoanalysis in her lecture
"Hate, greed and aggression" (1936), which complemented Klein's
"Love, guilt and reparation" lecture, which was presented that same

Figure 5.1 Joan Riviere in garden, Courtesy British Psychoanalytical Society, Copyright: Melanie Klein Trust.

Photo of Joan Riviere in garden, undated, Archives of the British Psychoanalytical Society, P02-D-09. The Archives of the British Psychoanalytical Society have granted us kind permission to reproduce this photograph. Copyright: Melanie Klein Trust.

Figure 5.2 Riviere aged 30 with her daughter Diana (Born 1908) – (picture taken circa 1912–1913). Courtesy British Psychoanalytical Society, Copyright: Melanie Klein Trust.

Photo of Joan Riviere and Diana Riviere, Archives of the British Psychoanalytical Society, P02-D-08. The Archives of the British Psychoanalytical Society have granted us kind permission to reproduce this photograph. Copyright: Melanie Klein Trust.

year. Moreover, her writings reveal how her clinical work, central to many of her papers, is guided by a Kleinian analytic stance and technique. But Riviere came to psychoanalysis before her encounter with Klein (which apparently first occurred in 1920). She entered a personal analysis with Ernest Jones in 1916 and began practising analysis herself in 1919, the same year that she joined the newly in-augurated British Psychoanalytical Society. She first met Freud in 1920, and entered analysis with him in 1922, the analysis with Jones having gone wrong in several ways. Her true devotion, no doubt, was to psychoanalysis itself, which she believed was most fully ex-pressed, both clinically and theoretically, in Klein's understanding of Freud's ideas, and thus she welcomed Klein upon her move to London in 1926 and became one of her staunchest supporters there.

Joan Riviere's main, significant, and unique impact on psychoanalysis, however, occurred not so much through the novelty or breadth of the ideas that she put forth or her extensive clinical practice (her patients including John Bowlby, Susan Isaacs, and Donald Winnicott; her supervisees including Henri Rey, Herbert Rosenfeld, and Hanna Segal). Rather, her special contribution was through the form of her writing, its accurate, vibrant, poetic quality, which helped make essential psychoanalytic ideas come alive in their full force and depth of meaning, and it was through her efforts to bring these ideas to life in promoting and nurturing the writing of others and sensitively translating their works. As Paula Heiman recalls in her obituary (1963): "she chose to spend her time and energy much more in helping others to write ... she had unlimited patience with people who wanted help with their ideas". It may be suggested that it is because of the subtle nature of her contribution, that "many psychoanalysts working today have", as Hanna Segal (1991) commented, "no idea of the debt that they owe to her".

It is in this context that Joan Riviere's contribution to *the International Journal of Psychoanalysis* can be best appreciated. Her official role was that of the *Journal's* translation editor, but in effect she played a much broader role: she reviewed and edited, wrote for the journal and helped others to do so (as may be seen from her correspondence with Melanie Klein (see IJP 2019 the compendium and Section C below), and influenced the shape and direction of the *Journal* in its formative years. Private exchanges with Freud, Jones, and Strachey testify to this.

One may think of the subtler nurturing nature of Riviere's contribution as, in a sense, feminine – a feminine stance, however, which was clearly at times imposed upon her by her male colleagues. For when Riviere sought overt recognition for her work, overcoming in this process a severe and exacting superego of which Freud speaks in letters to Jones and Riviere herself (and anonymously in his discussion of the negative therapeutic reaction in the *Ego and the Id*), she was, at times, met by reluctance that had sexist undertones. This is most notable in Jones's efforts to prevent her receiving the official title of "translation editor" of the *Journal*, efforts which were thwarted only by Freud's firm insistence in total disregard for Jones concerns (see Section A below). From 1922 until 1937, Riviere's name received modest mention on the inside cover of the *Journal* as she suggested to Freud, a solution which ultimately denied her recognition by later generations who encounter the *Journal* only through bound volumes (or later through PEP) which happen to omit that side of the cover.

Riviere's 1929 paper on "Womanliness as masquerade" describes women whose femininity is exaggerated to conceal the fact that, in phantasy, they castrated men and stole their potency, which, in turn, is tied to destructive rivalrous feelings in relation to the maternal object. In the formidable presence of Joan Riviere, recognized by all who encountered her, something of this kind of sense of potency seems to have found expression. She was without doubt a "powerful and impressive personality" (Segal, 1991 – see Section C below), her appearance "very tall, beautiful, but severe-looking, always dressed immaculately", fit well with her generous, deep, and yet fierce and demanding character. She was as demanding of herself as she was of others, including of the *Journal* and the translations it published, including her own (Section "Riviere on issues in translation into English of analytic texts"). In November 1930, Jones writes to Freud: "Your kind remark about the *Journal* is encouraging and I will transmit it to Mrs. Riviere who is always in despair at what she calls our low achievements (the *Zeitschrift* she thinks has sunk to hopeless depths!)" (Letter to Strachey).

Freud, in contrast, greatly appreciated Riviere's capacities and the quality of her translation and felt very warmly towards her (Section "On Riviere's role as "translating editor" and her potential"). In 1927, he writes to her:

> Although I complained about the tardiness of the English translation, you should not think that I have forgotten or underestimated the zeal and achievements of my English friends—above all, you… The only reproach I can hold against you is that you have so seldom sent me news of yourself and your work. Allow me to hope that you will be more generous in that respect in times to come.
>
> (23 February 1927)

Translation for Riviere was not a mere technical skill. It was part of a relationship to writer, reader, and text. In a letter to Strachey, upon the completion of Vol 1 of the *Standard Edition,* she writes: "Yes, you must feel lonely now parted from your first volume. I know this feeling. I don't forget how the tears ran down my cheeks as I wrote the last words of the Introduct. Lectures translation" (21 December 1952). And to Jones she confides: "I think that translation may have given me acute sensitiveness about the reader's point of view" (10 September 1956). For Riviere, translation involved a transformation of a "writer's thought in the spirit of his own language", which, like analytic writing itself, was for her a creative act, an act aimed at producing beauty and bringing forth truth. In a reflection on Freud, written on the occasion of the centenary of his birth, Riviere describes how she only gradually came to understand the urgent prescription Freud gave her to write ("Write it, write it, put it down in black and white"), how it allows one to create something *"outside you...give it an existence in-dependently of you"* (Riviere, 1958). Riviere goes on to speak of the creative and procreative qualities of Freud's writing process, and she does so with a pathos that suggests that she felt that in her own work – writing, helping others do so, and translating the writing of others – she too was partaking in this process. She writes of Freud:

> It was a deeper impulse in him—a capacity to construct and cre-ate something, a living body, to build up outside himself a body of knowledge that comprehends the single facts of which it is formed and yet transcends them...There was a marriage in him of the seeker after existing truth and the creator giving the world a new living truth—The scientist and the artist in one
>
> (1958)

A fervent search for truth and beauty drove Riviere in her analytic work and in her commitments to analytic writing. As Paula Heiman explains (1963): "To her what was beauty in art, was truth in science and love in human relationships", and to all three she was fully de-voted. It is this devotion that makes her description of insights into the depths of human experience so vivid and clear, and her contri-bution to psychoanalysis and more specifically to the formation of *the International Journal of Psychoanalysis* so valuable.

Selected Texts

A. On Riviere's role as "translating editor" and her potential

Excerpts from letters between Jones and Freud

1 April 1922, 111 Harley Street, London

Dear Professor,
    ... A day or two ago I received a handsome offer from Mrs. Riviere to take over the revision of translations for the Journal.

There is no one who could do it as well, and there is no work that I would more gladly be relieved of, for it is physically impossible to do it adequately alone. The delicate problem arises, however, about Rickman, whom I should like to see as assistant editor. He is far easier to work with and will also become a man of standing. But I have also to realise that this particular work he cannot do well. Owing, doubtless, to some remaining infantilism, he makes extraordinary mistakes in spelling and even in grammar, not the mistakes of an uneducated man, but those of a schoolboy, so that his work would all have to be checked carefully. I had known this previously, but forgot it in my urgent wish to find a good fellow-worker, and it was brought vividly to my mind in some recent manuscript he sent me. So Mrs. R. would logically have the better claim to the title so far as work is concerned. On the other hand I should not care to give such a slap in the face to the Americans as to put another lay person on the official staff of the Journal immediately after their strong representations to me on the subject of lay analysis. As you know, I am on the side of the lay analysts, but I hope to change the American view by some more persuasive method than this would involve. I also doubt whether Mrs. R. would attach any weight to the title. She speaks a lot about "recognition", but it seems to mean on the part of yourself, myself and a couple of others, rather than on the part of the outside public. I am glad to be able to shift this delicate matter on to your broad shoulders! I will write to her gratefully accepting your offer (Verschreiben for "her" because I know it is thanks to you that she has made it), but saying nothing about a title.

I am not surprised that she is shewing her best qualities at present, and she certainly has many, but I only hope that she will have an opportunity to bring out and overcome her bad ones. As she will not be with you in the critical ninth month, when she changed with me, it is a question if it might not be possible later on to regard her as an advanced patient, which of course she is in every respect, and provoke the feelings of disappointment by active therapy? As you remark, the feminine side does not lie far beneath the surface, but that fact I can honestly claim as a result of the analysis with me: the change in such ways, and also in her attitude towards children, has been very great indeed. I was surprised at your suspecting any sexual relations between us and think it must have been a Verlesen of the expression "declaration of love", which was of course on her side only. To satisfy her vanity she has always maintained the theory that I also was in love with her but was not honest enough to confess it, but I have never been able to confirm this in my self-analysis. She is not the type that attracts me erotically, though I certainly have the admiration for her intelligence that I would have with a man. But, speaking more generally, you need never have any fear about me in such respects. It is over twelve years since I experienced any temptation in such ways, and then in special circumstances; even should it arise in the future, which is very unlikely now, I have no doubt at all of my capacity to deal with it.

I am sorry you are not satisfied with the first two volumes of the Journal. Looking through the contents I see that of 27 articles half are translations, and of the others three only can be described as poor. Then the reviews have a good standard on the whole. Still it is better to be dissatisfied than the reverse, and I have every hope that by collecting a better staff of helpers we shall be able to improve steadily. Among English and American periodicals we already take a fairly high standing, so I gather...

6 April 1922, Vienna, IX. Berggasse 19
Dear Jones,
....I was glad to inform Mrs. Riviere that you had accepted her offer and would write her so. She seems to be a powerful helpmate and we should bring her to some good use. I further think if she does the work she has a right to claim a title and a position, or she would find no recognition with the other ones. Her own proposal is that she should be named as "translating editor" on the inside of the cover and her address given for all communications regarding translations. I do not think the Americans could object to this way of distinguishing her. (Nor can I lay any stress on the Americans' reluctance. It is well known all through the world of ΨA that Rank the editor of both our Periodicals is a layman.) I am of opinion besides that you owe her a compensation having aggravated her analysis by inconsequent behaviour as you confess yourself. I do not think there will be any need of artificial means to bring up her whims and claims but as long as these last are not more immodest, I am ready to support them with you.

B. Riviere on issues in translation into English
of analytic texts

A note to Strachey doubting whether one could ascribe to her the translation of Freud's "Interminable", stating that it was so horrid and nasty that she could only read the proofs of it while listening to a Mozart Mass. She asks of Strachey to list the translator as "unknown", and Strachey offers to put in an "imaginary name". It would seem, however, that he ultimately attributed it to Riviere (Figures 5.3 and 5.4).

In 1923, the *International Journal* publishes a review by Riviere of Freud's book on *Group Analysis* (1921), translated by James Strachey. There she addresses problems with translation, including special limitations of the English language and that of remaining true to the text at the expense of its beauty.

> this new science was entirely without a terminology in our language. Then the long literary traditions of English have so hardened and stereotyped the meaning of such numbers of our words, so many others have become degraded and colloquialized till they are unfit for use in an impersonal document, that we cannot fall back, to anything like the degree that is possible in German, on our ordinary speech for rendering these new conceptions. Our English shyness in matters of sex, our extreme sensitiveness in matters of 'taste', results in an almost insuperable difficulty in expressing ourselves at all, outside poetry, on anything relating to the emotions. Psycho-analysts have to grow accustomed to mentioning love, but even they cannot find an English word for *Verliebtheit,* the state of being in love. All these things increase the difficulties of the translator...
>
> Efforts have been made to bring the terms, or at least those used in authorized translations of psycho-analytic work, up to some standard of uniformity and accuracy. In this, beauty of language can only be a secondary consideration, however much those responsible may regret that it is so. But apart from technical terms, which matter comparatively little, a rendering of the original that furnishes the reader with a complete and clear expression of the writer's thought, in the spirit of his own language and undisturbed by any reminiscence of the original wording, has a beauty of its own.

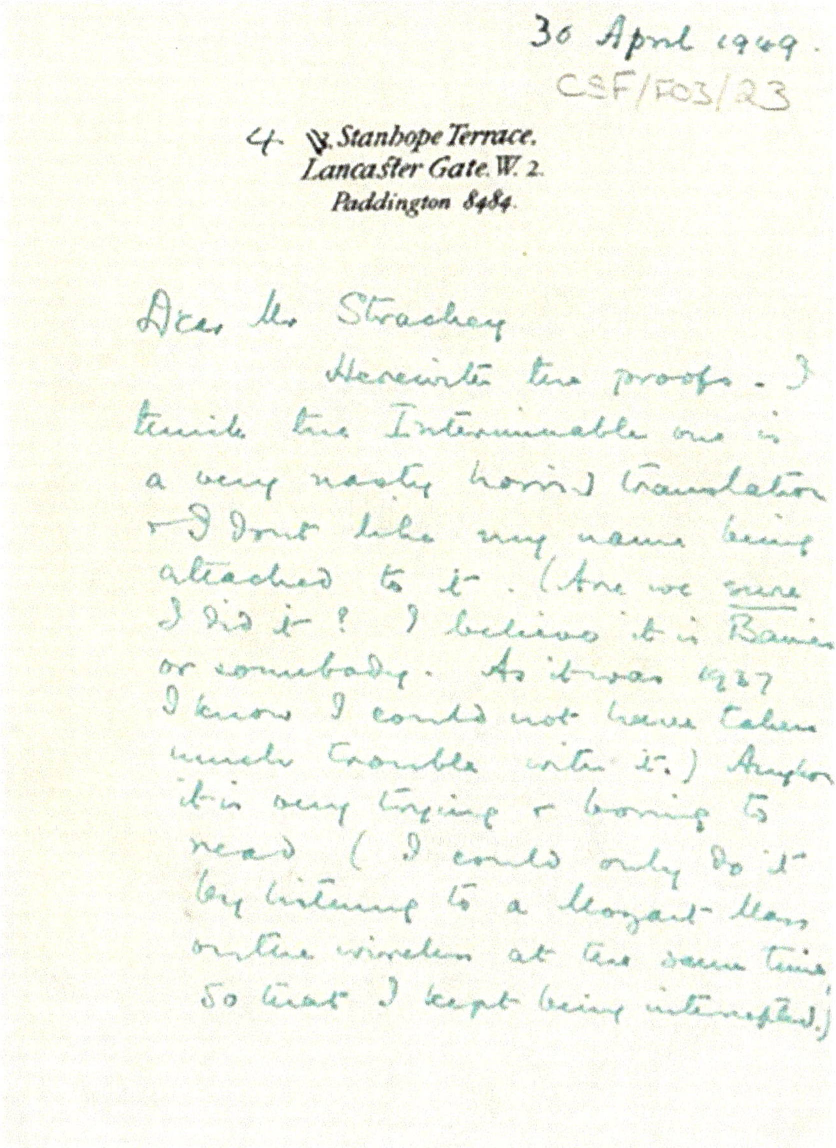

30 April 1949.

CSF/FO3/23

4 & Stanhope Terrace,
Lancaster Gate. W. 2.
Paddington 8484.

Dear Mr Strachey

Herewith the proofs. I
think the Interminable one is
a very nasty horrid translation
— I don't like my name being
attached to it. (Are we sure
I did it? I believe it is Baines
or somebody. As it was 1937
I know I could not have taken
much trouble with it.) Anyhow
it is very trying & boring to
read (I could only do it
by listening to a Margaret Mann
on the wireless at the same time
so that I kept being interrupted.)

Figure 5.3 Letter from Joan Riviere to Strachey 1949. Courtesy British Psychoanalytical Society, Copyright: Melanie Klein Trust.

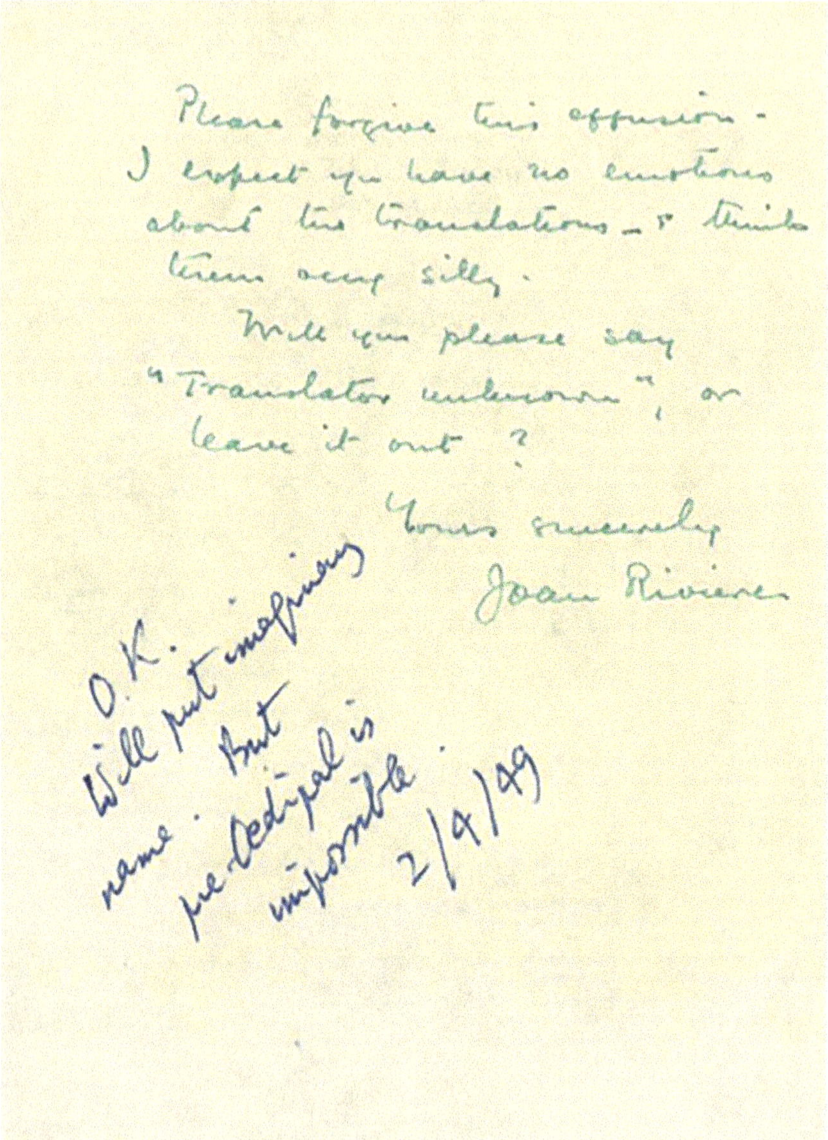

Please forgive this effusion -
I expect you have no emotions
about the translations - & think
them very silly.
Will you please say
"Translator unknown", or
leave it out?
Yours sincerely
Joan Riviere

O.K.
Will put inquiring
name.
But
pre-Oedipal is
impossible.
2/9/49

Figure 5.4 Letter from Joan Riviere to Strachey 1949. Courtesy British Psychoanalytical Society, Copyright: Melanie Klein Trust.

Letter from Joan Riviere to James Strachey, 30 April 1949, Archives of the British Psychoanalytical Society, P17-F-C-02. The Archives of the British Psychoanalytical Society have granted us kind permission to reproduce this photograph. Copyright: Melanie Klein Trust.

C. Powerful devotion: to psychoanalysis, to advancing life and truth, and to serving the *International Journal*

From Strachey's obituary of Joan Riviere, *the International Journal of Psychoanalysis*, 1963:

We were still in Vienna when early in 1922 she herself came out for analysis with Freud; and it was then that I got to know her better. When we were all back in London we were faced with the frightful work of bringing out the four volumes of the Collected Papers. But it is quite wrong to say 'we'. My wife and I did the straightforward job of the case histories. The organizing, translating, or revising other people's translations of the mass of miscellaneous papers in the other three volumes fell entirely on Joan Riviere. This was finally accomplished by 1925, and thereafter her translating activities were mainly devoted to the Journal. The only further volumes of Freud which she translated were The Ego and the Id and Civilization and its Discontents —the title of which, incidentally, is a brilliant proof of her gift for finding the mot juste. The later Freud volumes fell into other hands. Hers were in fact sufficiently filled with her Journal work. In those early days the greater part of the Journal consisted of papers translated from the German Zeitschrift and Imago. And her function was either to translate these papers herself or to correct the translations made by other and usually inadequate assistants. She was eventually given the rather miserable recompense of being described as the Translation Editor—a post which she occupied till the end of 1937, after which she felt that she might legitimately resign it in order to devote herself to things—clinical work and original writing—which interested her more. Those who knew her will know how time-consuming this Journal work was—how all her spare time every evening was devoted to it. But it was in fact the foundation on which all our English knowledge of psycho-analysis was first built.

.... Perhaps I was afraid of her. A lot of people were. I often felt sure, for instance, that Ernest Jones was. And indeed she was a very formidable person... I think she also regretted my non-committal attitude to questions of psycho-analytic theory. Non-committed was a thing she herself could never be. And that I think was, in spite of everything, what was so splendid about her. What she believed she believed; she was not afraid. And what she believed she would say, straight out and uncompromisingly. Such courage is a rare and precious thing.

From Paula Heiman's obituary, The International Journal of Psychoanalysis, *1963*

In the small community of two she was a most creative speaker, and produced many bold and original ideas, which she could have expressed in published articles for the benefit of many instead of only one listener. I often urged her to do this, without success. She chose to spend her time and energy much more in helping others to write. ... She was able to discern not only more clearly what the other person, fumbling for formulation, meant to say, but often she saw much sooner than the other the goal towards which his ideas moved and which they should reach. At the same time, she was exceedingly careful in her suggestions and clarifications not to impose on the other, and not to interfere with his specific individual style. She had indeed a very high respect for the individual.

I remember vividly how she once offered me a complete sentence for a draft of mine that expressed my ideas more clearly and carried them a step further. She had taken much trouble to compose it. She offered it to me with the full understanding that I might feel it as alien, and she was not offended when, precisely for the reason she had foreseen, I did not accept it.

... She expected from others the same concern for the essential and service to a cause that she herself was ready to give, and this made her unwilling to spare people's sensibilities. These she regarded as distracting and petty, and she would not waste time and trouble to avoid treading on people's corns. If it is necessary to walk, you walk, corns or no corns! Thus she could at times appear inexorable in her demands. But it was quite a different matter when she thought that a person was seriously in need of help....

The dominant force in her design of living, the key to her personality, was the striving after beauty, beauty in nature and in man-made things. This need for beauty had nothing in common with precious aestheticism nor with a Hedda Gabler's craving to die in beauty. To Joan Riviere the beautiful was the expression of the life instinct, and it demanded the exertion, the caring, the workmanship, the blood and sweat, the toil and tears that go into the act of creating or discovering beauty. Serendipity had little part in it. She was indeed contemptuous of easy achievements. When I once praised a writer's fluency, she said scornfully: 'Oh, but it is facile'. For herself the style in which she expressed her ideas was extremely important. But where other authors were concerned she distinguished sharply between substance and form, and could appreciate the former even when her sensibilities were offended by the latter.

She sought and found the beautiful in the three areas of life to which she devoted herself: in art, in science, and in human contacts. To her what was beauty in art, was truth in science and love in human relationships.

A common element of the greatest significance to her in these three fields of human experience was that of caring: to consider carefully, to pay attention to details, to take trouble, to be thorough, were imperative values to her. She abhorred flightiness, carelessness, and indifference, and seeing these as the constituents of the manic state, the 'manic defence' appeared to her to represent almost the quintessence of psychopathology, the pure expression of the death instinct...That she herself was capable of discerning and presenting the fullness of an experience with exquisite clarity and beauty finds expression in all her writings. I will quote a short passage from her paper: 'On the Genesis of Psychical Conflict in Earliest Infancy' (1936), describing infantile aggressive impulses.

Limbs shall trample, hit and kick; lips, fingers and hands shall suck, twist, pinch; teeth shall bite, gnaw, mangle and cut; mouth shall devour, swallow and "kill" (annihilate); eyes kill by a look, pierce and penetrate; breath and mouth hurt by noise, as the child's own sensitive ears have experienced.

The artist and the scientist were both at work in her writing. I once commented on the fact that a typewritten page through her corrections looked like a painting. Her lines, dashes, brackets, asterisks, signs of punctuation, and transpositions imparted a beautiful design. She was quite surprised at my remark: to her writing was painting.

Concluding comments

Joan Riviere's character and how she applied herself to the founding and furthering of the *International Journal* in its early years, as has been briefly described here, arouses admiration. Her devotion, her serious work ethic, her aspirations for excellence and beauty, her generosity in helping others develop their ideas and put them into writing, her desire and marked ability to convey ideas clearly, forcefully, accurately, and true to reality and to the mind of their originator, especially where translation is needed, and above all her love of analysis and fierce commitment to the deep truths it opens us to, have clearly shaped the *Journal*. And as one may feel towards a revered ancestor, one would like to hope that her influence is ongoing and continues to shape it; that the qualities that she brought to the *Journal* continue to guide and inspire all those who contribute to it.

References

Abram, J. Blass, R. Bruns, G. Diercks, C. McQuillan, D. Thompson, N. Tutter, A. Weiss, C. (2019). The Enigma of the Hour: Display Case Compendium: 100 years of Psychoanalytic Thought curated by Simon Moretti with Goshka Macuga and Dana Birksted-Breen. *Int. J. Psycho-Anal.*, 100(6):1481–1613.

Archives of the British Psychoanalytical Society.

Freud, S. (1923). Group Psychology and the Analysis of the Ego. *Int. J. Psycho-Anal.*, 4:183–199.

Freud, S. & Jones, E. (1993). *The Complete Correspondence of Sigmund Freud and Ernest Jones 1908–1939*, ed. R.A. Paskauskas. Cambridge, MA, and London: Belknap Press of Harvard University Press.

Heimann, P. (1963). Obituary. Int. J. Psychoanal., 44: 228–235.

Hughes, A. (1992). Letters from Sigmund Freud to Joan Riviere (1921–1939). *Int. J. Psychoanal.*, 19:265–284.

Riviere, J. (1929). Womanliness as a Masquerade. *Int. J. Psycho-Anal.*, 10:303–313.

Riviere, J. (1958). A character trait of Freud's. In The Inner World and Joan Riviere. Collected Papers: 1920–1958 ed. A. Hughes. London: Karnac Books, 1991

Segal, H. (1991). Foreword. In The Inner World and Joan Riviere. Collected Papers: 1920–1958 ed. A. Hughes. London: Karnac Books, 1991

Strachey, J. (1963). Obituary. *Int. J. Psychoanal.*, 44: 228–235.

MARJORIE BRIERLEY'S CONTRIBUTIONS TO *THE INTERNATIONAL JOURNAL OF PSYCHOANALYSIS*

Nellie L. Thompson

Marjorie Brierley's "'Hardy Perennials' and Psychoanalysis" (1969) was written for the fiftieth anniversary issue of *the International Journal of Psychoanalysis (IJP)*. Anne Hayman's excellent memorial paper on Brierley noted that her writing was "most elegant and fluid... often with an engaging dry wit" (Hayman, 1986, p. 384). This dry wit is on display in the title of Brierley's final paper. "Hardy Perennials" may be read as a self-reference since her middle name was Flowers. The OED defines "hardy" as bold, daring, and showing temerity, and "perennial" as enduring, a plant with deep roots. Brierley's title is a sly reminder that she is a psychoanalyst with "deep roots" and the temerity to think for herself.

Brierley's paper was written from the perspective of an analyst who had been a member of the British Psychoanalytical Society since 1927, participated in the Controversial Discussions in the 1940s, published ten papers in *the IJP*, and been a prolific book reviewer for the journal.[1] Her long-voiced view that psychoanalytic theory was not immutable was fundamental to her conviction that psychoanalysts should encourage independent minds and creative thought, however disruptive or antithetical new work might first appear in relation to received psychoanalytic concepts or technique:

> Some [psychoanalytic] concepts have stood the test of time, but it is none the less imperative to stress that theory is not Holy Writ and hypotheses are bound to need modification as knowledge grows. *This is one good reason for encouraging independent and creative thinking in our members and tolerating differences of opinion that may seem for a time to be diametrically opposed.*
>
> (Brierley, 1969, p. 448; italics added)

In considering an analyst's contributions to psychoanalytic literature, the influence they may exercise through their writing as book reviewers is seldom acknowledged. When analysts publish their collected papers, they often fail to include reviews they may have written, reinforcing the assumption that book reviewing is not integral to an appraisal of their contributions to the development of psychoanalytic theory and the controversies that often accompany it.[2] An outstanding review is distinguished by thoughtful critiques of important publications that highlight the nature and scope of the author's contributions, accompanied by incisive questions from the reviewer about the theoretical and clinical implications of the work under consideration. From a contemporary perspective, such reviews are a lens through which past analytic writing and thought, of both the author and reviewer, is brought to life for today's analysts. The reader gains insight into the intellectual character of the reviewer that, in turn, may contribute to an appreciation and understanding of how to read their work.

All of this is true of Brierley's contributions as a prolific reviewer of important works for *the IJP*. The psychoanalytic sophistication and rigour of her reviews often contrasts with more conventional reviews, whose aims are usually more prosaic, that is, to simply describe a book's content. Reading between the lines, the inescapable conclusion is that Brierley's work as a psychoanalytic reviewer and reader *par excellence* brought her intellectual gratification and pleasure in equal measure.

Beginning in 1931 and continuing for the next four decades, she published over 60 reviews in *the IJP*, of work by Edward Glove (*Psycho-analysis*), Melanie Klein and her circle (*Contributions to Psycho-Analysis 1921–1945; Developments in Psychoanalysis*),

Helene Deutsch (*The Psychology of Women, 2 Vols*), C.G. Jung, Karen Horney (*Our Inner Conflicts: A Constructive Theory of Neurosis*), David Rapaport (*Organization and Pathology of Thought: Selected Sources*), Heinz Hartmann (*Ego Psychology and the Problem of Adaptation; Psychoanalysis and Moral Values*), Ernest Jones (*Sigmund Freud: Life and Work, 3 Vols.*), R.D. Laing (*The Divided Self*), H.S. Guntrip (*Schizoid Phenomena, Object Relations and the Self*), among others. She also reviewed the 24 volumes of the Standard Edition of *The Complete Psychological Works of Sigmund Freud*.[3]

Brierley eschewed telling readers what to think of the ideas, arguments, and findings in the book under review; readers must decide for themselves what to think, drawing on their clinical experience and theoretical orientation. She credited the training she received from her second analyst, Edward Glover, "not least for the training which preserved to me the ability to think for myself" (Brierley, 1951, p. 5).

There is a readily observable relationship between Brierley's approach to book reviewing on the one hand, and her conception of the clinical encounter and the analyst's role on the other. In Brierley's 1937 paper, "Affects in Theory and Practice", she emphasized the singular role of affect in analytic work. "In practice we find our way only by following the Ariadne thread of transference affect, and go astray if we lose contact with this" (Brierley, 1937, p. 257). The analyst's capacity for empathy facilitates certainty concerning what the patient is feeling. "Analysis cannot proceed unless there is established between analyst and patient that mysterious affective contact which we call 'rapport' . . . It is only by empathy that we can be certain of what the patient is feeling" (ibid., pp. 266–267).

In a later paper, "Theory, Practice and Public Relations" (1943), Brierley wrote that while our knowledge of empathy and *rapport* may be inexact, "it is evident that feeling *with* the patient" is akin to an identification, while "thinking about the patient" implies an object relationship (Brierley, 1943).[4] There is a correspondence between the distinction that Brierley draws between the role of these two relationships in the therapeutic encounter and her approach to the role of the book reviewer. She begins a review with a fair, even sympathetic, account of the author's thesis, but then moves to an intellectual assessment of the cogency and value of the author's argument or findings against the current state of psychoanalytic theory and clinical technique. In other words, she commences her review by thinking with the author, and then thinks about author's ideas and arguments, and their cogency and value for enriching psycho-analytic theory and clinical practice.

Brierley's reviews of Melanie Klein and R.D. Laing Melanie Klein

Before and during the Controversial Discussions in the British Society in the early 1940s, Brierley adopted an agnostic position on Melanie Klein's theories, recognizing their clinical and theoretical value while expressing reservations about some of her conclusions. Her 1950 review of Klein's *Contributions to Psychoanalysis 1921–1945* (1948) opens by referencing the tensions that accompanied the Controversial Discussions and endured after the "Gentlemen's Agreement" was negotiated by Sylvia Payne and Anna Freud in 1945 (King and Steiner, 1992, pp. 906–907). These fissures led the Society's non-partisans, among whom Brierley counted herself, to form an informal "middle group" that "drew fire from both extremes but continued its unspectacular efforts to view the new work in rational perspective" (Brierley, 1950, p. 209).

In this vein, Brierley adopted a measured approach to Klein's contributions, urging readers to study her papers chronologically in order to follow the "germination, growth and establishment of specific ideas" in her work (ibid). She recognizes that a notable development in Klein's thinking is her paper, "Contributions to the Psychogenesis of Manic-Depressive States" (1935), where she depicted the onset of the depressive position in infants as occurring around the age of four months. This elevation of the centrality of the depressive position in psychic development made Klein's work more controversial. Addressing the reader, Brierley writes that analysts will have to decide for themselves whether Klein has "ousted the Oedipus complex from its priority in psycho pathogenesis" (p. 211). Klein's depiction of development has also been criticized as exclusively progressive, leading her to underestimate "the role of regression in pathogenesis, such as in the aetiology of manic-depressive states" (ibid).

In Brierley's view, two sets of considerations should be kept in mind when assessing the validity of Klein's work. First, it is not an alternative or substitute for psychoanalysis, but rather a contribution to psychoanalysis, the validity of which is still being assessed.

Second, the foundations upon which Klein has built her theories, "the mechanisms of introjection and projection, the occurrence of identification with introjected objects (melancholia), and the existence of pre-genital mental organization (primacies) were all recognized before Melanie Klein began her work" and may be found in the writings of Freud and Abraham (ibid). Beyond these considerations, the criterion for the validity of Klein's contributions cannot be whether they are in agreement with or differ from Freud. To adopt this standard is to stultify the development of psychoanalysis and deprive it of any claim to be a science (ibid). Clinical testing of new ideas and theories requires time and distance and cannot be compressed to suit the controversies of the moment. She concludes rather wryly that human considerations may frustrate a more cautious and measured approach to new ideas: "it is not the scientific problems that are insoluble", rather it is because they are linked to human actors that they are intractable (ibid).[5]

Brierley's 1953 review of *Developments in Psychoanalysis* by Melanie Klein, Paula Heimann, Susan Isaacs, and Joan Riviere expresses her disquiet with the air of certainty found in the writings of Klein and her followers (Brierley, 1953). The coherent picture of early infantile life that Klein has advocated causes unease among her critics since it "lends colour to the feeling that, in the opinion of its proponents, all that remains to be done is to fill in the gaps and modify details in what is otherwise a self-sufficient theory" (ibid). Brierley reiterates her position that "healthy growth" in psychoanalysis is nurtured by "allowing creative minds to follow their own bent to the full (as Melanie Klein has done) and tolerating the differences of opinion which result from differing angles of approach" (ibid). Psychoanalysis needs original thinkers "as much, or more, than any other science". Such thinking can become a danger, however, if "creative minds are tempted to feel that they have the 'Truth', the whole Truth and nothing but the Truth" (ibid., p. 158). Yet Brierley also expresses a note of optimism about the capacity of psychoanalytic theory to absorb and transform differing points of view by citing the fact there is little "common ground" between Heinz Hartmann and Melanie Klein. Nonetheless, "in so far as contributions from either of these very different types of mind are found to stand the test of time and experience, they will achieve co-ordination as theory expands" (ibid., p. 158).

While praising Susan Isaacs's lucid paper on phantasy, Brierley observes that many analysts do not accept her extension of the term phantasy to the whole field of unconscious mentation because

> it implies that unconscious processes are all alike, whereas the term 'phantasy', more narrowly defined, singled out a specific type of [unconscious] activity. Objection has also been taken to the apparent denial to the infant of any primitive sense of reality, if the earliest experiences are interpreted (felt) wholly in terms of inherited unconscious expectations.
>
> (Ibid. p. 159)

Although Klein has affirmed that the environment is important at every stage of development, there is yet "little that could be called precise knowledge about the preconditioning of the infant's first experiences" (ibid).

R.D. Laing

Brierley's review of R.D. Laing's *The Divided Self: A Study of Sanity and Madness* (1960) opens with praise for the author's sympathetic exploration of

> the subjective experience of borderline and fully developed psychotic persons . . . It is essentially an attempt to convey to readers, with the aid of relevant quotations from patients, what it feels like to be verging on insanity or to be completely mad.
>
> (Brierley, 1961, p. 288)

Accompanying Brierley's admiration for Laing's achievement is a plea that analysts allow him his own language to express his findings.

The foundations of Laing's efforts to understand the mad or near-mad are existential psychology, and "ontological insecurity" which Laing characterizes as the basic pathogenic experience of individuals who are mad or near-mad.

> Only existential thought has attempted to match the original experience of oneself in relationship to others in one's world by a term that adequately reflects this totality. Thus, existentially, the concretum is seen as man's *existence*, his *being-in-the-world*.
>
> (Brierley, p. 289)

In placing Laing's book within psychoanalytic literature, Brierley argues that there are affinities between Laing's conceptualization of the psychic experiences of schizoid and mad persons with those found in the writings of Harry S. Guntrip and D.W. Winnicott. For example, Laing writes that the anxiety that underlies "ontological insecurity" may take three forms: engulfment, implosion, and petrifaction and depersonalization. These states as described by Laing are compatible with Guntrip's description, using Fairbairn's language, of a split in the libidinal ego. Furthermore, Laing portrayed the "ontological insecurity" of schizoid, but still sane, individuals as an experience of a split between their mind and body where feeling is most closely identified with their mind.

> Normal people experience themselves as *'embodied'*, whereas the schizoid tend to feel themselves 'somewhat detached from their bodies' and therefore 'more or less unembodied.
>
> (Brierley, p. 289)

Brierley observes that here Laing has adopted Winnicott's notion of the "false" and "true" self to describe the schizoid individual. The body is the site of the "false" self – detached, disembodied – whereas the true self is looked upon by the individual with tenderness, amusement, or hatred, as the case may be (ibid).

Brierley opines that "apart from terminology", the affinities between Laing's conceptualizations and those of Guntrip and Winnicott demonstrate that Laing's theses are parallel to those of psychoanalysis. Since a writer's language is intrinsic to their conceptualization of new ideas, Brierley ends her review on a protective note towards Laing.

> This book does not set out to do more than throw light on the feelings and inter-relationships of 'divided' selves, but purely 'existential' interpretations seem a little thin ... However, this book is evidence that the young author is an acute and empathetic observer, well-endowed both intellectually and intuitively.
>
> (Ibid. p. 290)

Brierley expresses the hope that since Laing had undergone training at the British Psychoanalytical Society, eventually there would be a correlation between his existential approach and psychoanalysis.

181

Undoubtedly research workers do best when they use the conceptual tools most suited to them. Hence, psycho-analysis may have more to gain from encouraging him to continue on his own preferred lines than by deploring his dissatisfaction with some current psycho-analytical terminology and theory.

(Ibid. p. 290)[6]

Brierley's reviews of the Standard Edition (Appendix I)

Over a period of 13 years, between 1954 and 1967, Brierley reviewed *The Standard Edition of the Complete Psychological Writings of Freud* as the 23 volumes of his writings were published. Throughout, she is generous in her praise of James Strachey's Editor's Notes, annotations, and cross-references, while offering her own commentary on the volumes as they were published. They did not appear in chronological order; volumes IV and V, *The Interpretation of Dreams* and *On Dreams*, were the first to be published. The editorial considerations that resulted in the decision to have Brierley as the sole reviewer of the *Standard Edition* are unknown. A plausible assumption is that she was chosen because of her thorough grasp of the arc of Freud's intellectual development from his neurological orientation in the 1880s and 90s to his creation of psychoanalysis in the 1890s. Her reviews excel in integrating a description of the volume under review with a thread of commentary throughout all the reviews that highlights the generative theoretical ideas and clinical experiences that engaged Freud and led to important revisions in psychoanalytic theory.

When Brierley's reviews are linked chronologically to the *Standard Edition*, her discussion of Volume III (1893–1899) – *Early Psycho-Analytic Publications* (published in 1962) – and the last volume to be published, Volume I (1888–1899) – *Pre-Psychoanalytic Publications and Unpublished Drafts* (published in 1967) – are especially valuable for drawing out how concepts and discoveries found in his earliest writings, such as the aetiological importance of trauma, the concepts of "defence" and "cathexis", and the function of screen memories, which although later modified and transformed, found a place in his mature psychoanalytic thought. Paradoxically, the fact that Brierley reviewed the volumes of the *Standard Edition* as they were published, that is, out of chronological sequence, may have contributed to her emphasis on how the myriad papers and books written at different periods were theoretically and clinically related to one another and contributed to transformative creative moments in Freud's psychoanalytic thought.

At the conclusion of Brierley's review of Volume I, she rendered an assessment of Freud's work that remains germane:

> though the "psychic apparatus" described in *The Interpretation of Dreams* is obviously drawn from a neurological model, it is nevertheless a psychological scheme dealing with mental processes in terms of perception, memory ... and not with neuronal excitations ... His creation of psychoanalysis not only gave us the first effective instrument of mental research but laid the foundation of the first genuinely realistic understanding of mental and personal life and its relevance to the human situation in this troubled world.
>
> (Brierley, 1967, p. 325)

Editorial contributions

Brierley's contributions to *the IJP* were not confined to her reviewing. They included editorial work that has either been lost sight of or was undertaken anonymously. Edward Glover was appointed Director of Research of the London Institute of Psycho-analysis in the late 1920s. Under his direction, two Research Supplements, Nos. 3 and 4, on technique were published by *the IJP*.[7]

Supplement No. 3 (1928), *The Technique of Psycho-Analysis,* was comprised of six lectures given by Glover as a training course and published in *the IJP* in 1927 and 1928. The fourth supplement, *An Investigation of the Technique of Psychoanalysis* (1940), was edited by Glover, with Brierley's considerable assistance. The aim of this research was to "systematise and correlate work on the technique of psychoanalysis" in relation to typical problems encountered in clinical work (Glover, 1940, p. v). A questionnaire was created whose virtue in Glover's view was that it reflected a body of opinion that is otherwise seldom or never expressed (ibid). The original questionnaire (1932) was distributed to 29 practising analysts of the British Society, of which 24 were returned. The results of the questionnaire were discussed in a meeting of the British Psychoanalytical Society. A supplementary questionnaire was then distributed in order to obtain more information on some points; answers to the questionnaire were considered representative of the British Society up to 1938. But it fell to Brierley to sift and summarize the range of responses to the increasingly detailed and nuanced questions posed by the questionnaires. Glover acknowledged Brierley's not inconsiderable contribution to this research on psychoanalytic technique when it was published in 1940. "This by no means easy task was carried out by her with considerable skill and a reassuring measure of scientific detachment" (Glover, 1940, pp. v–vi). Years later when the report was reprinted as Part II in Glover's *The Technique of Psychoanalysis* (1955), his Prefatory Note was dropped, and with it Brierley's important role in this early research on psychoanalytic technique was erased from the record.

Brierley also anonymously reviewed manuscripts submitted for publication in *the International Journal of Psychoanalysis*. Her role as a reader was only publicly revealed when Willi Hoffer retired as editor of *the International Journal of Psychoanalysis* in 1959. On that occasion, he acknowledged:

> I am particularly indebted to the late Dr. John Rickman and to Dr. W. Clifford M. Scott, from whom I learned much during the period of our joint editorship from 1947 to 1949. From 1949 onwards, when I had become Editor-in-Chief, Dr. Marjorie Brierley has patiently and tirelessly given me a helping hand in assessing and improving manuscripts for publication; her judgement and advice have always been constructive and the thanks I have received from many authors are due to her.
>
> (Hoffer, 1959, p. 397)

Conclusions

Brierley's reviews are miniature essays that illustrate the seriousness with which she undertook the task of reviewing psychoanalytic literature, and of engaging with psychoanalytic thought. Her approach to an author's book mirrored her depiction of the analyst's dual role in the clinical encounter set forth in her paper, "Theory, Practice and Public Relations". That is, the analyst both thinks *with the patient* (identification with the author's thinking) and *about the patient* (an object relationship with author's work).

Brierley brought to reviewing a discerning analytic intelligence, intellectual rigour, clarity of thought, fairness, and an appreciation for authors whose writing brought to life the vast variety of human experience encountered by analysts in their consulting rooms.

Above all, she was unwavering in her conviction that psychoanalysts should encourage independent and creative thinking in their colleagues and tolerate differences of opinion in the interest of advancing psychoanalytic thought and clinical practice.

Appendix I

Marjorie Brierley's Reviews of The Standard Edition of the Complete Psychological Works of Sigmund Freud.

1953 Vols. IV and V

Brierley, M. (1954). *The Interpretation of Dreams. The Standard Edition of the Complete Psychological Works of Sigmund Freud*: Translated from the German under the General Editorship of James Strachey, in collaboration with Anna Freud, assisted by Alix Strachey and Alan Tyson. Vol. IV (1900) *The Interpretation of Dreams* (First Part). Vol. V (1900–1901). *The Interpretation of Dream (Second Part) and On Dreams.* 1953. *Int. J. Psycho-Anal.*, 35:68.

1953 Vol. VII

Brierley, M. (1954). *The Standard Edition of the Complete Psychological Works of Sigmund Freud*: Translated from the German under the General Editorship of James Strachey, in collaboration with Anna Freud, assisted by Alix Strachey and Alan Tyson. Vol. VII (1901–1905). *A Case of Hysteria, Three Essays on Sexuality, and Other Works.* 1953. *Int. J. Psycho-Anal.*, 35:360.

1955 Vols. X, XIII & XVIII

Brierley, M. (1956). *The Standard Edition of the Complete Psychological Works of Sigmund Freud*: Translated from the German under the General Editorship of James Strachey, in collaboration with Anna Freud, assisted by Alix Strachey and Alan Tyson. Vol. X (1909). *Two Case Histories (Little Hans and the Rat Man).* Vol. XIII (1913–1914). *Totem and Taboo and Other Works.* Vol. XVIII (1920–1922), *Beyond the Pleasure Principle, Group Psychology and Other Works.* 1955. *Int. J. Psycho-Anal.*, 37:476–477.

1955 Vols. II & XVII

Brierley, M. (1956). *The Standard Edition of the Complete Psychological Works of Sigmund Freud*: Translated from the German under the General Editorship of James Strachey, in collaboration with Anna Freud, assisted by Alix Strachey and Alan Tyson. Vol. II (1893–1895). *Studies on Hysteria*. Vol. XVII. (1917–1918). *An Infantle Neurosis and Other Works*. 1955. *Int. J. Psycho-Anal.*, 37:477–478.

1957 Vols. XI & XIV

Brierley, M. (1958). *The Standard Edition of the Complete Psychological Works of Sigmund Freud*: Translated from the German under the General Editorship of James Strachey, in collaboration with Anna Freud, assisted by Alix Strachey and Alan Tyson. Vol. XI (1910). *Five Lectures on Psychoanalysis, Leonard da Vinci and Other Works)*. Vol. XIV (1914–1916), *On the History of the Psychoanalytic Movement, Papers on Metapsychology and Other Works*. 1957. *Int. J. Psycho-Anal.*, 39:421–422.

1958 Vol. XII

Brierley, M. (1959). *The Standard Edition of the Complete Psychological Works of Sigmund Freud*: Translated from the German under the General Editorship of James Strachey, in collaboration with Anna Freud, assisted by Alix Strachey and Alan Tyson. Vol. XII (1911–1913). *The Case of Schreber, Papers on Technique, and Other Works*. 1958. *Int. J. Psycho-Anal.*, 40:339.

1959 Vols. IX & XX

Brierley, M. (1960). *The Standard Edition of the Complete Psychological Works of Sigmund Freud*: Translated from the German under the General Editorship of James Strachey, in collaboration with Anna Freud, assisted by Alix Strachey and Alan Tyson. Vol. IX (1906–1908). *Jensen's 'Gradiva', and Other Works*. Vol. XX (1925–1926). *An Autobiographical Study; Inhibitions, Symptoms and Anxiety; The Question of Lay Analysis; and Other Works of Psychoanalysis*. 1959. *Int. J. Psycho-Anal.*, 41:565–566.

1960 Vol. VIII

Brierley, M. (1961). *The Standard Edition of the Complete Psychological Works of Sigmund Freud*: Translated from the German under the general editorship of James Strachey, in collaboration with Anna Freud, assisted by Alix Strachey and Alan Tyson. Vol. 8. *Jokes and their Relation to the Unconscious (1905)*. 1960. *Int. J. Psycho-Anal.*, 42:123.

1960 Vol. VI

Brierley, M. (1961). *The Standard Edition of the Complete Psychological Works of Sigmund Freud*: Translated from the German under the General Editorship of James Strachey, in collaboration with Anna Freud, assisted by Alix Strachey and Alan Tyson. Vol. VI (1901). *The Psychopathology of Everyday Life*. 1960. *Int. J. Psycho-Anal.*, 42:288.

1961 Vols. XIX & XXII

Brierley, M. (1965). *The Standard Edition of the Complete Psychological Works of Sigmund Freud*: Translated from the German under the general editorship of James Strachey, in collaboration with Anna Freud, assisted by Alix Strachey and Alan Tyson. Vol. XIX (1923–1925) *The Ego and the Id and Other Works*. Vol. XXII (1932–1936) *New Introductory Lectures on Psycho-Analysis and Other Works*. 1961. *Int. J. Psycho-Anal.*, 46:251–254.

1962 Vol. III

Bricrlcy, M. (1962). *The Standard Edition of the Complete Psychological Works of Sigmund Freud*: Translated from the German under the general editorship of James Strachey, in collaboration with Anna Freud, assisted by Alix Strachey and Alan Tyson. Vol. III (1893–1899). *Early Psycho-Analytic Publications*. 1962. *Int. J. Psycho-Anal.*, 43:468–471.

1963 Vols. XV & XVI

Brierley, M. (1965). *The Standard Edition of the Complete Psychological Works of Sigmund Freud*: Translated from the German under the general editorship of James Strachey, in collaboration with Anna Freud, assisted by Alix Strachey and Alan Tyson. Vol. XV (1915–1916) *Introductory Lectures on Psycho-Analysis* (Parts I and II). Vol. XVI (1916–1917) *Introductory Lectures on Psycho-Analysis* (Part III). 1963. *Int. J. Psycho-Anal.*, 45:584–586.

1965 Vols. XXI and XXIII

Brierley, M. (1965). *The Standard Edition of the Complete Psychological Works of Sigmund Freud*: Translated from the German under the general editorship of James Strachey, in collaboration with Anna Freud, assisted by Alix Strachey and Alan Tyson. Vol. XXI (1927–1931) *The Future of an Illusion, Civilization and its Discontents, and Other Works*. Vol. XXIII (1937–1939) *Moses and Monotheism, An Outline of Psycho-Analysis, and Other Works*. 1965. *Int. J. Psycho-Anal.*, 46:521–525.

1967 Vol. I

Brierley, M. (1967). *The Standard Edition of the Complete Psychological Works of Sigmund Freud*: Translated from the German under the general editorship of James Strachey, in collaboration with Anna Freud, assisted by Alix Strachey and Alan Tyson. Editorial assistant: Angela Richards. Vol. I (1886–1899) *Pre-Psycho-Analytic Publications and Unpublished Drafts*. 1967. *Int. J. Psycho-Anal.*, 48:323–326.

Notes

1 Jan Abram's "Affects, mediation and countertransference: some reflections on the contributions of Marjorie Brierley (1893–1984) and their relevance to psychoanalysis today" highlights the myriad ways her 1937 paper "Affects in theory and practice" anticipates contemporary writing on countertransference.

2 A topic beyond the scope of this paper includes the questions of how past book reviewers were selected and books assigned to reviewers. These questions can only be answered if journals retain editorial archives that hold the needed information.

3 Brierley also wrote 24 abstracts for *the IJP* in the early 1930s, as well as 31 for the *British Journal of Medical Psychology* (*BJMP*), which published one of her 11 papers (Brierley, 1934). Many analysts wrote for the *BJMP*, also founded in 1920, as well as serving as editors of the journal, e.g. John Sutherland, Thomas Main, John Rickman.

4 Brierley further writes:

> I imagine that we vary greatly in the degree to which we individually combine identification and object relationship in our work, but I do not see how any of us can avoid sustaining both these relationships in some proportion. It is this combination or alternation of relationship to our patients that is all too often reflected in confused thinking about theory.
>
> (Ibid. p. 119)

5 Klein wrote to Brierley thanking her for her review, describing it as "a very helpful summary – both objective and stimulating. I am grateful for all the work you have put into it and for the fairness you have shown" (Klein, 1950). Klein did take issue, however, with Brierley's observation that she neglected the role of regression in psychic development.

6 Nonetheless, Brierley hoped that Laing's work "will not lead to the discarding of any of the basic findings of psycho-analysis, as too often happens with the introduction of 'new' ideas, to the detriment of both theory and practice" (Brierley, p. 291).

7 Altogether, there were four Supplements published by *the IJP*: Supplement No. 1 (1924) *A Glossary of Technical Terms For the use of Translation of Psycho-Analytic Works* edited by Ernst Jones with the assistance of Joan Riviere, James Strachey and Alix Strachey. In 1943, a revised and expanded version edited by Alix Strachey, renamed *A New German-English Psycho-analytical Vocabulary,* was published. Supplement No. 2 *The Development of the Psychoanalytical Technique of the Psychoses of 1893–1926* was authored by John Rickman.

References

Abram, J. (2015). Affects, Mediation and Countertransference: Some Reflections on the Contributions of Marjorie Brierley (1893–1984) and Their Relevance to Psychoanalysis Today. https://www.epf-fep.eu, 19 March 2015.

Brierley, M. (1934). Present Trends in Psychoanalysis. *British Journal of Medical Psychology*, 14: 211–229.

Brierley, M. (1937). Affects in Theory and Practice. *International Journal of Psychoanalysis*, 18: 256–268.

Brierley, M. (1943). Theory Practice and Public Relations. *International Journal of Psychoanalysis*, 24: 119–125.

Brierley, M. (1950). Review. Contributions to Psycho-Analysis 1921–1945 by Melanie Klein. The Int. Psychoanal. Library, no. 37, edited by Ernst Jones, 1948. *International Journal of Psychoanalysis*, 31: 209–211.

Brierley, M. (1951). Acknowledgements. *Trends in Psychoanalysis*. London: The International Psycho-Analytical Library, edited by Ernst Jones, 39. The Hogarth Press and the Institute for Psychoanalysis.

Brierley, M. (1953). Review. *Developments in Psychoanalysis* by Melanie Klein, Paula Heimann, Susan Isaacs and Joan Riviere. Edited by Joan Riviere with a Preface by Ernst Jones. London: Hogarth Press, 1952. *International Journal of Psychoanalysis*, 34: 158–160.

Brierley, M. (1961). Review. *The Divided Self: A Study of Sanity and Madness* by R. D. Laing. *International Journal of Psychoanalysis*, 42: 288–291.

Brierley, M. (1969). 'Hardy Perennials' and Psychoanalysis. *International Journal of Psychoanalysis*, 50: 447–452.

Glover, E. (1940). *An Investigation of the Technique of Psycho-Analysis.* Research Supplements to *the IJP* edited by Edward Glover with the assistance of Marjorie Brierley. London: Bailliére, Tindall and Cox.

Glover, E. (1955). *The Technique of Psychoanalysis.* New York: International Universities Press.

Hayman, A. (1986). On Marjorie Brierley. *International Review of Psychoanalysis*, 13: 383–391.

Hoffer, W. (1959). Change of Editor. *The International Journal of Psychoanalysis*, 40: 397.

King, P. and Steiner, R. (1992). *The Controversial Discussions 1941–45.* London and New York: Tavistock/Routledge.

Klein, M. (1950). Letter to Marjorie Brierley, 7 November. Archives of the British Psycho-Analytical Society.

THE INTERNATIONAL JOURNAL OF PSYCHOANALYSIS AS THE VOICE OF PSYCHOANALYSIS

United and different

Rachel B. Blass

Introduction

This chapter describes the establishment of *The International Journal* as the official organ and united voice of the IPA, and how in this role it has provided a central framework for debate of the essential differences of views, theoretical and clinical, that exist among IPA members. Through the study of the evolution of controversial debate within the *Journal* over time, light is shed on the evolving role of the *Journal* within the psychoanalytic community and its relationship to the IPA.

United voice

The 1920 Bulletin of the IPA announces the decision of the executive of the IPA to "inaugurate an official organ of the Association in English…under the direction of Professor Freud" to be called *The International Journal of Psycho-analysis* (*Int. J. Psycho-anal* 1:117).

The protocol of the business meeting of the Sixth IPA Congress, 1920, held in The Hague and chaired by Sándor Ferenczi, refers to the ratification of this decision. The following is stated:

7. Dr. Rank explained the circumstances connected with the foundation of the "*International Journal of Psycho-analysis*". Dr. Stern

and Dr. Bryan, as Secretaries of the New York and British Societies respectively, expressed their approval of the Journal in the name of their Societies. The meeting thereupon unanimously accepted the Journal as one of the official organs of the Association.

8. Dr. de Saussure and Dr. Pfister then proposed that all non-German speaking members should be permitted to subscribe to the *"International Journal of Psycho-analysis"* instead of to the two German journals, should they so desire. This proposal was accepted.

9. Prof. Freud thanked the English speaking Societies for their acceptance of the Journal and expressed his desire to hear the wishes of these Societies, particularly with regard to the question of editorship (remarking that Dr. Jones had been requested to act as editor provisionally until the time of the Congress).

After a discussion in which Prof. Freud, Dr. Pfister, Dr. Bryan, and Dr. Jones took part it was agreed that Dr. Jones should be the editor, with the assistance of an editorial committee, to be appointed later, consisting of three American and two British members.

(Int. J. Psycho-anal. 1: 209–10)

This report appeared in the second issue of the first volume of the *Journal*, in accordance with the decision that the *Journal*, like the *Zeitschrift*, would include the verbatim reports of the IPA. The very first page of the *Journal* is an open letter from the IPA president, Sándor Ferenczi, in which he emphasizes the value of creating the *Journal* in post-World War I psychoanalysis. He writes:

Among the many reconstructive problems awaiting the "International Psycho-Analytical Association" after its long period of enforced inactivity I judge none to be more urgent or important than the reconsideration of the position of our literary organs. It has become evident that, in view especially of the remarkable increase of interest in Psycho-Analysis in America and England during the past few years, the *Internationale Zetschrift für ärztliche Psychoanalyse* can no longer be expected satisfactorily to fulfil its function as the international organ, at least on its former lines ... I have decided that the most satisfactory method would be to found a distinct Journal in the English language, in close contact with the *Zeitschrift*, and if possible under a similar editorship. The new Journal would rank equally with the *Zeitschrift* and *Imago* as an official organ of the "International Psycho-Analytical Association", with special reference to the English-speaking public, and would contain the official Reports of the Association ... [I] conclude what I have to say here with expressing my warmest wishes for the success of the new venture, on the future of which so much will depend.

(Ferenczi, 1920, pp. 1–2)

This letter is followed by an Editorial by Ernest Jones (who, at Ferenczi's request, also temporarily replaced him as IPA president), in which he further explains the necessity of the *Journal* and its role as a unifying voice within the analytic world. Like the formation of the IPA, the *Journal* provides a way in which to "cooperate towards a common end" of "maintaining and developing hardly-won truths" of "the Science of psychoanalysis". In this editorial, Jones describes the rejection of the idea of establishing the *Journal* as a private venture, instead choosing the following complex arrangement:

It will be published by the "International Psycho-Analytical Press", with private financial help; the definite editorship and organization of the "Journal" will be arranged at the Congress of the "International Psycho-Analytical Association", of which it will rank, equally with the *Internationale Zeitschrift für ärztliche Psychoanalyse*, as the official organ.

(Jones, 1920, pp. 3–5)

As becomes apparent from his correspondences, Freud was not "the director" of the *Journal* in name only. Rather, he was actively involved in its formation and the details of its development, both technical and ideological, referring to it at times as "our *Journal*" (e.g., letter to Jones, 16 July 1920).

In 1938, the *Zeitschrift* and the *Imago* were not published, a fact explained in a later editorial note in terms of "political events in Austria". These journals then reappeared in 1939 in a joint publication, which continued to appear for only two more years. Thus, the *International Journal* remained the sole official voice of international psychoanalysis (Figure 7.1).

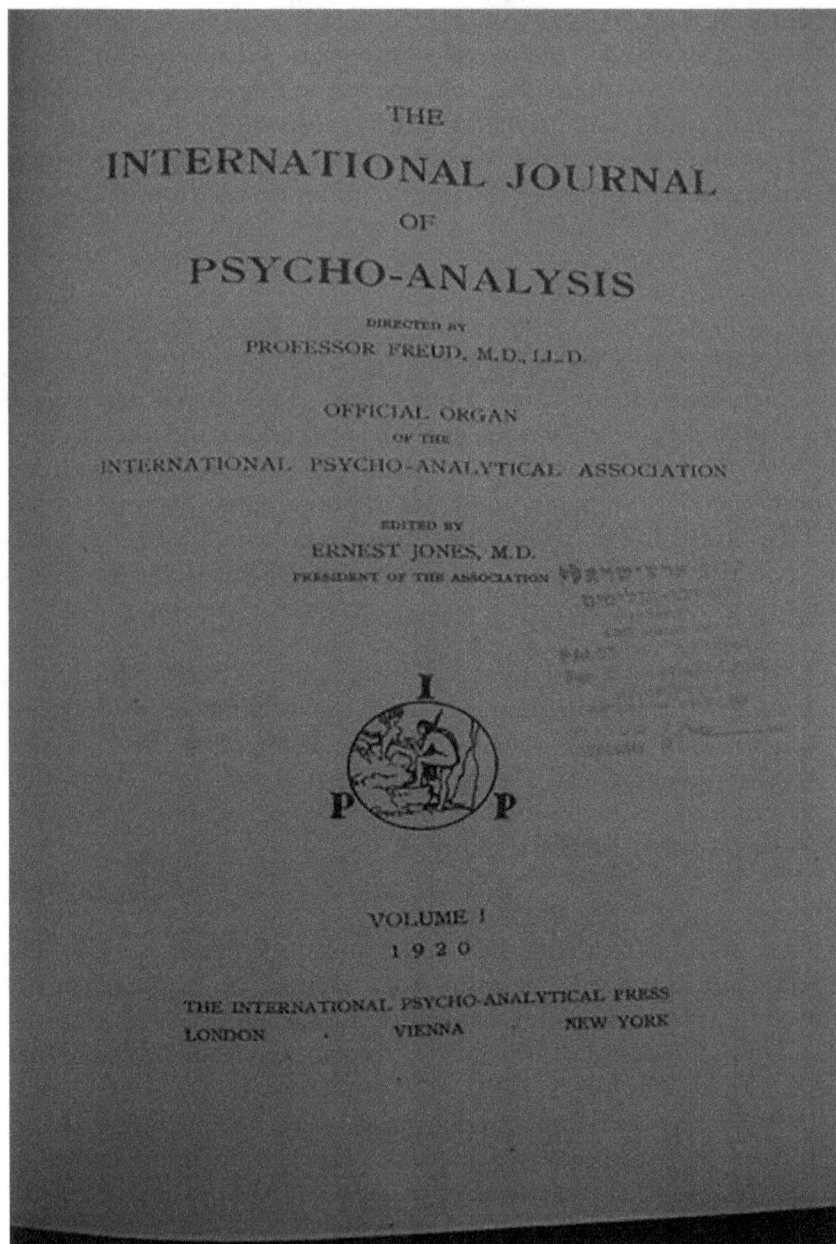

THE

INTERNATIONAL JOURNAL

OF

PSYCHO-ANALYSIS

DIRECTED BY

PROFESSOR FREUD, M.D., LL.D.

OFFICIAL ORGAN
OF THE
INTERNATIONAL PSYCHO-ANALYTICAL ASSOCIATION

EDITED BY
ERNEST JONES, M.D.
PRESIDENT OF THE ASSOCIATION

VOLUME I
1920

THE INTERNATIONAL PSYCHO-ANALYTICAL PRESS
LONDON · VIENNA NEW YORK

Figure 7.1 Volume 1 of *the International Journal of Psychoanalysis*, 1920.

Voices divided

For the *Journal*, being the voice of psychoanalysis meant allowing the diversity within the psychoanalytic world to be heard, even when it included sharply opposing views. This was made clear from the start. One of the earliest controversies discussed in the *Journal* regarded Anna Freud's ideas on child analysis, which stood opposed to those of Melanie Klein.

Jones writes to Freud in a letter from the 30 of September 1927:

When Anna read her paper at Berlin Mrs. Klein, who was still at that time a member of the Berlin group, sent a written contribution to the discussion, but this was suppressed. Rado [then editor of the Zeitschrift, RB] had previously barred the "Zeitschrift" to her, and so she came to me to ask what opportunity there was for her to defend herself against this attack on her life's work. I wrote to Rado asking if Anna's book [Introduction to the Technique of Child Analysis, RB] could be simultaneously reviewed, as has been done before, by two people from different points of view, and his reply indicated that only a favourable review of it could be published. There remained only the "Journal". I should, of course, publish the "Zeitschrift" review in translation in the "Journal", but I promised Mrs. Klein that our pages would also be open to any contribution of hers defining the points at issue between her and Anna and generally clearing up the situation. You may well imagine that it never once occurred to me that Anna would claim immunity from criticism of her writings, still less that [she] you would expect any such immunity for her. Extremely important scientific issues were at stake and an open discussion on all sides seemed the obvious course. I certainly could not sympathise with the possibility of one side of the case being artificially blocked.

Freud responds ten days later that he sought no such immunity and that he "will personally see to it that she [M. Klein] is given free access".

This exchange followed the publication in Volume 8 of the *Journal* of a series of critical papers presented at the Symposium on Child-Analysis, held at the British Society in May 1927. The authors engaged in this controversial discussion included Melanie Klein, Joan Riviere, M.N. Searl, Ella F. Sharpe, Edward Glover, and Ernest Jones.

A second significant round of discussions of the differences between London and Vienna is published in the *Journal* between 1935 and 1937. Jones opens the discussion with his famous 1935 paper on "Early female sexuality" and is followed by a paper by Joan Riviere on early psychic conflict and two response papers by Robert Wälder. Jones's introductory words shed light on the *Journal's* special role on furthering constructive debate in the analytic community. He writes:

> This lecture is intended to be the first of a series of exchange lectures between Vienna and London which your Vice-President, Dr. Federn, has proposed for a special purpose. For some years now it has been apparent that many analysts in London do not see eye to eye with their colleagues in Vienna on a number of important topics: among these I might instance the early development of sexuality, especially in the female, the genesis of the super-ego and its relation to the Oedipus complex, the technique of child analysis and the conception of a death instinct. I use the phrase 'many analysts' without attempting to enumerate these, but it is evident that there is some danger of local views becoming unified to such an extent as to enable people to speak of a Vienna school or London school as if they represented different tendencies of a possibly divergent order. This, I am convinced, is in no wise true. The differences are of just that kind that go with imperfect contact, which in the present case are strongly contributed to by geographical and linguistic factors. The political and economic disturbances of the past few years have not brought London and Vienna nearer to each other. Many English analysts do not read the *Zeitschrift*, and still fewer Vienna analysts read the Journal. And I have not as yet succeeded in making the interchange of translations between the two as free as I could wish... The fact is that new work and ideas in London have not yet, in our opinion, been adequately considered in Vienna.

Interestingly, the *Journal* did not publish the most famous of analytic controversies, the one held in London in the 1940s (with the exception of Susan Isaacs's well-known "The nature and function of phantasy", published a few years after its presentation). This may have to do with considerations of the editor at that time, James Strachey, who, while being one of the organizers of the Special Discussions to Consider Scientific Differences of the controversies, attended none of them (King & Steiner, 1991) (Figure 7.2).

> In my view, despite differences there existed a shared ground of psychoanalytic concern with attaining and furthering the truth regarding psychic reality that held the different groups together. I suspect that this was supported by the fact that both Melanie Klein and Anna Freud were primarily motivated by a concern with the well-being of psychoanalysis rather than by personal ambition.
>
> (Segal, 2006, p. 288)

The relationship between the *Journal* debates and the analytic community has been reciprocal. The *Journal* presents debates in the analytic community but also encourages them. The 1927 publication of a series of papers on "lay analysis" is an interesting case in point. It is introduced with the following editorial note:

Figure 7.2 Portrait of Melanie Klein, A. Freud, E. Jones.
Reproduced by permission of the Wellcome Collection and the Melanie Klein Trust.

197

The Central Executive of the International Psycho-Analytical Association informs us that it is their intention to bring forward the question of 'Lay Analysis' at the next Congress, so that opinions may be heard and, so far as possible, decisions arrived at in the matter. The Executive desires that the question shall be ventilated as fully as possible before the Congress meets, and has consequently requested the various Branch Societies to further this end by arranging for local discussions on the subject. In order to serve the same purpose we are opening our pages to an international discussion of the question of Lay Analysis.

(1927, p. 392)

Over 100 pages of views follow, including from Franz Alexander, Edward Glover, Karen Horney, Ernest Jones, Wilhelm Reich, Theodore Reik, and many other individuals and from several societies from around the world.

Freud's famous "Postscript" on this issue first appeared in the *Journal* in the context of this debate (1927, pp. 392–398, directly following the *Symposium* papers). In the *Journal* edition, Freud's "Concluding remarks" include a final statement by Max Eitingon who, in the name of the IPA Training Commission, puts forth practical resolutions to the question of Lay Analysis to be confirmed at the forthcoming Congress.

Central to the discussion of differences in the *Journal* is the aim of constructively furthering analytic theory and practice, not simply making corrections or airing objections. The line between the two can at times be fine but is important. Awareness of this may be seen in the Editorial introduction to a 1955 "controversy [that] has arisen between … two writers on the character and function of psycho-analysis in Japan", an American analyst on the one hand, and one of the translators of Freud's works into Japanese plus the editor of the *Tokyo Journal of Psychoanalysis*. This Editorial introduction to this controversy clarifies that while the objections and corrections that the Japanese writer makes in regard to a paper published by the American writer are of a kind that would normally be covered by a Letter to the Editor (and in the future should), in this case they warrant a more extensive discussion; the Editorial does not directly tell us why, but alludes to the idea that it is the cultural context of the objections and the importance of hearing from Asian colleagues that justify further discussion:

The Editor [Willi Hoffer, RB] is glad to give Mr. Kenji Ohtsuki an opportunity to state his objections to some of Dr. Moloney's conclusions, but unfortunately, owing to language and other difficulties, his manuscript could not be published as received. The Editorial Committee have therefore prepared an abridged transcript which they sincerely hope contains the gist of the main arguments which the author wishes to present. In accordance with custom in scientific journals, Dr. James Clark Moloney has been invited to make a final reply (to the original manuscript).

The Editor would like to take this opportunity of reminding members and readers of this Journal that it is the policy of the Editorial Committee to print such ... discussions only in exceptional circumstances, since they seldom lead to any positive advance in theory or practice. In general, corrections of misstatements, etc., should be made in a *Letter to the Editor....* It should, however, be emphasized that the pages of this Journal will always be open to any serious worker who has a contribution to make to our science or to its various applications.

(1955, p. 205)

The development of controversy and its impact on the role of the *IJPA*

Over the years, the discussion of the differences between analytic perspectives, both in relation to theory and practice, have taken different forms, determined in part by the growth of the field of psychoanalysis in its historical, demographic, and professional factors. These discussions have impacted upon and been impacted by the perceived roles of the *Journal* within the analytic community and specifically in regard to its role as the official and united voice of the IPA.

The first 30 years

In a sense, discussions of differences are pervasive. In 1927, Sándor Ferenczi writes a book review of Otto Rank's 1926 book *Technik Der Psychoanalyse: I. Die Analytische Situation* and he takes his colleague and former co-author sharply to task, for overemphasizing not only birth anxiety but also the relationship to the mother in the transference and the here and now interpretation of it to the neglect of historical determinants. As I have noted, the famous Controversial Discussions of the early 1940s did not appear in the *Journal* but in 1945, Susan Isaacs, a major contributor to those controversies, offers detailed comments on Marjorie Brierly's 1944 paper "Notes on Metapsychology as Process Theory", and Brierley's response to Isaacs appears in the same issue. The discussion of these differences allows for further working through the differences that arose in the Controversial Discussions regarding the understanding of Freud's metapsychology.

But there were more structured ways of expressing controversy as well. Most notably, there is the publication of Symposia from Congresses in which differences were presented and discussed. In the first 30 years of the journal, there were several of these. The sharp differences between the basic frameworks of thinking of two of the symposia point to an ongoing controversy between foundational attitudes to psychoanalysis that has guided many future controversial discussions until this day.

The first is a "Symposium on the Theory of the Therapeutic Results of Psycho-Analysis", which took place at the IPA Congress held in Marienbad in 1936 and was published in the *IJPA* the following year. The second, the "Symposium on the Evaluation of Therapeutic Results", similarly, but significantly differently titled, took place in Boston eight years later, and was published in 1945. The first symposium included leading European analysts such as Glover, Fenichel, Bibring, Strachey, and one American analyst Nunberg. The second symposium involved leading American analysts including Obendorf (a former The Ameican Psychoanalytic Association (APsA) president), Greenacre, and Kubie.

Glover's opening comments, which inaugurate a lively and clear exchange of views and different evaluations of developments, begin as follows:

> The decision to hold a Symposium on the nature of Therapeutic Results is a clear indication that theories on this subject which have been generally accepted for so many years are either no longer regarded as adequate or no longer entirely acceptable. At any rate it will add considerably to our freedom of discussion if we admit from the onset that legitimate differences of opinion have arisen as to both past and present therapeutic formulations. Moreover, to judge from earlier analytic controversies it would appear

200

that whenever differences of opinion exist in psycho-analytic circles, two safe generalizations can be made: first, that the original views put forward by Freud on that particular subject are still the best available and second, that as a result of more recent work, these original views are capable of, indeed require, more detailed correlation. I should like to add that in most cases the first of these two generalizations is the more valuable.

Reviewing earlier literature, there seems to be no question that Freud's original views, simple and schematic as they were, still constitute the most valuable and permanent contribution to the subject. These were in effect (1) the existence of transferences, (2) the development of the analytic or transference neurosis and (3) the degree to which the existence of these two manifestations (and in particular their negative forms) was hidden by repression or obscured by projection, thus giving rise to resistances. Successful results depended on the extent to which these three factors were analysed.

Later contributions can be divided into two main periods. The first of these was concerned for the most part with restatements. The theory of transferences and resistances was restated in terms of the newer ego-psychology. This led to more copious use of the terms super-ego and Id but did not add very much to the earlier clinical conceptions. The second and more recent group consists of speculations as to the effect of introjection mechanisms on transferences. This expansion of the concept of introjection together with increasing recognition of the importance in therapeutic processes of fusion and defusion of instinct added considerably to our technical range. But apart from this they did not widen very much our theory of analytic results except in so far as they compelled us to pour old wine into new bottles. Indeed, it might also be said that these later phases gave rise to a certain reactionary tendency in analytical theory. For it would appear from the contributions of various modern writers as if the emphasis placed on early phases of introjection and projection had led to a neglect of the fundamental importance of repression, particularly in the later infantile years.

Obendorf opens the second symposium in a strikingly different tone. He refers to Stekel's very early efforts to shorten analytic treatments and states:

To go back to Stekel, whose attitude directly defied Freud's epoch-making endeavour. The latter was primarily concerned with the discovery of the factors which enter in mental pathology and only secondarily with the therapeutic results which might accrue from the theoretically beneficial procedure he was constructing. To a certain, though perhaps lesser, degree this remained Freud's position throughout his long, extraordinarily productive career—that of research worker applying his own ever-widening theory to questions of anthropology, sociology, literature, art and culture rather than the cure of specific aspects of medical pathology. Freud's analysis developed into a procedure where the physician saw the patient six times a week for an hour session and in its normal course this might continue for a year or more. I recall that in 1921 Freud considered it a concession to see patients only five times a week instead of six.

He goes on to compare European and American analysts, viewing the distance from Freud, geographically grounded, mainly as an advantage:

The European groups loyal to Freud, largely dependent upon him for every new thought, directed and dominated by his genius, dared to deviate only in minor ways from his dicta. Dr. Horney, when she first came to this country, told me that she was surprised at the latitude which the American psycho-analysts had assumed, and said that it could not have been done abroad.

Freud's early adherents in America who were using the psycho-analytic method regularly did not exceed a dozen physicians until after World War I. While deprived of the advantages of close contact with Freud and his increasing number of able collaborators in Germany, France, Holland and Britain, they enjoyed greater freedom in experimentation with the clinical application of the psycho-analytic method in clinics, general hospitals, mental hospitals and in private practice. Thus while American contributions to the structure of the psycho-analytic theory have remained rather meagre, America early became a testing ground for psycho-analytic theory in a great variety of psychologically determined physical disorders and situations. For Freud this disregard for some of his most cherished precepts constituted a desecration of the essence of psycho-analysis.

Recently the Chicago group have reverted to the idea of brief analysis. Some of the cases described by them are reminiscent of the reports of Stekel nearly forty years ago.

In this instance too, what followed was a lively discussion of ideas, including differences. But it would seem that the differences <u>between</u> the symposia are more striking, having to do with basic attitudes about analytic aims, interventions, and setting (including frequency of sessions); the ways in which psychoanalysis is scientifically justified; what defines a therapeutic practice as analytic; and the extent to which theory, especially Freud's foundational thinking, is thought to determine the definition of analytic. The relevance of these considerations to contemporary discussions is notable.

The choice to submit the Boston symposium to the *IJPA* is interesting and seems to reflect a desire for more exchange with European colleagues and more generally with the IPA, despite differences. It is at this time that the idea of a rotation of the IPA presidency between North America and Europe is established. When Jones resigns as president in 1949, the next president is the American Leo Bartemeier.

This change occurs at the IPA Congress held in Zürich in 1949. This was the first IPA Congress to be held after an 11-year hiatus because of the impact of World War II on psychoanalysis in Europe, and it was also the first since the death of Freud in 1939.

1950–1979

During the next 30 years, symposia become the dominant form of controversial discussions within the *IJPA*, and, more specifically, the symposia of the biannual IPA Congresses; not only do they become the main format for the discussion of differences, but they gradually become the *Journal's* main source of material in general. It was as though the Journal's central format became that of debate. This took place under the editorships of Willi Hoffer (1949–1959), John Sutherland (1960–1968), and Joseph Sandler (1969–1978). The process was gradual, gaining strength in the late 1950s, completely dominating entire volumes in the 1960s, and then lessening towards the end of the 1970s. The issues discussed are as varied as the topics of the IPA Congress panels and include mainly leading analytic figures. For example, in 1957, one of the more clinical panels on

"Classical Psychoanalytic Technique" was chaired by Greeson, and, among others, included contributions from Lowenstein, Eissler, Annie Reich, Nacht, Rosenfeld; another panel on "Ego Distortion", which focused more on the definition and treatment of pathology, was chaired by Waelder and included papers by Gitelson, Gillespie, Glover, Nacht, and Rosenfeld. All the papers of these panels appear in the 1958 volume of the *IJPA*. Since the IPA Congress only had designated themes from 1965 onwards, for a long while, the topics of discussion were especially varied.

In the 1960s, the panels published in the *Journal* included discussions of depression, psychosomatics, psychosis, phantasy, selection for training, the ego ideal, parent infant relationships, curative factors, gender identity, and symptom formation; then, when themes were introduced, the *Journal* included the various panels on obsessive neurosis and acting out (all the papers were mainly published in the year following the Congress). On all these issues, the different analytic schools, coming from many different countries, were represented and the differences openly discussed. At this point, the *IJPA* was effectively the written version of the discussion within the IPA, and this version took a number of formats (paper followed by discussion, paper and discussion presented jointly as one publication, paper and reports from discussion groups, reports [in English of discussions in other languages, etc.]).

This profound tie between the *Journal* and the IPA may be seen also in the fact that the *Journal* not only published its Congresses (papers, introductory comments, discussions and all), but, in addition, it served as its main instrument for communicating with its members during the time leading up to the Congresses. The IPA would use the *Journal* to inform members (i.e., *IJPA* readers) about the forthcoming Congress, invite papers, and even at times direct presenters regarding how best to write them. This is noted in Lampl de Groot's 1969 introduction to the Congress in Rome that year, in her capacity as chair of the Programme Committee. She writes:

> ...we asked the speakers, especially those on the main theme, to make it very clear what they consider to be new in their contributions to psychoanalytical theory and/or practice; to show what is the gain of the new development, and what it is that is seen as an improvement and enlargement of our knowledge of human mental life.

We do hope that the various discussions will contribute to this aim and that the discussants will try to avoid the dangers of "one-sidedness" in regard to a possible neglect of well-documented psychoanalytic knowledge. Further, we hope that in the Panel Discussions the application of this knowledge to other disciplines which study human behaviour (sociology, anthropology, psychiatry, psychotherapy etc.) will contribute to a legitimate widening of the understanding of interpersonal relations.

(Lampl-de-Groot, 1969, p. 4)

From the other direction, the IPA basically served as the *Journal* reviewers and even editors. In the context of a 1972 Editorial that followed the IPA Congress held in Vienna the year before, Joseph Sandler writes:

The onerous task of selecting the papers to be given at the Congress from the large number submitted was, as always, undertaken by the Programme Committee of the International Psycho-Analytical Association. Because it was impossible to publish all the papers read, this Committee had the even more difficult and unenviable problem of selecting those papers which are to be published in the Journal as part of the Proceedings. There is no doubt that many of the papers which were not included in the final selection were of a high standard, and will doubtless also find their way into print.

As Editor, I want to express my own appreciation of the hard work carried out by those responsible for the organization of the Congress. The President of the Association, Dr Leo Rangell, and the Secretary, Dr Frances Gitelson, did everything in their power to facilitate the coordination between the Programme Committee and the Journal. The Programme Committee itself, under the co-chairmanship of Dr Samuel A. Guttman and Dr Arthur F. Valenstein, made heroic efforts to see that the authors of the papers to be published met the printer's deadlines, and that the papers were in suitable form for publication. In particular, the indefatigable Secretary of the Programme Committee, Dr Edward M. Weinshel, saw to it that liaison between the *Journal* and the Programme Committee of the International was pleasant and efficient. Difficulties in this area which had occurred in the past were completely absent, for which I am sincerely grateful.

(Sandler, 1972, p. 1)

The topics discussed at the Congresses and in the *Journal* in the 1970s included aggression, hysteria, affect, and more general topics such as "new developments in psychoanalysis" and "changes in psychoanalytic practice and experience".

Notably, in 1977, the IPA Congress is first held outside of Europe in Jerusalem. But as Israel belongs to the European region of the IPA and is a member of the EPF (the European Psychoanalytic Federation), this was only a harbinger of a more momentous change that was soon to come. The 1979 Congress was held in New York, and after three more Congresses held in Europe, there began the rotation of the Congresses between the three IPA regions – Europe, North America, and Latin America – which continues until this day.

It would seem that the increase in numbers of papers that were being presented at the Congresses, of which Sandler speaks in his 1972 Editorial, together with the expansion of the locations of the Congresses, ultimately limited the publication of all Congress papers and discussion, and, in turn, brought about a major change in the format of controversy in the coming years.

1979–2003

During the next 25 years, under the editorships of Thomas Hayley and David Tuckett, the discussion of controversies within the *Journal* takes a major turn. Given the volume of the Congress papers, the *Journal* could not automatically publish all papers or even major panels, but also with the Congress locations becoming truly international (a factor undoubtedly influenced in part by the growing accessibility of air travel), the issue of integrating large numbers of papers from other regions, including their translations, becomes a difficult task. A certain gap between the interests of the *IJPA* as a professional journal and the IPA as a framework for dialogue between analysts around the world emerges. On the one hand, the *Journal* goes to great efforts to encompass the entire IPA community. In 1984, it establishes editorial boards for both Latin America and for Europe, which allows for the submission of papers in Spanish and Portuguese; also, the possibility of creating an Annual in Spanish, which would include papers selected from the *Journal* each year, is considered (and is soon implemented). The idea of the prepublication of Congress papers in four languages (English, French, German, and Spanish) is also considered (but ultimately never implemented; Hayley, 1984).

On the other hand, these very efforts seem to indicate and high-light the fact that the *Journal serves* the IPA rather than being completely identified with it (as it was in the past). This is reflected in Hayley's 1988 Editorial. There he speaks of the original founding of the *IJPA* and the circumstances that led to its British ownership in order to explain the *Journal's* special outreach efforts, and he adds: "We feel a deep responsibility to fulfil this trust and extend it towards the international psychoanalytical community of the World" (Hayley, 1988, p. 1). Towards the end of the Editorial, he notes that the Bulletin of the IPA, which up until this point was published in the *Journal*, will from now on be published separately by the IPA in the four official languages for free distribution to all members, explaining that "This is another of the excellent developments in the administration of the IPA made possible by the setting up of its new offices in London and by modern methods of printing" (Hayley, 1988, p. 2). Interestingly, the paper version of the Bulletin continues to appear in the *IJPA* through the year 2000.

In line with these developments, the publication of the Congress papers is gradually reduced, and by 1991, with the first Congress held in Latin America, only a few keynote papers are immediately published in the *Journal* without any independent review by the *IJPA*, and this is done prior to the Congress in order to make the papers available. Alongside the limited prepublication of Congress papers, there is an increase in *Journal*-organized reports on Congress Panels, which offer brief summaries of their content. Interestingly, the IPA continued for many years to oblige authors whose papers were accepted to the Congresses to submit them to the *IJPA*, offering the *Journal* first rights to all Congress papers for publication in English.

With controversial debate no longer finding direct expression in the publication of the IPA Congress panels and discussion, a new framework for this debate emerges – Letters. In 1993, after five years of co-editorship with Thomas Hayley, David Tuckett becomes the sole editor, and the framework of letters and responses soars. The letters all address papers and reviews that appeared in recent issues of the *IJPA*. Without any formal notification or invitation in regard to this change of format, during the decade of Tuckett's editorship, there are, on average, ten letters and responses published per year, overall five times as many as those that appeared in the 72 preceding years of the *Journal's* existence. For example, in 1998, there are letters questioning Marcia Cavell's views on truth and objectivity, and she offers several responses. Gabbard twice responds to critiques of his film reviews; Danielle Quinodoz offers a clinical reflection on Berman's review of the film Vertigo; there is an exchange over Robert Caper's view of the mind of the analyst; Nathan Kravis responds to Mary O'Neil's critique of his book review that was critical of Sandor Rado; Robert Emde responds to critics regarding the question of what constitutes relevant empirical research; and David Scharff responds to critics of his views of Fairbairn.

In his Editorial for the seventy-fifth volume of the *IJPA*, Tuckett, like Hayley before him, describes the *Journal* as a service provider for the analytic community, but in Tuckett's description, emphasis is laid on its central role in facilitating dialogue, especially on controversial matters. He writes: "Freud founded the *Journal* to provide a coherent on-going setting in which all those who were taking part in the growing body of psychoanalytic thought and research could enter into dialogue with one another", and he adds that it is to Jones that the *Journal* owes the important tradition of maintaining a "non-partisan approach to controversy" (Tuckett, 1994, p. 1).

2003–

In 2003, Glen Gabbard and Paul Williams become co-editors of the *Journal*, with Gabbard being the first non-British person to assume this role. Among the innovations this team introduced is the special controversy section. In their first editorial, Gabbard and Williams write the following under the heading "Psychoanalytic Controversies":

> One of our initiatives, in response to our thrust towards internationalisation, was the establishment of a dialogue between analysts from different psychoanalytic cultures through our new feature 'The Analyst at Work'. Another innovation was the creation of our 'Community of Analysts' network. When we surveyed our colleagues in this network, we asked them for a candid evaluation of how well the *IJPA* served their needs as analysts. A recurrent refrain from respondents around the world was a wish for us to address cutting-edge controversies in the field. To this end, we are pleased to introduce 'Psychoanalytic Controversies' in this issue. This initiative will comprise two distinct, if not opposing, viewpoints to be published side by side. An analytic colleague will be

invited to present a position statement on an issue in our field that is controversial. A response will then be enlisted from another colleague. Finally, the author of the original position statement will have the opportunity to offer a rejoinder to the response.

(Gabbard and Williams, 2003, p. 1)

During the next four years, there were two to three Controversies in this format per volume, alongside the debates that took place through the Letters to the Editor, which continued to be used extensively.

The topics were varied, including on the analytic treatment of schizophrenia (Robert Michels and Richard Lucas), the relevance of repressed memories to analytic work (Harold Blum and Peter Fonagy), various aspects of analytic training (Egle Laufer and Cesar Garza-Guerrero and Paul Israel and Robert Michels), the psychoanalytic understanding of terrorism (Twemlow and Lawrence Friedman), the need for research in psychoanalysis (Otto Kernberg and Roger Perron), and matters of analytic technique (including Freud Busch and Betty Joseph and John Steiner and Edgar Levenson).

In 2007, when Dana Birksted-Breen and Bob Michels became joint editors-in-chief, I became editor for the Controversy section. With my assumption of this new role, I introduced several changes into the section's format, all aimed at ensuring that the heart of the controversial issues will be addressed, that discussants will directly respond to the points raised by presenters, rather than only present alternative perspectives, and that readers will come away with deeper understanding of the ideas presented and their significance. In practice, changes included my framing the controversial issues in terms of specific and focused questions, reviewing the papers before publication, and, where necessary, asking for modifications that would further the dialogue. In addition, I write a detailed introduction to each controversy, which places it in context in terms of historical and ideational developments in the field and clarifies the positions presented by the invited participants, highlighting points of similarity and difference and their broader significance to analytic theory and practice. A special effort has been made to ensure that the voices of analysts from different schools and regions be heard, and that the topics address issues between different analytic approaches, as well as within them.

Over the years, we have covered the following: "On the idea that analysts should acknowledge to their patients that they have failed them: A clinical debate" (contributors: Jessica Benjamin, Vic Sedlak); "Distinguishing psychoanalysis from psychotherapy" (contributors: Fred Busch, Horst Kachele, Daniel Widlocher); "The value of 'late Bion' to analytic theory and practice" (contributors: Rudi Vermote, David Taylor); "On the value of Winnicott's thinking to analytic practice with adults" (contributors: Jan Abram, Vincenzo Bonaminio, Michael Eigen); "What does the presentation of case material tell us about what actually happened in an analysis and how does it do this?" (contributors: Elias de Rocha Barros, Dale Boesky, Catherine Chabert); "How and why unconscious phantasy and transference are the defining features of psychoanalytic practice" (contributors: Lucy Lafarge, Donnel Stern, Michael Feldman); "Is the nature of psychoanalytic thinking and practice (e.g., in regard to sexuality) determined by extra-analytic social and cultural developments?" (contributors: Jorge Ahumada, Robert Paul); "On the value of the Lacanian approach to analytic practice" (contributors: Bruce Fink, Ricardo & Beatriz de León de Bernardi, Alfred Margulies, Sara Flanders, Lionel Bailly), and, currently, "Can we think analytically about transgenderism?"

In 2014, under the sole editorship of Birksted-Breen, an additional arena for debate within the journal was established – the "Contemporary Conversations" section. In this section, one or more analyst are invited to discuss a paper that has been accepted for publication through the regular submission and review process. I have had the good fortune to be one such discussant. This was on the topic of the relevance of neuroscience to psychoanalysis – an area of clear controversy and division within the analytic community. While the mind does not exist without a brain, does the study of the brain on the biological level of neurons contribute to the understanding of the mind? And is it not the mind, rather than the brain, with which psychoanalytic theory and practice is concerned?

While awaiting the receipt of the paper for discussion – which, as I had been informed, took issue with some of my earlier anti-neuropsychoanalytic work –I felt firsthand the excitement of participation in the *Journal's* controversial discussions, an eagerness to read and engage with the critique of my ideas and the sense of hope that my opponents would make the strongest and most challenging arguments, and in this way open me to a deeper understanding of reality, of truth, and of analytic practice.

Unity, difference and the role of *the IJP*

The IJP continues to provide a context for dialogue over differences within the psychoanalytic community. But indeed, some community, some union or unity, is needed for such dialogue to be meaningful and relevant to psychoanalysis. And here an important problem arises. Is it not the case that as psychoanalysis expands, as the field becomes more diverse, the nature of that unity is less clear, and in fact the question of what is psychoanalysis is in itself at issue in many of the Controversies? That is, are not the differences between the perspectives in regard to pathology, technique, theory, and so forth ultimately determined by more foundational differences regarding the very nature of psychoanalysis?

Based on the present study, I would maintain that while indeed all significant controversial discussions rely on more foundational issues regarding the essence of psychoanalysis, this is not a function of growing diversity. Rather, very early on, fundamental differences in regard to basic Freudian tenets and "the essence of psychoanalysis" emerge (Obendorf).

Moreover, this study has pointed to a certain tension between the value of opening the *Journal* to free debate and the value of maintaining clear standards both in terms of quality of argumentation and evidence and in terms of ensuring that the views expressed are in some significant way analytic in nature. The latter involves a critical evaluative dimension. Insofar as the IPA is not only the unified body of practicing analysts but also maintains this dimension as it intended at its inception, uniting its members by promoting a certain tradition of analytic thinking and practice based on Freud's notions of the unconscious, resistance, transference, internal conflict, drives, and so forth, and by together developing this tradition through rigorous clinical and theoretical work, the aims of the IPA and *the IJP* are clearly aligned. The role of *the IJP* may then be seen to be that of preserving and advancing what is important to the IPA's psychoanalytic objectives – in this proactive sense, it is its "official organ". But insofar as the IPA leans towards the value of providing its members with the most open possible context for discussion, putting aside any evaluative dimension, a gap evolves between its aims and those of *the IJP*.

The history of the *Journal*, and specifically its history in relation to the discussion of controversial issues, is significantly shaped by the way it has dealt with this tension. As we have seen, one way of dealing with it has been to take a more passive stance in relation to the IPA,

211

publishing all that transpires in the meetings of its members, putting aside its proactive role. But more common is the effort to find some better balance between the values. This may be seen in the way controversies are dealt with at present. All views prevalent in the analytic community, however radical, are invited to the table, but within the context of the Controversies section, the positions are contextualized, seen in relation to traditional analytic tenets, and their assumptions clarified and challenged through focused debate. In this way, the *Journal* serves the entire analytic community, while at the same time maintaining the critical standards that Freud intended for it when it was first established as the official organ of the IPA.

References

(1920). Editorial. *Int. J. Psycho-Anal.*, 1:3–5.

(1920). Reports of the International Psycho-Analytical Association— Sixth Congress of the International Psycho-Analytical Association. *Bul. Int. Psychoanal. Assn.*, 1:208–221.

(1927). Discussion: Lay Analysis. *Int. J. Psycho-Anal.*, 8:174–283.

(1937). Symposium on the Theory of the Therapeutic Results of Psycho-Analysis. *Int. J. Psycho-Anal.*, 18:125–189.

(1955). Discussion. *Int. J. Psycho-Anal.*, 36:205–208.

Ferenczi, S. (1920). Open Letter. *Int. J. Psycho-Anal.*, 1:1–2.

Gabbard, G.O. and Williams, P. (2003). A New Era. *Int. J. Psycho-Anal.*, 84(1):1–2.

Hayley, T. (1984). Editorial. *Int. R. Psycho-Anal.*, 11:1–1.

Hayley, T. (1988). Editorial. *Int. J. Psycho-Anal.*, 69:1–2.

Jones, E. (1927). Letter from Ernest Jones to Sigmund Freud, September 30, 1927. *The Complete Correspondence of Sigmund Freud and Ernest Jones 1908–1939*, 625–632. Cambridge, MA/London: The Belknap Press of Harvard University Press.

Jones, E. (1935). Early Female Sexuality. *Int. J. Psycho-Anal.*, 16:263–273.

King, P. and Steiner, R. (1991). The Freud–Klein Controversies 1941–45. *New Library of Psychoanalysis*, 11:1–942. London and New York: Tavistock/ Routledge.

Lampl-De Groot, J. (1969). Introduction to the Scientific Programme of the 26th Congress of the International Psycho-Analytical Association, Rome—(27 July 1969 to 1 August Inclusive). *Int. J. Psycho-Anal.*, 50:3–4.

Oberndorf, C.P., Greenacre, P. and Kubie, L. (1948). Symposium on the Evaluation of Therapeutic Results. *Int. J. Psycho-Anal.*, 29:7–33.

Sandler, J. (1972). Editorial. *Int. J. Psycho-Anal.*, 53:1–1.

Tuckett, D. (1994). The 75th Volume. *Int. J. Psycho-Anal.*, 75:1–2.

FORM AND REPRESENTATION

8

PICTURING OEDIPUS

Ingres, Bacon, Freud

Adele Tutter

An artist is originally a man who turns away from reality because he cannot come to terms with the renunciation of instinctual satisfaction which it at first demands, and who allows his erotic and ambitious wishes full play in the life of phantasy. He finds the way back to reality, however, from this world of phantasy by making use of special gifts to mould his phantasies into truths of a new kind, which are valued by men as precious reflections of reality. Thus in a certain fashion he actually becomes the hero, the king, the creator, or the favourite he desired to be.

—S. Freud[1]

For beauty is nothing but the beginning of terror, which we can just barely endure

—R. M. Rilke[2]

Of the collection of more than 80 papers on art, artists, aesthetics, and creativity published in *the International Journal of Psychoanalysis* (*IJP*) and surveyed in this essay commemorating the journal's centenary,[3] a mere handful train their focus on photography. In the first, Colson (1979) characterizes the characteristic ability of the photograph to both facilitate and to impede mourning; in two others, Reineman (2011) and this author (Tutter, 2011a) implicate mourning and defenses against mourning in photographs of the dead and missing in Argentina and in the auto-portraiture of Francesca Woodman, respectively. Along similar lines, Greenspan (2017) interprets the photomontages of Grete Stern, a German Jew who left Nazi Germany in 1933 for Great Britain, and then Argentina, as comprising an aesthetics of exile. One imagines that similar dynamics were in play when in May 1938, Edmund Engelman was commissioned to document Sigmund Freud's office and home at Bergasse 19; one of the resulting images is shown in Figure 8.1. As Werner (2002) explains in another essay on photography, Engelman made these photographs at great personal risk, just weeks before Freud, after much persuasion, at last capitulated and fled Vienna, but not before securing a set of proofs, which accompanied him to London and guided the minute reproduction of his new rooms there.

The association of art and loss was not central for Freud, who in 1908 formulated creativity as a sublimation of the libidinous drive.

Figure 8.1 Freud's office at Berggasse 19, Vienna, Edmund Engelman, May 1938. The white arrow designates the engraving of Ingres's *Oedipus and the Sphinx*. Freud Museum, London, reference number IN270. Used with permission.

Since then, psychoanalytic theories of art, artistic creation, and aesthetics have grown considerably in breadth and depth – developments often first elaborated in the pages of *the IJP*. The earliest such effort, Hans Sachs's essay "Aesthetics and psychology of the artist" (1921), surveys 40 published articles by various authors, including Lou Andreas-Salomé, Otto Rank, Theodore Reik, and others – including, curiously, one anonymous writer, whose 1914 contribution "Der Moses des Michelangelo" caught Sachs's attention. While allowing that "neither the starting point nor the result" of the paper "belong to the domain of psycho-analysis", Sachs nonetheless concludes that it, in its *method,* "answers fully to the psycho-analytic method in its best and purest form" (p. 8).

The unnamed author was, of course, eventually revealed to be Freud, whose attempt at anonymity belies his trepidation about publishing an essay on art, an area he stressed was wholly outside his expertise – let alone drawing inferences from his personal response to art. One is tempted to conjecture that at that point, Freud could give himself the freedom to roam in and rely on his countertransference only when analyzing a dead person, Moses – and, even more remotely, doing so via Michelangelo's aesthetic interpretation.

Given Freud's subsequent inability to further mine the rich theoretical vein of the countertransference, his essay on Michelangelo's Moses is remarkable for representing perhaps the first instance in which a psychoanalytic approach to visual – rather than literary – art anticipated an important new direction of psychoanalytic theory, if only unwittingly.

★ ★ ★

It was Melanie Klein who provided the first substantial advance in psychoanalytic theorizing about art by stressing its connections to loss and reparation. Reporting the analysis of an artist in the 1929 essay "Infantile anxiety-situations reflected in work of art and in the creative impulse", she concludes that the desire "to make good the injury psychologically done to the mother and also to restore herself was at the bottom of the compelling urge to paint" (p. 443). Explicating and extending Klein, Hannah Segal in her valuable "Psychoanalytical approach to aesthetics" (1952) writes that art is ultimately not merely "the outcome of a loss", but "a creative act involving the pain and the whole work of mourning" (p. 203). Art, then, is

217

powered by loss and at the same time comprises a means to mourn it. In a study of three sculptors, Felix Deutsche (1959) extends this framework to include aspects of the self: "creative passion… is based on the idea of the lost integrity of oneself, which has to be redeemed" (p. 49). In agreement, Chasseguet-Smirgel (1984) adds that if the creative act can "plunge its roots in the desire to repair the object", then it follows that "there exists creative activity in which the pursued goal is the reparation of the subject itself" (p. 400).[4]

Working within a Kleinian framework but approaching creativity from a more generative angle, Heimann (1942) understands artistic efforts as constructive attempts to improve or enhance internal objects "as distinguished from a compulsion to save them from unutterable destruction" (pp. 13–15). Also shaped by Klein while remaining utterly unique is the art writing of Adrian Stokes (1945), who, in his singular voice, specifies the artist as "a self-constituted priest of Eros, the synthesiser and the object-seeker" (p. 177).[5] Stokes and Heimann anticipate the metapsychology of Marion Milner, which, as summarized by Marks (2014), detects in the creative process a characteristic "rhythmic merging and emergence, alternating between 'oceanic' feelings of fusion with an object (one-ness), on the one hand, and surface ego or outer-world perception of two-ness" (p. 69). Like Klein, Milner has proved an important jumping-off point for analysts writing about art; as example, Marks (2014) and Podro (1990) apply her formulations to their studies of the artists Y.Z. Kami and Paul Cézanne, respectively. Parker's seminal essay "Killing the Angel in the House" (1988) extends Milner's thought via a reading of an essay by Virginia Woolf that underlines its identification of the aggression requisite for creativity, and the problems this poses for women in particular. So, too, do Milner's ideas inform Ferraro (2003), who considers creative work as a procreative product of maternal and paternal identifications – echoing Segal (1952), who asserts that "creating a work of art is a psychic equivalent of procreation" (p. 200). Sirois (2008) also draws on Milner to explore the role of "fascination" in aesthetic experience. Finally, Eigen (1983) offers a useful counterpoint to these appreciations in his careful critique of Milnerian metapsychology.

Endorsing the very different theoretical direction led by Anna Freud, Ernst Kris (1936) understood creativity as a "regression in the service of the ego" (p. 290). Despite the remarkably prescient warning of Gombrich (1954), Kris's formulation was eagerly adopted by a generation of ego-psychologists (e.g., Székely, 1967) who used it to underwrite what became a popular, if often misused paradigm: the analysis of art as result and reflection of the artist's psychopathology. In contrast, Kris's understanding of ambiguity as a singular feature of great art remains a widely accepted and valuable proposition (see Noy, 1972; Roland, 1972; Sirois, 2008).

★ ★ ★

Let us return to Engelman's photograph of Freud's consulting room and consider a small detail of particular interest (Figure 8.1). At the foot of the analytic couch hangs a small engraving of Jean-Auguste-Dominique

Figure 8.2 The engraved reproduction of Ingres's *Oedipus and the Sphinx* that hung at the foot of Freud's analytic couch (also see Figure 8.3). Freud Museum, London, reference number 6405. Used with permission.

Figure 8.3 Oedipus and the Sphinx, Jean-Auguste-Dominique Ingres, Musée du Louvre. Originally completed in 1808 when the artist was 28, the canvas was in 1827 modified for exhibition. Image © Scala / Art Resource, NY. Used with permission. © Seala/Art Resource, NY.

Ingres's *Oedipus and the Sphinx* (Figure 8.2; the original canvas is shown in Figure 8.3). As he tells Fliess, Freud gifted another reproduction of the painting to one of his more gratifying patients, one "E":

You are familiar with my dream which obstinately promises the end of E.'s treatment... It now appears that the dream will be fulfilled... I scarcely dare believe it yet. It is as if Schliemann had once more excavated Troy, which had hitherto been deemed a fable... [E.] demonstrated the reality of my theory in my own case... For this piece of work I even made him the present of a picture of Oedipus and the Sphinx.

(Freud, 1899a, pp. 391–392)

Freud's triumphal report of a dream of cure come true echoes a letter he wrote to Fliess six months before, wherein he describes reading Heinrich Schliemann's *Ilios*, the archaeologist's bestselling memoir. *Ilios* is notable for its author's claim that his heroic excavation of ancient Troy and "proof" of ancient legend achieved an early wish:

I gave myself a present, Schliemann's *Ilios,* and greatly enjoyed the account of his childhood. The man was happy when he found Priam's treasure [archaeological finds attributed to King Priam of Troy], because happiness comes only with the fulfillment of a childhood wish.

(Freud, 1899b, p. 353)[6]

Freud, too, would enjoy this special kind of gratification. On the occasion of his fiftieth birthday in 1906, a group of his followers presented him with a commemorative medal (Figure 8.4):

having on the obverse his side-portrait in bas-relief and on the reverse a Greek design of Oedipus answering the Sphinx. Around it is a line from Sophocles' *Oedipus Tyrannus*: ΟΣ ΤΑ ΚΛΕΙΝ'

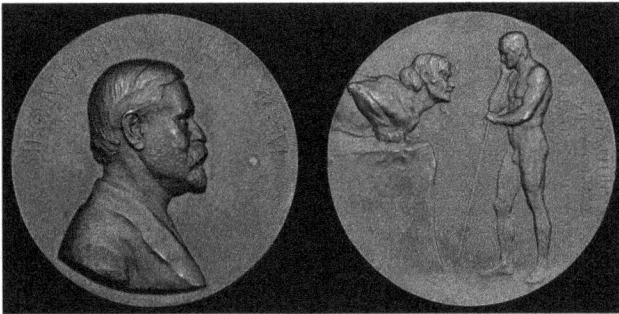

Figure 8.4 Commemorative medal by Carl Maria Schwerdtner given to Freud on the occasion of his fiftieth birthday. Freud Museum, London, reference number 4395. Used with permission.

ΑΙΝΙΓΜΑΤ' 'ΗΙΔΗ ΚΑΙ ΚΡΑΤΙΣΤΟΣ 'ΗΝ ΑΝΗΡ (He who solved the famous riddle and was the most powerful man)... When Freud read the inscription he became pale and agitated... He behaved as if he had encountered a revenant, and so he had... Freud disclosed that as a young student at the University of Vienna he used to stroll around the great Court inspecting the busts of former famous professors of the institution. He then had the phantasy, not merely of seeing his own bust there in the future... but of it actually being inscribed with the identical words he now saw on the medallion.

(Mattonet, 2002, p. 15)

Years later, Jones (1955) took it upon himself to consummate Freud's "youthful wish", presenting

to the University of Vienna, for erection in the Court, the bust of Freud made by the sculptor Königsberger in 1921, and the line from Sophocles has been added. It was unveiled on February 4, 1955.

(p. 15)

Reflecting his enduring fascination with the myth, Freud's collection of antiquities contains several excellent examples of Greek vessels featuring Oedipus and the Sphinx. The decoration of one red-figure *hydria* typifies the conventional classical iconography of the theme: Oedipus, with travelling hat and stick, sitting quite casually, legs crossed, before the commanding Sphinx (Figure 8.5). In keeping with this ancient treatment, Ingres's iconic 19th-century interpretation that Freud so valued also depicts a relaxed Oedipus, but here the subject is uncharacteristically unclothed: holding his hat and robe in his hand, he reveals his naked body for all to see. This overt display moreover divulges no trace of his childhood wounds, or indeed of any disability; indeed his athletic figure is incongruent with his legendary lameness. Further breaking with tradition, Ingres's Oedipus leans not on his iconographic walking stick (as seen, for example, in Freud's *hydria* and commemorative medal) but on two spears, more warrior than wanderer. Yet if one were to believe Ingres, Oedipus' most effective weapon is not his legendary quick wit, or newly evident physical strength, but sheer will: "it is hard

Figure 8.5 Red-figure *hydria* decorated with Oedipus and the Sphinx. From Freud's collection. Freud Museum, London, reference number 3117. Used with permission.

to resist the impression that the weapon with which this duel to the death is being fought out is the eyes" (Wollheim, 1987, p. 299). The Sphinx cannot sustain Oedipus' locked, knowing stare, and averts her eyes.

In the positivist tradition of the Enlightenment, a cornerstone of the intellectual heritage in which Freud's theorizing is firmly situated, Oedipus's heroism derives from his intellect, a quality of paramount value for Freud.[7] It is thus no wonder that he privileged Ingres's image with a prominent position in his consulting room: its unequivocally heroicizing treatment of Oedipus – powerful in mind, and also in body and will – would have reinforced any identification Freud might have had with the mythic figure. Exploring his tendency to identify with great men, Steiner (1999) stresses "the heroic self's specific need to identify and to surpass its peers, both past and present" (p. 706) – a variation on the very dynamic that Freud (1900) named after the Oedipus myth. In a stunning example of theory generated via art, his formulation of the Oedipus complex was cataluzed by his creative solution of *Hamlet*. It was heady stuff: after all, Freud was heir to the tradition voiced by the philosopher and statesman Sir Francis Bacon (1609), who notes:

> the riddle that enigma propounded to Oedipus (by means of which he obtained the Theban empire) belonged to the nature of man: for whosoever doth accordingly consider the nature of man, may be in a manner the contriver of his own fortune, and is born to command.
>
> (p. 117)

Recall here the commemorative medal that explicitly compares Freud to Oedipus: "he who solved the famous riddle and was the most powerful man." In a sense, in describing the Oedipus complex, Freud, too, solved "the riddle of man". With the discoveries of his dream book, at the turn of the century Freud was *on fire*. R. Steiner writes,

> the passages on *Oedipus Rex* and *Hamlet* in *The Interpretation of Dreams* are ideas belonging to the heroic, creative period of Freud's work, containing condensed, as it were, into a dense white-hot ball, an enormous series of problems which will take their own shapes later on.
>
> (p. 542)

By solving the Oedipal complex, and anticipating like solutions to myriad other puzzles, Freud sought to liberate man from his neuroses and set him free. If he could relieve man from neurotic misery, how could he *not* identify with Oedipus, who freed Thebes from that singular specter of horror, the Sphinx?

To this end, as an iconic component of Freud's cultural heritage, Ingres's heroicizing image of a victorious Oedipus, notably absent of any residue of trauma harmonizes with the optimistic expectation of cure that pervades Freud's earlier metapsychology, epitomized as it is by his conviction that difficulties issuing from a central and universal unconscious conflict – manifest in such significant cultural elaborations as *Oedipus Rex* and *Hamlet* – could be resolved via therapeutic means, ridding that complex of its pathogenic potential.

Given Freud's predilection for visual representation, the riveting beauty and self-assured power of Ingres's Oedipus may have more indirectly reinforced his confidence via a different sort of "cure": aesthetic pleasure, which he formulated as the:

> deeper pleasure connected with the cathartic effect of the phantasies veiled by this form, which allows for the liberation of certain tensions and masks the shame of the original phantasy presented in the work of art.
>
> (Sirois, 2008, p. 128)

We may also imagine that on some illusory level, the solid corporeality of Ingres's nakedly realistic treatment of Oedipus[8] additionally served Freud's purposes by credibly transporting the subject from the mythical past inscribed on ancient vessels into a more universal time, bolstering the idea that Oedipus – or, more accurately, the Oedipus complex – was indeed fact, and not fable.

★ ★ ★

An oft-overlooked aspect of the myth of Oedipus is that it is, at heart, a succession story. In Freud's formulation of the Oedipus complex, the son views his father as a competitor whom he wishes to overthrow (or kill) so as to take possession of his father' wife, his mother. Laius is just one of many fathers who, in legend at least, try to kill their sons for fear of patricide; but these fathers typically worry about forfeiting their throne, rather than their bed. Viewed from this perspective, a son's wish to possess his mother could be seen as secondary to his wish for his father's status – *to the victor go the spoils*. (This might be especially so when there is no love lost between mother and son.) Thus, alongside the triadic dynamics, dyadic aspects that implicate conflictual issues of succession and envy also contribute to the Oedipus complex.[9]

Even if father is not king, he must be "killed", so to speak, to make one's mark.[10] But there is no need to kill the father if one is not present. This is the essential proposition of the avant-garde: the wishful illusion that a great work of art can be entirely novel, indeed *suis generis*, and thus can unburden itself of another kind of dynastic succession, the indebtedness to history and tradition (an idea

225

promulgated by the modern myths of creative genius so elegantly deconstructed by Kris and Kurz [1934]). Analogous aspirations for freedom, couched in aesthetic terms, are embedded in some psychoanalytic theories of creativity: as example, Chasseguet-Smirgel maintains that "on a certain level, the creator expects nothing from anybody and attains total autonomy... *Creativity's deepest impulse, its living strength, as we know it, is essentially linked to freedom*" (1984, p. 405, emphasis original). Even if we accept that the prospect of "total autonomy" from one's predecessors and teachers may be a potent driving force, innovation and originality typically coexist, with varying degrees of conflict, with opposing wishes for a place in a dynastic lineage: longings to adhere and belong to a particular tradition. Here one detects derivatives of the ambivalent wish for dependent attachment, the wish to admire the father (or mother, or master), and to attain and share in their greatness.

The iconic cartoon of Ingres's *Oedipus and the Sphinx* that comprises *the IJP's* "coat of arms" has been the journal's signifying logo since its inception (Figure 8.6). It seems fitting that Freud hung his reproduction of Ingres's canvas next to a reproduction of the relief sculpture in the Vatican that William Jensen named "Gradiva" in his 1903 novel of the same name (Figure 8.1): Freud inaugurated the extension of psychoanalytic theory to visual art in his essay on Jensen's novel (1907), followed by papers on Leonardo (1910) and Michelangelo (1914). Unfortunately, the missteps in this troika – the wild analysis, theory-driven arguments, amateur ahistoricity, and reductive pathography – inspired like efforts, including essays by Heilbronner (1938) on Paleolithic art; Sterba and Sterba (1956) and Peto (1979) on Michelangelo; and Simon

Figure 8.6 The logo, or "coat of arms", of *the International Journal of Psychoanalysis.*

(1977), who reduces essentially the entire *oeuvre* of the Bloomsbury painter Mark Gertler to a consequence of primal scene trauma. More recently, Hartke (2000) revived this infelicitous formulation in a reductive interpretation of Picasso's *Guernica,* and Thanopulos (2005) looks to Freud's presumptive analysis of Leonardo in his no-less presumptive analysis of Freud. No doubt Oedipal dynamics –or defenses against them – play a role in preserving the tenacious sway of Freud's example.

A tension, between such emulative, deferential identifications with Freud's pioneering contributions on the one hand, and more creative responses and interrogative correctives to those contributions on the other hand, courses throughout in the pages of *the IJP.* Pointed correctives that exhaustively counter the reductive and overprivileged application of psychoanalytic theory to art (and other liberties) include the particularly valuable comments of eminent art historians, including Herbert Read (1951) and James Elkins (1994). Another academic, Ernst Gombrich (1954), chides efforts undermined by art-historical naiveté, using as example Ernest Jones's study of Andrea Del Sarto, which, as Jones points out, relies on flawed 19th-century notions about exaggerated talent ("the fault of faultlessness", p. 407). Using Cézanne as example, art historian Michael Podro (1990) explores the problematics of pathography and offers an alternative, more credible approach to a psychoanalytically informed formal analysis. And scholar Griselda Pollock (1994) offers a clipped Marxist critique of the idealizing cultural mythologies that corrupt both psychoanalytic and popular views of Van Gogh, deftly dissecting "the cultural and historical privilege with which [Van Gogh's] life has been endowed by the confusion between his mythicised life and his art" (p. 811) – a problematic that undermines the analyses of psychoanalysts Heiman (1976) and Valenstein & Wylie (1976). Academics from other disciplines have weighed in as well. Social scientist Michael Schröter (1994) unsettles long-standing, but erroneous psychoanalytic theories around Leonardo, beginning with Freud's, emphasizing the need to appreciate the "gap which separates them from the world of their subjects before they try to bridge it by empathy, i.e. by experiences familiar to themselves" (p. 96) – as exampled by a study of Leonardo by Grinberg and Paniagua (1991).

Psychoanalysts, too, chime in. Critiquing the facile extension of adult experience to infants and children, Esman (1983) roundly rejects Kutash's (1982) conjecture that minimal and abstract expressionist art conveys "early transitional experiences of the self and object world and their first representations" (p. 172). Per Esman, Kutash "falls victim to the seductive practice of treating speculations about infantile experience... as though they were facts" (p. 111) In something of an inverse of the pathologization of art, Esman (2004) depathologizes the art of the mentally ill, and, disagreeing with Kris, argues that it constitutes genuine art in its own right. Further emphasizing the dangers of pathography, Paniagua (1986) argues that "*precise* dynamic formulations and reconstructions are intrinsically impossible", and cautions that "psychobiographical speculations are fertile ground for projective novelization" (p. 449, emphasis original). Sensitive to these warnings, yet remaining largely theory-driven, are Hoffman (1984), whose exploration on Picasso from an ego–psychological perspective, and Abella (2007), who trenches on speculative pathography in an essay on Marcel Duchamp: "destructivity continues its work and turns against thought itself, entailing a subversion of logic and reason, a path that finally left Duchamp no other option but to abandon art" (p. 1054).

In a sharp riposte to psychoanalytic theories of creativity, Fossi (1985) concludes that "data gathered from the analysis of creative persons may constitute the only original contribution of psychoanalysis to the problems of creativity" (p. 227).[11] Exampling the centrality of the case history of the creative analysand to psychoanalytic theories are the contributions of Klein (1929), Heimann (1942), Segal (1952), Rose (1964), Roland (1972), Browne (1980), McDougall (1989), Laub and Podell (1995), and Steiner (1999), to name a select few. I would also aver that, if lacking in first-hand analytic material, psychoanalytic approaches to artists outside the consulting room, strengthened by art-historical rigour and clarifying sociocultural context, can shed fresh light on the underpinnings of creative efforts. Three illustrative examples include Adams (1990), who juxtaposes pertinent clinical material with an acute art-historical analysis of Velazquez's *Las Meninas*; Attia (2011), who integrates psychoanalytic concepts and longitudinal art-historical methodology to uncover new meanings in the preparatory studies for Picasso's *Guernica*; and Greenspan (2017), who presents a multifaceted interdisciplinary study of the photomontages of Grete Stern.

Some psychoanalysts writing on art challenge the traditional one-way application of psychoanalytic principles, and also look to reciprocally gain from the insights and observations of the creative artist. Enlisting interdisciplinary research as a valuable means to expand psychoanalytic theory, Werman (1989) addresses the Belgian painter James Ensor's relationship to physical place, a neglected topic in the psychoanalytic literature; this author's analysis of Nicholas Poussin's serial canvases of Narcissus informs a new perspective on narcissism (Tutter, 2014). And, as early as Fraiberg (1956), analysts have looked to Freud's art writing as a valuable window onto his process of theory building. Blass (2006), focusing on Freud's contradictory theorizing around the libidinal underpinnings of curiosity and epistemophilia – the very issues around which Oedipus's fate revolves – argues that Freud in his essay on Leonardo makes "explicit latent aspects of the foundations of psychoanalytic thinking which may be transmitted to contemporary psychoanalysts in part through Freud's seminal texts" (p. 1260). Indeed, Jurist (2006) in his critical reading goes further, observing that Freud's "focus on emotions in art is remarkable because it underscores what is missing in his scientific theory" (p. 1327). We have already discussed one instance of this: the pioneering use of countertransference in Freud's essay on Moses; there is even more to be found there. Literally step by step, Sigg (1990) meticulously deconstructs Freud's approach to this masterpiece. The sculpture of Moses was commissioned for a tomb of Pope Julius that was never completed, and its intended inhabitant was interred elsewhere. But Sigg discovers encrypted traces of Freud's late brother Julius hidden in the empty tomb.

★ ★ ★

As we have already touched on, no less than psychoanalytic thinkers, artists continually engage with the dialectics of dynasty: interrogating the "issue of how an artist, a true artist, should stand to the work of his predecessors" (Wollheim, 1987). Ingres, a serious student of the visual iconography of classical myth, is a most instructive case. Wollheim explains:

> it does not require any deep acquaintance with Ingres to recognize how important this issue was for [Ingres]. At times it seems to have been paramount, and Ingres often looked upon himself as a mere conduit through which the art of the past could flow smoothly, safely, into the future.
>
> (p. 301)

Figure 8.7 Hermes Tying His Sandal, Roman copy of the 2nd century CE after a Greek original of the late 4th century BC, from the Theater of Marcellus in Rome. Image, open source, https://commons.wikimedia.org/wiki/Category:Hermes_with_the_sandal_(Louvre,_Ma_83)#/media/File:Hermes_with_the_Sandal-Louvre.jpg.

While the dominating stance Ingres assigns his own Oedipus is nowhere to be found in traditional aesthetic representations of this subject, his posture quotes the ancient Greek statue of *Hermes Tying His Sandal* in the Louvre; this latter subject is especially notable for his attention to his *foot* (Figure 8.7). Not only does Ingres wipe away any trace of Oedipus's wounded feet, he also exchanges them, via this provocative allusion, for *winged* ones.

The statue of Hermes was also a likely source of an aspect of a *seicento* painting that predates Ingres by two centuries, Nicolas Poussin's *Et in Arcadio Ego* (Figure 8.8), specifically, the figure on the right who points to the eponymous phrase inscribed on a monument (perhaps best translated in context as "'And I, Death, also live in Arcadia"; see Panofsky, 1957; also discussed by Steiner, 1995). Mixing intimations of mortality and immortality, Ingres's

Figure 8.8 Nicolas Poussin, *Et in Arcadio Ego*, 1637–1638. Musée du Louvre. Image, open source: https://en.wikipedia.org/wiki/Et_in_Arcadia_ego#/media/File:Nicolas_Poussin__Et_in_Arcadia_ego_(deuxi%C3%A8me_version).jpg.

Oedipus thus draws both on a classical source and on Poussin's reference to that source. The linkage gains in significance given Ingres's genealogical relationship to Poussin, the founder of the French Neoclassical school of painting. Poussin's dynastic mantle was passed to Jacques-Louis David, one of the greatest exponents of Neoclassicism, who would, in turn, so honor his gifted student, Ingres, continuing the developmental line.

If, in quoting Poussin, Ingres identifies with his illustrious aesthetic predecessor, then in heroicizing Oedipus, the virtuoso artist identifies with his victorious subject. Overwhelmed by the archaic frontality and sheer size of Ingres's visibly intact Oedipus, the hero's history of mutilation as an infant remains occult: encoded by his spears, which suggestively graze his toes – as if to also caution that he himself is the weapon that will cause his final downfall – and which ultimately aim at the foregrounded human remains, which include, of interest, an intact *foot*. The painting also hints of his future exile

231

with a secondary figure, the terrified man at the right who flees the scene. Often called "Poussinesque" (Roseblum, 1968, pp. 80–81), this element was an afterthought, added by Ingres when, 20 years after he painted the original, he enlarged and added to it, transforming a figure exercise to a historical painting – the portrayal of a narrative – suitable for exhibition at the salon. In the process, Ingres rendered the Sphinx more prominent, too.[12]

In Greek legend, the Sphinx is usually depicted as a chimeric creature with the head of woman, body of a lion, and wings of a bird. Note that in Ingres's hands, the Sphinx is almost completely shadowed, except for her brilliantly lit, tumescent breasts. While this follows conventional iconography, exemplified by one of Freud's statuettes of the Sphinx (Figure 8.9), when contextualized within the mythical narrative, these highlighted, weaponized female parts – ironically, one of the "human" aspects of the monster – summon

Figure 8.9 Sphinx statuette, terracotta, on wooden base, from Freud's collection. Freud Museum, London, reference number 4037. Used with permission.

a dangerous human woman: Jocasta. The ultimate enabler, she colludes with Laius's attempt at infanticide; some versions of the myth have her, not her husband, piercing their son's ankles, using the same brooch with which Oedipus will blind himself. And, like the Sphinx, Jocasta knew the answer to a riddle – that of Oedipus's identity – for she remembered what the oracle told Laius, and was also witness to "the unspoken evidence", notes Steiner (1985), namely, "the scars on his feet" (p. 164). Hence her desperate attempts to halt his search for Laius's murderer: himself. Another parallel between Jocasta and the Sphinx is the latter's reaction after Oedipus solves the riddle: gesturing to himself in Ingres's canvas, he answers, "it's me: man", precipitating the Sphinx's fall from the cliffs, a lethal surrender that anticipates Jocasta's suicide after Oedipus solves the *other* riddle, the identity of Laius's murderer – with the same answer: "it's me!" Thus, Edmunds (1988) proposes, "the riddle-solving is an image of incest... the marriage to Jocasta, who is not explicitly connected with the Sphinx, is thus prefigured" (p. 57).

Even if we can conjecture that Ingres's Sphinx invokes Jocasta, and likewise, that the fleeing man does double duty by invoking both Oedipus's impending exile and his preceding nemesis, Laius (who would have been at least as horrified by his son's survival as he would have been by the Sphinx), this level of representation was likely lost on Freud, who appears to have understood Ingres's Oedipus in a more manifest way, at the height of triumph: here, recall his gifting an engraving of the painting to a patient in celebration of a moment of clinical success. This narrow view was, at least originally, the artist's manifest intent, too: after all, Ingres was a 28-year-old prodigy and recipient of the Prix de Rome when he first conceived *Oedipus and the Sphinx*, which, in 1808, was sent to Paris as proof of his progress abroad. He fleshed out its narrative and enhanced its monumentality for public display only after the death of his father, in 1814. The recursive Oedipal implications for the artist are evident: Ingres's father, a provincial artist of only nominal talent, placed his failed aspirations for greatness squarely on his talented son's shoulders, sending him from Provence to Paris to study with the master David.[13] Asked to provide an obituary notice for Ingres *père*, Ingres *fils* replied with respectful modesty and the exaggerated admiration that mitigates the guilt of victory:

My father was born with a rare genius for the fine arts; I use the plural, for he practiced painting, sculpture, and even architecture with success… if M. Ingres senior had been given the same advantages he accorded his son and had studied in Paris with the greatest of masters [David], he would have been the premiere artist of his day.

(Vigne, 1995, p. 16)

Poussin's paintings of the giants of classical myth highlight a boy's wish to identify with an omnipotent father (Tutter, 2018): in kind, Ingres's monumental painting of a glowering Jupiter, over 11-feet tall, dwarfs the viewer (*Jupiter and Thetis,* Musée Granet, Aix-en-Provence). While the painter's overly generous estimation of his father's talent might be expected from a grateful son who had long eclipsed the father that supported and advocated for him, Ingres may have also wished for a more accomplished father to emulate – a "rare genius" with whom he could really compete – rather than a man who, in Ingres's words of faint praise, provided "cartouches and ornaments of all kinds" to "decorate the rich hotels of that time with felicity and taste", and manufactured in quantity "terracotta garden sculptures of Sphinxes" (Ingres, quoted in Vigne, 1995, pp. 16–17). Posèq (2001) goes so far as to suggest that Ingres's painted Sphinx stood for his father and his garden ornaments; if so, the Oedipus canvas is more "oedipal" than it first appears.[14]

Despite its allusions to past and future, Ingres's canvas visualizes one moment in time. Similarly, Freud, in his theorizing, concentrated on one part of the myth: the fulfilment of the prophecy that Oedipus tried to defy. While at the end of his life, Freud, in exile in London, may well have identified with Oedipus and the singular anguish of banishment from one's home, as many have noted, he in his writing discussed neither Oedipus's childhood injury and exposure at the hands of his parents, nor his later exile in Colonus, blinded and disgraced. Nor, for that matter, did he explore the genesis of the curse that burdened Laius – his rape of a boy – or versions of the myth with prominent homosexual themes, about which he was well aware (Steiner, 1994). Freud:

nonetheless chose to recall selectively, in his written work, that which a particular tradition, the one stemming from fifth-century Athens and Sophocles, had already chosen to put in a certain order.

(p. 523)

Ingres and his idealizing Neoclassical treatment of Oedipus was thus consonant with this "particular tradition", the 19th-century German-speaking intellectual culture in which Freud was deeply rooted:

> characterised by a particular way of seeing Greek culture and of idealising it... a tendency to consider the art of Ancient Greece as something special, unique, perfect and serene, and they acknowledged its unique historical individuality, comparing it polemically with French Neo-classicism.
>
> (p. 529)

★★★

Just as Poussin and David of the French Neoclassical school shaped Ingres's art, so would Ingres shape the course of modern art. His seminal emphasis on line and form over physical accuracy was an important influence for Cézanne; in turn, Cézanne, Poussin, and Ingres were essential to Picasso. The British painter Francis Bacon (1909–1992) was inspired by all of them.

Like Ingres *père*, Bacon *père* had high hopes for his son, manifest in the name he gave him, after Sir Francis Bacon, from whose brother he descended. Unlike Ingres *père*, however, this father was disappointed by his effete son and his choice of an artistic career, and, intolerant of his flamboyant homosexuality, ultimately threw him out of the house. Lacking the filial support that Ingres, Cézanne, and Picasso enjoyed, Bacon had to find encouragement elsewhere. He remembers:

> I saw at Rosenberg's an exhibition of Picasso, and at that moment I thought, well I will try and paint too... [my parents] were horrified at the thought that I might want to be an artist... they were totally against it.
>
> (quoted in Sylvester, 2016, pp. 210–211)

Bacon's art-historical heroes took on a benevolent, literally paternal, role for him: "Picasso is the reason why I paint. He is the father figure" (quoted in Gruen, 1991, p. 122). He also places important credit on classical Greek tragedy, and two of its prominent aesthetic interpreters, Poussin and Ingres, and explicitly acknowledges his debt to the latter in the 1983 canvas *Oedipus and the Sphinx after*

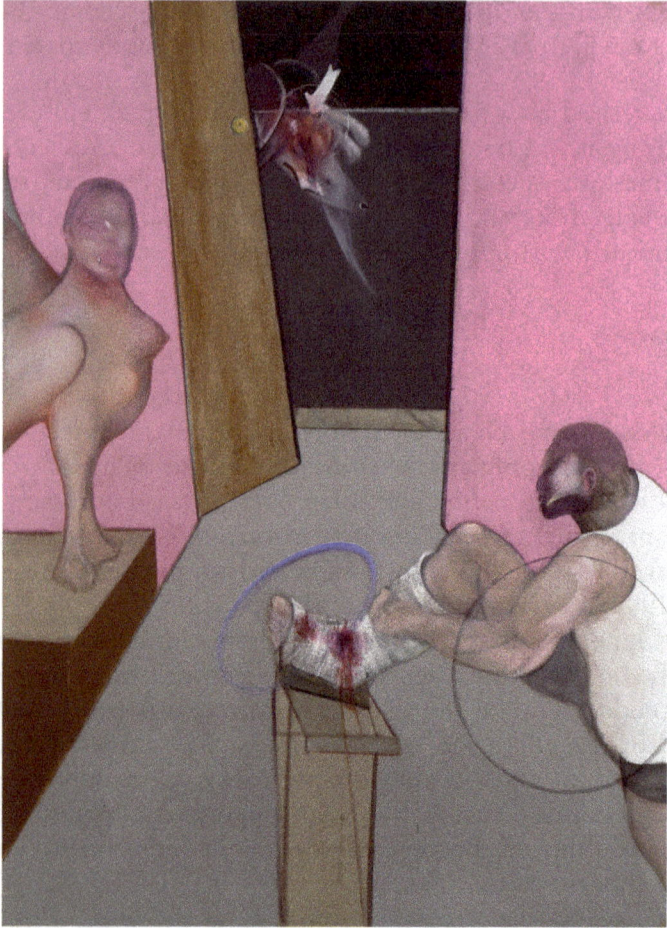

Figure 8.10 Oedipus and the Sphinx after Ingres, Francis Bacon, 1983, Museu Coleçao Berardo, Lisbon. © The Estate of Francis Bacon. All rights reserved, DACS, London/Artist Rights Society, New York, 2020. Photo: Prudence Cuming Associates Ltd, used with permission.

Ingres (Figure 8.10). Almost the exact size as Ingres's canvas, Bacon's adaptation follows its general arrangement of figures. But whereas Oedipus dominates the centre of Ingres's canvas, Bacon's Oedipus is pushed to the right, carrying little more weight than the Sphinx. We sense immediately that there is no victor here.

Kleinian theories of art opened the door to contemporary conceptualizations that view the creative process as an essential component

236

of the response to trauma, exemplified by the landmark articles by McDougall (1989) and Laub & Podell (1995), the latter of whom assert that "the art of trauma" aims to achieve "a representation of that which defies representation in both inner and outer experience" (p. 992), and thus able to "bestow form on chaos" (p. 993). This perspective informs the works on photography discussed earlier, as well as essays on the Norwegian sculptor Gustav Vigeland (Simons, 1984) and Poussin's Ovidian paintings (Tutter, 2011b, 2014, 2018).

Bacon's *Oedipus and the Sphinx after Ingres* is a most fitting illustration of "the art of trauma": its most striking aspect, its Barthian punctum, is the subject's bandaged foot, extended and elevated on a pedestal at the very centre of the canvas. Bacon gives it even more emphasis – indicating, "look *here!*" – by encircling the bloodied foot in blue. Thus privileged, and demanding examination, it is a literal elaboration of the name *Oidipous*, "swollen foot", echoing Edmunds (1988): "Oedipus *is* his feet" (p. 59). This Oedipus's history is evident: the hero to whom Ingres gave two spears now leaks blood from two round wounds, which also summon his future injuries – the eyes he will gouge out. The pedestal bearing Oedipus's foot aligns with the doorway above, which opens onto a blackened empty space; here hangs suspended an indeterminate object that resembles a bleeding heart, comparable in form and placement to the lit area in the rocky crevasse in Ingres's canvas. Like the blue circle that directs attention to Oedipus's wound, a white arrow points out this curious clumped mass, which Bacon identifies as the *Eumenides* (alternatively, the *Erinyes*, better known as the Furies), the three goddesses who, in Greek legend, mete out justice and vengeance.

Bacon made his acquaintance with these arbitresses of guilt in Aeschylus; he employs a similar representation in *The Eumenides: Triptych inspired by the Oresteia of Aeschylus* (1981, Astrup Fearnley Mu Moderne Kunst, Oslo, not shown). In legend, Orestes, the great-grandson of Pelops, fathers Chryssipus, the boy whom Laius abducted and raped, thereby earning the curse that sealed his fate and that of his wife and son. Pelops's wife, Hippodamis, conspired with their two sons Atreus and Thyestes to kill Chryssipus– their illegitimate half-brother – so that one of her own sons would inherit Pelops's throne. This crime begat another curse, that of the House of Atreus. The Houses of Laius and Atreus are thus linked not only by lineage, but also by parallel curses, both instigated by crimes against Chryssipus: Laius's crime of transgressive lust, and Atreus's crime of murderous succession. And these are precisely the two crimes that Oedipus commits: the Eumenides ensures that the sins of the father are visited on the son. Bacon's Eumenides, hanging over Oedipus, signals the guilt he is destined to inherit.

Adams (1990) asserts, "just as myth can elucidate psycho-analysis, so psychoanalysis can elucidate myth and its inclusion in an artist's iconography" (p. 608). Contextualizing the painting within the painter's history, let us examine the door in Bacon's *Oedipus and the Sphinx After Ingres*. It has a distinguishing feature – a round lock – that "unlocks" the presence of the Eumenides beyond a threshold. In 1971, the Grand Palais in Paris held a monumental retrospective of Bacon's work. Over Bacon's objections, his lover, George Dyer, insisted on joining him in Paris. Bacon had grown tired of the less worldly Dyer, and increasingly irritated by his worsening alcoholism and clinging dependence. Dyer, aware that the relationship was dwindling, was desperate. Two days before the exhibition opened, Bacon, sensing trouble, went to their hotel to check on Dyer, but could not open the locked door to his room. The museum staff reassured the exhausted Bacon, and persuaded him to return to the exhibition hall to take a final walk-through the show. That evening Bacon found Dyer dead from an overdose; he was moreover pressured to keep his passing secret until after the opening, so as to not taint the festivities with unwanted media attention.

> As he stood waiting for the President [Pompidou, to preview the exhibition], Bacon would not have missed the tragic irony of the red carpet that had been rolled down the steps of the Grand Palais for the opening ceremony; he was too conscious of the relevance of Greek drama to his own life not to see it. By "trampling the royal crimson," Agamemnon brought about his own swift destruction and unleashed the Furies' quest for further blood.
>
> (Peppiatt, 1997, p. 235)

Taking blame for his lover's death, Bacon never forgave himself for prioritizing his career over Dyer. His guilt is palpable in a series of paintings variously featuring his late lover: blackened doorways; a man attempting to open a lock with his toes; a red carpet; and the Eumenides, who, in *Oedipus and the Sphinx after Ingres,* wait for Oedipus behind an unlocked door.[15]

Prior to his 1983 homage to Ingres, Bacon executed several paintings on the theme of the Sphinx, a preoccupying theme; one of these, the 1979 *Sphinx—Portrait of Muriel Belcher* (Figure 8.11), was painted in the same year as his first Oedipus. Like Ingres's Sphinx, it hints at a maternal link, casting as the Sphinx Bacon's close friend Muriel Belcher, the sharp-tongued, openly lesbian proprietor of the Colony Club, the infamous gay bar where she held court daily. The champagne flowed all

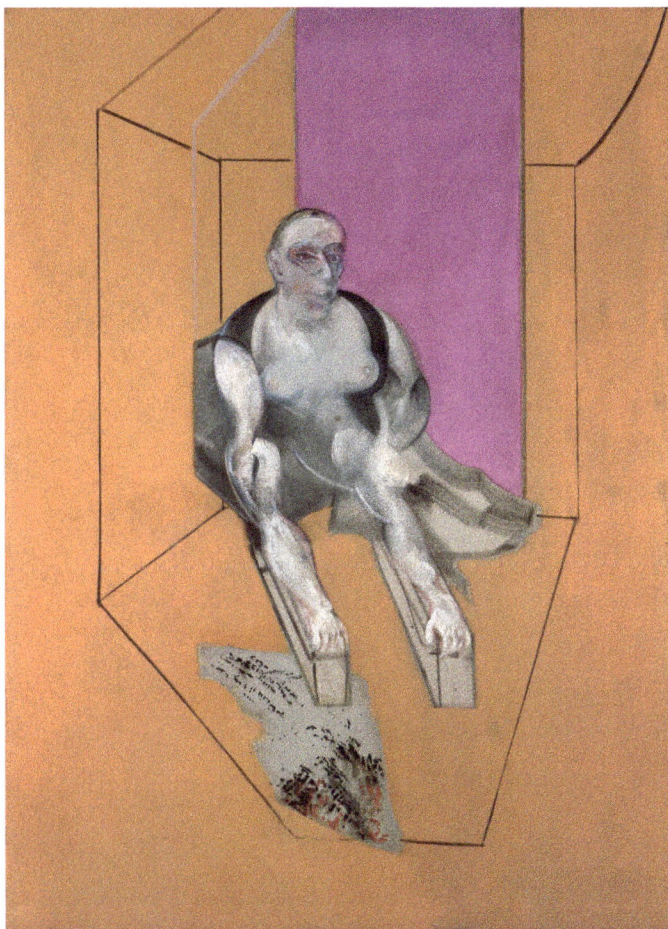

Figure 8.11 Sphinx – Portrait of Muriel Belcher, Francis Bacon, 1979, Museum of Modern Art, Tokyo. © The Estate of Francis Bacon. All rights reserved, DACS, London/Artist Rights Society, New York, 2020. Photo: Prudence Cuming Associates Ltd, used with permission.

day at the Colony Club, Bacon's home-away-from-home in the 1950s; he affectionately called Belcher "Mother".

Also in 1979, Bacon painted a solo *Oedipus* (private collection, Figure 8.12), which features a lone male figure leaning on a lectern,

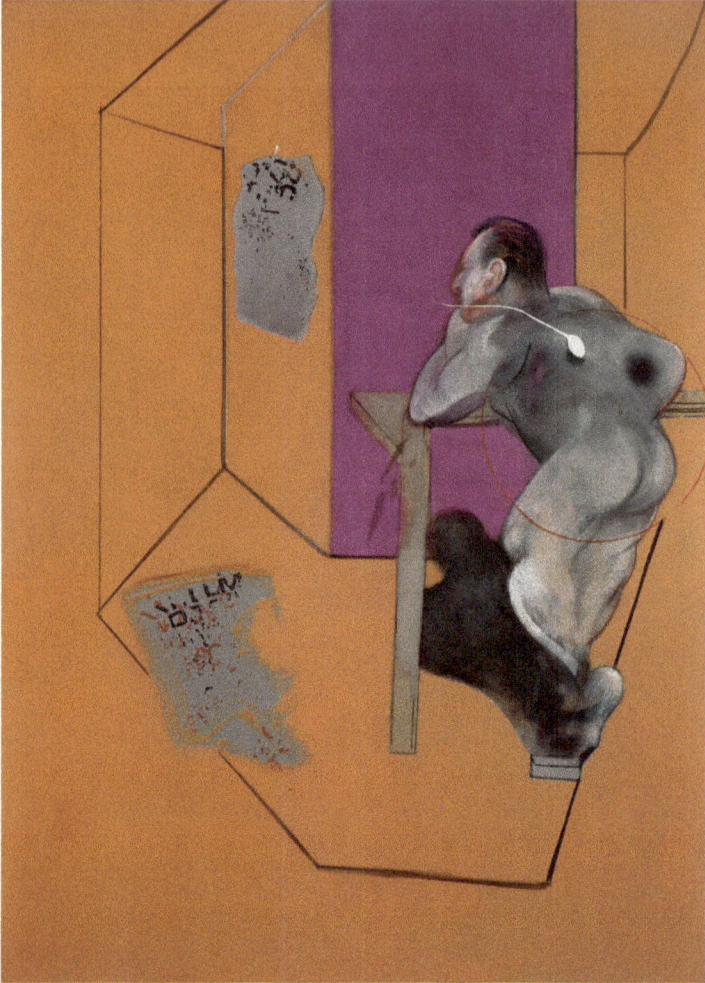

Figure 8.12 Francis Bacon, Oedipus, *1979, private collection. © The Estate of Francis Bacon. All rights reserved, DACS, London/ Artist Rights Society, New York, 2020. Photo: Prudence Cuming Associates Ltd, used with permission.*

contemplating crumpled sheets of illegible text, all enclosed within one of the artist's characteristic rectolinear cages. Anticipating the 1983 *Oedipus and the Sphinx*, the earlier Oedipus also has two wounds – not in his feet, but in his back. One is overlaid with a sperm-like shape, condensing his childhood injury with his father's violation of Chryssipus, a crime for which Oedipus was ultimately also punished. Placing the three Oedipus canvases in a developmental line, the single figures of the 1979 canvases occupy similar positions in the 1983 *Oedipus and the Sphinx* canvas. However, in lieu of a second figure, both 1979 canvases feature indecipherable textual elements not found in *Oedipus and the Sphinx*. The sequence of Bacon's Oedipus paintings thus recapitulates Ingres's elaboration of a figure study of Oedipus into a historical painting that stresses his confrontation of the Sphinx. But Bacon goes further than Ingres, and confronts the reality of Oedipus's wounds, which Ingres – and also Sophocles – only allude to and refuse to acknowledge outright.

At the outset of *Oedipus Rex,* Creon advises Oedipus:

> There's a wound that eats at the very heart of our city's soul.
> (Oedipus Rex: 90)

Creon here refers to the fact that Laius's murderer has not yet been caught and punished, but the audience knows that on a more implicit level, there is another, underlying trauma, one inflicted *on* – not committed *by* – his murderer: the murder victim's own attempted muder. Visualizing this brutal wound in *Oedipus and the Sphinx*, Bacon literally *fleshes out* Sophocles's enigmatic text, signified in the two preceeding canvases by the illegible fragments of type. Relating the mythical tragedy to Dyer's lethal overdose, Bacon would have remembered a line from the last play of the *Oedipus* trilogy:

> Can there be a bigger wound than that inflicted by an evil friend?
> (Antigone: 639)

In contrast to their crisp geometries, flattened planes, and abstracted props, Bacon's paintings are distinguished by figurative distortion. Leikert (2017) observes that despite their gross deformation, Bacon's faces nevertheless "bear an uncanny resemblance to the photographic portrait" (p. 675). In a letter to Michel Leiris, dated 20 November 1981, Bacon explains:

> For me realism is an attempt to capture appearance with all the sensations which that particular appearance has suggested to me... Perhaps, at its deepest level, realism is always a subjective thing.
>
> (quoted in Peppiatt, 1997, p. 306)

Something similar to Bacon's smeared handling of paint is found in the photographic-like portraits of Y.Z. Kami. Marks (2014) suggests that:

> the blur in Kami's portraits leads us to question what we are seeing, to adjust our focus and to gaze in a way which is different from the casual look we project onto the people who inhabit our outer world.
>
> (p. 78)

This impact also rings true for Bacon, who, in deforming the human face, seems to Winnicott "to be painfully striving towards being seen, which is at the basis of creative looking" (1971, p. 114).

Yet for all Bacon's attempts to express his subjectivity, at the same time he insists that his paintings be shown under glass, in which viewers see their reflection. If in Kami's work the "reflection of the human condition in the portraits transfers the viewer's gaze back to himself" (Marks, 2014, p. 79), then Bacon literalizes this, recalling Rose's (1964) assertion that:

> both art and analysis try to provide a framework within which a safe expansion of ego boundaries can occur... Art induces expansion from without by stimulating the imagination. It offers itself as a new skin (mirror, mask, body image) for the observer to try on for size. It invites the observer to step out of his own skin, to transcend his more narrow limits, and to step into the canvas, the dance, the music, the character of the role, via identification and empathy.
>
> (p. 81)

Despite its transparency, glass restricts that connection, separating us from the painting – both as a physical barrier and as a visual barrier –

its reflections and glare interfering with viewing the painting. There are limits to knowing the other. Anticipating Kris's comments on ambiguity, Freud (1914) notes:

> the apparently paradoxical fact that precisely some of the grandest and most overwhelming creations of art are still unsolved riddles to our understanding. We admire them, we feel overawed by them, but we are unable to say what they represent to us.
>
> (p. 322)

Ultimately, Bacon's cryptic images deny our quest to fully understand and thereby test our tolerance of indeterminacy, eliciting both awe and *horror vacui*. Perhaps like no other figurative painter, Bacon's work challenges us with that other great riddle, the enduring mystery of art in all its irreducible ambiguity, which dwells in "places inaccessible to the psyche" and renders visible "the terrible beauty, the horror rendered thinkable by art" (Civitarese, 2014, p. 1065). The wounds and guilt of subject and artist mingle with our own. We have come a long way from Ingres.

And what of Bacon's Sphinx? The statuesque figure does not as much look away from Oedipus as gaze impassively at us, and we observe ourselves meeting her gaze in the glass. The Sphinx, not Oedipus, is the thing of beauty now; now the thing of horror is Oedipus, not the Sphinx. If Ingres's Oedipus epitomizes Rilke's notion that "Beauty is nothing but the beginning of terror that we are still just able to bear" (quoted in Segal, 1952, p. 206), then Bacon's Oedipus locates the epicentre of that terror, giving full expression to what Segal finds "essential to the excellence of a tragedy: the unshrinking expression of the full horror of the depressive phantasy" (p. 204). If Ingres's Oedipus is omnipotent, then Bacon's Oedipus faces nothing but endless grief and guilt.

The psychoanalytic discourse around Oedipus constitutes a continual reappraisal, powered by "the force of the myth itself and its polysemic, ambiguous ramifications" and the "cultural, but also the social, context in which psychoanalysis has developed during this century" (Steiner, 1995, pp. 554–555). The path from Ingres to Bacon – from heroic to horrific – parallels the normal developmental steps that challenge:

> the adult's deep-seated need to place all responsibility for the Oedipus complex upon the child, and to ignore, whenever

possible, certain parental attitudes which actually stimulate the infant's oedipal tendencies.

(Devereux, 1953, p. 132)

Anticipating Laplanche, Devereux encourages us to reconsider Jocasta's response to what, in at least Ingres's imagination, is her sexually attractive adult son, and accordingly revises the Oedipus complex as "a consequence of the child's sensitiveness to its parents' sexual and aggressive impulses" (p. 139).[16] Likewise, Priel (2002) stresses Jocasta's repeated attempts to stifle Oedipus's search for the truth: "infanticide and the silencing of truth might have been enigmatic messages addressed to Oedipus by his two parental couples... translated by Oedipus into his primordial guilt and self-conviction" (p. 438).

Yet Oedipus is not altogether innocent, and his guilt not exclusively an inherited parental burden. The classicist Philip Vellacott (1964) points out that there was ample reason for Oedipus to doubt his parentage; thus, given the oracle's prophecy, he should have appreciated the risk entailed in killing a man the age of his father and marrying a woman the age of his mother, especially one whose husband has just been murdered. Oedipus's transgressions may not have been as unconscious as Freud believed. Likewise, Bacon had every reason to be worried about Dyer, a man he loved but wished would go away. The oppressive presence of the Eumenides in Bacon's *Oedipus and the Sphinx* represents this inescapable guilt: like Oedipus, Bacon should have known better.

J. Steiner (1985), drawing on Vellacott (1964), argues that Oedipus's guilt paradoxically enhances the heroism in which Ingres revels and that Bacon refutes: he stresses, not once but twice, that Oedipus is "truly heroic", because he dares to learn about and (at least temporarily) accept responsibility for his actions: "in a truly heroic moment he faces his guilt" (p. 164). Bion (1958) takes a different position: holding that Oedipus had no right to divine hidden knowledge, he aims to:

> rehearse the Oedipus myth from a point of view which makes the sexual crime a peripheral element of a story in which the central crime is the arrogance of Oedipus in vowing to lay bare the truth at no matter what cost.

(p. 144)[17]

Daring to know the forbidden, and balancing analysis and hubris, psychoanalysts face the same dilemma as Oedipus every day.

★★★

The categorization of psychoanalysis as science or art has always been contested, and claims for scientific objectivity continue to be challenged by confrontations with the indeterminate, the ineffable, the inarticulate – the very province of art. Early psychoanalysts took great interest in comparing the investigation of the world through science and the investigation of the self through art (Sharpe, 1935; Kris, 1939), and the field continues to deepen its engagement with the psyche as observed through an aesthetic lens. While the artist presents us "with a daydream which might have been his own, but which has become more than that" (Fraiberg, 1956, p. 94), "the analysand presents his inner state as a *painting to be contemplated*" (Sirois, 2008, p. 140, emphasis original). Civitarese (2014, 2016) situates Bionian theory within the aesthetics of the sublime, which "represents the arrival in the 18th century of a new poetic sensibility in reaction to a certain aridity of the Enlightenment vision of human affairs" (2014, p. 1080). Compared to Freud, a "man of the Enlightenment" who "investigates the magma of the drives and the opacity of the unconscious", Bion "bears witness to both the exhausting of a positivistic urge and to the movement, especially in his last works, towards a new paradigm which can itself be defined as 'aesthetic'" (2014, pp. 1080–1081). Psychoanalysis thus comes all the closer to art, which, "like an open-ended analytic interpretation", Rose (1964) notes, "carries a degree of aesthetic ambiguity while being rooted in basic issues" (p. 83).

The beautiful strangeness of Bacon illuminates this movement. So, too, does the strange beauty of Ingres, who in 1867 revisited Oedipus nearly six decades after his first rendering. In this, his third version, he reverses the subjects' position (Figure 8.13). Painted when the artist was 82, five years before his death, this heavier, resigned, almost weary Oedipus gestures no longer to the Sphinx, but towards the human remains below. He may not know his identity, but he knows his ultimate destiny. We are all in the same situation, exemplifying Winnicott's (1967) musings:

the myths which were a product of oral tradition could be said to be a cultural pool giving the history of human culture spanning

Figure 8.13 Jean-Auguste-Dominique Ingres, *Oedipus and the Sphinx*, 1862, Walters
Art Museum, Baltimore. https://en.wikipedia.org/wiki/Oedipus_and_
the_Sphinx_(Ingres)#/media/File:Jean-Auguste-Dominique_Ingres_-_
Oedipus_and_the_Sphinx_-_Walters_379.jpg.

six thousand years… It is these cultural experiences that provide the continuity in the human race which transcends personal
existence.

(p. 370)

Exemplifying this continuity, the lineage – Poussin, David, Ingres
Picasso Bacon – draws an unbroken line though three centuries,
offering eloquent elaborations of classical myth over the generations. The continual reinterpretation and transformation of aesthetic precedent illustrates "the interplay between originality and

the acceptance of tradition as the basis for inventiveness" – a tension that for Winnicott (1967) appears "just one more example, and a very exciting one, of the interplay between separateness and union" (p. 370). The relationship between an artist and his master implicates competitive oedipal dynamics, to be sure, but these often overshadow dyadic issues of dependence, identification, and succession. In creative persons, succession entails the balance between aesthetic identification and de-identification – a different sort of leave-taking. Thus, we may expand on Milner's conceptualization of the relationship between the artist, viewer, and the work of art, which informed Winnicott's transitional object – the formulation of which is itself a creative product – and imagine the work of art as a transitional entity that exists between the artist, his masters, and the tradition those masters represent, which serves to maintain the artist's connection to his predecessors while at the same time allows his aesthetic divergence from them, and the space to create anew.[18]

However illuminating the psychoanalytic investigation of art of can be, it remains the case that "the real work of art clearly achieves more than the satisfaction of a few analysable cravings" (Gombrich, 1954, p. 411); "thus, even though we may understand its dynamics and origin, we will still be unable to solve the riddle of creativity" (Noy, 1972, p. 243). The *utility* of art is more accessible than its mystery, as Rickman (1940) indicates in an essay on the "ugly" that brings much to bear on Bacon's oeuvre:

If we limit ourselves to what might be called the biographer's life of the artist we cannot explain the power these people have to affect nearly the whole of mankind. But if we take into consideration the intensity of infantile pain, the enormous courage and endurance of the child in the face of what it feels to be great dangers to itself and to loved ones, its passionate belief that in spite of the fact that its world is reduced to chaos nevertheless it will and can put things right, its good humour due to its belief that in spite of its own evil impulses it has the power to restore and recreate a good world again and that its good objects will remain, if we reckon with the fact that the child goes through periods when the face of familiar things is changed and all that it loves and trusts is crushed by its own violence and befouled by its hate, and if with all this we reckon with the influence and power of infantile phantasy and experience upon our adult perception and emotion: then we may see how the artist can lead us into and out of the world of suffering.

(p. 308)

Seventy-five years later, Leikert (2017) extends this line of thought:

rather as the analytic psychotherapy setting frames the analytic relationship, art by its formal structure provides a framework for representing human suffering, while the subject's aliveness is simultaneously protected and challenged. This leads to the emergence of an emancipatory impulse and to a process of psychic change.

(p. 678)

Thus do the aspirations of psychoanalysis best compare to the achievements of art.

Notes

1 Freud, 1911, p. 224.
2 Rilke, 2000, p. 5.
3 With rare exception, all of the sources quoted in this paper were published in *the IJP* or the *International Review of Psychoanalysis (IRP)*, which was merged into *the IJP* in 1993. Many other papers concerning sublimation, symbolization, literature, and the cinema germane to the essay, yet outside its scope, have been published in *the IJP* and *IRP*.
4 Beyond the scope of this essay, Székely (1983) understands loss as fueling another kind of creative product, namely, scientific theorizing. This appears to have been true for Freud (see Tutter, 2016).
5 See Meltzer's (1965) review of Stokes's *An Invitation to Art*, admiringly described as "the first comprehensive theory of the nature of art which can claim a firm link to psychoanalysis, and yet not fall under the shadow of being a psycho-analytic theory of art" (p. 533). The reception of Stokes's work was not always so positive: Klein reacted badly to the portrait that Stokes – her analysand – painted of her (Sayers, 2015).
6 Schliemann's claims of "evidence" of the reality of legendary figures (including, famously, the "death mask of Agamemnon") were widely derided from its announcement, and that Schliemann himself later acknowledged that he had fabricated the story of listening at his father's knee to his recitations of Homer (Traill, 1995). Freud seemed happy enough to accept, and adopt, the narrative of happiness gained from

the literal mining of heroes of legend: the achievement of a childhood wish.

7 The reader is referred to Steiner's (1994) tour de force, *In Vienna Veritas...?* for a rich discussion of Freud's cultural tradition.

8 Ironically, in the artist's characteristic fashion, Ingres's Oedipus is anatomically distorted, accuracy sacrificed in the service of pure geometric form. For example, his right leg is far shorter than his left, even when accounting for foreshortening, in order to achieve the right leg's desired right angles.

9 Recall René Girard's (1965) concept of mimetic desire: *I want mother because I wish to be like father: to want what he wants and to have what he haves.*

10 Or mother: see Parker (1988).

11 Usefully, Fossi (1985) rejects outright the "centuries-long tradition maintains that creativity and genius depend on some type of mental disorder", a viewpoint that was "bound to find confirmation in psychoanalysis, given its theoretical bias" and which underlies much of the reductive pathography that has characterized psychoanalytic writing on art. This author agrees with Fossi's observation that "psychopathology has only a negative effect on creativity" (p. 219).

12 Ingres's preparatory painting for the amended canvas (1826) hangs at the National Gallery, UK. Of note, it lacks the fleeing man, suggesting that this was a more last-minute addition.

13 Biographical information regarding Ingres is drawn from Fleckner (2007) and Vigne (1995).

14 Here, one recalls Freud's (1900) shame of his father's "unheroic conduct" when he suffered an anti-Semitic attack (p. 25).

15 Edmunds (1988) notes that in Hesiod's narrative, after Kronos castrated his father Uranus,

> blood from Uranus's severed genitals dripped upon the earth and produced the Erinyes [Eumenides]... born from the earth as the result of a castration, [the Erinyes] are associated with Oedipus in almost every one of his appearances in Greek poetry.
>
> (p. 63)

This observation underscores the aspect of succession in the Oedipus myth, and illuminates the raw, bloody character of Bacon's depiction of the Eumenides.

16 Steiner (1995) notes that as early as 1912, Ferenczi took note of Jocasta's seductiveness.

17 Here Bion anticipates Vellacott (1964), who states that for Sophocles, Oedipus's sin was "an obstinate neglect of divine warning in the pursuit of his passions and his ambitions; the taking of a risk which he had no right to take, one which put a whole city in peril" (p. 147).

18 Albeit without implicating the artist's aesthetic predessors, Weissman (1971) considers the created object to be derived from the transitional objects of infancy.

Works cited

Abella, A. (2007). Marcel Duchamp: On the fruitful use of narcissism and destructiveness in contemporary art. *Int. J. Psycho-Anal.*, 88:1039–1059.

Adams, L. (1990). The myth of Athena and Arachne: Some oedipal and pre-oedipal aspects of creative challenge in women and their implications for the interpretation of *Las Meninas* by Velazquez. *Int. J. Psycho-Anal.*, 71:597–609.

Attia, O. (2011). Separation and individuation in Picasso's *Guernica*. *Int. J. Psycho-Anal.*, 92:1561–1581.

Bacon, F. (1609). *The wisdom of the ancients, and New Atlantis.* London: Cassell & Co., 1900.

Bion, W.R. (1958). On arrogance. *Int. J. Psycho-Anal.*, 39:144–146.

Blass, R. (2006). A psychoanalytic understanding of the desire for knowledge as reflected in Freud's *Leonardo da Vinci and a memory of his childhood*. *Int. J. Psycho-Anal.*, 87:1259–1276.

Browne, N.D. (1980). Mirroring in the analysis of an artist. *Int. J. Psycho-Anal.*, 61:493–503.

Chasseguet-Smirgel, J. (1984). Thoughts on the concept of reparation and the hierarchy of creative acts. *Int. R. Psycho-Anal.*, 11:399–406.

Civitarese, G. (2014). Bion and the sublime: The origins of an aesthetic paradigm. *Int. J. Psycho-Anal.*, 95:1059–1086.

Civitarese, G. (2016). On sublimation. *Int. J. Psycho-Anal.*, 97(5):1369–1392.

Colson, D.B. (1979). Photography as an extension of the ego. *Int. R. Psycho-Anal.*, 6:273–282.

Deutsch, F. (1959). Creative passion of the artist and its synesthetic aspects. *Int. J. Psycho-Anal.*, 40:38–51.

Devereux, G. (1953). Why Oedipus killed Laius—A note on the complementary Oedipus complex in Greek drama. *Int. J. Psycho-Anal.*, 34:132–141.

Eigen, M. (1983). Dual union or undifferentiation? A critique of Marion Milner's view of the sense of psychic creativeness. *Int. R. Psycho-Anal.*, 10:415–428.

Elkins, J. (1994). The failed and the inadvertent: Art history and the concept of the unconscious. *Int. J. Psycho-Anal.*, 75:119–132.

Esman, A.H. (1983). Understanding form in painting. *Int. R. Psycho-Anal.*, 10:111–112.

Esman, A.H. (2004). Ernst Kris and the art of the mentally ill. *Int. J. Psycho-Anal.*, 85:923–933.

Ferraro, F. (2003). Psychic bisexuality and creativity. *Int. J. Psycho-Anal.*, 84:1451–1467.

Fleckner, U. (2007). *Jean-August-Dominique Ingres.* Translator, C. Shuttleworth. Königswinter, DE: Tandem Verlag.

Fossi, G. (1985). Psychoanalytic theory and the problem of creativity. *Int. J. Psycho-Anal.*, 66:215–230.

Fraiberg, L. (1956). Freud's writings on art. *Int. J. Psycho-Anal.*, 37:82–96.

Freud, S. (1899a). Letter from Freud to Fliess, December 21. In: *The complete letters of Sigmund Freud to Wilhelm Fliess, 1887–1904*, ed. J. M. Masson. Cambridge, MA: Harvard University Press, pp. 391–393.

Freud, S. (1899b). Letter from Freud to Fliess, May 28. In: *The complete letters of Sigmund Freud to Wilhelm Fliess, 1887–1904*, ed. J. M. Masson. Cambridge, MA: Harvard University Press, pp. 352–354.

Freud, S. (1900). The interpretation of dreams. *SE*, 4/5:1–627.

Freud, S. (1907). Delusions and dreams in Jensen's *Gradiva. SE*, 9:1–96.

Freud, S. (1908). Creative writers and day-dreaming. *SE*, 9:141–154.

Freud, S. (1910). Leonardo Da Vinci and a memory of his childhood. *SE*, 11:57–138.

Freud, S. (1911). Formulations on the two principles of mental functioning. *SE*, 12:213–226.

Freud, S. (1914). The Moses of Michelangelo. *SE*, 13:209–238.

Girard, R. (1965). *Deceit, desire, and the novel: Self and other in literary structure.* Translator, Y. Freccero. Baltimore, MD: Johns Hopkins University Press.

Gombrich, E.H. (1954). Psycho-analysis and the history of art. *Int. J. Psycho-Anal.*, 35:401–411.

Greenspan, R. (2017). Dreaming woman: Image, place, and the aesthetics of exile. *Int. J. Psycho-Anal.*, 98:1047–1073.

Grinberg, L., & Paniagua, C. (1991). The attraction of Leonardo Da Vinci. *Int. R. Psycho-Anal.*, 18:1–10.

Gruen, J. (1991). *The artist observed: 28 interviews with contemporary artists.* Atlanta, GA: A Cappella Books.

Hartke, R. (2000). The primal scene and Picasso's *Guernica. Int. J. Psycho-Anal.*, 81:121–133.

Heiman, M. (1976). Psychoanalytic observations on the last painting and suicide of Vincent Van Gogh. *Int. J. Psycho-Anal.*, 57:71–79.

Heimann, P. (1942). A contribution to the problem of sublimation and its relation to processes of internalization. *Int. J. Psycho-Anal.*, 23:8–17.

Hoffman, L. (1984). Picasso and the painter model theme: Multiple identifications and creative transformations of aggressive conflicts. *Int. R. Psycho-Anal.*, 11:291–300.

Jones, E. (1955). *Sigmund Freud: Life and work, Volume Two: Years of maturity 1901–1919.* London: Hogarth.

Jurist, E.L. (2006). Art and emotion in psychoanalysis. *Int. J. Psycho-Anal.*, 87:1315–1334.

Klein, M. (1929). Infantile anxiety-situations reflected in work of art and in the creative impulse. *Int. J. Psycho-Anal.*, 10:436–434.

Kris, E. (1936). The psychology of caricature. *Int. J. Psycho-Anal.*, 17:285–303.

Kris, E. (1939). On inspiration—preliminary notes on emotional conditions in creative states. *Int. J. Psycho-Anal.*, 20:377–389.

Kris, E., & Kurz, O. (1934). *Legend, myth, and magic in the image of the artist.* New Haven, CT: Yale University Press, 1979.

Kutash, E.S. (1982). A psychoanalytic approach to understanding form in abstract expressionist and minimalist painting. *Int. R. Psycho-Anal.*, 9:167–177.

Laub, D., & Podell, D. (1995). Art and trauma. *Int. J. Psycho-Anal.*, 76:991–1005.

Leikert, S. (2017). "For beauty is nothing but the barely endurable onset of terror": Outline of a general psychoanalytic aesthetics. *Int. J. Psycho-Anal.*, 98:657–681.

Marks, L. (2014). Creative surrender: A Milnerian view of works by Y. Z. Kami. *Int. J. Psycho-Anal.*, 95:67–81.

Mattonet, T. (2002). Und Freud erblaßte... Kulturpsychoanalytische Überlegungen zu einem Geburtstagsgeschenk. *Psyche–Z Psychoanal.*, 56:1227–1241.

McDougall, J. (1989). The dead father: On early psychic trauma and its relation to disturbance in sexual identity and in creative activity. *Int. J. Psycho-Anal.*, 70:205–219.

Meltzer, D. (1965). *The invitation in art:* by A. Stokes. With a preface by R. Wollheim. London: Tavistock, 1965. *Int. J. Psycho-Anal.*, 46:533–534.

Noy, P. (1972). About art and artistic talent. *Int. J. Psycho-Anal.*, 53:243–249.

Paniagua, C. (1986). Notes on a drawing by Leonardo Da Vinci. *Int. R. Psycho-Anal.*, 13:445–452.

Parker, R. (1998). "Killing the Angel in the House": Creativity, femininity and aggression. *Int. J. Psycho-Anal.*, 79:757–774.

Peppiatt, M. (1997). *Francis Bacon: Anatomy of an enigma.* New York: Farrar, Straus & Giroux.

Peto, A. (1979). The Rondanini Pieta: Michelangelo's infantile neurosis. *Int. R. Psycho-Anal.*, 6:183–199.

Podro, M. (1990). "The landscape thinks itself in me": The comments and procedures of Cézanne. *Int. R. Psycho-Anal.*, 17:401–408.

Pollock, G. (1994). The ambivalence of the maternal body: Psychoanalytic readings of the legend of Van Gogh. *Int. J. Psycho-Anal.*, 75:801–813.

Posèq, A.W.G. (2001). Ingres' oedipal *Oedipus and the Sphinx. Source: Notes Hist. Art*, 21:24–32.

Priel, B. (2002). Who killed Laius? On Sophocles' enigmatic message. *Int. J. Psycho-Anal.*, 83:433–443.

Read, H. (1951). Psycho-analysis and the problem of aesthetic value. *Int. J. Psycho-Anal.*, 32:73–82.

Reineman, J. (2011). Between the imaginary and the real: Photographic portraits of mourning and of melancholia in Argentina. *Int. J. Psycho-Anal.*, 92(5):1241–1261.

Rickman, J. (1940). On the nature of ugliness and the creative impulse. *Int. J. Psycho-Anal.*, 21:294–313.

Rilke, R.M. (2000). *Duino elegies.* Translator, E. A. Snow. London: Macmillan.

Roland, A. (1972). Imagery and symbolic expression in dreams and art. *Int. J. Psycho-Anal.*, 53:531–539.

Rose, G.J. (1964). Creative imagination in terms of ego "core" and boundaries. *Int. J. Psycho-Anal.*, 45:75–84.

Rosenblum, R. (1968), *Ingres.* Paris: Cercle d'art.

Sachs, H. (1921). Aesthetics and psychology of the artist. *Int. J. Psycho-Anal.*, 2:94–95.

Sayers, J. (2015). Adrian Stokes and the portrait of Melanie Klein. *Int. J. Psycho-Anal.*, 96:1013–1024.

Schröter, M. (1994). Two empirical notes on Freud's Leonardo. *Int. J. Psycho-Anal.*, 75:87–100.

Segal, H. (1952). A psycho-analytical approach to aesthetics. *Int. J. Psycho-Anal.*, 33:196–207.

Sharpe, E.F. (1935). Similar and divergent unconscious determinants underlying the sublimations of pure art and pure science. *Int. J. Psycho-Anal.*, 16:186–202.

Sigg, B.W. (1990). Moses hiding the empty tomb. *Int. R. Psycho-Anal.*, 17:205–222.

Simon, N. (1977). Primal scene, primary objects and nature morte: A psychoanalytic study of Mark Gertler. *Int. R. Psycho-Anal.*, 4:61–70.

Simons, R.C. (1984). Creativity, mourning, and the dread of paternity: Reflections on the life and art of Gustav Vigeland. *Int. R. Psycho-Anal.*, 11:181–197.

Sirois, F.J. (2008). Aesthetic experience. *Int. J. Psycho-Anal.*, 89:127–142.

Sophocles. (2004). *Antigone.* Translator, G. Theodoridis. https://www.poetryintranslation.com/PITBR/Greek/Antigone.php#highlightsophocles.

Sophocles. (2005). *Oedipus Rex.* Translator, G. Theodoridis. https://www.poetryintranslation.com/PITBR/Greek/Oedipus.php#highlightsophocles.

Steiner, J. (1985). Turning a blind eye: The cover up for Oedipus. *Int. R. Psycho-Anal.*, 12:161–172.

Steiner, J. (1999). Some notes on the "heroic self" and the meaning and importance of its reparation for the creative process and the creative personality. *Int. J. Psycho-Anal.*, 80:685–718.

Steiner, R. (1994). In Vienna Veritas…? *Int. J. Psycho-Anal.*, 75:511–583.

Steiner, R. (1995). 'ET IN ARCADIA EGO…?' Some notes on methodological issues in the use of psychoanalytic documents and archives. *Int. J. Psycho-Anal.*, 76:739–758.

Sterba, R., & Sterba, E. (1956). The anxieties of Michelangelo Buonarroti. *Int. J. Psycho-Anal.*, 37:325–330.

Stokes, A. (1945). Concerning art and metapsychology. *Int. J. Psycho-Anal.*, 26:177–179.

Sylvester, D. (2016). *Interviews with Francis Bacon.* London: Thames & Hudson.

Székely, L. (1967). The creative pause. *Int. J. Psycho-Anal.*, 48:353–367.

Székely, L. (1983). Some observations on the creative process and its relation to mourning and various forms of understanding. *Int. J. Psycho-Anal.*, 64:149–157.

Thanopulos, S. (2005). Leonardo's phantasy and the importance of Freud's slip: The role of the analyst's phantasies in applied psychoanalysis and in the analytic relation. *Int. J. Psycho-Anal.*, 86:395–412.

Traill, D. (1995). *Schliemann of troy.* New York: St. Martin's Press.

Tutter, A. (2011a). Metamorphosis and the aesthetics of loss: I. Mourning Daphne—The Apollo and Daphne paintings of Nicolas Poussin. *Int. J. Psycho-Anal.*, 92:427–449.

Tutter, A. (2011b). Metamorphosis and the aesthetics of loss: II. Lady of the Woods—The transformative lens of Francesca Woodman. *Int. J. Psycho-Anal.*, 92:1517–1539.

Tutter, A. (2014). Under the mirror of the sleeping water: Poussin's Narcissus. *Int. J. Psycho-Anal.*, 95:1235–1264.

Tutter, A. (2016). Prologue: Give sorrow words. In *Grief and its transcendence: Memory, identity, creativity*, eds. A. Tutter & L. Wurmser. London: Routledge, pp. xxv–xliii.

Tutter, A. (2018). Embodying disillusionment: Poussin's blinded giants. *Int. J. Psycho-Anal.*, 99:828–854.

Valenstein, A.F., & Wylie, A.S. (1976). A discussion of the paper by Marcel Heiman on "Psychoanalytic observations on the last painting and suicide of Vincent Van Gogh." *Int. J. Psycho-Anal.*, 57:81–84.

Vellacott, P.H. (1964). The guilt of Oedipus. *Greece & Rome*, 11:137–148.

Vigne, G. (1995). *Ingres.* Translator, J. Goodman. New York: Abbeville Press.

Weissman, P. (1971). The artist and his objects. *Int. J. Psycho-Anal.*, 52:401–406.

Werman, D.S. (1989). James Ensor, and the attachment to place. *Int. R. Psycho-Anal.*, 16:287–295.

Werner, A. (2002). Edmund Engelman: Photographer of Sigmund Freud's home and offices. *Int. J. Psycho-Anal.*, 83(2):445–451.

Winnicott, D.W. (1967). The location of cultural experience. *Int. J. Psycho-Anal.*, 48:368–372.

Winnicott, D.W. (1971). Mirror-role of mother and family in child development. In: *Playing and Reality*, New York: Basic Books, Inc., pp. 111–118.

Wollheim, R. (1987). Painting, omnipotence and the gaze: Ingres, the Wolf-Man, Picasso. In: *Painting as an art*. London: Thames & Hudson, pp. 249–304.

9

FREUD AND OEDIPUS–THE MEDAL GIFTED TO SIGMUND FREUD ON HIS FIFTIETH BIRTHDAY

Carina Weiss

On the 6th of May 1906, on his fiftieth birthday, Freud received a brass medal with his bust and name on the front (Figures 9.1a and 9.1b; 9.2a) and an episode of Sophocles's King Oedipus on the back (Figure 9.2b). The biggest medal of this type, it forms part of the Freud collection (Figure 9.1a and 9.1b) and was shown at the exhibition at the Freud Museum, "The Enigma of the Hour, 100 Years of Psychoanalytic Thought", marking the centenary of *the International Journal of Psychoanalysis* 2019.

Displayed in a special wooden frame, this extraordinary medal is outstanding in size, with a diameter of 14.2 cm, more than twice as large as the other known medals (cited later). There are several smaller types of Freud medals. The original has a diameter of 5.98 cm, marked at the rim with "MÜNZE WIEN" (Figure 9.2c), and some copies (with a slightly smaller diameter of 5.92 cm) were made at a later time without the mark (Weiß, 2012, p. 45, Figure 11). As far as we know, until now the small Freud medal (Figure 9.2a–c) is one of the rare originals of the Viennese mint (Wiener Hauptmünzamt), made during Freud's lifetime.

Nevertheless, the diversity in size of the different types of the Freud medals raises questions which deserve investigation. Is the large medal in the Freud Museum the original that he received for his fiftieth birthday, or is it a later copy? Bryony Davies from the

Figure 9.1 (a) The medal gifted to Sigmund Freud on his 50th birthday, front with Freud's bust, diameter 14.2 cm. Photo: Courtesy Freud Museum London. (b) The medal in Figure 9.1a. The photo was taken in 1976 (INO523, Photo: Courtesy Freud Museum London) and shows the medal in its wooden frame in one of the shelfs in Freud's study in Maresfield Gardens 20.

Figure 9.2 (a–c) A specimen of the smaller edition of the medal Figure 9.1a and b with the mark "Münze Wien", probably meant for relatives, friends, and followers. Private collection. Photo © J.S. Spering, Höchberg.

Freud Museum in London kindly informed me that the large framed medal has been in the Freud house since at least 1976 (Figure 9.1b), while Anna Freud was still the caretaker for the collection. So it seems likely that the big medal was meant to honour Freud himself, while the smaller ones (Figure 9.2a–c) were distributed to relatives, friends, and colleagues.

Let us take a closer look at the Freud medal made of Viennese mint (Figure 9.2a–c in private possession). On the front, Freud's bust looks to the right and is encircled by the inscription SIEGMUND FREUD WIEN MCMVI (note the misspelling of Sigmund, Figure 9.2a). On the back (Figure 9.2b), Oedipus stands in front of the crouching sphinx who is luring on a rock. Behind Oedipus, at a right angle to him and therefore in a position only visible to the sphinx, is Sophocles's famous saying, *Who divined the famed riddle and was a man most mighty*, appears in Greek letters: ὋΣ ΤΑ ΚLΕΙΝ᾽ΑΙΝΙΓΜΑΤ᾽ΗΙΔΕΙ ΚΑΙ ΚΡΑΤΙΣΤΟΣ ῏ΗΝ ΑΝΗΡ. Again there is an error in the Greek spelling, which alters the meaning.

How should we interpret the orthographic mistakes in both inscriptions? "Siegmund" instead of Sigmund in the name. And a Latin L instead of the Greek Λ in the third word of the Sophocles's quotation, which is believed by some researches (amongst them Regier, 2005, p. 115) to allude to the German word "klein" as 'little' instead of the Ancient Greek κλεινός, "famous", from Sophocles's text.

The first wrong spelling of Freud's name could be intentional to bring out the word "Sieg", "victory", in his first name. Indeed, Stefan Zweig notoriously used this form of Freud's name in his books which he dedicated to Freud; his books are full of inscriptions like the following: "Professor Siegmund Freud / In alter inniger Verehrung / Stefan Zweig 1926". The victory of psychoanalysis as a scientific discipline could not be expressed in a more condensed way than in this little Freudian slip.[1]

The second mistake in the Greek inscription is in my opinion a pure misspelling of somebody who was not trained to write or read ancient Greek lettering. Even Freud himself had difficulties to give the correct translation to Jones, who admits his own "Greek having rusted considerably" (II 15). The situation was even more complicated for the engraver who had to produce the negatives of the steel stamps, from which the medal was coined. There the letters are inverted, running to the left. The wrong form of the lambda could have appeared already in Schwerdtner's plaster model as it could have slipped into the hand of the engraver of the steel stamps. In Freud's ex libris, the Greek text is correct, and also in Jones's (1955, p. 15).

We know from Jones (1955, p. 15), who wrongly describes the medal as a "medallion", that the medal was given to him by Paul Federn and was commissioned by a small group of Viennese adherents. Carl Maria Schwerdtner (1874–1916), a known Viennese sculptor and engraver, drew the sketch and produced the plaster model. Jones reports that when Freud looked at the gift and read the inscription, he became pale and agitated, wanting to know who had come up with the idea of it. In a strangled voice, Freud explained that as a young student, he often strolled around the great Court of the Viennese University. There, he faced the busts of former famous professors and celebrities and imagined seeing his own bust there in the future, inscribed with the identical words he now found on the medal. Already at the end of his schooling when he passed the *Matura*, he talked to his friend Emil Fluss about a passage from King Oedipus (Freud, 1873, p. 3): for the exam, he had to translate 33 verses from the ancient Greek text into German, and he had translated them well. So it seems Freud encountered a real "revenant", not the only one in his lifetime. Indeed, in 1955, the bust of Freud with the lines of Sophocles was exhibited in the great Courtyard of the Alma Mater, Rudolphina Vindobonensis, and so Freud's daydream came true (Windgätter, 2016, p. 302, Figures 126 and 127).

It is sometimes said that the image of Oedipus in front of the sphinx is a direct adaption of the painting by August-Dominique Ingres (1780–1867) dated 1825 (Regier, 2005, p. 64, Figure 4.3); Freud possessed a reproduction of this picture, which hung on the wall over his couch (Engelmann, 1977, Figures 10–12; Windgätter, 2016, pp. 299–300, Figures 121 and 123). At the very end of a successful analysis, Freud would point to the reproduction of the painting by Ingres, telling his patient that Oedipus resolved the riddle of the sphinx (Wittels, 1924, p. 114; Regier, 2005, pp. 110–111). But Schwerdtner's composition of the figures on the medal differs from Ingres's painting. Much closer to the image on the medal is the image on Freud's ex libris (Windgätter, 2016, p. 300, Figure 122), created by the art nouveau painter and graphic artist Berthold Löffler (1874–1960). The ex libris dates back to the year 1901 and shows the same variation of the sphinx's position and the same misspelling of Freud's name, as in the medal (Siegmund). The positions of the figures, and especially the crouched and horizontal sphinx, are definitely derived from a picture by Franz von Stuck "Ödipus löste das Rätsel der Sphinx", from 1891 (Bierbaum, 1899, p. 42, Figure 43; Ostini, 1909, p. 24, with Figure). Stuck had not only painted Oedipus resolving the riddle but also the sphinx kissing her victim, inspired by a poem by Heinrich Heine (Regier, 2005, p. 95, Figure 6.1; 174 note 5). Here, again, the sphinx is lying in a nearly horizontal position.

In the medal, Oedipus's attitude is also different to Ingres's classicist paintings (Regier, 2005, pp. 64–65, Figures 43 and 4.4). In Ingres's painting, Oedipus is standing with one foot propped up a rock. This physical gesture is often found in heroic and victorious figures of Roman late-Republican and early imperial art. The sphinx is also classical: Ingres's sphinx is sitting upright, proudly presenting her female breasts, while her head more or less disappears in the shadow of the cave. Upright sitting sphinxes of this type can be seen in many representations of ancient Greek art, like the late classical terracotta figure in Freud's own collection (Figure 9.3; Gamwell, Wells, 1989, pp. 92–93) or on Roman coins and gems from the late-Republican time (Regier, 2005, p. 139; Figure 8.10) to the period of Emperor Augustus who used this figure on two of his seals (Zwierlein-Diehl, 2007, p. 12, pl. 3 Figure 8).

Figure 9.3 Terracotta statuette of a sphinx. Freud Museum London, Inv. 4387. Photo
© Carina and Heinz Weiss.

In contrast, the position of the sphinx on Freud's ex libris and his medal is inspired by von Stuck's painting, where the sphinx does not sit upright but appears like a winged, crouching snake, with a human head stretching out towards Oedipus. This strange appearance is consistent with her uncanny epiphany and in a way evokes her erotic danger. In von Stuck, Oedipus is not in straightforward contact with the sphinx. He stands with both feet firmly on the ground, some distance from the sphinx, supporting his head with his right hand in a gesture of reflection that dates back to classical antiquity (cf. Neumann, 1965, pp. 128–152; Zwierlein-Diehl, 2007, pp. 105, 401; Figure 414). In his interpretation of the ex libris/medal, Windgätter (2016, pp. 300–301) suggests that Oedipus's posture not only alludes to the therapeutic process but also presents Freud himself as the victorious Oedipus.

The Oedipus complex was the cornerstone of Freud's self-analysis as well as of his theory of infantile sexuality. Many of Freud's pupils and followers wrote about the Oedipal scene, including Otto Rank's 1912 contribution, "Das Inzest-Motiv in Dichtung und Sage: Grundzüge einer Psychologie des dichterischen Schaffens", which Freud praised highly. In the Sixth Volume of Imago in 1920, Theodor Reik published his work on the theme under the title "Oedipus und die Sphinx" (Reik, 1920). Towards the end of the 20th century, Peter L. Rudnytzky's study, "Freud and Oedipus", deserves a mention (Rudnytzky, 1987).

But interest in the Oedipus theme is not exclusively limited to Freud and psychoanalysis. The topic was in vogue in the 19th and early 20th century in the Viennese modern arts, as well as in classical philology and archaeology. At the beginning of his stay in Paris in 1886, Freud wrote to his fiancée, later wife, Martha: "I am under the full impact of Paris and, waxing very poetical, could compare it to a vast overdressed sphinx who gobbles up every foreigner unable to solve her riddles" (Freud, 1885, pp. 187–188). Here, the topic of the Oedipus story was part of the everyday discourse between Freud and his fiancée, to suggest that he found the people of Paris somewhat uncanny. Freud confesses that the classics, and especially the Oedipus theme, formed a strong thread throughout his literary sources (Papini, 1934 (1973), p. 101). But the young Viennese literati were dealing with the same subject, as illustrated by Hugo von Hofmannsthal, who in 1906 wrote his drama *Oedipus and the Sphinx* (Schoeller, 1979).

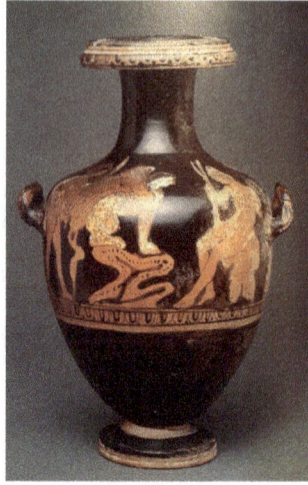

Figure 9.4 Attic red-figure kalpis, Apollonia Group (attributed Carina Weiss) 380–360 B.C., Oedipus sitting in front of the sphinx, Freud Museum London, Inv. 3117. Photo © Carina and Heinz Weiss.

In the meantime, the known group of Greek vases that depicted Oedipus in front of the sphinx grew in number (Simon, 1999). The first vases displaying that theme were revealed by Hetty Goldman, the known American archaeologist and excavator from Harvard, in the *American Journal of Archaeology*, 1911 (Goldman, 1911). One year after its foundation in 1912, the famous Loeb Classical Library published the texts of Sophocles's Oedipus trilogy in ancient Greek, with an English translation of the titles: *Sophocles I: Oedipus the King; Oedipus at Colonus; Antigone* (Storr, 1912; Weiß, 2012, p. 47; Figures 13 and 14).

And last but not least, Sigmund Freud, the founder of psychoanalysis, and James Loeb (1867–1933), the founder of the Loeb Classical Library, collector of antique art and possibly a patient of Freud, both possessed original Greek vases displaying Oedipus in front of the sphinx (Freud's Oedipus Vase, here Figure 9.4; Weiß and Weiß, 1985, p. 50).[2]

Notes

1 See also Arens 1995, p. 391, with another example by Hilda Doolittle.
2 Figures 19 and 20; Gamwell, Wells, 1989, pp. 94–95, Figure; Simon, 1999, p. 23; Figure 1. – Loeb's Oedipus Vase: Oakley, 1997, pp. 55–56

119 nr. 35; Simon, 1999, p. 34 Figure 7; Regier, 2005, p. 58 Figure 4.1; Carina Weiß, 2012, pp. 45–46 note 51 with lit. Figure 12.

References

Arens, K. (1995). H.D.'s Post-Freudian Cultural Analysis: Nike versus Oedipus. *Am. Imago*, 52(4): pp. 359–404.

Bannert, H. (2013). *Sophokles König Ödipus. Vatermörder und Retter der Polis.* Wien: Holzhaus.

Bierbaum, O.J. (1899). *Franz von Stuck. Künstler Monographien*, Bd. XLII, Bielefeld und Leipzig: Verlag von Velhagen & Klasing, p. 42, Figure 43.

Engelmann, E. (1977). *Berggasse 19. Das Wiener Domizil Sigmund Freuds.* Stuttgart, Zürich: Belser.

Freud, S. (1873). Letter from Sigmund Freud to Emil Fluss, June 16, 1873. Letters of Sigmund Freud 1873–1939, pp. 3–6.

Freud, S. (1885). Letter from Sigmund Freud to Minna Bernays, December 3, 1885. Letters of Sigmund Freud 1873–1939, pp. 187–188.

Gamwell, W. (1989). Sigmund Freud and Art. His personal Collection of Antiquities. *Introduction by Peter Gay*. Edited by Lynn Gamwell and Richard Wells. State University of New York, Freud Museum London: Ed Marquand Book Design.

Goldman, H. (1911). Two Unpublished Oedipus Vases in the Boston Museum of Fine Arts. *Am. J. Archaeol.*, 15 (1911): pp. 378–385.

Jones, E. (1955). *Sigmund Freud Life and Work, Volume Two: Years of Maturity 1901–1919*. London: The Hogarth Press, pp. 1–507.

Neumann, G. (1965). *Gesten und Gebärden in der griechischen Kunst.* Berlin: Walter de Gruyter.

Oakley, J. (1997). *The Achilles Painter.* Mainz am Rhein: Philipp von Zabern.

Ostini, von, F. (1909). Franz von Stuck. Das Gesamtwerk, Vorwort von Fritz von Ostini, München, fig. p. 24.

Papini, G. (1934). A Visit to Freud. In: *Freud As We Knew Him*, edited and introduced by Henrik M. Ruitenbeek. Detroit: Wayne State University Press, 1973, pp. 98–102.

Rank, O. (2010, 1912). *Das Inzest-Motiv in Dichtung und Sage: Grundzüge einer Psychologie des dichterischen Schaffens.* Classic Edition.

Regier, W.G. (2005). *Book of the Sphinx.* Phoenix Mill Thrupp, Stroud (Glostershire): Sutton Publishing.

Reik, Th. (1920). Oedipus und die Sphinx. In: Imago. *Zeitschrift für Anwendung der Psychoanalyse auf die Geisteswissenschaften.* Herausgegeben von Prof. Dr. Sigm. Freud. Redigiert von Dr. Otto Rank und Dr. Hanns Sachs. VI. Band 1920 Heft 2. Wien: Internationaler Psychoanalytischer Verlag, pp. 96–196.

Rudnytzky, P.L. (1987). *Freud and Oedipus.* New York: Columbia University Press.

Schoeller, B. (1979). Hugo von Hofmannsthal. Ödipus und die Sphinx. In: *Hugo von Hofmannsthal: Gesammelte Werke in zehn Einzelbänden. Dramen II. 1892–1905.* Hg. v. Bernd Schoeller. Frankfurt am Main: 1979.

Simon, E. (1999). Ödipus als mythische Persönlichkeit im Bewußtsein der Antike. In: Heinz Weiß (ed.), *Ödipus und Symbolbildung. Ihre Bedeutung bei Borderline-Zuständen und frühen Störungen.* Hanna Segal zu Ehren. Tübingen: Edition discord, pp. 20–47.

Storr, F. (1912). *Sophokles*: With an English Translation by Francis Storr. Loeb Classical Library. London: W. Heinemann Ltd.

Windgätter, Chr. (2016). *Wissenschaft als Marke.* Berlin: Brinkman+Bose.

Wittels, F. (1924). *Sigmund Freud. His personality, His Teaching, and His School.* Translated by Eden and Cedar Paul, New York: Dodd Mead.

Weiß, C. (2012). *Die Gemmen der Sammlung James Loeb.* Lindenberg im Allgäu: Kunstverlag Josef Fink, pp. 45–47.

Weiß, C., and Weiß, H. (1985). Ein Blick in die Antikensammlung Sigmund Freuds. In: Antike Welt. Zeitschrift für Archäologie und Kulturgeschichte 16. Feldmeilen: A. Golfetto, Raggi Verlag.

Zwierlein-Diehl, E. (2007). *Die antiken Gemmen und ihr Nachleben.* Berlin and New York: Walter de Gruyter.

10

FORM AND FEELING

Reflections on a century of psychoanalytic
discourse on meaning and poetry

Margot Waddell

In the 100-year history of *the International Journal of Psychoanalysis* and *International Review of Psychoanalysis,* we encounter an important shift from a time when a new and exciting paradigm for understanding the nature of interpersonal and individual relationships was being embraced and applied enthusiastically to specific works of art and literature. With time, an altered version of this position began to emerge – one that could throw light on the meaning and nature of personal and artistic creativity more generally. The account that follows describes a central aspect of the form and functioning of the creative imagination – of that which lies at the heart of the individual's capacity to develop internally and is thus indissolubly linked to the therapeutic process that enables change and growth to occur.

Tracing the history of articles on poetry and psychoanalysis in *The Journal* and *The Review* since their inception offers a fascinating and enriching picture of the development of psychoanalysis itself. For such a journey charts, in stark terms, what Wilfred Bion described as being, in the early days, the "victimisation" of literature by psycho-analytic interpreters and the reductiveness of much psychoanalytic criticism (*Memoir of the Future,* 1991, p. 588). Some years later, in his uncompleted anthology of poetry, Bion explains how he turned to the poets because they have the capacity "to say something in a way which is beyond my powers to reach" (*IRP,* 1981). The pages of *The Journal* and *The Review* confirm the rather bleak oversimplifica-tions in many of the early articles, in contrast, later on, with more contemporary psychoanalytic insights into the nature of creativity and the centrality of meaning in psychic and artistic life more generally. Such a reading tells a commanding story not only of the evolution of psychoanalytic thinking itself but also of the historiographic issues in the development of the human sciences.

These issues go to the heart of the ever-changing nature of psychoanalysis and lie, often unacknowledged, at the root of the wide-ranging debates about its goals, character, and, in particular, its status – as science or as art – in relation to its part in the respective emphases of psychological and cultural thinking more generally. The century-long sweep is especially instructive in the context of the historicity of ideas. For, if divorced from its roots in the scientific and cultural preoccupations of its time, psychoanalysis runs the risk of acquiring a self-conception as an interpreter of, rather than a participant in, the history of thought both in its broadest and its most intimate terms. As Philip Reiff (1959) rightly said, and as the 19th-century poets, novelists, and historians of science make so clear, these ideas were "in the air" at the time. Freud found a way of garnering them at the turn of the century and taking them further, and deeper, to start with almost entirely on his own.

A reading of psychoanalytic reflections on poetry during these years offers an impressive set of insights into what might be described as a slowly turning gyre in the history of culture and of artistic expression generally, and of the development of psychoanalysis in particular. For a setting-in-context makes more immediate some of the dimensions which tended to become altered or lost in the inter-war turmoil of the early days.

Thomas Ogden (*IJP*, 80, pp. 979–994), who published many articles in *The Journal* on the issues being discussed here, puts the matter very clearly in "'The Music of What Happens' in Poetry and Psychoanalysis".

Over the course of the past 50 years, there have been a number of important shifts in the theory and practice of psychoanalysis. Among them, is an increasing awareness that the most interesting and productive avenues of psychoanalytic enquiry seem no longer to be adequately addressed by the question, "What does that mean?" – that symptom, that set of dream images, that acting out, that rageful response to the sound of the analyst's coughing and so on. An enquiry into personal meanings has become inseparable from an understanding of the unconscious inter-subjective context in which those meanings are generated. Consequently, the question "what does that mean?" has gradually expanded in such a way as greatly to increase emphasis on such questions as: "What's going on here?" "What's happening between us consciously and unconsciously and how does that relate to other aspects of the patient's (and the analyst's) past and present experience, both real and imagined?". With this shift in our conception of the analytic process comes the need for commensurate change in the way we use language to speak to ourselves and to our patients. It seems to me important that we develop a capacity to use language that does justice not only to the task of understanding and interpreting the conscious and unconscious meanings of our patients' experience; in addition, our use of language must be equal to the task of capturing and conveying in words a sense of what it is "that's going on here" in the intrapsychic and intersubjective life of the analysis, the "music of what happens" in the analytic relationship.

A forerunner of this shift in psychoanalytic attitudes to the poetic is to be found, in the pages of *The Journal*, in the work of Ella Sharpe, work that could be described as strikingly innovative in her sensitivity to the precise words and meanings of her patients. Coming from a literary background herself, Sharpe has a keen ear for the "music" of language and for the ways in which, as Owen Barfield (1928) puts it in his *Poetic Diction: A Study in Meaning,* the role of metaphor "lies in its attempts to arouse cognition of the unknown by suggestion from the known" (p. 110). Ella Sharpe made constant comparisons between dreams and works of art. Her interest in the music of words, in the mechanisms of poetic diction, and, particularly, in metaphor shaped her clinical thoughts about her patient's communications. Her belief was, for example, that "the dream is a psychic work of art and the dream work as defined by Freud is more than a management device, it is a creative activity" (Whelan, unpublished manuscript).

Ogden's (1999) analysis of the first line of Frost's poem "Acquainted with the Night" makes the point with great clarity:

I have been one acquainted with the night.

"Even the syntax", says Ogden, "(which is "the nerve and bone structure of language" [Steiner, 1989, p. 159]) of the first sentence contributes to its sombre vitality: grammar is pushed to its limit, is unobtrusively broken just a bit, and is newly created. It is as if the structure of language itself is unable to contain "some strange resistance within itself...".

Acquainted with the Night: Psychoanalysis and the poetic imagination is the title of a fine volume in the *Tavistock Clinic Series*, edited by child psychotherapist Hamish Canham and poet Carole Satyamurti. As Al Alvarez writes in his Foreword to the book:

> Psychoanalysis and literature have been close partners from the start, not least because Freud himself read widely and wrote compelling prose. Both these accomplishments were unusual in a scientist and they generated in him an even more unusual respect for the arts. When, during the celebration of his 70th birthday, one of his disciples hailed Freud as "the discoverer of the unconscious", he answered, "the poets and philosophers before me discovered the unconscious. What I discovered was the scientific method by which the unconscious can be studied.
>
> (p. xiii)

Alvarez ends his Foreword thus:

> A good poem is as hard to find as a good analysis but, once found, the effect of both is to make you – the reader, the patient – more fully and pleasurably alive.
>
> (p. xv)

There are many examples of what Bion termed "victimisation" to be found in some of the early articles that offer readings of, for example, Blake, Shelley, Baudelaire, Verlaine, and Tagore. What we find here are contributions that purport to offer psychoanalytic insight but which, in fact, provide a reductionist set of interpretations either of the poet in question, personally, or of a certainty about the validity of psychoanalytic interpretation that is, in fact, based on a very crude formulation of symbolic representation. Albert D. Hutter (1982) points out that the early articles on poetry and psychoanalysis have left "an unfortunate legacy of partial and reductive misreadings". We encounter this in the very first issue of *The Journal* in an article on Blake which begins "Much of Blake's poetry labours under an obscureness that deprives it of any lasting human interest".

The "Prophetic Books" it goes on to say, "is remarkable for its obscure mysticism and general diffuseness", while suggesting, "the first of the lyrics in question 'the Garden of Love' for any but the psycho-analytically informed can have but little meaning". "Among the many gems" the author writes, "are a few which, though they sometimes charm the ear, rarely convey anything to the understanding" (1920, pp. 196–199).

A further illustration from an article in the early fifties offers an "ingenius" take on Coleridge's "Rime of the Ancient Mariner" (1951). At one point, the author enquires:

> But how does the Albatross-mother become a dangerous object, an object that must be killed? The answer must be sought in Coleridge's productions. His oral fixations prepare us for an unconscious conflict on a pre-genital level with its characteristic aggressive content.

And so on. What was, in those early days, almost wholly lacking, was any sense of what began to appear, in the *Psychoanalytic Review* in particular, of a questioning of "interpretations of literature" and, by contrast, a much deeper involvement in the significance of the presence or absence, the sound or the silence, in relation to words and to creativity more generally. Besides this, one might set a learned and much more recently published article on "Dante's 'Two Suns': Reflections on the Psychological Sources of the *Divine Comedy*" (2017). In this piece, David Black suggests that the power of the *Divine Comedy* "derives from the deep psychological truthfulness with which Dante deals with the painful personal crisis that underlies the poem and is his starting point". From this, we can trace the development from psychoanalytic characterizations, "albatross-mother", for example, to the question of the "psychic truth" that underlies the poetry.

It is difficult to know to what extent Freud's own thinking was affected by the nature and background of the Strachey translation of his work from German to English; or possibly also by the influence of Ernest Jones in conveying a much more scientific picture of things than Freud's own prose and cultural sensibilities had suggested throughout. This is clear in some of Joan Riviere's comments on her own attitude to translating his work. What has become apparent, as some of the articles of the 1990s corroborate, is that, as

Gay suggests (1985), Freud himself had a deeply sensitive artistic spirit which is evident in so many of his texts. The fact is that if one looks, in detail, into the inextricable relationship during Freud's lifetime of the personal, political, professional, and cultural issues that had so significant a bearing on the history of psychoanalysis, the limited nature of the account from within the psychoanalytic framework comes significantly to the fore. It was only in the 50s and early 60s that the work of Bion, Klein, Meltzer, Money-Kyrle, Riviere, Segal, Sharpe, Stokes, and Winnicott began to engage with the more substantial role of a psychoanalytic understanding of creativity itself, and, as a consequence, the language of poetry acquired a more central position in the thinking of psychoanalytic discourse. As the pages of these journals unfold, it becomes increasingly clear that psychoanalysis is a true child of literature rather than merely the interpreter or explainer. As I (1991) put it in my contribution to *The Chamber of Maiden Thought,*

> In considering how the embodiment in literature of the development of the life of the mind has illuminated the task of psychoanalysis, their congruent goals become apparent: to explore the process whereby truthful emotional experiences evolve and to participate in the growth of the mind. Founded, as it is, in the notion that all cognition is primarily emotion, that knowing is essentially an imaginative experience, [Keats's] "The Vale of Soul-making" offers a description of the human condition that is shared by the Romantic poets, by mid-nineteenth century thinkers and late-twentieth century post-Kleinian psychoanalysts alike. By establishing the necessity of placing emotionality at the heart of the matter, it focuses attention on recognising the place for meaning and value in human affairs – the absolute values of psychic reality as opposed to the relativity of social values. The promotion of the evolution of such values has always required that thought have its anchorage in feeling. In pursuing this same process in the context of psychoanalytic thinking, we follow the central preoccupation of the great creative artists, to oppose the dissociation of thought from feeling.
>
> (pp. 170–171)

This change of emphasis is inseparable, to reiterate, from the literary context of the time. The sociocultural forces bearing on the poetic development during these years are as distinctive as they were for,

for example, the metaphysicals, the Victorians, the Romantics, and as far as this piece is concerned, the postmodernists. When the first few volumes of *The Journal* appeared, World War I had only recently ended and the traumatic shadows of those years hung heavily over the whole world, especially in Germany, where three-quarters of a million people died of starvation between 1914 and 1918. From the 1920s onwards, issues of, to generalize, presence and absence, meaning and meaninglessness were a *terra incognita* in many cultural circles: lands that needed exploration in novels, poetry, art, film, but also in psychology, philosophy, and epistemology. It was a time, for example, when what became known as the Bloomsbury group were gathering force with their innovative ways of expressing how they saw and experienced the world, especially in relation to issues of time (quotidian or psychic time) and that "unmapped country within" that George Eliot had explored and defined in her final novel, *Daniel Deronda* (1876).

Bearing this in mind, it is interesting to speculate on what it was that accounted for the shift between the first paper that Bion gave at the British Society, "The Imaginary Twin" (1950) and his *Second Thoughts* (1967) about the material 17 years later. Here he makes explicit the development of his own thinking since giving this original and memorable presentation. The congruences he finds between the psychoanalyst, as an intuitive, creative interpreter, and aspects of the artistic process are striking. He criticizes his early formulations for not making clear how much

> the reader is to suppose that the account is a direct intuition of what was taking place and how much a report of selected facts. In psychoanalysis the psychoanalyst must discern the underlying pattern by a process of discrimination and selection. If the account given is a selection made to demonstrate the correctness of the original selection it is utterly worthless.
>
> (p. 131)

Later on, he speaks of the "artistic representation" necessary to an approximation of a truthful report of a session which is possible if one assumes, he says rather challengingly, "the requisite" degree of artistic capacity in the psycho-analyst which can bring about,

> a transformation during which selection and ordering of the material takes place. The interpretation given the patient is a

271

formulation intended to display an underlying pattern. It is therefore itself similar to the mathematical formula described by Poincaré.... It is also similar to some aspects of a painting, sculpture or musical composition. At their best these formulations make us aware of a coherence and order where, without them, incoherence and disorder would reign.

(p. 131)

In effect, he is exploring, as so often, the limitations of the psychoanalytic interpretive model, the limitation of this particular form:

These words I write are supposed to "contain" a meaning. The verbal expression can be so formalised, so rigid, so filled with already existing ideas that the idea I want to express can have all the life squeezed out of it. On the other hand, the meaning I wish to express may have such force and vitality, relative to the verbal formulation in which I would strive to contain it, that it destroys the verbal container.... Psychoanalysis itself provides an outstanding example of such a force, idea or individual in tension with its container, verbal formulation or society.

(p. 141)

Bion never ceases to tussle with this quandary: in effect, how can the psychoanalytic interpretive mode expand rather than limit the complex sensuality of emotional experience; how can it free rather than imprison embryonic thought?

Among the many strands in this discourse is a significant clutch of journal articles that were gathered together in *New Directions in Psychoanalysis* (1955). Here, a freeing of embryonic thought can be found in Joan Riviere's two contributions to the book, 'The Unconscious Phantasy of an Inner World Reflected in Examples from Literature", and her paper on Ibsen's *The Master Builder*, both of which are expansive, rather than reductive, psychoanalytic readings of the literature. Hanna Segal's "A Psycho-Analytic approach to aesthetics" in particular marked a significant change in how psychoanalysis would begin to "treat": works of art. Rather than analyzing the author or artist, Segal chose to explore the aesthetic experience itself, and the desire to create. "The task of the artist lies in the creation of a world of his own" (p. 388), she writes, followed by a poem by Shelley that ends "...and all that we/ Read in their smiles/ And call reality". Later in the article, "The artist withdraws into a world of phantasy, but he can communicate his phantasies and share them. In that way he makes reparation, not only to his own internal objects, but to the external world as well" (p. 398).

Thinking of this kind continued to find ever more varied expressions throughout the 1980s in particular. Meira Likierman (1989) expresses this point in her *International Review* article, "Clinical Significance of Aesthetic Experience". Noting the shift just described over the last 100 years, Likierman writes about the importance of form, rather than content, when it comes to poetic and artistic expression:

> It becomes clear that the crucial determining factor is form, and not content. Neither the subject matter, nor the underlying unconscious content of a work are in themselves sufficient to make it aesthetic. "To be, or not to be" would have been forgotten by now if Shakespeare had made Hamlet say "I have a conflict..." even though these different sequences describe the same truth. It is the particular composition of Shakespeare's sentence rather than only its meaning which is aesthetic and which turns it into art rather than a statement of facts.... For example, the choice of "to be" to represent both life and death alerts us to the thin line which separates the two states. These are one syllable words which make it an alarmingly easy phrase to utter, with an inevitable verbal slip into "not to be". This gives us a direct intuition of the nearness of Hamlet's state of mind to death.

Also enshrined in psychoanalytic thinking is the crucial insight that the capacity for symbolic thought is lodged in the prior capacity to bear separation and to mourn loss, and in the recognition that the wellsprings of creativity lie in a constant reworking of that most painful cluster of "depressive" emotions – so movingly and often searingly re-evoked in great poetry – emotions of love and hate, of guilt, remorse, anger, pining, destructiveness, and reparation. For example, in Day-Lewis's poem "Walking Away", the pain of letting go, and the conflicts involved in any of life's transitions, are engaged with in a way that emphasizes the inevitable stresses of "growing up". The acts of courage, be they on the part of parent or child, pervade this poem as Day-Lewis recalls the occasion of his son's first game of football. He describes how vividly this apparently trivial event has remained in his mind and suggests how deep an impact such a parting could make on both father and son. For the son, such partings mark the beginnings of selfhood; for the parent, the pain of letting go is a necessary part of love.

These are the transitions so often engaged with during the lengthy psychoanalytic processes of working through the ever-fraught necessities of separating and individuation, beautifully captured by Freud in 1905, in his "Three Essays on the Theory of Sexuality". Such a process may be caught, or held, in a few spare lines of poetry of which the impact tends less to be on the symbolic structures than on the engagement itself. Hanna Segal, discussing Salman Rushdie's work, writes, "an essential component of the aesthetic experience is our identification with the artist's creative process… Unconsciously, we learn from it about the creative experience itself. Every work of art carries within it the story of its own creation; it captures experience" (1994 "Salman Rushdie and the Sea of Stories: a not-so-simple fable about creativity"; *IJP*, 75, p. 611). Moreover, each medium, the poetic and the psychoanalytic, establishes the significance of the apparently mundane – the insistent quest to engage with all experience, without denial or evasion, however painful. The very writing of a poem represents an echo, a resonance, a reparative response. In this sense, the poem, like the analytic frame, acts as a container for the expression of powerful feelings that are thereby rendered manageable, both, as Segal suggests, for the poet and for the reader. For the lines express the poet's own internal struggles to find some kind of shareable, musical "pitch" which engenders in the reader or listener an experience of being held and understood.

That there are many congruences between poetry and psychoanalysis has long been recognized. As this chapter suggests, there is a huge literature on the psychic and the aesthetic, one that stretches across these past 100 years and many aspects of which appear, as a kind of treasure trove, in the pages of *The Journal*. Clive Bell (1914) put it with spare clarity, "what orders the work of art is, I suggest, the emotion which empowers the artist to create significant forms" (p. 13). Several decades later, Meg Harris Williams (1983) points out that, in poetry, the

> penumbra of significance beyond the lexical connotations of words begin to impinge on the observer as he ceases to be a mere observer… Feeling himself to be drawn into the aesthetic object,

and responding to the psychic tensions captured by its formal
qualities, his own inner mental structure is inevitably qualified.

(p. 182)

The relationship between the psychoanalytic and the poetic enables and communicates the meaning of emotional experience –
it moves "the sleeping images of things towards the light", in
Dryden's words. The emergence of that meaning is embedded in
a particular *quality* of relationship. To apprehend the poem, the
reader must put him/herself in the poet's place, and must make
the poem an outgrowth of one's own mind as well. Coleridge
compares mind to a living plant in that, absorbing into itself the
atmosphere to which its own respiration has contributed, it grows
into its own perfection (1816). This would seem to me to describe
the psychoanalytic process at its best.

The evolution of the thoughts expressed here, in the context of
The Journal's 100-year discourse, is supremely expressed in *The Four
Quartets,* where T.S. Eliot says that words or music reach the stillness
only by the form or pattern (Burnt Norton, V, ll. 4–7).

References

Barfield, O. 1928. *Poetic Diction: A Study in Meaning.* Middletown, CT:
   Wesleyan University Press.
Bell, C. 1914. *Art.* New York: Frederick A. Stokes Company Publishers.
Beres, D. 1951. A Dream, a Vision, and a Poem: A Psycho-Analytic Study
   of the Origins of the Rime of the Ancient Mariner. *IJP*, 32:97–116.
Bion, F. 1981. Memorial Meeting for Dr Wilfred Bion. *International Re-
   view of Psycho-Analysis*, 8:3–14.
Bion, W.R. 1950. The Imaginary Twin. Read to the British Psycho-
   Analytical Society, 1 November 1950.
———. 1967. *Second Thoughts.* London: Heinemann.
———. 1991. *A Memoir of the Future.* London: Karnac.
Black, D.M. 2017. Dante's 'Two Suns': Reflections on the Psychological
   Sources of the Divine Comedy. *IJP*, 98(6):1699–1717.
Coleridge, S.T. 1816. *Lay Sermons: 1. Statesman's Manual.* R.J. White, ed.
   Reprint. London: Routledge, 1972. pp. xiv–xv.
Eliot, G. 1876. *Daniel Deronda.* Reprint. London: Penguin Classics, 1986.
Eliot, T.S. 1963. *Four Quartets.* London: Faber and Faber.
Gay, P. 1985. *Freud for Historians.* Oxford: OUP.
Harris Williams, M. 1983. Underlying Pattern in Bion's *Memoir of the Fu-
   ture*. *IJP*, 10(75):75–86.

Harris Williams, M., and Waddell, M., eds. 1991. *The Chamber of Maiden Thought: Literary Origins of the Psychoanalytic Model of the Mind*. London: Tavistock/Routledge.

Hutter, A.D. 1982. Poetry in Psychoanalysis: Hopkins, Rossetti, Winnicott. *International Review of Psycho-Analysis*, 9:303–316.

Likierman, M. 1989. Clinical Significance of Aesthetic Experience. *International Review of Psycho-Analysis*, 16:133–150.

Ogden, T. 1999. "The Music of What Happens" in Poetry and Psychoanalysis. *IJP*, 80:979–994.

Preger, J.W. 1920. A Note on William Blake's Lyrics. *IJP*, 1:196–199.

Reiff, P. 1959. *Freud: The Mind of the Moralist*. Chicago, IL and London: The University of Chicago Press.

Riviere, J. 1955a. The Unconscious Phantasy of an Inner World reflected in examples from literature. In Klein, M., Heimann, P., and Money-Kyrle, R. eds. *New Directions in Psychoanalysis*. London: Maresfield Prints.

Riviere, J. 1955b. The Inner World in Ibsen's *Master Builder*. In Klein, M., Heimann, P., and Money-Kyrle, R. eds. *New Directions in Psychoanalysis*. London: Maresfield Prints.

Segal, H. 1955. A Psycho-Analytic Approach to Aesthetics. In Klein, M., Heimann, P., and Money-Kyrle, R. eds. *New Directions in Psychoanalysis*. London: Maresfield Prints.

Segal, H. 1994. Salman Rushdie and the Sea of Stories: A Not-So-Simple Fable about Creativity. *IJP*, 75:611–618.

--------------------------------- 11 ---------------------------------

PSYCHOANALYSIS AND MUSICALITY

Francis Grier

In this chapter I seek to address the question of why music and musicality originally played such a negligible part in psychoanalytic theory and clinical practice, and how and why that is starting to change. Some key IJP papers are examined, exploring Freud's paradoxical claims to musical deafness, and his influence on subsequent theoreticians. It's suggested that the advent of opening out and even reversing previous theories of countertransference set the stage for musicality within the clinical encounter to be recognised, considered and investigated, especially in the context of Winnicott's theory of transitional space, Bion's theories of reverie and alpha function, and Stern's theory of attunement. Birksted-Breen's notion of "reverberation time" is considered as an instance of a contemporary deepening and broadening out of psychoanalytic theory to include in a central position the intuitive and non-verbal dimension of musicality. The paper ends with a clinical example and my attempt to give definitions to the different usages of the term "musical" in a psychoanalytic context.

> This chapter adds to, and utilises some
> passages from, Grier (2019)

Music cannot be said to have had a central place in Freud's thought nor in the development of psychoanalytic theory, even to the present day. Given that psychoanalytic treatment consists of talking and listening, the exchange of sound, a moment's reflection will show that musicality is inevitably always present in the music of the patient's and analyst's voices and in the musicality of their interchange. A stranger to the field might be forgiven for assuming that musicality would have a primary place in psychoanalytic theory, and might be shocked at its virtually complete absence. I have therefore chosen as the main project of this chapter to try to show how, in *the International Journal of Psychoanalysis* over the years, this paradox has been addressed.

I aim to draw out a division between papers which address musical subjects directly and those which are involved with musicality, implicitly or even unconsciously. In this chapter, I have decided against exploring papers which are overtly devoted to the subject of music, the majority of them taking operas or composers as their subject matter, simply because their psychoanalytic-musical importance is thereby obvious, and any musically interested readers will find their way to these papers with no difficulty. I would only add that the editors of *the International Journal* have taken the view that musical (as with other artistic papers) should show not only a sophisticated knowledge of both music and psychoanalysis, but that such papers' argumentation should also demonstrate theoretical development in and between both disciplines. Richard Rusbridger, for example, shows not only how the theory of projective identification operates with regard to the narrative and the text in Shakespeare's *Othello* and Verdi's *Otello*, but also how projective identification can be seen to operate on a purely musical level (Rusbridger, 2013). The papers in this musical series are rich in such originality of insight, and can therefore be read not only with pleasure but also with professional interest by practising psychoanalysts, since such insights, though overtly centred on issues outside the consulting room such as the operatic stage, have a way of enhancing, perhaps through the analyst's free association, clinical practice.

It may seem contrary in such a survey to devote any time to non-existent papers. Nevertheless, I speculate that it is probably a symptom of the absence – even unconscious proscription? – of music within psychoanalytic theorizing that not a single paper has yet been published in the *International Journal* devoted to non-verbal, purely instrumental music, even though such music is accorded possibly the highest musical respect at least within the Western tradition, whether classical or jazz, sometimes referred to as "pure music". I suspect that psychoanalytic writers on music (myself included) have unconsciously needed to keep a reference to words, to keep in line with the primacy that psychoanalysis has historically accorded to verbal thought, and to avoid imputations of anything that might reek of "wild analysis", an almost unavoidable danger if tackling the non-verbal subject matter of "pure music". My contention here is that there is a direction of travel in contemporary psychoanalytic theory which brings us closer to this possibility.

To start with Freud's own notorious unmusicality, which I suggest had consequences for the absence of music in psychoanalytic theorizing for so long, I wish to explore three outstanding historical papers. Cheshire (1996) engages principally with questions of Freud's own personality and his own biographical history, whereas the primary foci of Vermorel & Vermorel (1986) and Barale & Minazzi (2008) are the broader cultural and scientific cultural trends of which psychoanalysis was a part, with a two-way traffic of mutual influence between them.

One cannot help but be impressed by the detail and breadth of Cheshire's historical knowledge, and of his intuitive psychoanalytic acumen as he applies it to the figure of Freud himself, with relation to all things musical. His respect for the founder of psychoanalysis does not prevent him from probing Freud's own musical claims and disclaimers. In the course of the paper, Cheshire points out various strange inconsistencies, for example, that Freud would say and even write that he had no musical acquaintances, when, in fact, no less than three of the original founder members of the famous Wednesday meetings were musicians, including the famous music critic and writer Max Graf, the father of "little Hans", who himself went on to shine in a successful career as an operatic stage designer – in which he would eventually collaborate with another of Freud's musical patients, Bruno Walter, one of the foremost conductors of his day, especially expert in the interpretation of the works of Mahler, whom Freud had also treated, to the composer's apparent satisfaction, in one single consultation.

Cheshire explores various avenues for Freud's antagonism to music, one being that one of his rival suitors for Martha was a musician, making Freud feel that students of the arts had an unfair advantage in matters of love over scientists like himself. Cheshire also wonders whether Freud's resentment of Vienna's anti-Semitism may have been expressed through his turning his back on Vienna's most cherished ideal, its music.

However, much of the paper is given to showing and discussing how, in various more or less unconscious ways, almost Freudian slips, Freud showed to the observant eye, or ear, that he did in fact possess quite a natural feel for music. He hummed, for example, a Mozart aria to his dog, and quite often associated to operatic themes in particular situations, both in his personal life and also when practising psychoanalysis: to an opera singer who consulted him about problems in her love life, he quoted Cherubino's famous aria from *The Marriage of Figaro*. The paper explores possible psychological reasons underlying the three operas which were apparently Freud's favourites, Mozart's *Don Giovanni*, Bizet's *Carmen*, and Wagner's *Meistersinger*. Cheshire notes that all three operas could be seen as exploring the problem of the id, and the close association between love, sex, and death, all central themes of Freud's psychoanalytic investigations. In *Carmen*, the id wreaks havoc; in *Don Giovanni*, it finally meets with ultimate superego punishment; in *Meistersinger* it is controlled, restrained – one might almost say, contained – and sublimated.

Cheshire considers the inevitable impression that Freud's interest centred on the words and ideas rather than on the music, in the light of Freud's own opinion that he did not like to not know why he was moved by something. Cheshire argues that music fell for Freud into the same category as mysticism (and, I would add, women). However, in making this statement, Freud precisely implies that music did indeed move him, and this is Cheshire's central point. He notes how, already at the age of 17, when Freud decided against being a lawyer and for being an explorer of the natural world, his way of referring to himself is telling. He describes how his ambition was to "eavesdrop on" or "listen-in to the eternal processes of nature". In terms of his teacher Charcot's categories, he was temperamentally an "auditif" rather than "visuel" or "motoric".

> This penchant for an auditory mode of expression and account-rendering, which made him prized by his children as a colourful raconteur in everyday life (M. Freud, 1957), also influences the form of his written expositions; and some would go further to say that it affects the form of his theoretical arguments and his use of clinical evidence.
>
> (Cheshire, p. 1128)

Regarding Freud's inability to sing or hum in tune, but his tendency nevertheless to do so (e.g. to his dogs (Freud, 1936)), Cheshire imaginatively quotes the 6th-century Boethius:

> he who cannot sing agreeably still hums something to himself, not because what he sings gives him pleasure, but because one takes delight in giving outward expression to an inner pleasure, no matter what the manner.
>
> (quoted by Strunck, 1965, p. 83)

With regard to Freud's intuitive, perhaps quite unconscious, musicality, Cheshire writes:

> One of his patients, who had undoubted aesthetic sensibility and talent, namely the 'imagist' poet Hilda Doolittle, has reported that Freud spoke English 'without a perceptible trace of accent', and that 'the beautiful tone' of his therapeutic voice had a 'singing quality that ... permeated the texture of the spoken word'. Whether or not these features were a legacy from his former role as a clinical hypnotist, they could not have been achieved and maintained by someone with a pervasively defective 'ear' (Doolittle, 1956, p. 75). This impression, that Freud's contributions to the analytic session bore the stamp of an artistic, if not specifically musical, performance, is confirmed independently by another witness, the Englishman James Strachey who is now so well known to us through the Standard Edition. From his experience of being analysed by Freud in 1920, he reported that as a therapist he was 'a brilliant artistic performer'.
>
> (Meisel & Kendrick, 1986, p. 30)

Indeed, Freud seems to have intuited this himself. For he has left us, in a letter to Fliess, a remarkable metaphor (remarkable, that is, for a completely unmusical person) which represents him, in the role of therapist, as a skilful musician who plays upon the psyche of the patient in such a way as to create a harmonious composition from the latent resources of his instrument. Thus he writes of the progress of a case ... : 'everything is going smoothly, and the instrument responds willingly to the instrumentalist's confident touch'.

(Freud 1901, p. 340). (Cheshire, p. 1135)

This paper gives a convincing and fascinating account of what has always seemed to me obvious about psychoanalysis, that musicality is a vitally important dimension in a treatment which consists primarily of sound. My contention is that psychoanalysts have, at least to some extent, unconsciously ignored the musical dimension in their allegiance to Freud. Paradoxically, it has been recognized that Freud's own writing and his ideas are delivered with musicality (as we shall see later in the chapter); this musicality is not a superficial wrapping of the all-important message but is itself an integral part of the communication. It could be that the musicality of Freud's expressive writing is what may convey to us the depth of his integrity, rendering his thought so persuasive. It was surely this aesthetic quality which gained for his writing the Goethe Prize in 1930. And it is this musical quality which links Freud's own writing, and, as Cheshire has shown, even his biographical dimension, with the musicality between patient and analyst in the consulting room which is such an important feature for those contemporary authors who have sought to explore the non-verbal aspects of psychoanalysis.

Moving away from the centrality of Freud's personality and its influence, we turn now to broader trends. Vermorel & Vermorel (1986) explore the immense and not properly acknowledged importance of Romanticism on Freud himself and psychoanalysis. Fittingly enough, given their central musical interpretation of Freud, the tone of their own paper (like Cheshire's) is, to my ear, thoroughly musical, and thus, presumably unconsciously, it demonstrates precisely what it explores.

The Vermorels' work is important for situating Freud firmly among the Romantics, not only in his ancestry but also in so many of the ways that he thought, dreamed, and behaved, and indeed regarding many of the culturally contemporary aspects of psychoanalysis. They write:

> … it is by way of the poetry which joins with science that Freud's language rediscovers music, which was a vital element in the German soul and in Romanticism; if music was relatively lacking in Freud's tastes and concerns, the reason is because it lies concealed in the flavour of his poetic style, where the mere words are pervaded by music in some ineffable region beyond language.
>
> (p. 26)

In these few words, the authors of this paper articulate concisely the musicality behind the poetic dimension behind the surface theoretical aspect of so much of Freud's writing, but which nevertheless makes its presence felt subliminally, giving the writing its particular quality of aesthetic resonance.

This point is also relevant to the discussion about the musicality of psychoanalysis in the consulting room: just as the emotional authenticity and vitality – or otherwise – of the participants may be sensed for the most part unconsciously through the musicality underlying the verbal engagement, so it is this same quality of aliveness, sensitivity, and emotional authenticity which comes across in reading Freud, conveyed particularly through the underlying musical qualities of his prose, even though for the most part readers may be quite unconscious of this dimension and their own communion with it. But perhaps it is this quasi-ineffable quality of Freud's writing that makes it so persuasive and convincing: you could say that his overt reasoning and argumentation is constantly supported, even buttressed, even furthered, by a quality of emotion and musicality which one can only sense, not directly demonstrate. To return to the core of the Vermorels' paper, this particular quality is thoroughly Romantic in its ethos and sensibility. The Vermorels imply thereby that Freud may have been much more engaged with a more "irrational", romantic, aesthetic, and emotional current than he perhaps quite liked to avow. Since we are now learning the centrality of non-verbal, musical aspects of psychoanalysis, it is interesting to consider that, in a hidden way, it always existed, not only in the analyst-patient encounter but also concealed in the resonance behind the surface of Freud's own writing.

Barale & Minazzi (2008) tackle headlong the problem alluded to in their title, of the way music has been psychoanalytically invisible, "off the beaten track". They point out that, in contemporary psychoanalysis, the non-verbal, sonic-musical aspects of the clinical analytic encounter are moving to the foreground of theoretical attention, with its emphasis on the emotional receptivity not only of the patient to the analyst, but also *vice versa*, whereas for many years during the establishment of psychoanalysis, interpretation claimed the theoretical foreground. They note the irony of this, given that psychoanalytic treatment is sound-based.

The authors develop their principal theme to explore why music was ignored at the inception of psychoanalysis. Adding to the contributions of Cheshire and the Vermorels, they cast substantial doubts amounting to frank disbelief that the reasons were genuinely that Freud himself was congenitally unmusical or that the cultural atmosphere was antipathetic to music in one of the most musical cities in the world. Nor was the contemporary scientific atmosphere at all unmusical or antagonistic to music:

> ... precisely within the positivist culture, interest in music was particularly evident and keen. This culture could not possibly have discouraged Freud from taking at least a theoretical interest in music.
>
> (p. 941)

The authors detail how the major positivist scientists of the time, particularly Helmholtz and Lipps, who both influenced Freud so profoundly, were both very interested in investigating music and in establishing a physiologically based system of aesthetics. In fact, music was central to both their bodies of work. However:

> If anything ... a problem lay hidden in other aspects of the cultural position of music at the time of Freud, squeezed as it was between the psychophysiological laboratories and the late-Romantic idea of the ineffable and of abandonment to the 'oceanic feeling' of fusion with Being — as well as, in particular, in the various manifestations of that idea that were widespread in the psychiatry of the time.
>
> (p. 943)

The authors focus on the work of Lipps, so important a reference in Freud's *Interpretation of Dreams,* and show how Freud put down a boundary (Masson, 1985, p. 325) when it came to Lipps's study of music, in which rhythm was the supreme focus:

> For Lipps, moreover, rhythm has to do with the general conditions of psychic experience, or of intentionality — or, as Lipps puts it, of the movement 'of the soul as it stretches out to the object'.
>
> (p. 944)

Even though Lipps

> sought a path that eschewed ... any spiritualistic or romantic vagueness... what 'stopped' [Freud] was manifestly the overall difficulty presented by the theme of music — a difficulty in relation to what it represented, and to its integration within the edifice [psychoanalysis] under construction.
>
> (p. 945)

The authors then turned to Freud's avowed discomfort with non-verbal affect:

> Freud describes his relation to aesthetic experience with exemplary clarity: in order to enjoy a work of art, he writes, he must "explain to myself what [its] effect is due to" (Freud, 1914, p. 211). By the phrase 'is due to', Freud of course means by way of 'what content' or representation, which may be unconscious. "Whenever I cannot do this, as for instance with music, I am almost incapable of obtaining any pleasure. Some rationalistic, or perhaps analytic, turn of mind in me rebels against being moved by a thing without knowing why I am thus affected and what affects me."
>
> (p. 945)

They continue:

> ... A man of the Aufklärung, Freud always distrusted, or indeed was positively averse to, any form of mysticism or irrationalism, spheres to which he assigned much contemporary art and almost all that of the avant-garde (Gombrich, 1966); to these he remained even more deaf than to music, albeit for similar reasons.
>
> In Freud's view, interest in art had nothing to do with 'oceanic feelings' (of which he almost proudly wrote that he could not find the slightest trace in himself), or with the 'magic of illusion'; it was instead connected with the capacity of the artistic form (like jokes) to permit the emergence of the repressed, the residue of our infantile history, and to make it tolerable and agreeable.
>
> (Freud, 1905, 1907)

285

... Freud's rationalism, the primacy of words and representations, avowedly constituted a shield against the uncanny aspect of aesthetic 'abandonment'...

(p. 946)

... psychoanalysis was to be organized as a hermeneutics centred on language and on the expression in language of the (representational) formations of the unconscious. This in itself excluded music, which contained 'something that seems refractory to psychoanalytic interpretation because it is outside language' (Imberty, 2002a, translated) — or, at least, outside representational language. Music, the direct language of live emotions, temporality, and the underlying tuning of psychic life, was relegated to the margins of psychoanalysis.

(p. 947)

The authors note how much has now changed, listing the various theoreticians who started to write about musicality, noting the immense influence of the philosopher Susanne Langer, whose ideas have been and continue to be so important to psychoanalysts seeking to understand the meaning both of musical works and also of the musicality of psychoanalysis itself:

A recurring reference is to the philosophy of Susanne Langer (1951, 1953, 1967), in whose conception music features very prominently, and who sees musical language as isomorphic not with particular contents of consciousness but with the very movement of psychic life, in its basal, preverbal structure.

(p. 939)

Bringing their contribution up to the date of their paper, they write:

In the last decade ... there have been many indications that the theme of music is 'exerting pressure' within psychoanalytic thought. Musical analogies have been used more and more frequently to describe aspects of the analytic situation. Contributions abound on 'psychoanalytic listening' or 'listening to listening', which is likened more and more often to its musical counterpart (Stein, 1999). The perception of the 'music of what happens' (Ogden, 1999) is stated to be a fundamental aspect of analytic reverie. Musical metaphors punctuate the writings of Bion and post-Bionian conceptions of the psychoanalytic field (Zanette, 1997) — for instance, the theme of being in 'unison' with the patient, or of reception of the un-heard for "expressing the music of humanity or the little bit of it which has got into your consulting-room".

(Bion, 1985, p. 74), (p. 939)

While I agree with their conclusion, I will go further and argue that an *actual* musical dimension needs to be recognized and acknowledged, not just metaphorically or by analogy (see Grier (2019).

Turning now to some examples of more recent theoretical developments, in which the musicality of the *clinical exchange* is brought out in more recent papers, the title of Rayner's (1992) paper immediately invokes a musical dimension: "Matching, attunement and the psychoanalytic dialogue". Rayner's thought is particularly influenced by the work of Daniel Stern (1985), as well as the philosophy of Langer. Addressing the non-verbal affect between patient and analyst, he considers that tuning in to this non-verbal level often precedes the analyst's readiness to give a verbal interpretation.

> To set the stage, our line of thought is as follows. At the start of any session the analyst gives his free-floating attention; he tunes in and resonates with affects and ideas from the patient until an underlying theme is distinguishable. He can then begin to think about verbal interpretation. Resonances and unfolding sequences early in an analysis are likely to be sporadic and undefined. However, later in treatment sequences are likely to have vital and distinctive features so that deep resonances often occur between patient and analyst and interpretive verbalization is richer.
>
> (p. 39)

I believe that when Rayner writes about "deep resonances", he is referring precisely to a musical level of emotional communication between them, that is, a literal – not metaphorical – expressing and responding to the actual musical qualities underlying their speech-duet. He continues:

> Music, being presentational and an efficient vehicle of affect, might also be an appropriate form of communication about the

indistinct largely pre-verbal analytic times that are the subject of this paper, for there is then perhaps a dance or tune of the two protagonists' interpenetrating moods. But poetry or music is an esoteric skill; Freud did not use concepts derived from them, and most of us have followed his example. Perhaps partly because of this region of analytic poverty, reportage of pre-verbal gesture and intonation tends to remain unstudied and ill-conceptualized.

(p. 40)

It is rare to find such a confession of psychoanalysis's musical deaf-spot declared in such plain and direct language. In this passage, Rayner clearly appreciates the central place music might have been having at the heart of psychoanalysis and rightly attributes its absence to Freud's own abjurance of music and the collective identification of the original group of psychoanalysts with their discipline's founder. It is particularly striking that Klein, though she was precisely interested in the earliest months and years, also ignored musicality. Moreover, although she contributed the first paper on opera in the *International Journal* (Klein, 1929), she explicitly focused on the text, not once mentioning the music.

There is, however, a certain irony in Rayner's description of poetic or musical skill as "esoteric", given that the paper alludes to the ordinariness with which mothers respond musically to their children, and *vice versa*, as part of the affective cross-modal interchanges described by Stern. Rayner himself goes on to try his hand as an amateur poet in this very paper. It is as though the Freudian example with its implicit admonishment to avoid the musical dimension is paradoxically affecting Rayner and demanding his submission simultaneously as he critiques it. My suspicion is that this might represent a slightly more visible version of the effect of an internal prohibition affecting many psychoanalysts who might otherwise have allowed themselves more flexibility with experimenting with musical metaphors. Rayner goes on:

If our contention about the value of attunements in the analytic dialogue has substance, we should then be enquiring about an affective duet, or 'tune', between the two protagonists. Such a duet would be a far cry from the simple pre-verbal rhythms of infancy; the dialogue of patient and analyst is full of conflict, anxiety and resistance, it is complex and also highly verbal. What is more, the movement out of attunement to discord is probably as important to insight as moving in.

(p. 45)

I believe Rayner to be correct in describing how, in any session, a musical duet between analyst and patient is always taking place. He is also correct in emphasizing that music might just as much tend towards discord as concord. Discord is in fact just as musical as concord, and it is just this kind of writing that can perhaps help the analyst tune into the presence of discord. This might be obvious in many cases when the words between the psychoanalytic couple are also discordant, for example, aggressive or argumentative, but this can also happen at times when the surface is apparently calm or cool. The only indication that something very different may be happening at an unconscious level might be that the analyst hears, as it were, a dissonant music. If analysts can train themselves to tune into experiences of internal, dissonant music, and then to use their secondary-process, verbal-thinking skills to probe and question its meaning, they may find themselves on the track of something of vital emotional importance. Rayner goes on:

> Formulated verbalization by the analyst was described classically by Strachey (1934), giving the criteria of mutative interpretation. The suggestions of the present paper extend Strachey somewhat. They are that fully verbal formulated interpretations are still vital for stable and coherent psychic change. But they may fail to be mutative without prior deepening and loosening of fixated affect structures by unconscious and preconscious attunements and discords in the duet between patient and analyst. New meaning is given to feelings when they are known to be shareable. Important in these attuning and discord stages would be gestures and intonations, possibly by both protagonists to be read by the other.
>
> (p. 45)

Rayner points out here how Strachey's classic discussion of what makes an interpretation truly mutative is nevertheless impoverished by its omission of the musical dimension: the "unconscious and preconscious attunements and discords in the duet between patient and analyst" are crucial. An otherwise mutative interpretation will remain emotionally incomplete, possibly over-intellectual and over-rational if the musical dimension is lacking. This may point to those moments, presumably quite common in many an analysis, when either a sense of intuitive, "musical", and affective understanding may be achieved between the analytic couple which nevertheless lacks sufficient verbal elaboration, or the converse case in which an intellectual understanding may be reached but which nevertheless lacks the musical and emotional resonance so vital for the understanding to be able to be digested, for it then to become properly potent, and thereby truly mutative (see Nacht, 1963; Dufresne, 1992; Schwaber, 1998).

Regarding more recent authors writing more specifically about the musical dimension in psychoanalysis, the crucial background is that almost all contemporary psychoanalytic theoreticians have been greatly influenced by Bion's notion of reverie (1962), Stern's notion of attunement (1985), and Winnicott's theory of transitional space (1953). In their different ways, all three notions emphasize the processing of emotion by the analyst more intuitively, using less secondary process thinking. It is one of the fundamentals of Winnicott's theory that the creative, transitional space between, in his discourse, "me" and "not me" should not be impinged upon nor intruded into by premature interpretation. Within Bion's theory of containment, the highly active process of alpha function is nevertheless unconscious; much of it is related to the dimension of dream life, even if dreaming when awake, and very little is related to conscious, secondary process thinking. Stern, similarly, describes how mothers tune into their infants' emotional states and communicate their understanding through their vocal responses, which are intuitive and not marked by excessive rationality (though they are not irrational).

These three bodies of theory have made an enormous, ongoing impact on psychoanalytic theorizing. Their emphasis is on non-rational, intuitive, dreaming, creative, imaginative, inventive responses, within analyst and patient. By contrast, Freud and the first analysts, Klein, Anna Freud, and the ego psychologists all, of course, engaged with their patients' emotional states, and all spoke of dreams, but their own processes of reverie were usually downplayed in their theoretical or clinical accounts, and have to be inferred by the reader. Theorizing about the musical dimension, which coincides pre-eminently with the non-verbal, intuitive, atmospheric, and dreaming aspects of the analyst's mind, were effectively, if unconsciously, proscribed. This all began to change with the new theories of countertransference promoted by Heimann (1950), Racker (1953), and Searles (1959). Intuition, which perhaps had been originally feared as giving licence to "wild" analysis, began to find its legitimate place – and, I would suggest, there may be no intuition without musicality. Whether the first stirrings of intuition give rise initially to musicality, or whether musicality comes first, I do not know, though I suspect the latter, as I intuit that the beginnings of intuition occur in a region of the psyche distant and distinct from anything approaching verbal thinking. The OED defines intuition as "the ability to understand something instinctively, without the need for conscious reasoning", and that first, non-verbal proto-understanding in the realm of feeling is highly likely to achieve its first expression in some sonic, proto-musical form, which might perhaps be expressed in the duet invoked by Rayner between patient and analyst in verbal hesitations and mumblings (on either part). In-articulate mms, ahs, ohs, and pauses, including the quality of breathing in its audible aspect – although usually entirely overlooked – can surely be the musical expression of intuition gathering momentum towards verbal, secondary-process-thought articulation.

The musicality of analysis is increasingly evoked particularly by analytic writers emphasizing the qualities I have just described, of dreaming, intuition, and imagination, for example, Anzieu (1979) and Ogden (1999). Many other authors refer fleetingly to music, and many others imply a strong musical quality.

Dana Birksted-Breen has concentrated recently on articulating often delicate, non-verbal, intuitive and often dreamlike, imaginative events within analysis, whether within the patient or within the analyst, and always in the patient-analyst interrelationship. Her work seems intuitively to have concentrated on musical dimensions, particularly of tempo and rhythm: tempo even finds its way into the title of one of her papers (2012).

A central musical aspect she describes – without bringing out its conscious musicality – is the dimension of mother-infant, analyst-patient relating, she calls, "reverberation time" (2009). Birksted-Breen describes the infant's or patient's need to find in his mother or analyst a capacity to let his communication in and allow it to reverberate, or resonate within her. This need is so fundamental that it does not always require the next step, of the maternal object reflecting back her understanding, through the story of a patient who needed to tell her analyst a dream just in order to receive precisely this non-verbal, and, I would add, musical experience of resonance. Birksted-Breen's emphasis here is almost exclusively on non-verbal, pre-verbal, non-rational (but not irrational), intuitive, imaginative, dreaming levels of mental and emotional functioning. The voices, the sound of the voices, and specifically the musicality of mother–infant or of patient–analyst in their duets are, I suspect, vital in what they convey through musical qualities of harmony and dissonance to what ensues, transpires, and develops between the couples. The patient was singing the song of her dream within her speaking voice to the musically – n.b. literally, not just metaphorically – resonating chamber of her analyst's mind, where there may be more than one musical response, of, say, not only mother but also father, which may themselves be in concordant agreement or disharmonious disagreement.

I will now give a clinical example of how, on one occasion which can stand for many others, an important element in a psychoanalysis was only realized through its musical quality. A patient made mention of some bad weather, some lowering clouds, and it was only after several minutes passed that I woke up to the fact that the patient was almost certainly making an unconscious observation about my own state of mind, of which I myself had been unconscious (or preconscious) as I had been trying to ignore my own unpleasant feelings. I realized that it was some quality of the musicality of the patient's expression which had got through to me, triggering a sympathetic resonance, for his words drew no special attention to themselves, the subject matter (about the clouds) fitting quite unobtrusively into the superficial context of the session. Not that the patient's music was obviously or flagrantly musically demonstrative. He had been speaking about conscious issues in a rather overtly expressive, musical way, whereas when he alluded to the lowering clouds, the music of his communication modulated to a softer, more tentative tone. It was precisely this inhibited musical quality that awakened a sympathetic resonance in me, and then a verbal curiosity.

My patient, I believe, intuited my unconscious mood, quite unintentionally and unconsciously, attributing it not to me but to the external weather. He then verbalized it metaphorically, but, more importantly, sang musically about it in a way that my musical ear picked up. I do not reckon that my secondary process thinking was alerted by his comment about the external weather. I make no particular claim for my musical ear on account of my trained musicality.

This was an instance of a quality of musicality that is general and widespread, possibly universal (including Freud's own undoubtedly musical ear, notwithstanding all his infamous protestations to the contrary).

I judged that I needed to make some rejoinder to my patient's comment about the weather. I said that I thought that he felt that he may have intuitively picked up some underlying depressed mood in me. I did not develop this point, believing it not to be helpful for analysts to divulge much information about themselves to patients, whereas I consider analysts should go at least partway to confirming their patients' perceptions. Given my usual reticence in this area, my patient was obviously surprised by my interpretation, but also accepted it quietly, saying that he had not thought about it consciously at all, but perhaps it could be so. After a pause, he – and we – picked up from where he had left off with his previous train of thought. It felt important to respond in a simple, low-key manner, which matched (perhaps an example of sympathetic affect attunement?) the muted musical tone in which he had stated his observation about the clouds in the first place. With this rather sensitive patient, this may have enabled him to feel that the focus of my attention remained essentially on him rather than on myself.

In the immediate term – meaning not only for the remainder of the session but for about two years afterwards – no further reference was made to this incident. The patient then referred back to it through a chain of associations, and it turned out to be an important event for him, confirming his own capacity, which he had severely doubted, for tuning in intuitively to someone else's frame of mind, and to find that when this was received by the other person, the analyst, it apparently led to no harm to the couple. This disproved his unconscious phantasy of catastrophic, dissonant consequences, in which the music would express my fury or my pain (or both) through his penetrative – to him synonymous with hostile – observation. He anticipated being guilty of setting off a train of destructive events damaging to the couple, whose duet would then become a miserable one. Instead, his experience had become of a couple both sensitive but also robust, in which his observation about the other's mind and feelings, even though the song in question was a sad one, could contribute to the musical creativity of the couple.

I can use this example because, evidently, I became conscious of it. I am sadly confident that many such examples occur regularly in which I am not properly attuned to the musicality of my patient's communications, for any number of different possible reasons, particularly – as nearly happened on this occasion – because of my resistance to the content of the communication. By "content" I include its verbal content, but I mean much more its musical content. I do not mean "musical" as synonymous with "emotional", but, rather, as the vehicle through which the core of the emotion is expressed. The particular emotion in question then needs to be articulated within a psychoanalysis in terms of secondary process verbal understanding, yet it needs also to be acknowledged that the musicality underlying the verbal expression will often point to an ineffable, literally non-verbalizable quality of emotionality conveyed through the music of the voice.

On this occasion, my patient was highly sensitive to my private disturbance of mind, but even so I had to fight through an internal struggle to allow this communication to become conscious. On many an occasion, such a penetration of intuitive insight from the patient can feel unwelcome, intrusive, disturbing, and even insulting. This is ironic, because the patient is constantly making himself vulnerable and exposed to the analyst's intuitive insights, simply by way of being a patient. As analysts, we can sometimes become desensitized as to how hostile even our compassionate intuitions can feel to the patient – until, that is, we have experiences such as the one I have described, ones that bring home to us the vulnerability of the patient's responses. Analysts have all been patients, but we may be quite invested in denying, ignoring, and forgetting just how unnerving it is to receive psychologically penetrating observations and interpretations, all the more so when they are truthful. Whichever way round it is between patient and analyst, the deep emotional truthfulness of such insights inevitably involves an ingredient of pain, and the intensity and degree of authenticity of the exchange along with its accompanying insights will always be mediated via the music of the encounter.

In the light of the foregoing theoretical and clinical material, it is now more possible to pose questions more clearly about the musical dimension of psychoanalysis, including the different meanings of the term "musical". Most obviously, "musical" can sometimes refer to the entire – and vast – non-verbal domain, deriving from pre-verbal and intra-uterine life, but continuing throughout childhood and adult life in a dimension related to, but not identical with, primary process thinking, which partially overlaps with verbal speech. This is mainly expressed through pitch, tone, and volume (including crescendos and diminuendos).

"Musical" can also refer to the entire emotional domain, sometimes used synonymously with "emotional", presumably because it is hard to conceive of emotions being registered and/or expressed in any way other than musical. Even when overt emotional expression is lacking, as in the flat tone of a depressed or schizoid patient, the very fact that the analyst registers the importance of its tonal absence points to its affective centrality, and presumably the hope would be that a successful analysis would revive and develop the patient's musical expressivity.

"Musical" is often also equated with intuition. A particular quality of voice – again expressed through musical parameters – alerts the analyst to the patients exercising their intuitive, not merely rational, capacities: the patient may well intuit a similar quality of intuitiveness through a subtle change in the music of the analyst's voice. This also occurs intrapsychically, in that the analyst – or patient – may catch a different quality of musical tone in their own voice, even in their own thinking, which may alert them to the fact that they are now operating on a different, non-verbally rational dimension. Both these processes, interpersonal and intrapsychic, may be quite unconscious in either or both analytic parties.

"Musical" may also refer to either analyst or patient finding themselves thinking of, or, less rationally, immersed in a piece of music which has somehow sprung to mind.

"Musical" refers also to the attunement to qualities of consonance or dissonance in the musical tone in the current discourse, again in either analytic player. An analyst may be quite unaware, for example, that he may be beginning to push a point too forcefully, but the patient may – consciously or unconsciously – sense the new music of coercion even if the analyst's conscious point is a delicate one. The patient will probably react automatically by closing herself off, the analyst may start to interpret resistance.... There may be no verbal cues whatsoever to these issues, which can sometimes become chronically repetitive, seriously undermining and spoiling an analysis to the bewilderment of both analyst and patient, since there may be no clue as to the cause of the problems in the verbal content of the discourse. It may not be easily remedied in supervision, either, since the supervisor does not hear the patient. A supervisor, however, who is attuned to the fundamental importance of musicality might, however, begins to suspect that the problem might lie in this area; this would also apply to the possibility of an internal supervisor helping the analyst to arrive at second thoughts.

"Musical" can also refer, firstly, to the quality of the mother's response to her infant, as a sonic–aural–musical element of her Winnicottian mirroring which is then internalized by the infant, and, secondly, to the analytic version of this same all-important inter-communication – Anzieu's (1979) "sound-bath".

Music is often described as the most abstract of the arts, yet paradoxically it is also completely centred in the body. I have underlined the aforementioned musical importance of hearing from the beginnings of uterine life, long before seeing or talking. In a recent paper, Birksted-Breen explores the body of the analyst as a receiver and proto-container of the patient's primitive communications of anxiety (Birksted-Breen, 2019). Freud always insisted on the importance of the body, and in analytic musicality, both parties automatically engage in communications which are at once both entirely bodily and yet, in their musical, non-verbal, sometimes non-rational, dimensions; these communications can seem disembodied, sometimes even spiritual.

Finally, musicality also refers to a temporal dimension within analysis. The music of the patient's (or analyst's) voice can obviously express a pre-verbal, infantile quality which may accompany, enrich, and deepen their conscious, rational verbal communication. It may, however, be in conflict with it. The totality of the patient's utterances may therefore not only express that their feelings and their verbal sense of themselves are in conflict, but that, at a much deeper level, the patient may be unconsciously operating on quite different psychic levels of maturation simultaneously. For example, in the case of a patient whose childhood trauma has not been recognized, let alone worked through, I have sometimes found a habitual musicality of speech which is dissonant with their verbal expression.

I have also worked, however, with more complex and subtle cases, in which the patient's musicality and verbal thought may be habitually quite harmonious, until the patient begins to explore areas that may lead to the area of childhood disturbance and trauma. At these moments the music may alter, for example, sounding vulnerably childlike or unexpectedly aggressive and threatening in pitch and tonal quality, even whilst the patient is still talking relatively comfortably, apparently quite unaware of the different music he is "singing". The analyst may have to pinch himself to attend consciously to this split presentation, as the conscious cues from the patient push the analyst to remain attentive solely to the surface, verbal content. This may be especially difficult when the trauma has not hitherto even been mentioned within the analysis, or hardly so: this strange musicality may be the only harbinger of a deep unconscious level of distress and disturbance. Getting to a point where this can be verbalized – where the musical identifications with a vulnerable small child or with a frightening adult aggressor can become consciously experienced and named – may take a long time, and the journey may be difficult for all the reasons stated earlier in the paper. Working through the issues arising from the trauma may have been the primary unconscious motive for the patient to seek analysis: it may be only through the music that this whole area of damage and disturbance could be proffered by the patient, discovered by the analyst, and then worked through together by both parties in such a way that the patient can begin to cease from splitting his mental and emotional functioning and instead take genuine steps towards true integration. This is a very obvious example of something very bodily: the trauma, almost lost to mind through repression, splitting off, and denial in the patient's early childhood, can become taken up eventually again through the body, this time via the musicality of the voice and ear, finally worked through via the duet between both patient and analyst.

I am trying to convey how traumatic elements may not be as principally external as they may initially seem, but are unconsciously drawn within the interior, the very citadel of the soul by the patient, who then becomes identified both with his child-self as victim and also with the aggressor, repeating this disturbing and destructive relationship internally between parts of the self as well as with others externally, especially the analyst in the transference. The principle instrument of the expression of this usually hidden or camouflaged sadomasochistic drama is inevitably the musical domain – songs and duets of fear, submission, terror, seduction, excitement, appeasement, coercion, triumph, despair – often occurring dynamically without the involvement of words or any conscious secondary process thinking. True exorcism can only occur through the analyst's availability for musical, non-rational immersion into this disturbing realm, and then through the analytic couple's striving for understanding and development as they work towards integration and deep knowledge. A trauma that was only superficially known – though producing seriously destructive acting out – now becomes, *après coup*, deeply known, its truth perhaps experienced in its fullness only now for the first time, affecting the whole of the personality, hopefully in a creative and containing direction of interiority and understanding. This will certainly involve the use of words and rationality, but the experiential depth of the whole psychological journey will be constantly communicated by music of different kinds from beginning to end, somewhat as in an opera.

Throughout this chapter, I have emphasized the importance of the non-verbal, intuitive, and musical level of relating between analyst and patient, at the expense of the usually privileged secondary process, verbal level. (See Grier, 2019, for further thoughts in this area.) However, this intuitive, musical level needs to become verbalized in the process of time. In Bion's theory, alpha function leads to verbal formulations; in Winnicott's theory, the patient eventually becomes able to describe and understand himself verbally; Birksted-Breen's patient comes to articulate her emotional life verbally and to take responsibility for her life, as did mine. So the ghost of Freud need not worry that mainstream analysis is going wild or mystical, losing his emphasis on verbal, rational thought. But the journey to that destination is increasingly understood as inevitably and necessarily travelling through primal, elemental, emotional regions which are themselves non-verbal, and, in my opinion, always musical.

My thanks particularly to Dana Birksted-Breen for her editorial help.

References

Anzieu, D. (1979). The Sound Image of the Self. *Int. R. Psycho-Anal.*, 6:23–36.

Barale, F., & Minazzi, V. (2008). Off the Beaten Track: Freud, Sound and Music. Statement of a Problem and Some Historico-Critical Notes. *Int. J. Psycho-Anal.*, 89(5):937–957.

Bion, W.R. (1962). The Psycho-Analytic Study of Thinking. *Int. J. Psycho-Anal.*, 43:306–310.

Bion, W.R. (1985). *Seminari Italiani*. Rome: Borla. [(2005). Italian seminars, Slotkin P, translator. London: Karnac.]

Birksted-Breen, D. (2009). 'Reverberation Time', Dreaming and the Capacity to Dream. *Int. J. Psycho-Anal.*, 90(1): 35–51.

Birksted-Breen, D. (2012). Taking Time: The Tempo of Psychoanalysis. *Int. J. Psycho-Anal.*, 93(4):819–835.

Birksted-Breen, D. (2019). Pathways of the unconscious: when the body is the receiver/instrument. Unpublished.

Cheshire, N.M. (1996). The Empire of The Ear: Freud's Problem with Music. *Int. J. Psycho-Anal.*, 77:1127–1168.

Doolittle, H. (1956). *Tribute to Freud*. Oxford: Carcanet Press, 1971.

Dufresne, R. (1992). The Lady with the Raincoat and the Little Button: The Turning Point of an Analysis—Reflections on Desire, Listening, Resonance, and the Birth of a Mutative Interpretation. *Psychoanal. Inq.*, 12(2):314–367.

Freud, M. (1957). *Glory Reflected*. London: Angus and Robertson.

Freud, S. (1901). Letter to Wilhelm Fliess, 19 September 1901. In *The Complete Letters of S. Freud and W. Fliess*, trans. J. M. Masson. Cambridge, MA & London: Harvard University Press, 1985, pp. 449–451.

Freud S. (1905). Jokes and Their Relation to the Unconscious. *Standard Edition*, 8:9–236.

Freud S. (1907). Creative Writers and Day-dreaming. *Standard Edition*, 9:143–153.

Freud, S. (1914). The Moses of Michelangelo. *SE*, XIII:211–236.

Freud, S. (1936). Letter to M. Bonaparte, 6 December 1936. In *Letters of Sigmund Freud, 1873–1939*, ed. E. L. Freud. London: Hogarth Press, 1961, pp. 430–431.

Gombrich, E.H. (1966). Freud's Aesthetics. *Encounter*, 26:30–40.

Grier, F. (2019). Musicality in the Consulting Room. *Int. J. Psycho-Anal.*, 100:827–851.

Heimann, P. (1950). On Counter-Transference. *Int. J. Psycho-Anal.*, 31:81–84.

Klein, M. (1929). Infantile Anxiety-Situations Reflected in a Work of Art and in the Creative Impulse. *Int. J. Psycho-Anal.*, 10:436–443.

Langer, S.K. (1951). *Philosophy in a New Key*. Cambridge, MA: Harvard UP.

Langer, S.K. (1953). *Feeling and Form*. New York: Charles Scribner's Sons.

Langer, S.K. (1967). *Mind: An Essay on Human Feeling*. Baltimore, MD: Johns Hopkins UP.

Masson, J.M., editor and translator (1985). *The Complete Letters of Sigmund Freud to Wilhelm Fliess 1887–1904*. Cambridge, MA: Belknap Press of Harvard University Press.

Meisel, P., & Kendrick, W. (1986). *Bloomsbury/Freud*. London: Chatto & Windus.

Nacht, S. (1963). The Non-Verbal Relationship in Psycho-Analytic Treatment. *Int. J. Psycho-Anal.*, 44:334–333.

Ogden, T.H. (1999). 'The Music of What Happens' in Poetry and Psychoanalysis. *IJP*, 80(5):979–994.

Racker, H. (1953). A Contribution to the Problem of Counter-Transference. *Int. J. Psycho-Anal.*, 34:313–324.

Rayner, E. (1992). Matching, Attunement and the Psychoanalytic Dialogue. *Int. J. Psycho-Anal.*, 73:39–54.

Rusbridger, R. (2013). Projective Identification in Othello and Verdi's Otello. *Int. J. Psycho-Anal.*, 94(1):33–47.

Schwaber, E.A. (1998). The Non-Verbal Dimension in Psychoanalysis: 'State' and Its Clinical Vicissitudes. *Int. J. Psycho-Anal.*, 79:667–679.

Strunck, O. (1965). *Source Readings in Musical History: Antiquity and the Middle Ages.* Reprinted from 1950 ed. New York & London: Norton.

Searles, H.F. (1959). Oedipal Love in the Counter Transference. *Int. J. Psycho-Anal.*, 40:180–190.

Stein, A. (1999). Well-tempered bagatelles: A meditation on listening in psychoanalysis and music. *Am. Imago*, 56:387–416.

Stern, D.N. (1985). *The Interpersonal World of the Infant: A View from Psychoanalysis and Developmental Psychology.* New York: Basic Books.

Vermorel, M., & Vermorel, H. (1986). Was Freud a Romantic?. *Int. R. Psycho-Anal.*, 13:15–37.

Winnicott, D.W. (1953). Transitional Objects and Transitional Phenomena—A Study of the First Not-Me Possession. *Int. J. Psycho-Anal.*, 34:89–97.

Zanette, M. (1997). Metafore musicali in Bion [Musical metaphors in Bion]. *L'erba Musica*, 7:28.

A MIDPOINT IN TIME

The dual aspect of the Wolf Man's dream

Lucy LaFarge

I dreamt that it was night and that I was lying in my bed. (My bed stood with its foot towards the window; in front of the window there was a row of old walnut trees. I know it was winter when I had the dream, and night-time.) Suddenly the window opened of its own accord, and I was terrified to see that some white wolves were sitting on the big walnut tree in front of the window. There were six or seven of them. The wolves were quite white, and looked more like foxes or sheep-dogs, for they had big tails like foxes and they had their ears pricked like dogs when they pay attention to something. In great terror, evidently of being eaten up by the wolves, I screamed and woke up. My nurse hurried to my bed, to see what had happened to me. It took quite a long while before I was convinced that it had only been a dream; I had had such a clear and life-like picture of the window opening and the wolves sitting on the tree. At last I grew quieter, felt as though I had escaped from some danger, and went to sleep again.

(Freud, 1918, p. 28)

Telling his dream to Freud part way through his long analysis, Serge Pankejeff, whom we have come to know through this dream as the Wolf Man, illustrated his verbal account with a picture.

Pankejeff's dream, repeated in many iterations in the course of the analysis, was central to Freud's formulation of the case. After termination, the dream and the accompanying sketch became iconic for Pankejeff as he constructed his identity over his life cycle, and in the century that has passed, the dream has become iconic for the field of psychoanalysis as well. For patient and field, as I will show, the dream has served as a durable structure, or framework, which preserves and memorializes a piece of the past and at the same time encloses and structures change and growth. At different times, for the Wolf Man, one aspect or the other was paramount; that is, the dream served him, at times, more to preserve, and, at others, more as a matrix for change. Similarly, in the field of psychoanalysis, different analysts' readings of the dream have emphasized one side or the other of this duality; their use of the dream conserves their tie to Freud and the past of analysis, while they simultaneously create something new, reworking and challenging Freud's ideas.

Dream, recurrent dream, screen memory

As we consider the Wolf Man's dream as a site for both conservation and change, it is useful to think of what it means to represent a memory or a phantasy in a dream. Encoding a version of a phantasy in a dream marks it in a special way. It becomes conscious; represented visually, it can be seen, remembered, and potentially shared. As Freud shows us with the Wolf Man's associations and his interpretations, the elements of a dream come together as a structure, a single unit. Freud takes pains to show us the way this dream structure—of waking, watching, and observing parental intercourse—follows in an exact way the much earlier historical scene that he constructs. Once crystallized, such a dream structure has the capacity to link further successive versions. For the Wolf Man, the addition of a sketch would have further formalized the dream structure.

In this regard, it seems significant that the Wolf Man's dream was a recurrent one; Freud notes that in the course of his analysis, the Wolf Man reported many versions of the dream, with varying details. Although Freud does not make this point explicitly, the famous first version reported to him was itself a new iteration, recollected or constructed in the context of the analysis and, like other recollections of childhood, subject to "distortion and refurbishing" (Freud, 1918, p. 9) by the adult who was looking back. In her report of her subsequent analysis of the Wolf Man, Ruth Mack Brunswick (1928) describes a series of versions of the dream, which were central to the analytic work.

Any dream reported in analysis potentially links analyst and patient in a special relationship, one where they are explicitly observers of a shared experience. This is particularly true of recurrent dreams which are reworked in the course of the analysis. Successive versions often come to represent focused moments in the history of the analysis. The underlying dream structure, which is carried forward from one version to the next, provides a continuity, an organization within which change can be located and tolerated.

It is illuminating to place recurrent dreams such as the Wolf Man's, and the scenes that underlie them, in relation to screen memories. In his discussion of the Wolf Man, Freud himself likens dreams to screen memories: "Indeed dreaming is another kind of remembering, though one that is subject to the conditions that rule at night and to the laws of dream-formation" (Freud, 1918, p. 51). Both dreams and screen memories, he points out, combine historical reality with phantasy, and both are constructions that reflect instinctual wishes and the defences against them. Although Freud's emphasis is less on this aspect, screen memories are of course less fluid and more conservative than dreams; they are durable solutions that, once crystallized, are highly resistant to change. As I have written elsewhere (LaFarge, 2012), screen memories memorialize both specific constructions of the past and the act of remembering them. That they are predominantly visual in form reflects their link to trauma (Greenacre, 1949) and their closeness to sensory experience; we do not recall them so much as re-evoke them. Formed primarily in childhood, they also reflect the act of taking in a relationship where remembering and constructing are possible, the formation of an individual, subjective point of view that is no longer dependent upon the object.

A recurrent dream may be seen as standing between a screen memory and an ordinary dream: as with screen memories, a visual structure is preserved, while at the same time new phantasies and resolutions can be worked out in successive versions. Like the analytic frame (Bleger, 1967), the structure of the recurrent dream provides a stable background, or scaffolding, which permits awareness of the vicissitudes of internal and external reality while buffering the dreamer from their full impact. During an analysis, recurrent dreams acquire dynamic transference meanings, and, at the same time, become imbued with the sense of the analyst's listening; they become in effect a part of the unchanging setting of the analysis. Recurring after the analysis, they can carry this function forward, providing what is felt to be a shared space for further analytic work.

The dream's importance for Pankejeff in his analysis and afterward

Freud does not tell us the exact moment in the analysis that Pankejeff first reported the wolf dream, but he makes clear that it became a central motif, dreamed over and over in "innumerable variations" (Freud, 1918, p. 35). The interpretation of the dream extended over several years, as Pankejeff provided further associations and Freud clarified his understanding. Freud tells us that from early on in their work on the dream, the patient shared his belief that the causes of his infantile neurosis lay behind it (Freud, 1918, p. 33). Freud's final construction of the antecedents of the Wolf Man's neurosis was met by a sense of conviction, that it could not have been otherwise.

Freud's overarching conceptualization was that the dream reflected the reworking of an early primal scene experience at a moment of later oedipal disappointment. He lays out his understanding of the specific elements of the dream, reached through much shared analytic work, in an extended footnote (Freud, 1918, pp. 42–45). I will summarize the most important of these: The window opening represents the awakening of the young child; the idea of looking also appears in the image of the wolves' strained gaze. The walnut tree with wolves in it, the key image in the dream, is what is seen through the window, a construction that reflects at several levels the Wolf Man's disappointment in his wish for his father's love and the dangers which this wish presents. The tree is built upon the day residue of the Christmas tree and the child's disappointment in his gifts. The wolves in the tree represent the primal scene that was observed in infancy; their erect tails accentuate their phallic quality and ward off emerging castration fears; the fear of being eaten up by wolves, which ultimately awakens the child, is a displacement of the castration fears that accompany the child's negative oedipal desires.

Reading the case with a modern eye, we wonder about the place of Freud's interpretation of the dream in Pankejeff's analysis and the different meanings that the dream and the work on it may have had for Freud's famous patient. Neither Pankejeff's first report of the dream nor continuing analytic work on it led to a turning point in the analysis. This occurred, and the Wolf Man broke out of his "obliging apathy" (Freud, 1918, p. 11) only when Freud set a time limit for the analysis. It was during this short final phase that the patient's resistance gave way, Freud tells us. "All the information… which enabled me to understand his infantile neurosis is derived from this last period of work" (1918, p. 11), and it was only then that interpretation led to symptom resolution.

Pankejeff was well aware of his role and the place of his dream in Freud's theoretical edifice and he prided himself on this. The importance that Freud gave to his case stirred up both grandiosity and envy in the Wolf Man. In his recollections of his analysis, he tells us that he felt himself "less as a patient than as a co-worker" (Wolf Man, 1971b, p. 140), that Freud told him that he had an unusually strong understanding of analysis and disclosed information about other patients to him. Although Freud emphasized to him the importance of limiting the personal nature of the analyst–patient relationship in order to allow the transference to emerge and be interpreted, Pankejeff, over the course of his long analysis, became acquainted with the Freud family and, as Brunswick tells us, thought himself almost a member of it. Enhanced by the Freud connection, he also felt diminished, less than, particularly when the narcissistic tie was loosened. In his memoir, recalling the termination of the analysis with Freud, on the eve of World War I, Pankejeff describes his encounter with the coffins of the assassinated Archduke and Archduchess. The scene is melancholy, rainy, and torchlit, and he notes that "the coffins were transported in two hearses, one following the other with a considerable distance between them" to indicate that the Archduke had married a woman of lesser birth (Wolf Man, 1971a, p. 91).

It seems likely that Pankejeff's narcissistic tie to Freud, supported by Freud's writing and Freud's continuing interest and financial help, stabilized him in the period immediately following his analysis. These were extraordinarily difficult years as the upheavals of war and revolution led to the loss of Pankejeff's country and fortune. Although much has been written about the severity of the Wolf Man's pathology (Brunswick, 1928; Blum, 1974, 2013; Schafer, 2013; Woods, 2013), he demonstrated considerable resilience in these circumstances, moving wife and mother to Vienna and in the face of massive unemployment securing a job in an insurance company where he worked, gradually advancing, until his retirement.

When the Wolf Man learned of Freud's illness, this equilibrium collapsed. He gradually became paranoid towards Freud, and after a series of minor surgical procedures, he developed a somatic delusion: that the practitioner's error had left him with an irreparable scar on his nose. "The whole world turned on its axis. The structure of his life collapsed... he could not go on living" (Brunswick, 1928, p. 446). He fell into a bottomless despair, worse than he had previously suffered during his earlier illness. He turned to Freud for help, and in 1926, he was referred to Ruth Mack Brunswick for further analysis. In this analysis, he was able to put the wolf dream to use again to shape the discourse and re-establish a link to Freud within which a residual negative transference could ultimately be analyzed.

Brunswick found the Wolf Man to be much more disturbed than Freud had described, a change she describes as a change of character. He was walled off, she says, hypocritical and scheming. For a long period he maintained a superficial alliance with her, unwilling to speak of anything but his nose, or to explore the meaning that his symptom might have and its relation to his transference to Freud.

In this situation of potential impasse, the Wolf Man presented the first dream of the analysis. Brunswick tells us that it was

> a version of the famous wolf dream... One amusing change had occurred: the wolves, formerly white, were now invariably gray. When visiting Freud, the patient had on more than one occasion seen his large grey police dog, which looked like a domesticated wolf.
>
> (Brunswick, p. 452)

What did this re-emergence of the "famous wolf dream" mean in the new analysis? Although Brunswick reports it, she does not appear to give the dream's return very great significance; she labels the changes in it "amusing", and she does not report it verbatim as she does later versions. She tells us that in his associations, the Wolf Man said that the appearance of the dream corroborated his belief that his problems stemmed from his relationship with his father. He was glad to be in analysis with a woman because he would avoid this sort of transference. It seems likely that although the Wolf Man explicitly excludes Brunswick from the transference drama portrayed in the dream – one in which Freud is linked to the Wolf Man's father - by re-dreaming and reporting the wolf dream, he establishes with her the background transference that had developed in the earlier analysis. Recreating with Brunswick a stable space imbued with Freud's special interest, he is able to resume with her the discourse he has had with Freud, within which analytic work could be done.

As their work continues, the Wolf Man begins to report other dreams, which are not linked to the wolf dream. He becomes more accessible, beginning to work with Brunswick on his paranoid and grandiose transferences to Freud. In this context, he reports a second version of the wolf dream, in which Brunswick has entered the transference drama:

> In a broad street is a wall containing a closed door. To the left of the door is a large, empty wardrobe with straight and crooked drawers. The patient stands before the wardrobe; his wife, a shadowy figure, is behind him. Close to the other end of the wall stands a large, heavy woman, looking as if she wanted to go round and behind the wall. But behind the wall is a pack of grey wolves, crowding toward the door and rushing up and down. Their eyes gleam, and it is evident that they want to rush at the patient, his wife, and the other woman. The patient is terrified, fearing that they will succeed in breaking through the wall.
>
> (Brunswick, p. 459)

In the Wolf Man's associations, the door is the window of the original wolf dream; his wife also represents a feminine version of himself; and the tall woman contains a reference to Brunswick. The wolves' gleaming eyes (understood by Freud as a projection of the Wolf Man's own scoptophilia) now are linked to a symptom that he has not previously reported: as a child, he could not stand to be looked at fixedly. As the Wolf Man has become less "walled off", analyst and patient are both threatened by the ravening wolves.

In this context, the Wolf Man begins to reveal the extent of his paranoia, or "persecution mania", and his rage at both Freud and Brunswick: "He threatened to shoot both Freud and me", Brunswick tells us (p. 461), and his threats no longer seemed empty. Work with the patient's murderous rage as well as an emerging maternal transference now led to a remarkable third version of the wolf dream, one in which the observed primal scene is beautiful rather than terrifying:

> The patient stands looking out of his window at a meadow, beyond which is a wood, The sun shines through the trees; the stones in the meadow are of a curious mauve shade. The patient regards particularly the branches of a certain tree, admiring the way in which they are intertwined. He cannot understand why he has not yet painted this landscape.
>
> (Brunswick, p. 462)

Now, perhaps a reflection of a shared sensibility or a shared background of imagining that has emerged, it becomes uncertain from Brunswick's description what are the Wolf Man's associations and what are her own formulations. It seems clear to both analyst and patient, however, that the Wolf Man can now look with wonder at the primal scene, where the branches, now empty of wolves, are entwined, and that he feels that this is an entirely new experience. Brunswick writes:

> The reconciliation to what formerly terrified him can only mean that he has overcome the fear of his own castration, and can now admire what others find beautiful — a love scene between a man and a woman. So long as he identified himself with the woman he was incapable of such admiration; his entire narcissism reacted against the acceptance of the implied castration. If, however, he has abandoned his identification with the woman, he need no longer fear castration.
>
> (Brunswick, p. 462)

Brunswick tells us that the patient could not stay with the wonder of the dream; he could not renounce his passivity. One wonders if her interpretations went too far, or if among other meanings, the dream represented a transference to Brunswick herself, a depiction of a love scene with her, which carried its own dangers; in this case, her interpretation at a more abstract level also bore the meaning of a rejection. In any event, the Wolf Man reported the next day a fourth version of the wolf dream. Brunswick writes that it is:

... a dream in which he is lying at my feet: a return to his passivity. He is in a skyscraper with me, whose only means of exit is a window... from which a ladder extends dangerously to the ground. To get out he must go through the window. That is to say, he cannot remain inside, looking out, as in the other dreams but must overcome his fear and go out. He wakes up in great anxiety, looking desperately for another way of escape.

(p. 462)

In her formulation of the dream, Brunswick tells us that the window represents the narrowed choices that now face the Wolf Man: either he must accept his castration or he must return to the primal scene represented in his childhood nightmare – the scene viewed through the window – and unravel it. In his associations, the Wolf Man is now able to place his wish to be passively loved by his father at the centre of his neurosis.

He now realized that all his ideas of grandeur and fear of the father and, above all, his feeling of irreparable injury by the father were but cloaks for his passivity. And once these disguises were revealed the passivity itself, whose unacceptability had necessitated the delusion, became intolerable... had the patient been capable of assuming the feminine role and admitting his passivity to the full, he could have spared himself this illness...

(p. 462)

This was the last version of the wolf dream to appear in the analysis, and one wonders if the image of the window and the Wolf Man's felt desperation also have to do with the conflict that he felt as he anticipated relinquishing both the analyst – as his insight clearly opened the way to termination – and the discourse and structure that the dream in all its variants provided. Of the elements of the original dream, only the window clearly remains in this final version; there is no tree, and the bed and bedroom have been replaced by the cold, man-made skyscraper – the work-space constructed within his analysis, where he lies at the feet of his analyst. Seeing out only through the window, he sees the world and himself as Freud saw him – an organizing and powerful shared vision. Leaving Brunswick and moving through the window to the other side, he is able to resolve the

309

distortions of the constructed primal scene, but the world beyond the window –the world outside the shared vision –is rickety and dangerous and threatens him with a precipitous drop.

Following the analysis of the final wolf dream, the field of the Wolf Man's analysis expands. Reporting other dreams, unlinked to the wolf dream, he explores the complexity of his attachment to his father and the restrictions that this placed upon his sublimations; there are glimpses of an erotic heterosexual transference. He is able to deal sufficiently with his anger and paranoia towards Freud, related to money and favour, so that his somatic delusion resolves, and he ends the analysis, restored to his former state of mind. Brunswick tells us:

> ...at last gifts, which at the time of the patient's fourth birthday, on Christmas Day, had precipitated the wolf-dream and indeed the entire infantile neurosis and had played a leading role in all his later life and analytic treatment, were now robbed of their libidinal value.
>
> (p. 465)

The Wolf Man is able to relinquish, at least in part, his intense negative oedipal wishes towards his father and Freud and move towards new wishes and aims.

In the tumult and trauma that beset him as his life continued, however, the sense of openness and potential that Brunswick describes faded, and Pankejeff came to rely more and more strongly on his identity as Freud's famous patient. Continued periods of analysis were life-saving for him, particularly after the suicide of his wife immediately following the Anschluss in 1938. Contacts with analysts were a touchstone that animated what appears to have been a dreary life. He attempted to establish a semblance of identity as a psychoanalytic thinker, but his papers – among them one titled "Psychoanalysis and Free Will" – were not always accepted for publication. The analytic world welcomed him most in his identity as the Wolf Man, and his most remembered writing was a memoir of his analysis with Freud, which was published under the name "The Wolf Man" rather than Pankejeff (1958). Pankejeff was able to joke about his identity as an analytic icon. Writing to Muriel Gardiner, who became a lifelong friend, he comments on her daughter's love of animals: "Nothing can be of greater value to a young person than a love of nature and understanding of natural science, particularly animals. Animals played a large part in my childhood also. In my case they were wolves" (Gardiner, 1971, p. 316). The writing of further memoirs, which were ultimately published in a volume with Freud's and Brunswick's reports, again under the name "The Wolf Man", occupied his later years and seemed to help him to stave off recurrent depressions. In these last years, the sketch he had made for Freud once again became important, as, at the request of Gardiner and other analysts, he painted many versions of it, which were sold and served to supplement his modest pension.

Freud's use of the wolf dream in his theory

Pankejeff was rightly proud of his role in Freud's work, for Freud placed the wolf dream at the centre of his evolving theoretical edifice, using it to support his views of temporality and the relation between early and later experience. Freud located the dream at a midpoint in time: dreamt on the eve of the Wolf Man's fourth birthday, the dream pointed backwards toward a posited *observation* of the primal scene at age one and a half, while its construction as a *dream* reflected and attempted to manage later oedipal conflicts. What occurred in the act of dreaming was a revivifying and reworking of an impression so far in the past that it did not fully register at the time and could become known only when later wishes and capacities emerged. Freud used the dream to develop the concept of "nachtraglichkeit", whose translation alternately as "deferred action" and "apres coup" points to the potential for bidirectional action (Faimberg, 2005). An early moment in psychic reality may only acquire meaning afterwards; earlier meanings are reworked at later times. Events in psychic and external reality are potentially open to an endless series of revisions under the pressure of successive desires and fears.

Freud's conceptualization of the nature of the early event which would be the subject of this reworking remained ambiguous. His detailed reconstruction of the very early primal scene and his emphasis on the sense of reality that the Wolf Man associated with the dream accord with his wish, here and elsewhere, to ground this early event in historical fact. Nevertheless, towards the end of "From the History of an Infantile Neurosis" (1918, p. 120), he contemplates the possibility that, in many cases, the earliest primal scene was itself

311

a construct; the child may bring together partial observations or draw upon phylogenetic phantasy to form a needed representation of the parents' sexual life. As Freud put it in *Introductory Lectures on Psycho-Analysis*, written during the same period:

> The only impression we gain is that these events of childhood are somehow demanded as a necessity, that they are among the essential elements of a neurosis. If they have occurred in reality, so much the good; but if they have been witheld by reality, they are put together from hints and supplemented by phantasy.
>
> (1917, p. 369)

More important than the history of the event in external reality – its accuracy as a depiction of actual events – was its history in psychic reality – the importance of the original representation, or mixture of reality and phantasy, at a moment in early mental life:

> The phantasies possess *psychical* as contrasted with *material* reality, and we gradually learn to realize that *in the world of the neuroses it is psychical reality which is the decisive kind.*
>
> (1917, p. 367)

In addition to the question of their relation to historical reality, the very early events that set in motion a succession of reworkings also raise the question of causality. Why these and not others? Freud argues that it was their standing as "primal phantasies" (1917, p. 370) that gave early impressions like the Wolf Man's observation of parental intercourse at age one and a half the importance to serve as the material for later reworking at age four. The later version reflected in the reported dream preserves this force, this core of psychic importance, while at the same time presenting a new schema that responds to later instinctual pressures. And the same force links the new psychic reality to external reality, as the reworked event is felt as a new trauma, a happening in historical as well as psychic reality.

The conservative and change-promoting functions of the dream in psychoanalytic thought

In the 100 years since Freud published his history of the Wolf Man's analysis, generations of analysts have engaged with the wolf dream and reached new formulations of it. For these re-interpreters, as for Pankejeff, the dream has often served the purpose of maintaining a connection with Freud, claiming an identification with him, and through that an identity. A selected piece of the dream is often felt to suffice for this purpose. Comparing the widely different meanings that Freud, Klein, and Lacan gave to the wolf dream, Bernardi (1989) demonstrates that each analyst has selected isolated elements because they are felt, often outside awareness, to fit her initial paradigm. In consequence, each author tends to reconfirm the broad outlines of her existing theory, leaving little space for new discovery. Bernardi writes:

> These paradigms tend to become *devices to solve enigmas whose recognition and formulation they themselves have made possible,* or to produce interpretations in situations that they have made interpretable. However they are not tautological, or at least not totally circular, *so long as they can bring back in their nets something more than what they put in,* that is, *for so long as they can extract something from the experience, though it may have been digested, metabolized, taken apart and put together again.*
>
> (p. 342, italics Bernardi's)

Turning Bernardi's argument around, the selected elements may be seen as a tie to Freud, but also as a continuing stimulus to new thought. A reading of the widely divergent uses that analytic authors have made of the wolf dream does confirm Bernardi's assertion that theorists, like analysts working in the clinical situation, have heard and understood in a way that is shaped by their pre-existing models. Yet a close look at three disparate contributions – those by Klein; Blum, an ego psychologist; and Laplanche – gives the sense that in addition to the potential circularity that Bernardi emphasizes, their use of the dream also supports a more optimistic view of the possibility of creative development. Albeit from different perspectives, each of these authors struggles with the unresolved questions that emerged for Freud in his own reading of the wolf dream: the questions of temporality and the relation between past and present; of the force that propels phantasies, dreams, and their reworking; and of the relation between external and psychic reality.

Klein (1932) develops a conceptualization of temporality that is very different from Freud's. Looking primarily at the image of the devouring wolves, she questions Freud's assertion that the wolf image represents a regression from oedipal wishes. For Klein, the wolves show instead the persistence of the Wolf Man's cannibalistic phantasies; they are surviving relics of very early psychotic anxieties that have never been mastered. Time is linear, and it is measured in the evolution of psychic reality; and regression, while possible, is not central. The Wolf Man's dangerous negative oedipal desire for his father is not the instigator of a regression to anal sadism; rather, anal sadistic phantasy is too intense to permit his positive oedipal desire, and the negative oedipal situation is consequently reinforced.

Like Freud, Klein gives great importance to very early observations of the primal scene and feels that these experiences are re-evoked at later developmental stages. Her own patient, Erna, she writes, was exposed to parental intercourse in her third year and was stimulated to recollect it when she shared a room with her parents at age five, although there was no sexual intercourse between them at that time. However, for Klein, the re-evoking of the earlier observation is not linked to the profound reorganization that Freud characterized with the term "nachtraglichkeit". Instead, later conflicts are shaped, or even dominated, by earlier ones, and, in infantile neuroses, in contrast with the adult variety, many different disorders and levels of conflict and defence operate at the same time (p. 156). There is a sense of past and present, not simply side by side but intermingled, and of development as occurring through the gradual modification of aggression by libido rather than a hierarchical series of transformations.

Klein sees the force underlying the Wolf Man's phobia as instinctual rather than traumatic or arising in great measure from external reality. What is at stake is a massive amount of early aggression, which dominates unconscious phantasy and needs to be managed and modified. She contrasts her view of a phobia with Freud's: Freud (1926, p. 126, cited in Klein, 1932) argues that although a phobia is driven by an instinctual wish, that wish is dangerous because it poses a real external danger, that of castration. Klein counters that the threatening father is felt to be dangerous because the child has projected his own aggression, first onto the figures of his introjected parents and then onto the external parents. "What lies at the root of a phobia is ultimately an internal danger" (1932, p. 158).

External reality comes into play in the evolution of a child's animal phobia, not in the establishment of the fundamental anxiety but in its stepwise modification. Mapping the course by which childhood animal phobias ordinarily develop and are resolved, Klein contrasts the Wolf Man's animal phobia with that of the more normal case of Little Hans: at an early stage of development, the child first projects his oral sadism onto a persecutory internal father and father's penis, the core of the early superego; then the persecutory superego is projected onto a wild animal, a displacement which enables the child to move the danger farther from the centre of his psychic reality to a place in external reality where it can be avoided; ordinarily, as for Little Hans, the phobic animal, gradually modified by libido, then goes on to acquire a friendlier cast and becomes a less terrifying animal such as a horse; and with further working through, it can ultimately be relinquished. For the Wolf Man, the second displacement, to a friendly animal, has never taken place; sadism and the anxiety associated with it cannot be worked through. In this vision of phobic development, the child's ability to place his anxiety outside is potentially a developmental step toward overcoming it. Difficulties arise when the cycle of projection and introjection is interrupted, and Klein depicts the stalemated situation of the child who holds internal and external reality apart, maintaining a dream world, in which idealized as well as persecutory objects may be found and protecting it from the impact of real experience.

Like Klein, Blum (1974, 1977, 1980) places the Wolf Man and his dream primarily in a linear temporality, but for Blum, temporality is firmly linked to external reality. What is in question is a "psychoanalytic developmental framework" (1974, p. 727) in which the sequence of ego development shapes and is shaped by drive and phantasy. In this spirit, Blum places the primal scene and the wolf dream within Margaret Mahler's (1971) timetable, linking the terrors in the dream to a disturbance of the separation-individuation process. The devouring wolves represent a conflicted wish for symbiotic fusion –to be swallowed by the object and reunite with her as a single being.

In this linear, developmental timeframe, phantasies may be reworked as early ego functions are succeeded by later ones, and regression may revive archaic ego states and phantasies, but the striking reorganization linked to Freud's nachtraglichkeit is de-emphasized. What is in question is a continuing narrative rather than a sequence of scenes. The process that Freud depicts, one where an early scene comes to life and is represented via the conflicts of a later developmental phase, is lost. In this sense, the dream as a *structure*—as the detailed representation of an earlier experience – is also lost, although Blum interprets specific elements of it. Blum enquires, "Was this single early primal scene such a traumatic developmental influence for this patient?" (1974, p. 731), and takes Freud's shifting view of whether the Wolf Man's early experience fell within historical or psychic reality as evidence that "The reconstruction of the primal scene under these complicated circumstances strained Freud's credulity as it does ours today" (1974, p. 732). Reconstruction, for Blum, entails not so much the apprehension of a single moment – of either the early primal scene or the wolf dream – but rather the construction of a developmental history and the embedding of key moments within it. Intrapsychic reality is intertwined with external reality; the resulting narrative takes on meaning and is strengthened for both patient and analyst because it is located within developmental, historical reality. In keeping with this approach, Blum supports his argument by placing Freud's reconstruction of the Wolf Man's infancy within the timeline of Freud's own personal history, linking the reconstructions done in the Wolf Man's analysis to reconstructions that Freud did in his own self-analysis during the same period.

Blum uses the dream image of the window opening and the Wolf Man's statement that the dream seemed so real that he could not return to reality immediately upon awakening, to explore the relation between internal and external reality in normality and in symptom formation. The Wolf Man, Blum argues, could not maintain a distinction between psychic and external reality. He points to The Wolf Man's later avowal that he saw the world from behind a veil, which tore open when he defecated (Blum, 1974, p. 729) as evidence of the Wolf Man's chronic, blinding denial and the dream window as a reflection of his conflicted wish to see. Once seeing is permitted, the channel between psychic and external reality is open and cannot be closed again; the Wolf Man, flooded by the terrifying images of his dream, cannot easily return to reality when he awakens. In effect, with his emphasis on reality testing and the loss of it, Blum illuminates the other side of the problem laid out by Klein. Both argue for the key importance of the child's ability to permit psychic reality to be modified by external reality; Klein's concern is that the disturbed child may hold the two apart, protecting idealized internal objects but shielding phantasy from the modulating effect that external reality may have; Blum points to the danger that external reality will be entirely dominated by phantasy rather than modifying it, and the child will be lost in a psychotic world.

In contrast to both Klein and Blum, Laplanche (Laplanche and Pontalis, 1968; Laplanche, 1992), in his analysis of the wolf dream, emphasizes not the individual images – the wolves, the window – but the dream's overarching structure and its homology with the earlier primal scene that Freud constructs. Temporality, in Laplanche's conceptualization, is not linear, as it is for Klein or Blum; it is discontinuous, a series of new translations of an original core phantasy, in which the structure of the original phantasy is preserved. Retracing the history of Freud's conception of trauma, Laplanche observes that throughout the development of Freud's thought, what is in question is a two-step process; an original event becomes a trauma when it is re-represented in a new form later on. What is found in the unconscious is a "sequence of images" (1968, p. 16), a series of scenes, in which one version succeeds another. In the timelessness of the unconscious, both early and late versions are preserved: "What is involved here is a psychic phenomenon which is at one and the same time a cataclysm (like the engulfment of Pompei) and a permanent preservation (like the burial of Tutankhamen's objects in his tomb)" (1992, pp. 435–436). Nachtraglichkeit is central to this conception of the "unconscious as a structural field, which can be reconstructed, since it handles, decomposes, and recomposes its elements according to certain laws" (1968, p. 8). The important history of the scenes – the structures that persist from one to the next and the pressing questions that these raise – is found within the content of the scenes themselves; a linear, historical narrative is unnecessary or even deceptive.

For Freud, the question of the historical reality of the Wolf Man's observation of the primal scene was a vexing one, and he shifted back and forth from an assertion of its veridical nature to an explanation resting upon the concept of phylogenetic phantasy. For Laplanche, the dichotomy posed by Freud fails to capture the nature of the unconscious that Freud has depicted. There is not an original factual event, Laplanche argues: "... the historical life of the subject is not the prime mover, but rather something antecedent, which is capable of operating as an organizer" (1968, p. 8). Nor does the subject generate the scenes that are made and remade with perfect freedom. What is in question is a "third domain, which is not material, factual, perceptual reality, but which is also not subjectivity, that which is 'merely a presentation'" (1992, p. 436).

317

Laplanche uses the wolf dream to develop a conceptualization in which Freud's framework of internal and external is recast in terms of signifiers imposed on the child. "*Infantile scenes—the ones with which psychoanalysis is concerned—are first and foremost messages*" (1992, p. 437). What is presented to the infant in the first instance is a series of enigmatic communications, scenes experienced or observed with the parents, which cannot be understood both because of the infant's immaturity and because they are in important measure unconscious to the parents themselves. In their sexual relations and other actions as well, the Wolf Man's parents and his other important objects have communicated messages that press to be understood, meanings that they do not recognize or understand themselves. "Freud has omitted to note that repression and the unconscious exist in the Other before being present in the child: in the Wolf Man's parents, in Grusha and in the beating father [of "A Child is Being Beaten"]" (1992, p. 439).

The early messages transmitted to the infant press for translation, while at the same time they are distorted defensively and pieces of them remain repressed. The history of these messages must inevitably be discontinuous, not only because of their organization as individual scenes, but because they are broken up between subjects; what the child receives is never identical, either to the parent's conscious communication or to the parent's unconscious one. The analyst's task is to trace the history and meanings of the scenes that the patient has constructed, and the elements of these scenes that the patient has excluded, and to deconstruct them, so that the patient can construct new scenes and, correspondingly, a new fate (1992, p. 442).

Conclusion

Tracing the place of the wolf dream in Pankejeff's own narrative and in Freud's theorization, and sampling the uses it has had in the work of analysts after Freud, I have shown that the dream serves in each case both a conservative and a change-promoting function. How can we understand these two aspects? Here, the two visions of temporality, contained in Freud's term "nachtraglichkeit", suggest different conceptualizations.

For Laplanche, temporality is best seen as a series of discontinuous scenes. From this perspective, we can see both the dream and the theories that arise from it as instances in a single string of signifiers. Laid down in the Wolf Man's infancy by his parents, the earliest

conscious and unconscious communications have pressed for translation, first in his representation of a primal scene, and then in the
many versions of a recurrent dream. What is conserved in this series
of transformations is something that Simpson (2019) calls a "paradigm", a sequence or group that operates by analogy, in which each
individual instance is neither fully singular nor fully a member of a
general class. In the analyses with Freud and Brunswick, the Wolf
Man's communication of the dream has stimulated further transformations, first into constructions made by the analyst, and subsequently, for these analysts and for later theoreticians, in a series of
theoretical conceptualizations. This Laplanchean perspective tends
to bring forward the overall structure of the dream; it is in its underlying paradigm that each version is linked to earlier versions and
to subsequent ones.

Klein conceptualizes time as linear, and the questions of movement and stasis are linked to the idea of development and imped-
iments to it. Klein brings to our attention specific dream images,
which she argues are reflections of unconscious phantasy. Each image fits within a larger structure of phantasy –the hungry wolves, for
example, contain the child's projected aggression – but we have the
sense that each individual image also acts a structure in itself, one
that preserves and memorializes a concrete element of the dream
while leaving that element open to further interpretation. The images and the structures of which they are part have remained unchanged during development, Klein argues, because the Wolf Man's
use of splitting has shielded the phantasies underlying them from
exposure to external reality and from consequent working through.
The analyst must work as Brunswick does to bring them into the
transference and permit further integration.

Blum also holds the idea of time as linear, but for him the timeline of development overshadows the individual image or dream.
Although specific images from the wolf dream are evocative and wor-
thy of further attention, neither the dream nor the construction that
Freud builds upon it is of paramount importance. Blum suggests that

> the analysis was more enriching for Freud than it was for his fa-
> mous patient, a reflection of Freud's scientific and literary genius
> and possibly also an indication that the analysis was elucidated and
> organized in the mind of the analyst.
>
> (1974, pp. 721–722)

From this perspective, the usefulness of the dream for Pankejeff – his reason for holding onto it – is related to the timeline of analytic work: Pankejeff's dream and his subsequent use of it may be seen as indications of a process of internalization. Although Pankejeff dreamt the first version of the wolf dream long before he began his analysis with Freud, the dream came to hold lifelong importance for him because it served to conserve his relationship with Freud and the discourse that arose within it. The dream served as a stable frame for an ongoing discourse in which change could take place; and in a second analysis, he used it to re-establish a sense of Freud's presence through which he could do further work. He was able to internalize Freud's presence sufficiently to re-evoke it by means first of the dream, and later through self-identification as Freud's famous patient, but he did not develop the capacity to function without these concrete tokens.

Neither Klein nor Blum's conceptualization appears to account as fully as Laplanche's for the enduring interest that the wolf dream has held for analysts; that is, there is no essential continuity between their understanding of the importance of the dream and its images within the analytic process and within the continuing field of psychoanalysis. Here perhaps it is useful to look at the dream from outside the field of psychoanalysis proper; we might add that the structure and imagery of the dream resemble the structure and the figurative speech of a novel or the form and individual images in a painting; they convey the conscious and unconscious meaning that the author or artist has placed in them while remaining ambiguous, open to the meaning given by the audience. Laplanche, Klein, and Blum, and all of us and others as well are both audience and creators in this drama, finding the meaning that the dream contains and constructing new meanings as well.

In the end, the analysis of any dream is always a work in progress. Freud wrote of the navel of the dream (1900, p. 111) the deepest meaning that cannot be reached. And dreaming itself, particularly the repetition of a recurrent dream, is also a moment in an unending sequence. As Freud said to Dora, explaining why she had had a recurrent dream three nights running: "...your dream recurred each night, for the very reason that it corresponded with an intention. An intention remains in existence until it has been carried out" (1905, p. 66). Whether we see this intention as an infantile wish, as Freud did, or as a signifier pressing for translation, the work of both dreaming and interpretation is never complete.

320

References

Bernardi, R. (1989). The role of paradigmatic determinants in psychoanalytic understanding. *International Journal of Psychoanalysis*, 70:341–357.

Bleger, J. (1967/2013). *Symbiosis and Ambiguity: A Psychoanalytic Study.* Churcher, J. and Bleger, L., eds. London: Routledge.

Blum, H. (1974). The borderline childhood of the Wolf Man. *Journal of the American Psychoanalytic Association*, 22:721–742.

———. (1977). The prototype of preoedipal reconstruction. *Journal of the American Psychoanalytic Association*, 25:757–785.

———. (1980). The value of reconstruction in adult psychoanalysis. *International Journal of Psychoanalysis*, 61:39–52.

———. (2013). Wolf Man: Concluding commentary. *International Journal of Psychoanalysis*, 94:963–966.

Brunswick, R.M. (1928). A supplement to Freud's 'History of an Infantile Neurosis'. *International Journal of Psychoanalysis*, 9:439–476.

Faimberg, H. (2005). Apres-Coup. *International Journal of Psychoanalysis*, 86:1–6.

Freud, S. (1900). The interpretation of dreams. *Standard Edition*, 4:ix–627.

———. (1905). Fragment of the analysis of a case of hysteria. *Standard Edition*, 7:1–122.

———. (1917). Introductory lectures on psycho-analysis. *Standard Edition*, 16:241–463.

———. (1918). From the history of an infantile neurosis. *Standard Edition*, 17:1–124.

———. (1926). Inhibitions, symptoms and anxiety. *Standard Edition*, 20:75–176.

Gardiner, M. (1971). Meetings with the Wolf Man. In *The Wolf-Man by the Wolf-Man*, ed. Gardiner, M. New York: Basic Books, 311–333.

Greenacre, P. (1949). A contribution to the study of screen memories. *Psychoanalytic Study of the Child*, 3:73–84.

Klein, M. (1932). *The Psycho-Analysis of Children*. London: Hogarth Press.

LaFarge, L. (2012). The screen memory and the act of remembering. *International Journal of Psychoanalysis*, 93:1249–1265.

Laplanche, J. (1992). Interpretation between determinism and hermeneutics: A restatement of the problem. *International Journal of Psychoanalysis*, 73:429–445.

Laplanche, J., and Pontalis, J.B. (1968). Fantasy and the origins of sexuality. *International Journal of Psychoanalysis*, 49:1–18.

Mahler, M. (1971). A study of the separation-individuation process and its possible application to borderline phenomena in the psychoanalytic situation. *Psychoanalytic Study of the Child*, 26:403–424.

Schafer, R. (2013). Rorschach interpretation of Freud's "Wolf Man" at age 69. *International Journal of Psychoanalysis*, 94:955–957.

Simpson, R. (2019). The drive as paradigm—Laplanche's *Sexual* as paradigm shift. *International Journal of Psychoanalysis*, In Press.

Wolf Man, T. (1958). How I came into analysis with Freud. *Journal of the American Psychoanalytic Association*, 6:348–352.

———. (1971a). After my analysis. In *The Wolf-Man by the Wolf-Man*, ed. Gardiner, M. New York: Basic Books, 90–110.

———. (1971b). My recollections of Sigmund Freud. In *The Wolf-Man by the Wolf-Man*, ed. Gardiner, M. New York: Basic Books, 135–152.

Woods, J.M. (2013). On the Rorschach Protocol. *International Journal of Psychoanalysis*, 94:959–961.

Index

Note: *Italic* page numbers refer to figures and page numbers followed by "n" denote endnotes.